The Sitcom Reader

The Sitcom Reader

America Viewed and Scewed

Edited by

Mary M. Dalton
and
Laura R. Linder

STATE UNIVERSITY OF NEW YORK PRESS

Published by
State University of New York Press, Albany

© 2005 State University of New York

For information, address State University of New York Press,
194 Washington Avenue, Suite 305, Albany, NY 12210-2384

Production by Marilyn P. Semerad
Marketing by Fran Keneston

Library of Congress Cataloging-in-Publication Data

The sitcom reader : America viewed and skewed / edited by Mary M. Dalton and Laura R. Linder.
    p. cm.
  Includes bibliographical references and index.
  ISBN 0-7914-6569-1 (hardcover : alk. paper) — ISBN 0-7914-6570-5 (pbk. : alk. paper)
    1. Comedy programs—United States—History and criticism. I. Dalton, Mary M., 1962– II. Linder, Laura R.

PN1991.8.C65S57 2005
791.45'6—dc22

2004028407

10 9 8 7 6 5 4 3 2 1

For my father and my sister.
M. M. D.

For Gary.
L. R. L.

Contents

List of Illustrations   xi

Acknowledgments   xv

Introduction   1

PART ONE
CONVENTIONS OF THE GENRE

1 Origins of the Genre: In Search of the Radio Sitcom   15
   David Marc

2 Breaking and Entering: Transgressive Comedy on Television   25
   Michael V. Tueth

3 American Situation Comedies and the Modern Comedy
   of Manners   35
   David Pierson

PART TWO
REFRAMING THE FAMILY

4 Who Rules the Roost?: Sitcom Family Dynamics from the
   Cleavers to the Osbournes   49
   Judy Kutulas

5 From Ozzie to Ozzy: The Reassuring Nonevolution of the
   Sitcom Family   61
   Laura R. Linder

 6 Against the Organization Man: *The Andy Griffith Show* and
    the Small-Town Family Ideal   73
       John O'Leary and Rick Worland

                              PART THREE
                         GENDER REPRESENTED

 7 *I Love Lucy:* Television and Gender in Postwar Domestic
    Ideology   87
       Lori Landay

 8 *Our Miss Brooks:* Situating Gender in Teacher Sitcoms   99
       Mary M. Dalton

 9 Talking Sex: Comparison Shopping through Female Conversation
    in HBO's *Sex and the City*   111
       Sharon Marie Ross

                              PART FOUR
                          RACE AND ETHNICITY

10 The Hidden Truths in Black Sitcoms   125
       Robin R. Means Coleman and Charlton D. McIlwain

11 Segregated Sitcoms: Institutional Causes of Disparity among
    Black and White Comedy Images and Audiences   139
       Amanda Dyanne Lotz

12 Negotiated Boundaries: Production Practices and the Making of
    Representation in *Julia*   151
       Demetria Rougeaux Shabazz

                              PART FIVE
                      SITUATING SEXUAL ORIENTATION

13 *Ellen:* Coming Out and Disappearing   165
       Valerie V. Peterson

14 Sealed with a Kiss: Heteronormative Narrative Strategies in
    NBC's *Will & Grace*   177
       Denis M. Provencher

15 Poofs—Cheesy and Other: Identity Politics as Commodity in
South Park 191
Karen Anijar, Hsueh-hua Vivian Chen, and Thomas E. Walker

PART SIX
WORK AND SOCIAL CLASS

16 Women, Love, and Work: *The Doris Day Show* as Cultural
Dialogue 205
Phyllis Scrocco Zrzavy

17 Liberated Women and New Sensitive Men: Reconstructing
Gender in the 1970s Workplace Comedies 217
Judy Kutulas

18 "Who's in Charge Here?": Views of Media Ownership in
Situation Comedies 227
Paul R. Kohl

PART SEVEN
IMPLICATIONS OF IDEOLOGY

19 Sex and the Sitcom: Gender and Genre in Millennial Television 241
Christine Scodari

20 *Cheers:* Searching for the Ideal Public Sphere in the Ideal
Public House 253
Robert S. Brown

21 "It's Just a Bunch of Stuff That Happened": *The Simpsons* and
the Possibility of Postmodern Comedy 261
H. Peter Steeves

Bibliography 273

List of Contributors 293

Index 297

Illustrations

FIGURE 1.1. Gertrude Berg as Molly Goldberg in *The Goldbergs*, 1929–1954 (radio 1929–1948 and television 1949–1954). Photo courtesy of Photofest. Used by permission.   18

FIGURE 3.1. Donna Douglas as Elly May Clampett, Buddy Ebsen as Jed Clampett, Irene Ryan as Granny, and Max Baer Jr., as Jethro Bodine in *The Beverly Hillbillies*, 1962–1971. Photo courtesy of Movie Star NewsFair.   38

FIGURE 3.2. Jason Alexander as George Costanza, Jerry Seinfeld as himself, Michael Richards as Cosmo Kramer, and Julia Louis-Dreyfus as Elaine Benes in *Seinfeld*, 1990–1998. Photo courtesy of Larry Edmunds BooksFair.   41

FIGURE 4.1. Hugh Beaumont as Ward Cleaver, Barbara Billingsley as June Cleaver, Jerry Mathers as Beaver (Theodore) Cleaver, and Tony Dow as Wally Cleaver in *Leave It to Beaver*, 1957–1963. Photo courtesy of Movie Star NewsFair.   50

FIGURE 5.1. David Nelson, Harriet Nelson, Ozzie Nelson, and Rick Nelson as themselves in *The Adventures of Ozzie and Harriet*, 1952–1966. Photo courtesy of Photofest. Used by permission.   63

FIGURE 5.2. Ozzy Osbourne, Sharon Osbourne, Jack Osbourne, and Kelly Osbourne as themselves in *The Osbournes*, 2002–2005. Photo courtesy of Photofest. Used by permission.   65

FIGURE 6.1. Andy Griffith as Andy Taylor, Ronny Howard as Opie
Taylor, Don Knotts as Barney Fife, and Jim Nabors as Gomer Pyle
in *The Andy Griffith Show*, 1960–1968. Photo courtesy of Movie
Star NewsFair.   74

FIGURE 7.1. Lucille Ball as Lucy Ricardo and Desi Arnaz as Ricky
Ricardo in *I Love Lucy*, 1951–1961. Photo courtesy of Movie Star
NewsFair.   89

FIGURE 8.1. Robert Rockwell as Philip Boynton, Gale Gordon as
Osgood Conklin, Richard Crenna as Walter Denton, and Eve Arden
as Connie Brooks in *Our Miss Brooks*, 1952–1956. Photo courtesy
of Photofest. Used by permission.   103

FIGURE 9.1. Cynthia Nixon as Miranda Hobbs, Cristin Davis as
Charlotte York McDougal, Kim Catrall as Samantha Jones, and Sarah
Jessica Parker as Carrie Bradshaw in *Sex and the City*, 1998–2004.
Photo courtesy of Larry Edmunds BooksFair.   113

FIGURE 10.1. Spencer Williams Jr., as Andy Brown, Tim Moore
as George "The Kingfish" Stevens, and Alvin Childress as Amos
Jones in *Amos 'n' Andy*, 1951–1953. Photo courtesy of Movie Star
NewsFair.   129

FIGURE 10.2. (top row, left to right) Tempestt Bledsoe as Vanessa
Huxtable, Sabrina Le Beauf as Sondra Huxtable Tibideaux, and
Malcolm Jamal-Warner as Theodore Huxtable. (bottom row, left
to right) Lisa Bonet as Denise Huxtable Kendall, Bill Cosby as
Dr. Cliff Huxtable, Keshia Knight Pulliam as Rudy Huxtable, and
Phylicia Rashad as Clair Huxtable in *The Cosby Show*, 1984–1992.
Photo courtesy of Larry Edmunds BooksFair.   131

FIGURE 11.1. (top row, left to right) Tamala Jones as Bobbi Seawright,
Dedee Pfieffer as Sheri Winston, D. W. Moffett as Dean Winston,
and James Lesure as Mel Ellis. (bottom row, left to right) Edafe
Blackmon as Reggie Ellis and Holly Robinson Peete as Malena Ellis
in *For Your Love*, 1998–2002. Photo courtesy of Photofest. Used by
permission.   141

FIGURE 12.1. Diahann Carroll as Julia Baker, Lloyd Nelson as
Dr. Morton Chegley, and Marc Copage as Corey Baker in *Julia*,
1968–1971. Photo courtesy of Larry Edmunds BooksFair.   158

FIGURE 13.1. Joely Fisher as Paige Clark, Jeremy Piven as Spence Novak, Ellen DeGeneres as Ellen Morgan, David Anthony Higgins as Joe Farrell, and Clea Lewis as Audrey Penney in *Ellen*, 1994–1998. Photo courtesy of Photofest. Used by permission. 167

FIGURE 14.1. Sean Hayes as Jack McFarland, Megan Mullally as Karen Walker, Debra Messing as Grace Adler, and Eric McCormack as Will Truman in *Will & Grace*, 1998– . Photo courtesy of Movie Star NewsFair. 179

FIGURE 15.1. Big Gay Al in *South Park*, 1997– . Photo courtesy of Photofest. Used by permission. 193

FIGURE 16.1. Rose Marie as Myrna Gibbons and Doris Day as Doris Martin in *The Doris Day Show*, 1968–1973. Photo courtesy of Photofest. Used by permission. 211

FIGURE 18.1. Richard Deacon as Melvin Cooley, Rose Marie as Sally Rogers, Morey Amsterdam as Maurice "Buddy" Sorrell, Mary Tyler Moore as Laura Petrie, and Dick Van Dyke as Rob Petrie in *The Dick Van Dyke Show*, 1961–1966. Photo courtesy of Movie Star NewsFair. 230

FIGURE 18.2. (top row, left to right) Edward Asner as Lou Grant and Ted Knight as Ted Baxter. (middle row, left to right) Gavin MacLeod as Murray Slaughter, Mary Tyler Moore as Mary Richards, and Georgia Engel as Georgette Franklin Baxter. (bottom) Betty White as Sue Ann Nivens in *The Mary Tyler Moore Show*, 1970–1977. Photo courtesy of Photofest. Used by permission. 233

FIGURE 19.1. Calista Flockhart as Ally McBeal in *Ally McBeal*, 1997–2002. Photo courtesy of Larry Edmunds BooksFair. 243

FIGURE 20.1. (top row, left to right) John Ratzenberger as Cliff Gavin, Roger Rees as Robin Colcord, Ted Danson as Sam Malone, Woody Harrelson as Woody Boyd, and George Wendt as Norm Peterson. (middle row, left to right) Rhea Perlman as Carla Tortelli LeBec, Kirstie Alley as Rebecca Howe, and Shelley Long as Diane Chambers. (bottom row, left to right) Kelsey Grammar as Dr. Frasier Crane and Bebe Neuwirth as Dr. Lilith Sternin in *Cheers*, 1982–1993. Photo courtesy of Larry Edmunds BooksFair. 256

FIGURE 21.1. Marge, Maggie, Homer, Lisa, and Bart Simpson in *The Simpsons*, 1989– . Photo courtesy of Larry Edmunds BooksFair. 265

Acknowledgments

We want to thank our contributors for their compelling and insightful contributions to this volume. Their hard work, attentiveness to deadlines, and cheerful compliance during the writing and revising of their chapters has made our task as editors more manageable and certainly more pleasant.

Similarly, we want to thank our friends, students, and colleagues at Marist College, the University of North Carolina at Greensboro, and Wake Forest University. Bill Adler and Brian Householder provided research assistance. On numerous occasions when another pair of eyes was required to arbitrate editing questions, Gary Kenton rose to the task unfailingly.

And, as always, the support of our friends and family members has been sustaining throughout the process of developing this volume.

Introduction

Headlines of this type appear with a regularity that renders them as invisible by now as the cultural influence of the medium they describe: "Children Spend More Time Watching Television Than in School Classrooms," "TV Saturation in American Homes Close to 100%," and "Hours Spent Watching TV Continues to Rise Among Americans." Critical essays and books that complement these empirical studies have been published since the 1960s, and it only took a few years for media studies courses and entire programs to creep into the academy at locales outside of Los Angeles, where they first appeared alongside the main business and production center of the entertainment industry.

Long past are the days when scholars had to justify writing about television. The pervasiveness and persuasiveness—implicit as well as explicit—of the medium make critical and historical analyses of television programming, its various meanings for audiences, and the industry that produces these cultural artifacts an enterprise of considerable relevance and importance. This volume features twenty-one original works on American television situation comedies, one of the oldest and most ubiquitous forms of television programming.

The chapters are arranged into seven topical sections, which were carefully considered as the anthology was conceptualized to address the following topics: conventions of the form, the family, gender, race and ethnicity, sexual orientation, work and social class, and ideology. Perspectives represented include critical media studies, cultural studies, feminist theory, queer theory, and a number of interdisciplinary approaches. The range of theoretical and critical tools employed by the authors of chapters was also an intentional choice on the part of the editors, meant to parallel the richness and range of the programming itself.

This project originated as a way of filling a void in the television literature. From our examination of the journal articles on sitcoms and books on broader topics related to television that included some material on sitcoms, we found that these proposed topics are well established and represented by the scholarship in media studies. What has been missing, however, is a single volume that comprehensively examines the genre of situation comedy and applies sets of critical lenses to contextualize the programs and help readers think about the shows, and, perhaps, even about themselves, in new contexts.

The first part of this anthology begins, fittingly we believe, with an exploration of the conventions of the genre. The chapters in this part set forth the characteristics that establish situation comedies as a distinctive genre. These chapters explore the historical underpinnings of the genre as well as the evolution of the signifiers that establish and reinforce situation comedy. While sitcoms may be defined by their structure—thirty-minute episodes, photographed in a three-camera studio set up in front of a live audience, and built around the situations within the program—the term has been contested, especially in recent years. Can animated programs be classified as situation comedy? Some of our contributors certainly believe so. What about an hour-long, single-camera program shot on sets without a live audience? Another contributor writes about *Ally McBeal*, which pushes the perimeters of the form on all sides. While the terms defining the form may be contested, the appeal of the sitcom cannot. We believe it is no accident that situation comedy is the one television genre that has maintained a consistent level of popularity, and the explanation for its enduring popularity resides in the conventions of the genre.

David Marc has written extensively on comedic forms, and his work has been very influential among scholars writing about mass media. It is appropriate for this volume to start with his chapter on the conventions and history of the situation comedy during the critical time when sitcoms made the transition from radio to television. In "Origins of the Genre: In Search of the Radio Sitcom," Marc identifies the origins of the term "sitcom" and traces its integration into the larger culture to describe a discrete and influential form of early television programming. This chapter includes an important discussion of the "dialect comedies" that made the transition from radio to television, the sitcom–variety show hybrids, and the influence of developing radio and television technologies on the mediums' programming. Marc sets the larger context for the chapters across the topical sections and for Michael V. Tueth and David Pierson, who follow in the introductory part of the anthology with chapters that contextualize the situation comedy within two other historical traditions: the transgressive comedy and the comedy of manners.

In "Breaking and Entering: Transgressive Comedy on Television," Tueth writes that most television comedy has "behaved itself" over the years, but he focuses on programs that have pushed the boundaries of network standards and practices and other commonly held ideas about what constitutes good taste. In addition to a survey of network programs that have challenged social conventions, the author looks more closely at *South Park* and the looser regulations that govern cable programming. The analysis of *South Park* is grounded

in historical examples and theories of transgressive humor and in the oppositional interpretation of popular texts. Despite the phenomenal success of this
transgressive sitcom, *South Park* has its share of critics, which is to be expected
of any text designed to shock audiences. A more pressing question is posed by
Tueth regarding whether or not oppositional programming designed to vio-
late cultural taboos can continue without spawning a slew of successful imitators and, in the process, losing its power to shock audiences.

The theatrical comedy of manners genre is characterized by an emphasis
on "a strong sense of style, deportment, and a witty repartee that is used to conceal the raw emotions that lie just beneath the surfaces of the dramatic lives of
its characters," according to Pierson in "American Situation Comedies and the
Modern Comedy of Manners." Just as Teuth examines *South Park* in the context of transgressive comedy, in this final chapter of the first part of the volume
Pierson argues that characters in situation comedies are just as obsessed with
and frustrated by the dominant social conventions as characters in the English
Restoration comedies of Congreve and Sheridan are. In this chapter, the discursive elements of sitcoms from two distinct time periods, the 1960s and
1990s, are examined, and the author concludes through his analysis of *The Beverly Hillbillies* and *Seinfeld* that the situation comedy is a "worthy descendant"
and a "modern variation" of the theatrical comedy of manners.

The family has long been a staple of situation comedy. Part two, "Refram-
ing the Family," looks at some of the ways television families have evolved over
the years and, curiously, the way it seems that sometimes the more things
change, the more they stay the same among TV families. From the radio days
that established the formula to the earliest days of sitcoms on television, family sitcoms have formed the foundation of this type of programming. Through
the years, the picture-perfect family has evolved from the traditional working
dad and stay-at-home mom nuclear family to include unlikely but seemingly
exhaustive configurations of nontraditional families. The roles of mothers,
fathers, and children have been rearticulated in many forms, including
blended families, step-families, adoptive families, multigenerational households, multicultural households, school families, friendship families, and work
families. Still, the basic paradigm remains intact, as Laura R. Linder demonstrates aptly by comparing Ozzy and Harriet Nelson to Ozzie and Sharon
Osbourne. She finds remarkable similarities between the two superficially disparate TV families. The three chapters in this part will situate the family sitcom within a larger cultural context.

Judy Kutulas's expansive overview of sitcom familes, "Who Rules the
Roost?: Sitcom Family Dynamics from the Cleavers to the Osbournes," argues
that the family lies at the heart of the American situation comedy. She begins
with an examination of the 1950s sitcom families and explores how these idealized narratives complemented the desire in postwar culture for stability and
clearly delineated gender roles in fiction, if not in fact. The mid-1960s marked

the opening of a generational gap that would widen in real life and on television by the 1970s. When *All in the Family* premiered in 1971, it was clear that the Bunker family provided a marked contrast to the idealized Cleavers. It gave some legitimacy to youth's rebellion against their elders, while at the same time paving the way for the social relevancy family comedies of the 1970s. By the 1980s, television parenting styles had changed, and boomer parents actually cultivated independence in their children and ran their families more democratically than ever before. By the final decade of the century, family sitcoms had increasingly become pitched to a Gen X audience and the emblematic head of household has moved from Ward Cleaver to Ozzy Osbourne, but, as Kutulas maintains, there are similarities linking the two dads: "[Ozzy] certainly is not Ward Cleaver and maybe not even Cliff Huxtable; still, he cares about his wife and children, and they care about him." The survey of family situation comedies over time provides a valuable context for the other two chapters in this part.

Laura R. Linder's unlikely linkage of two sitcom families that appear dramatically different on the surface suggests that the conventions of the genre transcend time and culture. In the second chapter of part two, "From Ozzie to Ozzy: The Reassuring Nonevolution of the Sitcom Family," the contrast between Ozzie Nelson—who epitomizes the bland sitcom dad of the 1950s—and shock rocker Ozzy Osbourne—who is better known for profane lyrics, scary makeup, and antics on stage that some would label satanic—is shown to be more superficial than substantive when considered within the generic conventions of the family sitcom. This chapter offers an insightful look at the parallels between the two personas and their respective series. The fascinating historical background of each series is combined with a compelling textual analysis of the shows. While the problems these musical celebrity families deal with are different and related to the time periods in which the shows were produced, the defining elements of the family sitcom are intact: there are parents with kids; there are problems arising in day-to-day life that must be handled; and a loving family is able to handle whatever comes its way because of the closeness of the family unit. Whether or not the TV dad wears eyeliner is secondary to the core values that define the genre.

John O'Leary and Rick Worland offer us a chapter that has the gentle, affirming tone of the series itself in "Against the Organization Man: *The Andy Griffith Show* and the Small-Town Family Ideal." Their thoughtful critique begins by providing a historical context for the series that places it in the subgenre of rural situation comedies. Then they explore links between the popular series and the populist films of Frank Capra during the 1930s, especially *Mr. Deeds Goes to Town* and *Mr. Smith Goes to Washington*. One thread that runs through the chapter is the theme of family and small-town values that marked Mayberry as a mythic ideal even during its enormously popular prime-time run in the 1960s. While sitcoms of the 1970s would explore issues explicitly and build narratives around "work families," and defining series of the 1980s would begin to focus primarily on isolated suburban nuclear families, *The Andy Griffith Show* is distinguished by its emphasis on the extended family and the interdependence of that group with a small community.

The politics of gender have been implicitly represented but seldom explicitly addressed in television situation comedies. Part three, "Gender Represented," looks at the politics of representation and explores how this genre has constructed the male/masculine and the female/feminine. Women have undoubtedly come a long way from the earliest days of television, when most played mothers or spinsters on situation comedies, but the multilayered critique of gender in sitcoms remains an important political project. When compared to other forms of mass media, notably Hollywood cinema, television today offers a wide range of roles for women, particularly leading roles for women in their thirties and forties. At the same time, most women in sitcoms play characters that fit fairly conventionally into the programs. These chapters offer a discourse that looks at how situation comedies alternately challenge and reinforce the hegemony of gender in historical and contemporary culture.

Lucy is probably the single most dominant icon of the sitcom throughout history. Lori Landay offers an important critique of how gender informs this iconography in ways that have been publicly visible as part of Lucille Ball's phenomenally popular television characters and ways that have been less visible to the viewing public. In "*I Love Lucy:* Television and Gender in Postwar Domestic Ideology," Landay explores the history and influence of the series and how the program is a venue for Lucy's public and private selves. On the series, Lucy Ricardo is a dizzy housewife dissatisfied with staying home while her bandleader husband is in the public spotlight; she is eager to get into show business at any cost, and the antics she engages in to try to snare her own spotlight are predictably hilarious. Behind the scenes, Lucille Ball is a savvy businesswoman working as actively at producing as at performing. The contrast between Lucy Ricardo and Lucille Ball is distinct, while at the same time the lines are blurred in publicity that touts parallels between Lucille's real-life marriage to co-star Desi Arnaz and the birth of Lucille and Desi's son on the same day their characters welcome a baby into the household in the sitcom. This chapter explores how differently the power relations of the sexes work onscreen in the series *I Love Lucy* and offscreen in the real lives of Lucille Ball and Desi Arnaz.

If Lucille Ball's face is emblematic of the sitcom because of the indelible characters she has established over the years, her influence over the genre has been felt in other ways that are not so visible, such as through other shows brought to the small screen through her production company. The popular and long-running radio sitcom chronicling high school teacher Connie Brooks's skirmishes with her principal and her relentless pursuit of a colleague as a romantic partner was brought to television by Desilu Studios. The disconnect Landay identifies in the previous chapter between the personas of the character Lucy Ricardo and the creator of that character, Lucille Ball, sets the stage for Mary M. Dalton to examine Eve Arden's portrayal of the main character in *Our Miss Brooks*. Dalton does so in the context of other teacher narratives on film and television and also contrasts the television sitcom with the film of the same title. Dalton reads this sitcom and the resulting motion picture against the grain to argue that Miss Brooks's pursuit of Mr. Boynton and wisecracking about her desire to get married may be more fantasy than fact. Because of the conventions of teacher narratives related to gender and because of the mores of her small town, perhaps the only way Connie Brooks can remain independent in her 1950s community is to appear interested in the ideals set forth for her, marriage and children, and she chooses a most unlikely conquest to effectively retain her professional identity and autonomy.

While Connie Brooks alludes to her supposed desire for "frog boy," the biology teacher down the hall, the women friends on contemporary cable programs are much more decided and direct about desires of all types. In the final chapter of part three, "Talking Sex: Comparison Shopping through Female Conversation in HBO's *Sex and the City*," Sharon Marie Ross argues that representing female sexual desire as limitless is a construction that is compatible with many of the goals of feminism as a political movement. Her piece uses the HBO series as a frame for examining female sexual desire and its connection to other desires. Specifically, episodes are discussed that show women discussing their sexuality and sexual actions, that show women discussing gender roles in modern-day society, and that show women discussing their consumption of material goods. Ross believes that such representations are important in that they expand our notion of female sexuality and female friendship and, further, that popular culture should explore lesbian, bisexual, and racially and ethnically diverse narratives of female agency and desire.

What is the role of race and ethnicity in the situation comedy? As the chapters in part four demonstrate, there are multiple perspectives on the question, only a few of which can be considered in an anthology of this scope, and one of those perspectives is historical. There were a few examples of ethnic sitcoms in the early days of television, followed by almost two decades of "Whiteout." In the early days, roles for African Americans were confined mostly to maids or gross stereotypes—such as those seen on *Amos 'n' Andy*—followed by years of invisibility until breakthrough programs like *Julia* and *The Cosby Show*. Early shows, as noted by David Marc in the first chapter of this volume, also featured a number of immigrant families, but the trend was not sustained through the 1950s and 1960s, when White sitcoms became the norm. More recently, programs featuring mostly Black characters have been relegated to start-up networks to fill what is perceived as a niche programming need. The current marginalization of Black sitcoms begs the question whether it is better to be seen a little or not at all. Still fewer are the shows that feature Hispanic and Asian characters. This part will address issues of identity and representation in the context of racial determinacy and indeterminacy, taking into account trends toward a racial segmenting of both programming and the audience. The continuing invisibility of most racial and ethnic groups on commercial television is a topic raised in part four and explains why each of the chapters in this part focuses mainly on Black sitcoms. It seems logical that as people of color play an increasingly larger role in American society, the diversity of characters represented in sitcoms will expand accordingly. We anticipate that future critical studies of the genre will include this area of analysis.

Robin R. Means Coleman and Charlton D. McIlwain launch part four with an important survey of the historical and cultural significance of Black sitcoms. "The Hidden Truths in Black Sitcoms" draws on Means Coleman's earlier work, *African American Viewers and the Black Situation Comedy: Situating Racial Humor*, and establishes the Black sitcom as a definable subgenre by tracing the history of the form and integrating an analysis of industry practices related to the production and promotion of Black sitcoms. The earliest days of television (1950–1953) are identified as the TV Minstrelsy Era, followed by the Nonrecognition Era (1954–1967), the Assimilationist Era (1968–1971), the Social Relevancy and Ridiculed Black Subjectivity Era (1972–1983), Black Family and Diversity Era (1984–1989), and the Neo-Minstrelsy Era (1990–1998). It remains to be seen what patterns will emerge in coming years, but Means Coleman and McIlwain argue that audiences need to become more active, to understand how the "comedic mediation of Black identity impacts and informs African Americans' lives," and to demand programming that includes more diverse images of Blackness.

Amanda Dyanne Lotz pays even closer attention to audiences and reception of the Black sitcom in the second chapter of this part. She notes that comedy has historically been the first narrative form on television to break barriers but adds that people of color, particularly Asian Americans and Latino/as, have yet to find a presence outside of comedies in her chapter, "Segregated Sitcoms: Institutional Causes of Disparity among Black and White Comedy Images and Audiences." She looks at changes in television distribution—the movement away from programs being solely broadcast to programs being delivered by cable and satellite, with a resulting expansion in the number of networks—and how that transition has shaped programming and audience demographics. At the same time, the imperative for Black sitcoms to appeal to both African American and White audiences has been reduced or eliminated, and the audiences for comedies and other programs have become more and more segregated. Specifically, Lotz looks at the institutional and formal causes of audience segregation in the 1990s and offers a case study of the series *For Your Love* to support her argument.

In a sense, Demetria Rougeaux Shabazz brings another case study to this volume in the final chapter of part four, "Negotiated Boundaries: Production

Practices and the Making of Representation in *Julia*." This chapter demonstrates quite strikingly just how form and content are inextricably linked in television texts. Shabazz places *Julia* in its cultural and historical context, but she quickly moves on to show how television's standardized language already "had its own grammar of race and way of encoding racial bias" in 1968, when Diahann Carroll assumed the central role in this sitcom. The author's detailed reading of the sitcom explores how *Julia* "disrupted the color-coded language" at the same time the series' "staging techniques and genre repetition reinforced racist stereotypes." This chapter examines how elements such as the set design and the "posh" décor of Julia's apartment, the camera angles and lighting used to frame the character Julia Baker, the casting conventions of the time period, and the themes that complement the family sitcoms of the 1950s, come as close as possible to stripping the title character of *Julia* of her racial identity and, at the same time, make a mainstream audience more comfortable with the groundbreaking show.

Until the mid-1990s, sexual orientation had seldom been represented overtly in American situation comedies; the apparent assumption was that everyone in America was straight. Two chapters in part five, "Situating Sexual Orientation," focus on close textual readings of the two popular sitcoms most closely identified with the increasing acceptance of gay characters in half-hour comedies. With the coming out of Ellen Morgan on *Ellen*, portrayals of gay characters on television have become both more prevalent and more direct than ever before in sitcoms. In fact, one could argue that current programs, such as *Will & Grace*, advance the cause of "normalizing" homosexuality to the general public, even if the approach on these programs is exceedingly cautious. Perhaps these programs represent a distant echo of the relevancy television programs of the 1970s, with their overt political agenda supporting social change and progressive movements; on the other hand, these sitcoms may signify that issues of sexuality represent little more to network executives and program producers than an interesting "twist" on stock characters situated in staple scenarios.

This part begins with a thick reading of an important television text. In "*Ellen:* Coming Out and Disappearing," Valerie V. Peterson analyzes the "puppy episode" of Ellen DeGeneres's series that aired on April 30, 1997 and became more media event than prime-time sitcom. Peterson argues that this episode did little to challenge mainstream biases against gays because it presents an overly simplified process of coming out and an essentialist version of lesbianism, a version that allows only an intractable and singular set of properties for those who claim this identity. In this episode, Ellen's character comes out in four discrete and compressed stages: shared meaning, self-labeling, confiding, and announcing. The show's focus on a simplistic process rather than the complex construction of an identity within a larger cultural context is certainly reductive, as sitcoms often are, but the stakes for this media event were somewhat larger for viewers who hoped the episode might challenge the social order and demonstrate the potential for larger forms of liberation.

Denis M. Provencher explicates a set of texts rather than a single episode in "Sealed with a Kiss: Heteronormative Narrative Strategies in NBC's *Will & Grace*," but he confronts some of the same problems identified by Peterson in the preceeding chapter: the series conflates character types and avoids presenting particularly complex or controversial social issues that might prove too challenging for a mainstream audience. Provencher looks beneath the surface constructions and makes the implicit strategies employed on the show to link Will with Grace and Jack with Karen (and even Jack with Rosario) as "couples" explicit for readers of this chapter. He notes how same-sex affection is avoided on the series at the same time these couples regularly lock lips. The author offers close readings of two episodes of the series and concludes that the absence of the "gay kiss" and recurrence of the "straight kiss" on a gay sitcom exemplify how *Will & Grace* "foregrounds heterosexuality, heteronormativity, and family values" while the gay male characters are essentially closeted in terms of same-sex affection and intimacy.

One might expect the otherwise explicit and over-the-top *South Park* to make more obvious connections and offer overt commentary on homosexuality and politics, as it does with other progressive social issues addressed by narrative elements of the program. Karen Anijar, Hsueh-hua Vivian Chen, and Thomas E. Walker argue, however, that the opposite is the case in "Poofs—Cheesy and Other: Identity Politics as Commodity in *South Park*," the final chapter in part five. The authors argue that the Big Gay Al character on *South Park* falls into the category of "benevolent, White gay depictions that are marketed for easy consumption" by audiences, a category that includes Will and Jack on *Will & Grace*. If the identity politics of television sitcoms is simplistic, the interplay between these characters, lived experience, history, and consumer culture are much more complex, and this piece explores those connections.

Whether the collar in question is white, blue, or pink, work in the television situation comedy is invariably linked to social class and, often, to gender. Part six, "Work and Social Class," discusses how the complexity of class in America is explored and ignored as sitcom characters pursue, but never quite achieve, the American Dream. In their quest, however, the characters tacitly accept the validity and possibility of achieving this dream, with little political or economic critique to the contrary. Chapters in this section examine specific programs in the context of actual, cultural change played out in the fictive workplaces of television sitcoms and also look beyond the programs, in some cases, to explore the interplay between the real work of producing them and work as it is depicted within the sitcom narrative.

In the first chapter of this part, "Women, Love, and Work: *The Doris Day Show* as Cultural Dialogue," Phyllis Scrocco Zrzavy makes a compelling case that the *Doris Day Show* has been overlooked by critics and television historians. The author documents a character's transformation that essentially parallels the sort of changes women were experiencing in the culture at the time. Season by season, as the sitcom evolves and Doris Martin becomes more autonomous, Doris Day was making some of those same transitions offscreen. When her husband and agent died suddenly in April of 1968, Day discovered that he had left her in a precarious financial situation and contractually obligated to perform in a situation comedy, a format she "loathed." Over the next five years, the character Doris Martin, also a widow, makes the move from the family farm and bucolic bliss across the Golden Gate Bridge to an urban apartment of her own and a career in publishing. At the same time, Day eventually took responsibility for her sitcom in front of the camera and behind the scenes. In a sense, both the character and the performer came of age with a television series that mirrored the changes related to gender and the workplace that were taking place simultaneously in the culture at large.

In the decade following Doris Martin's big career move, workplace comedies became a staple of the sitcom genre and proved a rich venue for exploring gender and social change. Judy Kutulas links work and gender studies in the second chapter of this part, "Liberated Women and New Sensitive Men: Reconstructing Gender in the 1970s Workplace Comedies." By the late 1960s, baby boomers were diverging from patterns established by their parents by becoming more educated, marrying later, and having fewer children, which made them attractive to advertisers. The family sitcoms that had appealed to their parents were not compelling for the boomer, however, and television networks responded with social relevancy programs and workplace sitcoms. Males were still in charge of television workplaces, as they were in charge of real workplaces, but women made gains on television programs without doing so at the expense of men. Women were liberated, gained some degree of sexual freedom, and found themselves drawn to a new type of romantic partner: the sensitive man. Not incidentally, the "liberated woman and the new sensitive man carefully separated the most palatable aspects of feminism and packaged them into a neat consumer-friendly idea." By the 1980s, the workplace sitcom began to lose its momentum while the family sitcom began a revival. Although the liberated woman and new sensitive man have lost a lot of the traits that once defined them in workplace sitcoms, Kutulas notes that these characters continue to influence "our television-normalized sense of reality."

The third chapter in part six shifts lenses to look at sitcom texts in a context that is not limited to social conditions but also examines the industry that produces the programming. Paul R. Kohl suggests that collaboration is generally a misnomer when describing the process of producing television shows because of the imbalance of power between production executives, network programmers and advertising representatives, and the writers and creative personnel charged with "creating" a particular program. In "'Who's in Charge Here?': Views of Media Ownership in Situation Comedies," Kohl offers resistant readings of three classic situation comedy series. He uses an episode of *The Dick Van Dyke Show* as a vehicle for illustrating Marx's theory of the alienated worker. The final episode of *The Mary Tyler Moore Show* provides an exemplar for exploring "the resistance potential of carnival to ridicule the corporate end of the media." And a series of *Seinfeld* episodes in which the program's origins are "self-reflexively parodied" provide a forum for employing the carnivalesque technique of the grotesque for contextualizing the owner-worker relationship. The author argues that even though they are handsomely compensated for their work, television writers are subject to alienation because the product of their labor is removed from their control. There is the opportunity, however, for these writers to include competing messages in the texts they create that reveal some of the tensions they feel under the guise of humor.

The final set of chapters, part seven, begins to explore the implications of ideology. Critical theorists write extensively and compellingly of the competing messages embedded in popular texts, and situation comedies certainly reinforce the argument that popular texts are made up of layers of meaning under the guise of entertainment. Explicating these messages is critical to a fuller understanding of the genre and its influence on culture. Clearly, the pervasiveness of sitcoms coupled with the frequent and tacit acceptance of the values found in them is justification for the study and critical analysis of these texts. There can be no fear that sitcoms will inculcate untold generations with a dominant ideology that may not represent their interests without dissent, negotiation, and competing ideas so long as relevant and persuasive theoretical tools are used for reading and critiquing the texts. This final part will pull together the ideologies explored in previous parts and form new links to theoretical constructs.

Christine Scodari identifies an emergent subgenre of the situation comedy referred to as the "sexcom" in the first chapter of part seven, "Sex and the Sitcom: Gender and Genre in Millennial Television." She examines two sitcoms, *Ally McBeal* and *Sex and the City* as exemplars of sexcom, a subgenre defined by its curious privileging and trivializing of concerns of the private (feminine) sphere. This leads to increasing audience segmentation by gender while the programs purport to celebrate an emancipated, multifaceted, millennial woman. Scodari argues that the net result of this trend, in terms of audience and program content, is to further dissociate the masculine sphere from the feminine sphere.

Robert S. Brown takes a different tack by framing a series within a single theoretical construct. In the second chapter of part seven, "*Cheers:* Searching for the Ideal Public Sphere in the Ideal Public House," Brown argues that the bar where the vast majority of scenes in the long-running and highly popular series were staged is a model for the modern ideal public sphere as envisioned by Jürgen Habermas. This space was a place where a "community of independent, educated people existed as equals between the state and the masses, [where] opinions on matters of general interest were openly debated in the salons, reading rooms, and coffee houses of Europe." But this realm of ideas was shortlived in the late seventeenth and early eighteenth centuries and was criticized by Keith Michael Baker as a construction that was more private and exclusive than public. It was further criticized by David Zaret for privileging the role of economics in creating a public sphere over the influences of religion, science, and printing. Brown finds that the bar Cheers comes much closer to meeting Habermas's goals for the ideal public sphere and, at the same time, meets other concerns that a wider spectrum of the public be represented and have an equal voice in all discussions. For the eleven years the series ran in network prime time, bar patrons discussed popular culture and social issues in addition to the personal and anecdotal; in every case, even the most heavily contested ideas are discussed and debated until participants have arrived at a peaceful conclusion.

This volume concludes with an elegant chapter by H. Peter Steeves that is funny, expansive, and located in that powerful and evocative space somewhere between theory and fandom. " 'It's Just a Bunch of Stuff that Happened': *The Simpsons* and the Possibility of Postmodern Comedy" makes a number of interesting and compelling connections. Immanuel Kant, Thomas Hobbes, Henri Bergson, and Umberto Eco join a host of pop culture icons in a chapter that reads rather like an episode of the sitcom it contextualizes. What is the context? Postmodernism, consumer culture, theories of the comedic, and linguistics are tools for contextualizing an animated family living in Springfield, a family that is inexplicably and unapologetically yellow. What does it all mean? Many things. After all, television sitcoms, as we have come to know over the years, may be entertaining, but they are never *just* entertainment.

PART ONE

Conventions of the Genre

Origins of the Genre

In Search of the Radio Sitcom

David Marc

The introduction of a mass communication medium normally occurs when an economically viable commercial application is found for a new technology. A third element necessary to the launch, content (i.e., something to communicate), is often treated as something of an afterthought in this process. As a result, adaptations of popular works and of entire genres from previous media tend to dominate the introductory period of a new medium, even as they mutate under the developing conditions. Such was the case in the rise of the television sitcom from the ashes of network radio.

While a dozen or more long-running network radio series served as sources for early television situation comedies, it is in some ways misleading to describe these radio programs (for example, *Father Knows Best*, *Amos 'n' Andy*, or *The Life of Riley*) as "radio sitcoms." According to the *Oxford English Dictionary*, neither "situation comedy" nor "sitcom" were terms that achieved common usage until the 1950s, the point at which this type of entertainment had become completely absent from American radio. *TV Guide* appears to be among the first general circulation publications to use the term "situation comedy" in print, with the following passage cited by the *Oxford English Dictionary* from a 1953 article: "Ever since *I Love Lucy* zoomed to the top rung on the rating ladder, it seems the networks have been filling every available half-hour with another situation comedy' *(TV Guide)*." The abbreviated form, "sitcom," which probably enjoys greater usage today, has an even shorter history. It is dated in print by the *OED* only as far back as a 1964 *Life* magazine article announcing Bing Crosby's upcoming (and ill-fated) attempt to work in the genre: "'Even Bing Crosby has succumbed . . . and will appear in a sitcom as an electrical engineer who happens to break into song once a week' (*Life* Magazine)."

The integration of the term "sitcom" into the American language, like much of popular culture, was driven by the promotional needs of the entertainment industry. The *Life* article cited above provides a case in point. One of the most popular singers in early twentieth-century American show business, Crosby was well known to the public, first through his records and then as a radio personality and movie star. As the star of a radio variety show in the 1930s and 1940s, he demonstrated abilities to deliver gag lines, play the straight man, and trade snappy banter with guests, which led to his pairing with Bob Hope in the Paramount "road" pictures.[1] While variety programming was as popular on early television as it had been on radio, the genre went into a gradual decline in the 1960s; it eventually became virtually absent from prime time.[2]

With feature film production also in decline during the 1960s, many aging, studio-era movie stars—including Crosby, Donna Reed, Robert Young, Ida Lupino, Fred MacMurray, and Jimmy Stewart—attempted to reinvest their celebrity into situation comedy. Sitcoms had been experiencing a continuous surge of growth since 1951, when *I Love Lucy* sprinted past Milton Berle's *Texaco Star Theater* and half a dozen other comedy-variety shows to the top of the prime-time ratings.[3] Furthermore, residual fees from reruns of sitcoms were proving to be an extraordinary cash cow (Schatz, "Desilu").

Though a situation comedy may be accurately described as a "comic drama" or a "narrative comedy," to distinguish it from variety (or comedy-variety) programming, such terms were no doubt considered too eggheaded for promoting the product. Thus, "situation comedy" emerged from its origins in back office show biz lingo to become part of popular discourse.[4] Its abbreviation to "sitcom" was perhaps all but inevitable in accordance with the grammar of public relations.

DIALECT COMEDIES

Two of the longest-running and most popular "radio sitcoms" to be adapted for television were *The Goldbergs* (premiering on the NBC radio network in 1929 as *The Rise of the Goldbergs*) and *Amos 'n' Andy* (premiering locally in Chicago in 1928 and going national on CBS the following year). Both series began as live fifteen-minute programs that aired Monday through Friday, a broadcast format more akin to radio soap opera than television sitcom, and both were restructured into weekly half-hour series during the early 1940s. Both were adapted for television early in the life of the medium (*The Goldbergs* in 1949; *Amos 'n' Andy* in 1951) as weekly, half-hour, filmed series with audience response tracks, all characteristics that became basic to the genre. The two programs shared significant content attributes as well. Both made primary use of ethnic dialect comedy, a source of popular humor traceable in American culture to the nineteenth-century minstrel and vaudeville stages.[5]

The Goldbergs was written and produced on both radio and television by its star, Gertrude Berg, one of only a very few women who produced their own network programs.[6] The thick Ashkenazic (i.e., eastern European) Jewish accents of the program's immigrant-generation characters provided much of the show's humor. The younger, born-in-America characters spoke something more akin to standard radio English, sporadically adding inflections to acknowledge the series' Bronx location. Plotting was generally based on the exploitation of character stereotypes, especially live-in Uncle David's failure to catch the gist of things American (in one episode we learn that he has named his goldfish "Karl Marx" because of his respect for philosophers). But, despite its reliance on stereotyping, *The Goldbergs* could rarely be accused of anything more noxious than a kind of chicken-soup sentimentality in its content.

Amos 'n' Andy, centered on African American characters living in Harlem, was written, produced, and performed on radio by Freeman Gosden and Charles Correll, Whites who had grown up in the Jim Crow South. The pair had performed blackface "race humor" onstage in vaudeville and had done stints with several of the surviving minstrel shows of the early twentieth century. Their *Amos 'n' Andy* radio series—loosely based on Sam and Henry, two earlier characters they had created—grew from a local program on WMAQ-Chicago to what was arguably the most listened to prime-time entertainment series in the history of radio.[7]

When the television adaptation of *Amos 'n' Andy* came under attack by the NAACP and other civic organizations following its 1951 premiere, Gosden and Correll claimed to be nonplussed, even hurt, by claims made about the show's perpetuation of negative stereotypes. They argued that they were performing the same type of dialect humor in their depiction of "Negroes" as other sitcoms used in their comic depictions of any number of ethnic groups (*The Goldbergs*'s Jewish characters being a prime example; *I Love Lucy*'s Hispanic character, Ricky Ricardo, being another). In viewing *Amos 'n' Andy* today, it is difficult to ignore the series' unrelenting focus on negative stereotypes derived from the slavery era. The level of stupidity that emerges from the relentless use of farfetched malapropisms makes it difficult to characterize the effect of the sitcom as anything but racist at its core (Cripps 33–54).

The efforts of civil rights organizations to pressure CBS into canceling *Amos 'n' Andy* in 1953, despite the program's bankable Nielsen ratings, is

FIGURE 1.1. Gertrude Berg as Molly Goldberg in *The Goldbergs*, 1929–1954 (radio 1929–1948 and television 1949–1954). Photo courtesy of Photofest. Used by permission.

counted by some as among the first battles won in the post–World War II civil rights movement. If there is tragedy in the incident, it fell upon the African American performers. Gosden and Correll, who had performed as the title characters in three feature films for MGM, were dissuaded from taking on the roles in the television series and had replaced themselves and others in the cast with African American actors.[8] As these performers had predicted in arguing for the continuation of the show, the cancellation left them without any role to play in "all-White" television.[9] An ensemble of masterful African American comedians, including Tim Moore (who played the Kingfish), Ernestine Wade (Sapphire), and Johnny Lee (Algonquin J. Calhoun), simply disappeared from public view. Amanda Randolph (Mama), Kingfish's hilarious "battle ax" mother-in-law, was the sole exception. She took the part of the family maid on *The Danny Thomas Show*.[10]

Sitting atop the radio ratings with audiences numbering in the tens of millions, comedies such as *The Goldbergs* and *Amos 'n' Andy* seemed obvious choices for television, as did other radio hits that depended heavily on dialect humor. These included *Life with Luigi* (Italians in Chicago), *I Remember Mama* (Norwegians in San Francisco), and *Beulah* (African American servants in middle American suburbia).[11] While dialect humor was a natural for an aural medium, it proved to be a short-lived phenomenon on television and a poor fit for the emerging culture of postwar America.

The ethnic sitcoms suffered from the popular promotion of assimilationism that accompanied the mass migration of immigrant and second-generation White families from inner-city neighborhoods to suburban tracts. The exaggerated accents and malapropisms of radio comedy may have become more embarrassing than funny to a significant segment of the early television-viewing audience, which was located almost exclusively in large metropolitan areas.[12] Thomas Cripps has suggested that African American war veterans played a significant role in opposing the television adaptation of *Amos 'n' Andy*, which they saw as an instrument for perpetuation of the long-standing stereotypes that stood behind Jim Crow laws (Cripps).

Though it had run for two decades on radio, *Amos 'n' Andy* was gone from television in two seasons. *The Goldbergs* managed to remain on the air for six seasons, but this was largely due to Gertrude Berg's savvy as a producer. She repeatedly made new deals to save the show, switching television networks three times and even agreeing to change the twenty-five-year-old format by moving the family from the Bronx to the suburbs and renaming the sitcom *Molly*. In the end, ridding the show of what was now seen as its Depression-era, immigrant baggage left it a limp imitation of itself. Following *Molly*'s cancellation in 1955, not a single radio dialect comedy was left on the air. Suburban families with names such as Stone *(The Donna Reed Show)* and Anderson *(Father Knows Best)* moved in to dominate the genre.

THE SITCOM–VARIETY SHOW HYBRIDS

Like *The Goldbergs* and *Amos 'n' Andy*, *The Jack Benny Program* and *The George Burns and Gracie Allen Show* were among radio's most popular hits. These shows present complex genre problems when considered as sources for the television programs of the same name. On radio, *Benny* and *Burns and Allen* made frequent use of seamless aural segués to shift rhetorical modes between direct-address presentation (the vaudeville-derived variety format) and representational narratives of domestic life that seem very much like radio prototypes of contemporary television sitcoms.[13] Genre theory has thus far been unable to account for these shows in any satisfying way, and so they are treated as "radio sitcoms" by a kind of critical default.[14]

The purposeful confusion of the two principal genres of broadcast comedy (sitcom and variety), which radio accomplished by a mere shift of language, required much more work for presentation on television. *I Love Lucy* and *The Adventures of Ozzie and Harriet*, two sitcoms featuring bandleaders as husband-fathers, made use of "backstage" narrative in order to work variety elements, such as music, song, and dance, into the dramatic framework.

In *I Love Lucy*, Lucy's husband Ricky is a nightclub performer, and she is a hopeless show biz wannabe. A plurality of episodes concerns her efforts to sneak into shows at the Tropicana. The nightclub stage functions to allow variety segués. In *Ozzie and Harriet*, Ozzie's son, Ricky Nelson, has a garage band and performs at parties or practice sessions. *Ozzie and Harriet* was a pioneer in cross-media promotion, with Ricky Nelson launching a string of Billboard Top Ten hits on the show.

It is worth noting that *The Bing Crosby Show* (1964–1965), which inspired *Life* magazine to use the word "sitcom" in print, incorporated a backstage device as well. A closer look at the failed effort reveals an evocatively frenzied attempt at generic, masscult cookie-cutting with subgeneric elements borrowed from a half-dozen sitcom hits of the period. Like Danny Thomas (Danny Williams in *The Danny Thomas Show*) and Andy Griffith (Andy Taylor in *The Andy Griffith Show*), Crosby invokes a persona in the sitcom narrative. His character, Bing Collins, is a suburban suit-and-tie professional, married with children (á la Robert Young in *Father Knows Best* and other archetypal sitcom dads). His daughters are a study in contrast between boy-crazy bobby-soxer Janice, and child prodigy Joyce, in what seems to be a nod to the contrast between Patty and Cathy Lane of *The Patty Duke Show*.

The narrative thrust of the series has Bing eschewing stardom for the higher calling of being a "normal" family man, a familiar and popular theme in American mythology that perhaps reached its film apogee in Frank Capra's *It's a Wonderful Life* (1946). Using Bing Collins's aversion to fame and fortune as a diversion, the storyline incorporates Bing Crosby through the backstage door. Bing's wife (Beverly Garland) is, like Lucy, an incorrigible show business wannabe. She attempts to drag Bing back onstage as a way of realizing her suppressed ambitions. Borrowing another tactic from *The Danny Thomas Show* for the episode finish, Bing breaks into song as he delivers dad's weekly words of wisdom, with appropriate musical accompaniment rising from behind kitchen appliances, living room furniture, or garden tools.

IMPROVING THE HORSE AND CARRIAGE

When searching for the roots of situation comedy and other television genres in radio, it is worth remembering that radio enjoyed an extremely short moment as a primary (or *the* primary) medium for commercial American entertainment, perhaps too short to fully realize any genres of its own. Invented just before the turn of the twentieth century as a "wireless telegraph" whose purpose was to provide two-way communication systems for ships at sea and for places not reachable by telegraph cable, it was improved to carry analog sound in the 1910s. This led to a wave of hobbyists (known as "hams," another word for "show-offs") who began performing for each other with the new desktop communication system: telling jokes, reading poems, creating false identities, and otherwise prefiguring Internet chatting by the better part of a century.

It was not until after World War I that the mass production of cheap, downstream receivers for the consuming public was attempted. The first commercially owned local radio stations were put on the air in the 1920s by electronics manufacturers to stimulate sales of these models. In 1927, the Radio Corporation of America (RCA), the country's biggest maker of sets, launched its subsidiary, the National Broadcasting Company (NBC), thus imposing centralized quality control on broadcasting entertainment products by feeding content to a network of cross-country stations from its corporate studios.

Radio achieved a position at center stage of American culture during the national traumas of the Great Depression and World War II but went into decline after 1948, as the three major network broadcasting companies (NBC, CBS, and ABC) accelerated their commitment of the medium's profits to the development of another medium—television. Radio's golden age ends with a whimper in 1953 when its last great star, Jack Benny, gets the word from CBS that his radio show must go. Dying in its twenties and dead at around thirty, prime-time entertainment radio was only beginning to define its generic texts when they were either killed, kidnapped, or subjected to forced mutation in the service of the needs of visual representation on television.[15]

The case can be made that the artistic life of radio was hampered by the anticipation of television, which was patented in 1927, the very same year that network radio went on the air.[16] As early as 1929, David Sarnoff, the RCA executive who founded NBC, gave an address at the Harvard Business School in which he announced the existence of television, expressing a belief that it would "replace" radio (Morgenthau). By 1939, television broadcasting was within the capabilities of RCA, which publicly demonstrated it through daily telecasts from the New York World's Fair. There were more than a thousand set owners in the New York metropolitan area at the time, though most were employees of either RCA and/or several other companies at work on the technology.

World War II delayed television's implementation as a mass medium until after 1945, but the handwriting was already on the cue cards for radio. At the very height of its popularity, with daily audiences for specific programs numbering in the tens of millions, radio was functioning as little more than a stepping stone to television for the people who controlled the money that might have been used to develop radio art.

Henry Morgenthau, III, a pioneer maker of documentary films for television and the producer of Eleanor Roosevelt's syndicated television talk show during the 1950s, heard Sarnoff express his views on the future of radio in person in 1947. Morgenthau had just read Charles A. Siepmann's *Radio's Second Chance*, in which the author argued that radio was only beginning to suggest its artistic and educational potentials. Inspired to want to work in radio by Siepmann, Morgenthau had his father, then Secretary of the U.S. Treasury, arrange a meeting for him with Sarnoff, who was now chairman of the board at RCA. Morgenthau described it this way:

> I have a memory of walking down endless corridors, sort of like approaching the Sun King at Versailles, and meeting Sarnoff and talking to him briefly about my ambition to go into FM radio, which was new. I talked about the static-free sound and the opening of new channels and how exciting this all seemed to me. He stopped me and said that he thought going into radio was the worst possible thing to do. He said FM radio was like inventing an improved horse carriage just at the time that automobiles were coming in. "Forget radio and get into television!" he said and walked away, as if I were the mad man. (Morgenthau)

Though radio was already being dismissed as an obsolete technology in the late 1940s, the phenomenon it had done so much to create—mass audiences—had grown more valuable than ever to those who had the future of radio in their hands. Accordingly, they cannibalized the medium for its content. It is remarkable, however, to see how little attention was paid to the intricacies of adaptation, even for hit shows.

According to Paul Henning, who began writing radio scripts for *The George Burns and Gracie Allen Show* in 1942, the show's staff was sent a memo in April of 1950 informing them that they would be doing "the show" on television, beginning in October. "I remember George saying, 'Let's all go down to Palm Springs and we'll sit around the pool and talk about what we're going to do for television,'" Henning said (Henning).

Ralph Levy, the producer, evolved the idea for the show: a simple situation comedy with the cut-out set of the Burns's house, and another one for their neighbors, and, downstage, an area where George could stand and talk directly to the audience, to explain about his wife, Gracie, and predict what was going to happen [in the plot], and comment on his daily life in and around their neighborhood. (Wilk 176–77)

When Henning's wife, Ruth, suggested to Levy and Burns that they might need something more "visual" to interest audiences that were *seeing* the action, Burns came up with the idea of placing a television in the den of George and Gracie's television house. When the plot of the sitcom got too convoluted, the writers had the option of sending George up to the den to watch an action picture on television, usually a Western. These might play on the screen during a broadcast for as long as ten seconds. "You could do that kind of stuff back then, because nobody knew what a sitcom was," Paul Henning said. "We just did comedy."

NOTES

1. The *American Heritage Dictionary* lists "variety show," but does not list "comedy-variety" or "comedy-variety show." The *Oxford English Dictionary* lists neither. What we would today call a "comedy-variety show" was, during the radio era, usually called either a "comedy show" (if hosted by a comedian) or a "variety show." The term "comedy-variety" became useful or perhaps necessary during the television era to distinguish this type of programming from two proliferating forms: the situation comedy (e.g., *I Love Lucy*) and the variety show (i.e., "vaudeo" shows hosted by noncomedians, such as *The Ed Sullivan Show*, also known as *Toast of the Town*).

2. While dormant in English-language American television, the comedy-variety and variety genres remain vital in Spanish-language programming in the United States and elsewhere.

3. Rating is the percentage of households watching a particular program out of the total households in the area with TV sets. Share is the percentage of households watching a particular program out of the total households in the area with TV sets turned on.

4. Several radio comedy writers, including Everett Greenbaum and Paul Henning, recall the use of terms such as "situational comedy" and "situation comedy" in shop talk as early as the 1930s. It was used to distinguish comic drama from the more popular vaudeville style of that era, which today is remembered as comedy-variety. See the oral history collections of the Center for the Study of Popular Television, Syracuse University.

5. See Robert Toll, *Blacking Up: The Minstrel Show in 19th Century America* (NY: Oxford University Press, 1974) for a detailed discussion of the minstrel show and its extraordinary role in American culture.

6. Irna Philips (1901–1973), who virtually invented the daytime soap opera for radio and single-handedly adapted it for television, was the most prolific and influential of the handful of women producers in broadcasting. For a useful concise biography of Philips, see the entry concerning her in Oxford University Press's *American National Biography Online* at www.anb.com.

7. For more detail on *Amos 'n' Andy*, see Melvin Patrick Ely, *The Adventures of Amos 'n Andy: A Social History of an American Phenomenon* (NY: Free Press, 1991).

8. There were three Amos and Andy movies, with the title roles performed by Gosden and Correll in blackface: *Check and Double Check* (1930); *The Rasslin' Match* (1934); and *The Lion Tamer* (1934).

9. See J. Fred Macdonald, *Blacks and White Television* (Chicago: Nelson Hall, 1983) for the most comprehensive history of African Americans on early American television.

10. No criticism of *The Danny Thomas Show* is meant here. The show's producers, Danny Thomas and Sheldon Leonard, insisted on employing African American performers at a time when almost none were on television. Leonard and Thomas made another political statement by knowingly employing writers who had been blacklisted for their political beliefs. For example, Frank Tarloff (credited with the pseudonym David Adler) wrote for at least three of their sitcoms, *The Danny Thomas Show*, *The Andy Griffith Show*, and *The Dick Van Dyke Show*. Tarloff recounts this in an interview in the oral history collections of the Center for the Study of Popular Television at Syracuse University Library.

11. *Beulah* (ABC, 1951–1953), whose title female character had been played by a White man on radio, was less popular than *Amos 'n' Andy* and was therefore less of a cause célèbre. It was also cancelled in 1953, however, under similar circumstances. After its first season on television, the program's star, Ethel Waters, had quit because of the negative stereotypes she felt were perpetuated in her character.

12. The FCC issued 108 television station licenses before 1948, almost all of which were allocated to cities in three megalopolitan regions: the northeast coastal corridor stretching from Boston to Washington, D.C.; the Great Lakes rim, from Cleveland to Milwaukee via Chicago; and urban California, including Los Angeles and San Francisco. In 1948, the FCC put a freeze on new licensing that lasted until 1952.

13. For a detailed discussion of modes of television narrative, see the author's *Demographic Vistas* (Philadelphia: University of Pennsylvania Press, 1996), pp. 11–33.

14. In the 1990s, *Seinfeld* attempted to reintroduce the technique of creating genre tension between situation comedy and comedy-variety by opening and sometimes closing the show with stand-up clips.

15. For a rare account of the process of imagining content for television, see Gilbert Seldes, "The Errors of Television," *Atlantic Monthly* (May 1937), pp. 531–41. Seldes, a Harvard-educated popular culture and radio critic, was hired by CBS in 1935 as a consultant to its television development program.

16. In 1927 Philo T. Farnsworth patented his image dissector, which included key elements of the cathode ray tube. That same year, the Radio Corporation of America, whose research and development team was led by Russian emigré Vladimir Zworykin, patented its *eikonoscope*.

CHAPTER 2

Breaking and Entering

Transgressive Comedy on Television

Michael V. Tueth

Over the years, most television comedy has behaved itself. In the early days, however, a few memorable exceptions tried to break the rules. In the 1950s, when *Father Knows Best* and *The Adventures of Ozzie and Harriet* provided the models for husbandly behavior, Jackie Gleason approached forbidden territory in his portrayal of a loudmouthed braggart on *The Honeymooners*. Gleason's character would threaten to retaliate against his wife's remarks, "one of these days," by sending her "to the moon, Alice, to the moon!" Milton Berle's drag routines, Red Skelton's drunken characters, and Ernie Kovacs's effeminate Percy Dovetonsils were similar mild violations of the social taboos of middle America that kept well within the traditions of slapstick and vaudeville comedy. Such outlandish comedy, however, was apparently too risky for the networks. *The Ernie Kovacs Show* survived only a few months on nationwide television in 1952–1953. *The Honeymooners* lasted only one full season (1955–1956) in its situation comedy format. Gerard Jones claims that its portrayal of a working-class couple barely making ends meet and constantly on the verge of argument "played on deep anxieties" and were a "harsh reminder of a conflict being ardently denied by popular culture" (G. Jones, "Honey" 113).

Fifteen years later, Norman Lear's creations dared to speak the unspeakable, provoking frequent complaints from defenders of good taste. In Lear's breakout success, *All in the Family*, Archie Bunker's bigotry, his daughter Gloria's feminism, and his son-in-law Mike's liberal atheism all served to shock sensibilities across the ideological spectrum of the 1970s (Adler). Lear continued this pattern with the treatment of abortion on *Maude*; homosexuality on *Mary Hartman, Mary Hartman*; and the anger of African Americans verging on reverse racism on *Sanford and Son* and *The Jeffersons*. The programs were followed by two of the most popular situation comedies of the 1980s and 1990s, *Roseanne* and *Married . . . with Children*, both of which thrived on offensive attitudes, outrageous behavior, taboo topics, and the language of insult.

Almost all of these instances of groundbreaking comedy appeared on major networks during prime time, and most of them were cast in the conventional context of family situation comedies. They were all subject to the pressure of network standards and practices, the threats of viewer boycotts, the sensibilities of their sponsors, and the usual consensus in favor of "least offensive programming" to appeal to the huge viewership commanded by the three major networks (MacDonald, "One Nation" 118–24). A new pattern has emerged with the advent of cable television, however. Less burdened with FCC regulations, less dependent on sponsor support, and less hampered by the need to achieve blockbuster ratings, cable television has enjoyed the opportunity to appeal to a narrower demographic. In some cases, this has resulted in bold new comedy that dares to offend, transgressive comedy that revels in shock and tastelessness. The most successful of these new comedies has been Comedy Central's biggest hit, *South Park*, an animated cartoon that made its debut during the summer of 1997. Despite its TV-MA rating (unsuitable for children under 17) and its later time slot of 10 P.M., it became instantly popular, achieving a record-high rating for a cable series of 6.9 by February 1998. Its popularity has continued.

South Park, with its presentation of "alien abductions, anal probes, flaming farts, and poo" has been described as "gleefully offensive and profoundly silly, juxtaposing cute and crude, jaded and juvenile" (Marin 56–57). Using childlike cutout figures, the show follows the adventures of four nine-year-old boys in a small mountain town (named after an actual county in Colorado notorious for alien sightings). The show's creators, Trey Parker and Matt Stone, portray it as a "poisoned place in the heart, a taste-free zone where kids say the darndest, most fucked-up things" (Wilde 34). The foul-mouthed boys, Stan, Kyle, Cartman, and Kenny, constantly heap abuse on each other, utter racist and other politically insensitive epithets (like "Stan's dog's a homo"), question all authority, and obsess about flatulence, excrement, and other bodily functions. Stan, the leader of the group, vomits every time he encounters his semi-girlfriend, Wendy. Kenny, criticized by the others because he is poor, faces a horrible death in almost every episode only to reappear the following week. Other prominent characters include: Stan's Uncle Jim, a gun-rights fanatic; Jim's Vietnam-vet buddy, who speaks through a voice box; the school cook, Chef, the only African American in the town, who shares his fantasies and advice about sexual matters with the awe-struck boys; and Cartman's mom, described by the other boys as a "crack whore." The other adults—teachers, parents, and town officials—are generally portrayed as repressed, frantic, or otherwise unworthy of any child's respect. The one exception may be Jesus Christ, who, dressed in his familiar white robe and sandals, serves as the nice-guy host of a local cable-access show. It all adds up to a ribald, irreverent comedy with a "joyous lack of self-restraint . . . stridently, relentlessly, gloriously, and hilariously outrageous" (Mink).

Like the alien visitors who menace their town, these four nasty little boys have invaded the world of American pop culture and taken it by storm. The inevitable feature film, *South Park, the Movie: Bigger, Longer, and Uncut*, was released to high critical praise and big ticket sales in the summer of 1999. Meanwhile, its phenomenal success emboldened both cable and broadcast networks to attempt their own treatments of taboo subjects with varying degrees of success. In September 1999, for example, the FOX Network introduced with heavy marketing fanfare its new comedy, *Action*, replete with four-letter words (bleeped-out but easy to lip-read), outrageous sexual misbehavior, and viciously self-absorbed characters. The network executives were counting on what they saw as "the rapid disappearance of most taste and language restrictions in mass media," with *South Park* as the prime example (Cartier and Mifflin C10).

Not everyone has shared the general enthusiasm for *South Park*. Peggy Charren, founder of Action for Children's Television, suspects that despite the TV-MA rating, many children watch the program. She was particularly concerned about the characters' use of racial slurs, indicting such language as "dangerous to the democracy" (Huff). Dale Kunkel, a professor of communication at the University of California, Santa Barbara, questioned the motives of the producers and the network. He noted that "the humor and the whole orientation of the show is adolescent-oriented humor, rejecting authority, flouting convention. . . . They say they don't want the teen audience, yet the nature of the content is significantly targeted to appeal to that audience" (Huff). Two grammar schools in New Jersey went so far as to send letters home urging parents to stop their children from watching the show (Starr).

Concern about the influence of mass communication on the general citizenry has followed every advance in mass circulation, from the penny-presses and lurid dime novels of the nineteenth century, to the nickelodeons at the turn of the century, to the hysteria-inducing *War of the Worlds* radio broadcast in 1938, and on into the present. But the debate increased in volume when television invaded the living rooms of the nation, often serving as the new baby-sitter. What McLuhan envisioned as the new family hearth has become unusually powerful, not only in shaping but also reinforcing mainstream values. Television has become the culture's primary storyteller and definer of cultural patterns by providing information and entertainment for an enormous and heterogeneous mass public.

The success of *South Park* and similar television comedy represents the mainstreaming of a new comic attitude previously displayed only in more marginal settings. This attitude is new enough to television to shock yet creative enough to fascinate viewers. Transgressive comedy, climbing through the window of television, has broken into the American home.

This type of comedy is best identified in terms of its purpose. In his study of "the purpose of jokes," Freud first considers "innocent" jokes, such as puns and other plays on words, that are enjoyed for their cleverness and playfulness with no further purpose and which usually evoke a chuckle of moderate amusement. He then deals with "tendentious jokes" that seem to provoke much more laughter and therefore are probably serving some deeper psychological purpose. Freud sees only two such types of purposive humor: "it is either a hostile joke (serving the purpose of aggressiveness, satire, or defense) or an obscene joke (serving the purpose of exposure)" (Freud 97). His explanation of the higher amount of pleasure derived from these two types of humor, especially the obscene, derives directly from his view of "civilization and its discontents":

> It is our belief that civilization and higher education have a large influence in the development of repression, and we suppose that, under such conditions, the psychical organization undergoes an alteration (that can also emerge as an inherited disposition) as a result of which what was formerly felt as agreeable now seems unacceptable and is rejected with all possible psychical force. The repressive activity of civilization brings it about that primary possibilities of enjoyment, which have now, however been repudiated by the censorship in us, are lost to us. But to the human psyche all renunciation is exceedingly difficult, and so we find that tendentious jokes provide a means of undoing the renunciation and retrieving what was lost. (Freud 101)

Since civilization and education remove "the primary possibilities of enjoyment" found in uninhibited aggression and sexual activity, in Freud's view, certain types of humor allow us to "retrieve what was lost," to regress to the more primal state of childhood with its accompanying lack of inhibitions. It is particularly pertinent to this study that, as Freud proceeds to analyze the operation of the smutty joke, he observes that its sexual material can include anything that is "common to both sexes and to which the feeling of shame extends, what is excremental in the most comprehensive sense" (Freud 101). He specifically refers to "the sense covered by sexuality in childhood, an age at which there is, as it were, a cloaca within which what is sexual and what is excremental are barely or not at all distinguished"

(Freud 97–98). The farting, vomiting, and verbal spewing of the South Park boys vividly display such interconnection.

Freud distinguishes the obscene joke, with its purpose of exposure, from the hostile joke, which serves the purpose of aggressiveness or defense. Satirical comedy is one form of such aggression, attacking its target from a sense of outrage and with the hope of some reform. Juvenal catalogued the moral corruption of Rome; Molière ridiculed the religious hypocrites, the lying doctors, and the miserly parental tyrants of Louis XIV's Paris; Pope and Dryden derided the vanity and foppery of London society; Heller, Vonnegut, Kubrick, and other twentieth-century artists have employed absurdist techniques to oppose the stupidities of modern warfare and military culture. Such is the grand aggressive tradition of satire: human reason's warfare on human folly.

Transgressive humor has no such moral purpose. Instead of trying to change or eliminate human foolishness, certain comic writers and performers deliberately revel in the lower forms of social behavior. Unlike the intellectual wit and verbal sophistication of the satirical tradition, transgressive humor regresses to the infantile. Rather than portraying the objects of its humor in hopes that witty ridicule and public shame might provoke change, transgressive humor does not expect or even desire a change, for then the fun would end.

Transgressive humor does share one element with satire: both comic methods depend upon a basic consensus of standards and boundaries, otherwise the joke would not be pleasurable. The societal taboos must remain, so that one can experience the delight of the entry into forbidden realms, a childish joy in simply breaking all the adult taboos, a pleasure indulged in for the sake of exposure of the impulses we have all been forced to repress.

In another overlap with satire, transgressive humor, purposely or not, can sometimes serve general satirical purposes by its faux-innocent or playful criticism of ignorance, prejudice, or stereotypes. For example, in a transgressive context, the articulation of an offensive word or the performance of an offensive action operates to transform stigmatization into empowerment. The appropriation of the insult by the intended target disempowers the insult. The use of the word "nigger" by Black comedians, rappers, and urban street-talk in general and the use of the epithet "queer" by gay groups from academia to performance art serve precisely this purpose while adding an element of threat to those who would attempt to use these words against them. Gay comedy reverts to "camp" and Black comedy employs "homey" style for much the same purposes (Core 5–15). Appropriation of the insulting attack disempowers the attacker.

Transgressive humor sometimes adds a subtle twist to this formula. While the comic speaker may not be a member of the target group, the speaker may attempt to signify his or her solidarity with the group by joining in their appropriation of the hostile or outrageous language or actions. Such seems to have been the intent of an attempt at transgressive humor which resulted in considerable confusion and offense, a blackface act performed by the television star Ted Danson at a Friars Club roast of the African American comedian Whoopi Goldberg in 1993. The routine had been written primarily by Goldberg, who was in a relationship with Danson at the time. In the long tradition of the Friars Club roasts, Danson's routine was sexually explicit with many references to Black sexual stereotypes, outrageous sexual positions, and Goldberg's anatomy. Danson also joked about racist social stereotypes, reporting that when he brought Whoopi to meet his family, they asked her to do the laundry and wash the dishes and offered to drive her to the nearest bus stop when she had finished. Many prominent African Americans in the audience were deeply offended, including former Mayor David Dinkins and television talk-show host, Montel Williams, who cancelled his membership in the Friars (Williams).

In the ensuing controversy, Goldberg defended the routine as their response to the volume of hate mail and openly racist threats she and Danson had received. "We thought it would be a good idea if we sort of dispelled that word" (qtd. in Williams). The comedy writer Bruce Vilanch, who may have contributed material to the sketch, added, "Ted's plan was to defuse the whole (racial) thing with jokes up front" (Williams). The actor Burt Reynolds offered two arguments in favor of the humor: first, the traditionally raucous context of Friars roasts that combine tastelessness with affection; and second, Goldberg's sensitivity to racial offensiveness, saying, "She's tuned in to what would be degrading to Blacks. Times have changed, and we've gone past that" (Thomas). In an interview on the Black Entertainment Television Network, Danson added another argument in defense of the sketch, saying, "We are a racist nation. It's time maybe we started talking" ("Danson 'Proud'"). In other words, such humor brings unpleasant realities into public consciousness. Even academic experts offered some defense of Danson's comedy. Elise A. Williams, associate professor of English at the University of the District of Columbia and an expert on African American humor, commented that even though jokes based on racial stereotypes are particularly troublesome in a mixed-race setting, "I would rather have a comedian push the truth as far as he or she possibly can . . . tease, or move the stereotype to a kind of caricature as a way of *deflating* it" (Mills) [emphases mine].

Another oblique technique is to place the transgressive remarks or actions in the mouth or body of a character for ironic effect. For instance, in *All in the Family*, when Archie Bunker refers to "jungle bunnies," "chinks," or "fags," his obvious ignorance was intended by Lear to serve as a satire of racism. Audience surveys at the time of the show's initial run, however, indicated that many viewers identified with Archie's bigotry and failed to see the irony that Lear intended; they saw the show not as satire but as an outrageous expression of many viewers' socially forbidden racial resentments (Vidmar and Rokeach, qtd. in Adler, 123–38). Similarly, the South Park children's emotional and mental immaturity and undeveloped impulse-control allow them to speak the unspeakable and act out the forbidden behavior. The adults to whom the program is ostensibly targeted are presumed to understand and enjoy the irony and satire, but such a viewer reaction cannot be guaranteed. One viewer's satire may be another viewer's secret truths.

In fact, if the humor is truly outrageous, it is not properly considered satire, but merely a case of truly bad taste. Freedom to engage in such transgressive humor has even found a legal basis, most famously in the case of Larry Flynt, who was sued by Jerry Falwell for intention to inflict emotional distress. In 1983, Flynt's *Hustler* magazine ran a parody Campari liquor ad depicting the famous televangelist as intoxicated and confessing that his first sexual experience had been with his mother in an outhouse. This crude joke qualifies as transgressive rather than satirical. It was not intended as a criticism of any specific behavior of the Reverend Falwell; there was no evidence or public awareness in 1983 of any alcoholic or sexual misbehavior by Falwell. It is better understood as misbehavior on the part of the magazine, a besmirching of a respected moral authority, like the eternal portrayal by adolescents of their high school teachers or administrators in outrageous behavior. In the same spirit, Flynt could just as easily have decided to target Mother Teresa or the Dalai Lama. Such was the understanding behind the decision in the first court's decision on the case before it finally made its way to the Supreme Court as a First Amendment case. It was precisely the general understanding that the portrayal of Falwell was not intended to be taken as truth that robbed the joke of any satirical or libelous power and made the prosecution change its case to one of "emotional distress." The unanimous Supreme Court decision reaffirmed the protection of parody as included in "the recognition of the free flow of ideas." Chief Justice Rehnquist's decision stated, "freedom to speak one's mind is not only an aspect of individual liberty, . . . but essential to the quest for truth and the vitality of society as a whole" (*Hustler Magazine v. Jerry Falwell* 51). It is worth noting in this context that the Supreme Court decision came at a time when many of the Reverend Falwell's televangelist colleagues were being exposed for financial fraud and sexual misconduct, and such a portrayal of Falwell could have been interpreted as an accusation of guilt by association, yet the Supreme Court ignored such an interpretation.

While precedents for the outrageous comedy of *South Park* could readily be found in the practices of various folk cultures, the more mainstream influence can be traced to the long tradition in European societies of organized periods of anarchy and official societies comprised of common people as well as the highly educated that regularly violated, and often criticized, the standards and practices of their culture. In Enid Welsford's classic study of the social and literary history of the fool in Western culture, she describes the phenomenon of "misrule" which appeared in European culture from Roman days until the Renaissance. She refers us to Lucian's *Saturnalia* and its description of the "Liberties of December" at the time of the winter solstice, when "for a short while masters and slaves changed places, laws lost their force, and a mock-king ruled over a topsy-turvy world" (Welsford 201). In the first centuries of the Christian era, there were even instances of the clergy engaging in public folly, in which "mighty persons were humbled, sacred things profaned, laws relaxed and ethical ideals reversed, under the leadership of a Patriarch, Pope, or Bishop of Fools" (Welsford 201). In the cathedral towns of twelfth-century France, the Feast of Fools was an annual occurrence, during which even the Mass was burlesqued. Instead of waving censers of incense, the clergy would swing chains of sausages. Instead of sprinkling the congregation with holy water, some of the sacred ministers would be doused with buckets of water. Sometimes an ass was brought into the church, and "on these occasions solemn Mass was punctuated with brays and howls" (Welsford 202). The celebrant would conclude the liturgy by braying three times *(ter hinhannabit)*, and the people would respond in similar fashion. According to Welsford, such sacrilegious frivolity was often accompanied by satirical verse, topical plays, and burlesque sermons as expressions of the lower clergy's criticism of the Church for whom they were the official exponents.

The official Church, of course, persistently condemned such behavior, so that eventually people in secular associations took up the roles of seasonal fools. Groups such as the Societes Joyeuses flourished from the end of the fifteenth to the middle of the seventeenth century. Welsford describes them as:

> associations of young men who adapted the traditional fool's dress of motley, eared hoods, bells and baubles and organized themselves into kingdoms under the rule of an annually elected monarch known as *Prince des Sots, Mere-Folle,* etc. . . . which enabled them to keep up a running commentary on the affairs of their neighbours and to indulge a taste for satire and social criticism. (205)

With the disappearance of the religious festivals of folly, we seem to lose any account of this behavior among the lower classes, but there is considerable documentation of the continuation of such frivolity among the upper classes. This pattern of annual interruptions of the ordinary routine, with temporary suspension of law and order, remained popular in England, with the traditional feast of the "boy-bishop" among the choirboys of the English cathedrals and in the Christmas Revels of the Lord of Misrule among university students, at the Inns of Court, and in the English and Scottish royal courts of the fifteenth and sixteenth century. In France, the holiday tradition became a permanent feature among the upper classes. What had been seen as a social safety-valve, an "annual interruption of the ordinary routine, marked by a temporary suspension of law and order" developed into a "permanent and legal recognized institution, whose members . . . were pledged to more or less continuous representation of the whole of society as a 'great stage of fools'" and the social satire that had been "the occasional by-product of the Feast of Fools became the whole business of the Societes Joyeuses" (Welsford 205). Welsford describes the development as a change in the understanding of the purpose of a fool:

> The Enfants-sans-souci emphasized the idea of folly as a mask for the wise and armour of the critic. Their "Misrule" was no temporary relaxation of law and order, but a more subtle and permanent reversal of ordinary judgments. It was the wisdom of Mere-Folle to display the folly of the wise. (218)

One is left with the question of whether the transgressive humor of *South Park* and similar television shows is meant to be a mere relaxation of all prevailing norms, like the early Saturnalia and Feasts of Fools, or as a constant satirical commentary on the powerful and famous. Should the foul-mouthed children of *South Park* be considered our boy-bishops (fools for a day) or our *Enfants-sans-souci* (year-round fools)? Since such comedies appear on a weekly basis throughout the year, should they be understood as a break in the week's routine or the regular weekly meetings of the global village idiots? Can the viewing of such programming offer an opportunity for a "more subtle and permanent reversal of ordinary judgments"? Can such programming be truly oppositional and not just a holiday from the prevailing hegemony?

Fiske's approach to the "pleasure and play" of television viewing seems to opt for the oppositional interpretation, describing some readings of the television texts as expressions of resistance to the prevailing norms. He points to Lovell's study of female oppositional readings of soap operas and Schwichtenburg's account of the stylistic excessism and fetishism in *Miami Vice*, where "it is important to render pleasure out of bounds" (Lovell, Schwichtenburg 47). Fiske comments:

> This sort of pleasure lies in the refusal of the social control inscribed in the "bounds." While there is clearly a pleasure in exerting social power, the popular pleasures of the subordinate are necessarily found in resisting, evading, or offending this power. Popular pleasures are those that empower the subordinate, and they thus offer political resistance, even if only momentarily and even if only in a limited terrain. (*Television Culture* 230)

The crude language and the offensive actions of the characters on *South Park* seem to develop what Fiske goes on to describe as "an alternative semiotic strategy of resistance or evasion" (240). As a model of such cultural resistance, Fiske uses the example of the carnival:

> . . . not in its more overtly political or even revolutionary [sense] of attempting to overthrow the social system. Rather it refers to the refusal

to accept the social identity proposed by the dominant ideology and the social control that goes with it. The refusal of ideology, of its meanings and control, may not of itself challenge the dominant social system but it does resist incorporation and it does maintain and strengthen a sense of social difference that is a prerequisite to any more direct social challenge. (*Television Culture* 242)

One final observation of Fiske's is particularly relevant to the comedy of *South Park* and other animated comedies of recent years. The self-referential nature of much of the humor creates what Fiske has called an "empowering inversion of viewer relations" (242). Beavis and Butthead spend considerable time watching and commenting on the music videos typical of MTV, the very channel that carries the show. *The Simpsons* and *King of the Hill* provide frequent visual jokes about the art of animation and the existence of their characters as products of animators and not actual persons. One of the most sophisticated examples was *The Simpsons* episode that took the viewers behind the show, as MTV does with *Behind the Music*, and interviewed each of the main characters as if they were actual actors looking for other work. This conspiracy between the creators and viewers to acknowledge the artifice of television primes the viewer to question the legitimacy of any televised versions of "reality."

If the comedy of *South Park* can be understood as genuinely oppositional, how long can it continue? Will its ability to shock and offend be somehow disempowered and "domesticated," as Gitlin maintains happened to the Norman Lear comedies of the 1970s ("Prime-Time Ideology" 522)? Will it spawn enough successful imitators, as television megahits tend to do, that eventually the irreverence, irony, and shock will become the familiar comic landscape of television? Since Gitlin ascribes the softening of *All in the Family*'s edges to commercial decisions, perhaps the greatest hope for transgressive comedy lies in the viewer-driven nature of cable television as opposed to the broadcast networks' subservience to their advertisers. Alan Ball, Academy Award–winning writer of *American Dream*, has remarked that he chose to write his dark comedy, *Six Feet Under*, for HBO because "network TV works as a vehicle for marketing. . . . They want as large an audience as possible . . . primed by the fantasy in the shows for the fantasy of the products" (qtd. in Friend 83). Ball and others believe that commercial-free cable television offers an alternative situation, connecting more esoteric programming with a more select but highly appreciative target audience. This seems to be borne out by the popularity of several taboo-breaking cable programs like *Oz, Sex and the City, The Osbournes*, and *The Sopranos*, as well as the less sophisticated revelry of *WWE Smackdown*. If this is the case, cable television offers viewers who delight in the violation of cultural taboos their best hope of indulging their antisocial appetites. Every week, they can join the foolish company of Stan, Kenny, Cartman, and Kyle and enjoy the carnival while it lasts.

CHAPTER 3

American Situation Comedies and the Modern Comedy of Manners

David Pierson

David Hirst argues that the main subject of the theatrical comedy of manners genre is the complex ways in which people behave and the social manners they employ within a distinct social context. The central concerns of the genre's characters are sex and money, and thus the form addresses the main topics of "marriage, adultery, and divorce" (Hirst 1). These dramas are characterized by their emphasis on a strong sense of style, deportment, and a witty repartee that is used to conceal the raw emotions that lie just beneath the surfaces of the dramatic lives of its characters.

The dramatic universe of the comedy of manners is a world comprised of a vast assortment of social rules: rules for engaging and disengaging in romantic and sexual relationships, rules for marriage and courtship, rules for friendship, rules for raising one's children, rules for truth telling and outright deception, rules for conducting a dinner party, and so on. These rules are essential to the members of these societies primarily because a person's comprehension of these rules dictates whether he or she is socially accepted within this society (Greene 79). As Hirst maintains, "these rules are society's unwritten laws regulating behaviour, the dictates of propriety which, though they may differ in detail from age to age and class to class, are always basic to the conduct of the characters in the comedy of manners" (2–3). The characters who succeed within this dramatic world are those who are the most adept at discerning these rules and manipulating them to their own advantage.

At first glance, it may seem absurd to suggest that American television situation comedies have anything in common with the witty, refined upper-class worlds of Molière and Goldsmith. The characters in sitcoms, however, are just as obsessed and frustrated with following and often circumventing the prevailing social codes (of an American middle-class civility) as the characters in the English Restoration comedies of Congreve and Sheridan. In *The Beverly Hillbillies*, the backwoods-raised Jethro repeatedly fails every attempt to obtain a captivating career position, as well as to marry a refined woman from the city. In *Seinfeld*, Jerry, George, Elaine, and Kramer continuously debate a multiplicity of changing social rules and customs that constitute contemporary American society.

Because the comedy of manners genre involves the critical exploration of the social manners and mores of a particular society, it also serves as an appropriate form for social satire. In the Restoration comedies, there is usually at least one free-styled, hedonistic character who openly defies the social taboos of marriage and custom, and thereby mocks the moral rigidity of the seventeenth-century English upper-class societies. Douglas Canfield points out that while these defiant characters and their perceived threats to the ruling class are usually neutralized at the end of these Restoration comedies, nevertheless these characters serve to reveal defects in the social-class fabric. Canfield argues that the corrective nature of the comedies' social satire, ending by restoring the traditional order, often appears strained and absurd, which represents the order as socially false and hollow (1–32).

Modern comedy of manners playwrights have used the form's social satire to highlight and expose the social hypocrisies within these closed societies. Oscar Wilde, for example, employed the dramatic form to invert dominant Victorian values and to reveal and attack social hypocrisy (Hirst 49–57). The act of exposing the social hypocrisies of modern societies serves as a type of social-leveling device to bring the upper-class societies down to the egalitarian stratum of the rest of the wider society. In many ways, there is an emancipatory tendency lying beneath the surface of the manners drama, an inclination to reveal and release the larger society from the social dominance of social codes and rules devised largely from upper-class societies.

Because American situation comedies feature a wide range of dramatic characters either following, struggling with, or circumventing dominant social codes and manners, sitcoms can be understood as a particular televisual form of the modern comedy of manners. This chapter focuses on the thematic and discursive elements represented in popular television sitcoms from two distinct time periods: the 1960s, with *The Beverly Hillbillies*; and the 1990s, with *Seinfeld*.

THE BEVERLY HILLBILLIES

In *The Beverly Hillbillies*, Jed Clampett and his entire familial clan (Granny, Jethro, and Elly May) serve as comic rustic characters who unwittingly challenge and thereby parody the cultivated, modernist perceptions of the inhabitants of one of America's wealthiest neighborhoods, Beverly Hills. The central premise of *The Beverly Hillbillies* is that Jed, a poor Ozark farmer, accidentally discovers oil on his backwoods land while shooting at wild game. The discovery turns the poor Clampett family into millionaires overnight. A reluctant Jed is then convinced by "status-conscious Cousin Pearl" to move his entire clan to California for the sake of his daughter, Elly May, and Pearl's son, Jethro (Marc, *Demographic* 45–46). To the horror of their neighbors, the Clampetts convert their lavish, twenty-six-room mansion into a hillbilly ghetto, complete with roaming farm animals. The culture of Beverly Hills, and urban and suburban societies by implication, is consistently satirized as dominated and obsessed with social-climbing, money, and the latest fashion fads and trends. In other words, a modern type of society not unlike those represented in the comedy of manners genre. In the improbable comic world of *The Beverly Hillbillies* reside the persistent social and cultural tensions between America's agrarian, traditional past and its modern, technological present and future.[1]

The avaricious nature of a modern capitalist society is best exemplified in this sitcom by the character of Milburn Drysdale. As the banker and personal caretaker of the Clampett's millions, there is probably no level to which Drysdale will not stoop to keep the family happy, thus keeping their millions in his bank. In the course of the show, Drysdale is not above using extortion and blackmail to fulfill the Clampett's every whim and desire. For instance, when Jed attempts to enroll Jethro in the fifth grade of a prestigious Beverly Hills private school, the principal refuses to allow the twenty-year-old, backwoods young man into her school. She is, however, convinced of the wisdom of Jethro's admission when Drysdale reminds her that his bank holds the mortgage on the school. The sitcom's narratives repeatedly emphasize that money is the overriding factor in the modern, capitalist culture of Beverly Hills.

Furthermore, Drysdale is not above humiliating himself, his secretary Miss Jane Hathaway, his wife, Margaret, or even their family dog—a neurotic, high-strung poodle—to keep the Clampetts' millions in his bank. In one episode, Jed decides to buy and convert an exclusive women's fashion boutique into the House of Granny to sell Granny's handmade, gaudy gingham dresses. Drysdale is consumed with worry that the store will not have any customers for its grand opening, and to please the Clampetts, he and Miss Hathaway endure the humiliation of bad haircuts, supposedly an extra perk for Granny's dress shop customers. Along with Drysdale, the Clampetts must contend with a steady stream of con men, gold diggers, and schemers, all after a share of the Clampetts' millions, in episode after episode.

FIGURE 3.1. Donna Douglas as Elly May Clampett, Buddy Ebsen as Jed Clampett, Irene Ryan as Granny, and Max Baer Jr., as Jethro Bodine in *The Beverly Hillbillies*, 1962–1971. Photo courtesy of Movie Star NewsFair.

In *The Beverly Hillbillies*, the logic and supremacy of modernity is consistently challenged and undermined. Granny's effective homemade folk remedies, for example, repeatedly defy the logic and dominance of modern medical science. In "Granny vs. the Weather Bureau," Granny's innate weather-predicting skills challenge the authority of a professional meteorologist. By examining the movement of a beetle, Granny is able to predict that it will rain. The meteorologist, intent on convincing Granny of the superiority of his company's scientific prediction that it will not rain, shows her a film illustrating the technological advances that are a part of modern meteorological science. The meteorologist's presentation, however, is interrupted by a tumultuous rainstorm. At the end of the episode, the meteorologist is not only resigned to follow Granny's folk methods, but discovers that his father, founder of the company, was also a "beetle man." Although Granny's folk ways are not as appreciated in Beverly Hills as they were in the Ozarks, they serve nevertheless to challenge many of the dominant assumptions of modern science and technology.

Another distinct characteristic of the comedy of manners is that each play usually has a character that is the "truewit" of the drama. The truewit is the play's certified pragmatic philosopher who produces much of the drama's verbal humor, and who always speaks the truth no matter how impolite it may be. This person is usually the most contented character in the play, primarily because he acts instinctively and freely on his own impulses. The truewit is also the person who truly knows and accepts his own nature (Greene 80–81).

In *The Beverly Hillbillies*, the wisest character is the family patriarch, Jed Clampett. The popular sitcom, however, gives this comedy of manners' character its own unique twist by making him a common folkloric character: the wise rube (Staiger 76–77). The wise rube is a transgressive character who, because of his unwitting lack of knowledge about proper social customs and manners, is best positioned to speak the unbridled truth about people and situations. Jed's lack of understanding of modern city life and its customs becomes an enduring virtue rather than a serious character flaw. In many of the episodes, Jed's simple wisdom cuts through the duplicitous behaviors of most of the city folk the Clampetts meet.[2] Unlike most of the city people Jed meets, whose actions and moral conduct are governed by money, social class, and the latest media fads, Jed is guided by an unwavering moral center as he follows his own "code of the hills." It is Jed who implicitly realizes that, despite the family's impoverished living conditions back in the hills, he and his family have lost a spiritual dimension in moving from their rural birthplace. He has moved his family mainly for the sake of his daughter, Elly May, so she will find an appropriate husband, and his nephew, Jethro, so he'll find a good career (Marc, *Demographic* 45–46). Ironically, Jed's agrarian, Jeffersonian-style wisdom is itself an anachronistic type of wisdom, a wisdom found in America's past and therefore, inaccessible and impractical for most Americans living in a modern society.

The most ambitious member of the Clampett clan is Jethro, a social climber. Unlike the other members of the family, Jethro is easily influenced by the latest media fads and fashions. This susceptibility, coupled with his lack of intelligence and common sense, leads him to pursue an improbable range of fantasy-like occupations, including brain surgeon, secret agent, movie star, and astronaut. Jethro is repeatedly frustrated in his attempts to land a glamorous or socially respected job, as well as to marry a polished, refined city woman. Despite his apparent lack of formal education, experience, and intelligence for these positions, the Clampetts' millions function to buy him at least access to these occupations. In keeping with the show's representation of modern society, money is the magical force that opens doors, not the hard work and luck of the American success myth.

Although *The Beverly Hillbillies* is generally perceived as having a conservative perspective toward gender roles and politics, the sitcom is not without its share of contradictions. For instance, Jane Hathaway's unrequited romantic attraction to Jethro presents a situation rarely seen in television sitcoms—an older woman lusting over a much younger man. Traditionally, this particular character type in comedies and dramas has been represented as an unlikable, unsympathetic stereotype (Rowe, *Unruly* 105–06, 116–25). In *The Beverly Hillbillies*, however, Jane is the most decent, honorable, non-familial character in the show. She continuously risks her job to protect the Clampetts from unscrupulous outsiders, along with assuaging Drysdale's more excessive and extravagant schemes.

Elly May is also presented in a contradictory manner. On the one hand, she is a beautiful, innocent young woman whose primary purpose in life, as defined by the patriarch, Jed, is to find and marry a suitable, respectable young man from the city. Her prescribed role as the object of the male gaze is best exemplified by the show's frequent cheesecake poses of her in her swimsuit playing with her animals by the backyard "cement pond." On the other hand, though Elly May is naive and innocent, her true love for all types of animals and her tomboyish behavior usually sends her male suitors running for the door. Elly May has unusual physical strength, which is illustrated by the fact that she always beats Jethro in wrestling matches. While I am not asserting that Elly May be understood as representing a proto-feminist position, it is interesting how her love for animals and tomboyishness serve as forms of resistance to Jed's patriarchal designs to relegate her to the happy housewife role.

SEINFELD

Frank McConnell has suggested that *Seinfeld* may be best described as a "modern comedy of manners," rather than a traditional domestic television sitcom. One of the central differences between *Seinfeld* and more traditional

FIGURE 3.2. Jason Alexander as George Costanza, Jerry Seinfeld as himself, Michael Richards as Cosmo Kramer, and Julia Louis-Dreyfus as Elaine Benes in *Seinfeld*, 1990–1998. Photo courtesy of Larry Edmunds BooksFair.

television sitcoms is that the main characters know they are involved in an elaborate, largely contrived social game of witty dialogue, false deceptions, and elusive desires. Unlike the characters of the standard sitcom genre, they continuously watch themselves play out these absurd situations even as they realize they cannot avoid the "comic pull of the absurd." Within the world of *Seinfeld*, the absurd does not exist in well-conceived comic gags or wisecracks, but rather in the small social blunders that comprise the spectrum of social manners in the 1990s (McConnell 19–20).

While *Seinfeld* features a typical, stable sitcom group, which does not change from one episode to the next, its characters do not appear to be consistently consumed with either personal growth or advancing themselves out of their own social status or social group.[3] Instead, the main characters are continuously preoccupied with discerning, following, and sometimes evading, the complexity of social manners that exists both within and outside their own social group.

Of course, the main difficulty with associating *Seinfeld* with the comedy of manners genre is that its characters clearly inhabit a middle-class lifestyle rather than the genre's usual stylish drawing room world of societal elites. But Hirst points out that the manners genre is not simply relegated to an exclusively upper-class universe. English playwrights Orton, Pinter, and Osborne have each chosen this dramatic form to collectively explore the conflicting social moralities and manners of working-class, middle-class, and upper-middle-class English societies. Hirst argues that the comedy of manners is a form thematically flexible enough to dramatize and examine the moralities and manners of any social class in Western society (116).

One of the underlying assumptions of these dramas is that people primarily act out of self-interest and therefore have few commitments to anybody or anything but themselves. The primary goals of this self-interest are the pursuit of intellectual and sensual pleasures along with acquisition of material wealth and social privilege. The characters of *Seinfeld* are just as self-interested and self-absorbed as the characters that inhabit the comedies of Congreve and Wilde. In many of the episodes, Jerry and his friends satirize the highly discriminating and noncommittal ethos of the 1990s single adult dating scene. The characters constantly debate the implicit protocols of dating, from what signs constitute a girlfriend or boyfriend to how many dates one must endure before dumping a girlfriend or boyfriend. The characters demonstrate a high level of creativity in finding new grounds for breaking off romantic and sexual engagements. Jerry has dumped his girlfriends for a wide range of peculiar character traits, from not laughing at his jokes to laughing too strangely to eating peas one at a time. Elaine's dumping criteria includes not cleaning one's bathtub to the improper use of punctuation. In *Seinfeld*'s world, anyone who violates these unstated social rules is socially punished. When Elaine stops to buy a box of Jujyfruit candy after hearing that her boyfriend has been injured in a car accident, her transgression leads to her boyfriend dumping her. Because these characters are not firmly bound by any long-term relationship or career responsibilities, their self-identities become intimately linked to the idiosyncratic nature of changing social manners in contemporary American society. The characters' status of being thirtyish, middle-class, unattached adults, with plenty of unfettered time on their hands, places them in the opportune position to experience and contemplate most of the social manners that comprise American civility.

Perhaps one of the main reasons for *Seinfeld*'s popularity is that it implicitly acknowledges a deep-seated cultural ambivalence and anxiety over the consistently shifting social codes, attitudes, and manners of a rapidly evolving American society. On the one hand, the show's characters are partly dependent on these social codes to form their individual identities and they receive great pleasure from the richness of American cultural life. On the other hand, the characters must struggle to keep up with the sheer multiplicity of changing social codes and manners—from new dating rules to the tenets of political correctness.

Seinfeld, as a highly successful television series with impressive ratings and critical acclaim, takes as its main interest the social codes and manners of an urban, middle-class American lifestyle, and comically elevates them into highly absurd situations (McInerney 15). In "The Pen," Jerry's acceptance of an "astronaut pen" inadvertently erupts into a huge scandal within his parents' retirement community. In "The Red Dot," George's gift to Elaine of a cashmere sweater with a small red dot contributes to his getting fired from Pendant Publishing. *Seinfeld*, through its comical concern with social manners and customs, seems to assert not the decline of civility but rather its preponderance in American society.

Seinfeld shares many narrative and thematic concerns with the comedy of manners genre. Donald Bruce relates that one of the central comic themes of the English Restoration comedies, or comedy of manners, is that basic human impulses and inclinations must be disguised in reason in order to mask passion and appetite with decorum (89). Essentially, the comedy of manners acknowledges that all human social behavior is socially structured through societal social manners and customs. In *Seinfeld*, the main characters' inherent drives and desires (sex, money, friendship) must be disguised while often being comically frustrated and complicated by the impending requirements of a range of social manners. In the sitcom, Jerry's libidinal desires are frequently hindered by the dictates of established contemporary social manners. In "The Junior Mint," Jerry's uproarious comic attempts to learn his new girlfriend's name, which supposedly rhymes with a part of the female anatomy, leads to her storming out of his apartment.

Another underlying theme that cuts across the comedy of manners genre and *Seinfeld* is an overwhelming concern with maintaining social appearances.

Hirst relates that the final line of Joe Orton's modern comedy of manners play, *Loot*, "People would talk; we must keep up appearances," reflects not only a belief basic to Orton's plays but to the genre as a whole (2). Because the characters in these plays are caught in an intricate social game in which all of their actions are circumscribed by social rules, presenting an acceptable social image is the most important social rule they must follow. The most serious social blunder a character may commit is to fail to maintain one's public image and thus reveal to others one's concealed intentions and desires.

Likewise, *Seinfeld*'s main characters are just as concerned and obsessed with the intricate social manners and details that comprise their own social appearances. Although Kramer is definitely concerned with his social image, he consistently follows his own innate, often uncontrollable impulses and inclinations, often oblivious to any resulting social consequences. For instance, in "The Conversion," Kramer's innate sexual magnetism, referred to by a Latvian Orthodox priest as the "Kavorka," impels a devoted Sister to contemplate leaving the Church. Kramer, however, stops her from leaving the Church by wearing several rings of smelly garlic around his neck, a folk remedy which supposedly blunts his natural sexual appeal.

Although it may seem apparent that Jerry, with his sarcastic wit and ironic posturing, is the show's truewit, nonetheless he frequently neglects to tell the truth in his romantic and family relationships. The show's actual truewit is Kramer. While Jerry, George, and Elaine spend most of their time and energies on following and circumventing social rules, Kramer, for the most part, simply and instinctively acts on his own desires. In the episode "The Nose Job," George, with the help of Jerry, is painfully striving, in a very coy manner, to convince his girlfriend, Audrey, to get a "nose job." When Kramer is first introduced to Audrey, he bluntly remarks that she could be stunning; all she needs is a nose job. When Audrey's first operation is botched, George decides to break up with her. Kramer appears to be Audrey's only true friend; he even helps her find a new plastic surgeon. At the end of the episode, George is dismayed to find out that Audrey has become a radiant beauty and that Kramer is her new boyfriend. In this episode, as well as others, Kramer's impulsive and honest behavior easily wins out over his friends' frantic scheming and self-satisfied, moral pretensions of goodness. Through Kramer's truewit character, the sitcom affirms the belief that those who follow, evade, or gain ego satisfaction from society's social manners will invariably become social casualties of them.

Unlike the English Restoration comedies or traditional comedy of manners, *Seinfeld* is extremely egalitarian in its satirical thrust. The series asserts that personal idiosyncrasies and eccentricities are not the sole properties of the socially elite. In fact, the show comically maintains that people from all walks of life are primarily defined by their pet peeves, social habits, and concerns. From an obsessive auto mechanic who abducts vehicles he feels are being

abused by their owners to a dry cleaner with a predilection for wearing his customers' clothes, the sitcom satirically illustrates the complexity of social manners that comprise contemporary American civility. An interesting irony
behind the post-1960s expansion of social group diversity and individualism,
with their inherent social demands, is that most Americans must keep up
with, and contend with, an ever-increasing range of social manners. *Seinfeld*,
as a comedy of manners, constructs its comic narratives to satirize and lam-
poon a surplus of social manners in the 1990s.

CONCLUSION

Wayne Booth describes television programming as "the most frequent artistic experience in America today," more widely shared than any other art form
(387). While a relatively new art form, television creators draw from a long,
rich aesthetic history of dramatic and literary works to produce popular programs that effectively engage their large, diverse audiences. Television's most
popular form, the situation comedy, is a worthy descendant and a modern
variation of the theatrical comedy of manners genre. As with the comedy of
manners genre, the American sitcom features characters who must contend
with an array of social manners and rules in order to satisfy their desires for
sexual intimacy, elevated social status, and close relationships. These sitcoms,
through the process of having their main characters pursue their desires,
highlight, exaggerate, and satirize many of the social codes that comprise
American society. As such, the sitcom can be understood as a historical and
cultural document for observing and scrutinizing dominant social manners at
any particular time period, especially those relating to gender, social class,
and relationships. Despite the comically absurd situations in which sitcom
characters frequently find themselves entangled, they must follow the same
social edict as all comedy of manners characters—they must strive to "keep
up appearances."

NOTES

1. David Marc is one of the few television scholars who recognized Paul Henning's rural situation comedies *(The Beverly Hillbillies, Green Acres, Petticoat Junction)* as
worthy of critical attention. At the time, many critics disavowed these sitcoms for their
failure to address important social issues and their seemingly single-minded penchant
for obvious gag jokes. Marc, however, argues that the humor of these sitcoms rests on
the oldest thematic strain in American cultural history: the tensions that exist between
the city and the country. He adds that Henning's backwoods characters are "recognizable figures from American popular tradition" *(Demographic* 42).

2. In "Cool School Is Out, Part 2," Drysdale tries to convince Jed to evict a group of beatniks because their beards make them look like "hobos," they wear old clothes, like to dance, and are scornful of society's materialistic values. Jed responds by saying that he has a few whiskers himself, he likes to dance, and definitely agrees that there are more things in life than just money. Jed's response not only illustrates his ability to perceive beyond dominant standards of appearance and convention, but also associates the Clampetts (and America's pastoral past) with the expressive individualistic values of the beatnik and youth generation.

3. In the series, George and Elaine both change their job positions. While George moves from being an unsuccessful real estate agent to unemployment to a management-level position with the N.Y. Yankees, Elaine's job shifts include being a manuscript reader at Pendant Publishing, personal assistant to Mr. Pitt, and copywriter at J. Peterman's catalog company. These job changes do not occur because of any personal initiatives on their part, but rather due to chance circumstances. In "The Opposite," George adopts the opposite of his usual, self-loathing behavior and lands a front office job with the Yankees. In this same episode, Elaine's Jujyfruit candy habit leads to the loss of her job and the financial demise of Pendant Publishing.

PART TWO

Reframing the Family

Who Rules the Roost?

Sitcom Family Dynamics from the Cleavers to the Osbournes

Judy Kutulas

At the heart of the American sitcom lies the family, nuclear, extended, blended, and created. We have seen it all, from families headed by automotive matriarchs to astronauts married to genies. Family is the one experience to which virtually all viewers can relate. It evokes symbols and images advertisers like. And its plot possibilities are endless. According to Stephanie Coontz, "our most powerful visions of traditional families derive from images that are still delivered to our homes in countless reruns of television sit-coms" (Coontz 23). Yet, the modern audience is conflicted by those images. We see in the Cleavers *(Leave It to Beaver)* and other television families a vision of perfection, the embodiment of security, stability, and togetherness that haunts us as we grapple with our real, less-than-perfect, families. At the heart of these television families is the clear articulation of roles and responsibilities and the gentle lines of authority that flow from wise dad and understanding mom to obedient children (May 208). Objectively, we know that the Cleavers represent an ideal rather than a norm, and one that confines and constricts individuality. Emotionally, though, we cannot escape the sense that life would be so much better if our lives were just like the Cleavers.

FIGURE 4.1. Hugh Beaumont as Ward Cleaver, Barbara Billingsley as June Cleaver, Jerry Mathers as Beaver (Theodore) Cleaver, and Tony Dow as Wally Cleaver in *Leave It to Beaver*, 1957–1963. Photo courtesy of Movie Star NewsFair.

The 1950s sitcom family idealized a "qualitatively new phenomenon" (Coontz 25). The Depression and World War II blurred American memories of "normal" family life, even as they induced intense longing for stability. The Cold War introduced a new set of social expectations: family was to be a secure, consumerist, conformist bulwark against Communism (May 10–11). Television provided an intimate family prototype, beamed weekly into domestic space; it was natural, didactic, but still theatrical (Spigel 157), starring a white-collar father, stay-at-home mother, and a flock of children all nestled in their safe small-town cocoon. Material affluence contributed to the image's allure, but it was the television family's dynamic that was so seductive. Everybody got along, everybody was happy, and everyone wanted to be together. There was just enough conflict to drive plots. By the time the half-hour was over, everybody was happy again. The Cleavers and other 1950s television families were the wish fulfillment of several decades of social disruption, economic dislocation, and political fear.

The ethnic and racial sitcoms that made the transition from radio to television, *The Goldbergs*, *I Remember Mama* (called *Mama* on television), and *Amos 'n' Andy*, could not compete with these new family stories. Their focus on hardship or difference or the conflicts that existed between husbands and wives or parents and children suddenly seemed old-fashioned. *I Love Lucy* marked the transition. Originally a battle of the sexes comedy set in a New York City apartment, the series added a child to the mix, which softened the title character. Eventually it was reset in suburban Connecticut (G. Jones 73). A new dynamic emerged post-*Lucy*, one where television families respected authority, modeled conformity, and followed social rules.

In the new television families, dad was the leader, but not the boss. Only ethnic hotheads like Ricky Ricardo (*I Love Lucy*'s Cuban head of household) or Danny Williams (*Make Room for Daddy*'s title character, who, television name aside, was Lebanese) believed in the old-world patriarch. Sociologists noted the transformation from the "positional" family to the "personal" one, which was more democratic and less authoritarian (Skolnick 167–68). The new ideal, reinforced by several decades of social fears about too-strong women, rested on complementary gender roles in marriage (Weiss 18–19). The modern husband was involved in family life, helping out by occasionally drying the dishes, playing with his children, and modeling appropriate gender roles for his sons (Spock 254–55). In real life, dad's centrality to the family was slipping away as the family became more of a consumer entity (mom's specialty) and as dad worked longer hours and learned to fit into a corporate culture (Kimmel 236–37). On television, though, dad was always around, the impeccable reflection of the new ideal. Mom, meanwhile, was supposed to be dad's complement, the "steady, loving person" who met children's day-to-day emotional needs and cooked their suppers (Spock 484). On television she was more invisible, to help prop up dad's declining household status (Leibman

121–33). Stability was the result of carefully balanced roles. Father knew best, mother understood, and children obeyed. In television households without such division of labor—the households of television neighbors, sidekicks, and friends—chaos prevailed. The problem child on *Leave It to Beaver*, Eddie Haskell, lives in a dysfunctional family with a father who (depending on the episode) hits, yells, criticizes, or ignores his son. But in successful 1950s television families, members worked together, understood their individual roles, and did what was expected of them.

By the mid-1960s, networks were willing to disturb this domestic harmony for a particular segment of the audience. Advertisers instinctively recognized the potential of the baby boom, that vast postwar demographic bulge of Americans born between 1947 and 1960, and television courted it with a host of children shows like *The Mickey Mouse Club* and *The Flintstones*. The spending possibilities of boomers as they moved into adolescence did not escape the television industry. Certainly, *The Adventures of Ozzie and Harriet* benefited from the simple expedient of tacking on a song at the end of episodes by son Rick, a real-life teen singing sensation. The popularity of the Beatles, reflected in the sales of records, movies, magazines, bubblegum cards, and a Saturday morning cartoon show, reminded network programmers that teens had money and, unlike other components of the audience, were eager to spend it. But, immersed in a postwar peer culture, teens did not always believe that father knew best, either on sitcoms or in real life (J. Gilbert 17).

The emerging generation gap was treated gently on two mid-1960s shows, *Gidget* and *The Patty Duke Show*. On *The Patty Duke Show*, Duke plays, as the theme song explains, "identical cousins" who are "different as night and day"—sedate, studious, English Cathy and all-American, boy-crazy, frug-dancing Patty. Cathy rarely finds herself at odds with her uncle and aunt, but Patty lives in a world of peers and peer temptations. She falls in and out of love, tries on new roles, and often drives her parents crazy. She does not, to the disproportionately teen and preteen audience's delight, always do what her parents want her to do. As the first boomers edged into adulthood, their conflicts with real-life parents were likewise reflected and refracted on TV, as in the late-1960s series *The Mothers-in-Law* and *That Girl*. In both programs, the younger generation politely rejects their parents' lives. Ann Marie's *(That Girl)* decision to move to New York City and become an actress is about finding one's own way in the world rather than meeting parental expectations or following social rules. By the late 1960s, a few sitcoms began to undermine television parents' authority by privileging the independence of their adult or nearly adult children.

Within the next few years, the generation gap split wide open, both in real life and on television. College students rebelled against their parents' authority and materialism. The counterculture, the women's liberation movement, and the sexual revolution alienated youth from traditional institutions like the family. By 1970, one-third of America's college-aged population rejected marriage and having children (Schulman 16). Television stereotypes symbolized much of what they rebelled against. Young women feared becoming like June Cleaver—sweet, servile, and invisible, vacuuming in her pearls and high heels. Young men were equally dubious of Ward Cleaver, particularly his relationship with his boss and the psychological costs of keeping the Cleaver family in white picket fences and new Fords. This generation defied the networks' previous assumptions about audience. They were, as a group, freer spending, certainly by comparison to their Depression-raised parents. They were single longer, so less of their income was given over in fixed ways to mortgages and car payments. They were, in short, a highly desirable audience for advertisers. But they were also less likely to watch television than their elders because their lives were more self-absorbed, their time less structured into television-watching routines, and they saw little around the dial that spoke to their life experience (G. Jones 187–88).

As with so many aspects of American society, the baby boomers had the numerical weight to force change. Networks began to single them out as an audience, and advertisers pitched their ads at them. CBS dumped the "hayseed comedies" (*The Beverly Hillbillies, Green Acres,* and *Mayberry RFD*) that appealed to the older and rural viewers who watched the most television in favor of more sophisticated "relevance" fare geared toward a freer-spending younger audience (G. Jones 192). In January 1971, *All in the Family* premiered, sending shock waves because of its rendering of a family decidedly unlike the Cleavers. Its main characters are Archie and Edith Bunker, their daughter Gloria, and Gloria's husband, Michael. Gloria and Michael are baby boomers, open to the new political, social, and cultural possibilities of the 1960s. Archie and Edith represent the older generation, raised on the deprivation and sacrifice of the Depression and the unabashed patriotism of World War II. The generations fight all the time, about the war in Vietnam, sexual attitudes, race, religion, and women's roles, but the subtext is nearly always the same. Archie expects to be the patriarch of his family, and expects the attendant status and power. Gloria and Michael reject both Archie's authority and his model of the family; their rejection is privileged by the show's presentation of Archie as ignorant and bigoted (Marc, *Comic* 183). Even though his wife still offers up the trappings of his power (the can of beer, his own chair in front of the television), Archie is clearly not the lord and master of his castle.

All in the Family legitimated youth's rebellion against its elders. Its implicit subject was the boomers' critique of the 1950s family dynamic. Edith trots after Archie, smoothing over conflict, yet Archie treats her like a servant, not a partner or an equal. She tries to bolster his authority; he keeps telling her to "stifle." He uses similar tactics to keep his wayward daughter and son-in-law in line. The invisible, automatic hierarchy of the Cleaver household is neither normal nor easy at the Bunkers. *All in the Family* replicated the real-world collapse of

authority that followed the war in Vietnam and the counterculture. A generation of Americans became as sensitive to power and authority issues as Gloria
and Michael. Archie symbolizes the abuse of power and the unreasonable
expectation of obedience they saw everywhere, from the White House to their
universities. *All in the Family* also reveals the seamy underside of the 1950s family, the hurt, disappointment, and denial that are sometimes all that hold the
Bunkers together. It served a different function than happy family comedies,
mocking rather than modeling, offering up a deliberately imperfect vision of
family life to replace the deliberately perfect Cleaver model.

The show spawned a series of relevancy family comedies by *All in the
Family* creator Norman Lear—*Good Times, Maude, Sanford and Son, The Jeffersons*, and *One Day at a Time*. MTM Productions, founded by Mary Tyler
Moore and her then-husband, Grant Tinker, followed suit with its own set of
relevant domestic comedies, including *The Mary Tyler Moore Show, Rhoda,
Phyllis*, and *The Bob Newhart Show*. None were as shocking as *All in the Family* had been, but none featured families like the Cleavers either. Reality
intruded—divorce, unemployment, crime—and plots were not happily
resolved in half an hour. Dad and mom did not have all the answers. Family
did not live in harmony or balance; they clashed and fought and hurt one
another. By the 1973–74 season, relevancy comedies occupied half of the top
ten Nielsen spots, and they were the only sitcoms to make that list. Their target demographic was "a young, liberal upscale audience making the transition
from turbulent college campuses to the workplace" (Taylor 56), in other
words, baby boomers. While Saturday night, America's traditional date night,
used to be a big family broadcast night that included such family-friendly
shows as *My Three Sons, Green Acres*, and *Petticoat Junction*, CBS drew bigger
ratings with a 1974 Saturday night line-up aimed at baby boomers, *All in the
Family, The Mary Tyler Moore Show*, and *M*A*S*H*. College students watched
in dorms and young singles watched in their apartments. Young women, particularly, became a desirable audience, not as wives and mothers, but as single
women pursuing education, independence, and careers (Rabinovitz 145). This
baby boomer audience had the numerical and social weight to expect that its
critical view of family life would prevail.

In 1970s relevancy family shows, fathers' authority disappeared because—
to baby boomers—fathers were not central family members. The boomer
audience might have grown up watching Ward Cleaver, but its lived experience and the counterculture's social critique suggested that real fathers were
rarely as available or as engaged as Ward had been. They were too busy at the
office for family (Weiss 108). Relevancy sitcoms did not so much question
whether father knew best as whether he had any power in a domestic space
ruled by mom. Unlike Archie, other 1970s television fathers only rarely bothered to claim authority, having long since learned that a kind of domestic
ignorance was bliss. So superfluous were some of them that, like Phyllis's hus-

band Lars on *The Mary Tyler Moore Show*, they were not even shown or, if they were, they made occasional appearances in their children's lives, like Julie and Barbara's divorced father on *One Day at a Time*. As boomer children aged, they came to suspect that Ward Cleaver's den was a retreat away from the actual domestic power figure, mom.

Since moms were represented as the true authority figures on 1970s relevancy sitcoms, they became prime targets for ridicule and attack. Females were disproportionate viewers of sitcoms and the "single-female household" was a valuable 1970s demographic target (Marc, *Comic* 169). Thanks to the women's movement, young women looked at their mothers and saw "models to avoid," women who parlayed domesticity into power they extracted via guilt (Breines 77). If fathers disengaged in 1970s sitcoms, then mothers waged constant passive-aggressive guerilla actions to legitimate the housewife's role, a role that, in 1970s currency, was significantly devalued. Television housewives of the 1970s fervently believed in the value of what June Cleaver did all day, so fervently that they wanted their daughters to be like her, and them. There was a constant tug of war on shows like *Rhoda* between those mothers and their daughters, who were more attracted to the single, childless career woman modeled by Mary Richards *(The Mary Tyler Moore Show)*. Such struggles exaggerated the real-life generational break delineated by the women's movement while they allowed the all-important young, female demographic the vicarious thrill of besting mom.

As parental authority declined on 1970s relevancy television, family was redefined. There had always been truncated families on sitcoms—widows and widowers and bachelor uncles—but off-screen death forced those structures. On *Rhoda* and *One Day at a Time* and *The Mary Tyler Moore Show*, family came apart when family members opted out. Biological family no longer offered the security it had in 1950s sitcoms because, for many prized boomer viewers, family was not a stable institution. A lot of 1950s families stayed together out of economic necessity. By the 1970s, women had economic options other than marriage, and the swinging singles lifestyle tempted both men and women. The divorce rate rose, the marriage rate dropped, and the baby boom gave way to the birth dearth (Frum 73–81). Lifestyle choices also alienated many boomers from their parents. Sitcoms of the 1970s explored these facts of modern life culturally. Television's biological families became more fragmented and unstable at the same time television viewers representing prized demographic groups sought out alternatives to the nuclear unit. Constructed family composed of peers, friends, or coworkers who functioned as "support group[s]" provided the kinds of affirmation biological family did not always give (Marc, *Comic* 169). Originally a radical idea with roots in the counterculture, the sitcom's quick embrace of constructed family helped normalize this alternative, thanks to such hits as *WKRP in Cincinnati, M*A*S*H*, and *Three's Company*.

Unlike biological family, constructed family was family by choice, family without the hang-up of family roles, family without hierarchy.

Television of the 1970s was antiauthoritarian in structure as well as style, reflecting the influx of boomers into the production process. The result was programming that embraced 1960s values and was irreverent, topical, and mocking of institutions and traditions. *Saturday Night Live*, itself a constructed family of boomer performer/writers, epitomized the style of television made by and for people "who had grown up watching television" (Marc, *Demographic* 151). Its most popular target was television and, especially, 1950s family stereotypes, which appeared in segments as diverse as a "Hearst Family Christmas" and "The Coneheads" (Shales and Miller 155). In one classic sketch, guest host Rick Nelson *(The Adventures of Ozzie and Harriet)* finds himself trapped in a series of 1950s family sitcom homes, endlessly doomed to circulate from the set of *Leave It to Beaver* to *Father Knows Best* to *Make Room for Daddy*. Boomer television used the Cleaver metaphor as a generational touchstone, a nostalgic cultural reference point, and a sacred cow to be prodded and poked. No longer a model, the happy family ideal could be rendered sweetly in *Happy Days* or sarcastically in *Mary Hartman, Mary Hartman*, but always with a nudge and a wink toward the boomer audience.

By the end of the 1970s, the young, single television market became less important, largely because "it was simply difficult to keep those affluent, educated young people at home in front of the set" (G. Jones 244). The demographic center of gravity shifted as more boomers began their own families and as "family values" became a 1980s political catchphrase. The family sitcom was revived in the early 1980s with two enormous hits, *The Cosby Show* and *Family Ties* (Thompson 45). These shows featured neither the complementary parental roles of the 1950s nor the frustrated housewives and invisible dads of the 1970s. Their dynamic was modern. Clair Huxtable *(The Cosby Show)* and Elyse Keaton *(Family Ties)* work outside the home, their husbands cook and clean, and parenting is a shared enterprise. Both shows also played on boomers' generational identities. The Huxtables had marched on Washington in 1963 and the Keatons had been hippies. But what most distinguished these programs from 1970s family stories was that now the boomers were in charge, both behind the scenes and in front of the camera. Family sitcoms of the 1980s revealed how boomers intended to do family differently.

In the 1950s, parents raised their children to be crowd followers and people pleasers, conformist and obedient (Breines 68). In the 1980s, boomer parents cultivated independence in their children. Television parenting styles also changed. Ward and June Cleaver knew what was right for their children; Cliff and Clair Huxtable wanted their children to learn it for themselves. Families ran democratically as parents helped to educate and advise, but rarely laid down the law. Most of all, parents practiced tolerance, a value rebellious boomers wished their parents had shown them. The ideal in 1980s family sitcoms created by boomers was what sociologist Arlene Skolnick describes as a "personal, democratic style" of childrearing, where "an emphasis on autonomy" replaces obedience as a parenting goal (170). Family comedies of the 1980s aspired to model a more flexible and autonomous family unit, even if, as Cliff Huxtable often discovers, children raised in such an environment are not always respectful of parental authority.

While boomers often controlled the sitcom production process and, thereby, family representations on 1980s sitcoms, they had to take into account the broader audience for family stories. In addition to boomer parents, the primary audience for the new generation of family comedies was 'tweens and teens. Indeed, on *Family Ties* and another 1980s family comedy, *Growing Pains*, the teenage sons, played by Michael J. Fox and Kirk Cameron respectively, became so popular with preteen girls that they gained more airplay and, at some point, more dominance in shows once about their television parents. The bifurcated audience meant that 1980s family sitcoms had an undercurrent of youthful subversion, of rebels and bad boys like Fox and Cameron challenging parental authority. Younger viewers, identified as Generation X (defined as those born between 1961 and 1981), were well acquainted with the happy family sitcom ideal, thanks to reruns of *Leave It to Beaver*, *My Three Sons*, *The Partridge Family*, and *Happy Days*. Their interaction with family sitcoms was different, however.

If their boomer parents grew up in families influenced—for better or worse—by the Cleaver ideal, then Gen X's primary interaction with the Cleavers was through television. As Gen Xers grew up, old reruns often served both a baby-sitting and escapist function, a trend captured in the film *Pleasantville*. As they watched, they longed for "a happier, more simple time when families weren't as dysfunctional" (Owen 18), even though, as an age cohort, they had assimilated their parents' antiauthoritarian values. They were, in short, ambivalent about the ideal family dynamic, appreciating independence and autonomy, but wondering if too much autonomy fractured the family unit beyond repair. In the end, whether or not the Cleaver family model was realizable, they knew they would never themselves live it and for that their parents' generation was to blame. Like their parents before them, they blamed *their* parents for whatever deficiencies they found in their upbringings and represented the result in sitcoms they helped write and direct for their peers. The Gen X response to the happy family ideal first appeared on the margins of mainstream television, partially fueled by producers' desire to attract and keep the youngest edge of the young, single demographic. *The Simpsons* and *Married . . . with Children*, two Gen X visions of family, were crucial to the success of a new network, FOX, which targeted the "young-adult audience" (Jamie Kellner, president of FOX, qtd. in Owen 57). The adults in these shows were boomer parents, not as boomers might see them, but as their children did.

The classic Gen X representation of a boomer parent is Homer Simpson. Homer's creator, Matt Groening, is a boomer, not a Gen Xer, but, like most members of both age groups, he "grew up completely overwhelmed by television" (Doherty 36). Although Homer lives in Springfield, a name borrowed from *Father Knows Best*, he bears little resemblance to any 1950s father, a fact that tickles both boomer viewers and their children. But members of the two generations enjoy Homer for slightly different reasons. For boomers, he is an example of bad parenting, of what would happen if fathers simply indulged themselves rather than being responsible for their children. For Gen Xers, Homer represents the illogical extension of the boomer pursuit of autonomy, what Daniel Yankelovich describes as the "ethic of self-fulfillment" (Skolnick 167). Homer seeks immediate gratification and is completely governed by his id. Yet viewers of both generations like watching the show because Homer is a bad role model. *The Simpsons* is naughty, rebellious fun, a breath of fresh air in a television world where families richer and more perfect than our own predominate. We can all feel superior to the Simpson family. Still, they survive, sometimes thrive, and they certainly love each other, and that is reassuring to anyone whose family seems flawed.

In the 1990s, as more sitcoms were aimed at the Gen X market, boomers lost representation, except on shows like *Everybody Loves Raymond* that were pitched at an older audience. Boomer characters appear only infrequently on shows like *Will & Grace* or *Friends*, and when they do, they play the imperfect parents of continuing characters. Like Homer, most are too id-driven to have much authority. They are embarrassingly sexual, having affairs, changing sexual identity, or getting involved with much younger partners. Their motives are selfish, and their actions shatter their children's security, identity, and sense of morality. Joey Tribiani's parents on *Friends*, for example, are both okay with the fact that his father is having an affair, but Joey is not. He plays what the audience recognizes as the parental role, trying to force his father to behave morally, only to get yelled at by his mother, who likes the status quo because his father treats her better out of guilt. "Things just aren't the same here on Walton's Mountain," comments Joey's roommate, Chandler, invoking a Gen X television family model. Joey has a distinct notion of what a family ought to be like, one, as Chandler's comment suggests, that is partly derived from television. But Joey's parents do not fit that notion of family. Joey's cognitive dissonance between his real parents and the parents he grew up with on television is typical of Gen X's relationship with the Cleaver family ideal. Unlike his boomer parents, who are comfortable rebelling against that ideal, Joey feels cheated that he never got to live it, even if, like Chandler, he knows in his heart of hearts that it is a seductive ideal fabricated by television.

The 1960s have triumphed in American society to the extent that families are a more diverse lot. Their diversity is mirrored in the proliferation of television options aimed at different demographic groups. No single vision of family predominates anymore. Today, the endless reruns of television families past mingle with television families present on cable stations and networks. But the reference point of the Cleavers remains the cultural ideal in American society; whether accepted, rejected, or reconfigured, it always looms over television's renderings of family. Like Rick Nelson, we as audience seem forever trapped in a *Twilight Zone* of 1950s family sitcoms, never quite at home but always hopeful. *The Osbournes*, MTV's newest hit, aims at Generations X and Y, the youngest adult components of the still-desirable audience demographic. Although it focuses on a real family, its appeal is the wonderfully absurd juxtaposition of the self-proclaimed Prince of Darkness, former Black Sabbath singer Ozzy Osbourne, and the 1950s family ideal. Like Homer Simpson, Ozzy seems like he ought to be a bad parent, but he is not. He certainly is not Ward Cleaver and maybe not even Cliff Huxtable; still, he cares about his wife and children, and they care about him. Ozzy has his *Father Knows Best* moments, despite the Goth outfits and tattoos. And, if the Osbournes can find family bliss, so can the rest of us remake the 1950s family ideal in ways that work for us, too.

CHAPTER 5

From Ozzie to Ozzy

The Reassuring Nonevolution of the Sitcom Family

Laura R. Linder

My introduction to rock 'n' roll music was through Ricky Nelson on the television situation comedy *The Adventures of Ozzie and Harriet* in the early 1960s. The first rock 'n' roll album I ever bought was *Ricky Nelson Sings "For You."* It featured my favorite of his songs at the time—"Fools Rush In." On the other hand, I have never been a fan of heavy metal rock 'n' roll, and although I have heard of Black Sabbath, I have never really listened to any of their music. So what do these two short trips down memory lane have to do with situation comedy families? Ricky Nelson grew up on television, appearing in the situation comedy *The Adventures of Ozzie and Harriet* with his family, and fifty years later the lead singer of Black Sabbath, Ozzy Osbourne, has appeared with his family in a reality sitcom called *The Osbournes*. These two sitcoms have a great deal more in common than one might suspect, given the wildly different cultural orientations of the Nelsons and the Osbournes. Both show us what it means to be a family, and together they offer reassurance that the formula for presenting families on television has not changed much over the decades.

The Adventures of Ozzie and Harriet began in 1944 and was on the air for twenty-two years—eight on radio and fourteen on television (Brooks and

Marsh 16). Ozzie Nelson had been a bandleader during the 1930s and 1940s and Harriet was the band's singer. They developed a large following after they appeared on the Red Skelton radio show as a bandleader, singer, and young, married couple (which they were) for three years, and then replaced Skelton's show for the summer (Simon 378; G. Jones 27). They were sold as "America's favorite young couple" and portrayed themselves as regular folk—a husband and wife with kids—even though their radio show also featured celebrities and musical numbers (G. Jones 27). For the first five years of the show, Ozzie and Harriet's two sons were portrayed by actors, but for the remaining seventeen years, David and Ricky played themselves *(Ozzie and Harriet)*.

Although the show was very popular on radio, Ozzie had to produce the television pilot with his own money to convince the network executives that his show could make the transition to television. (Ever the shrewd businessman, he then released the pilot as a feature film in theaters to recoup his investment.) The television version of *The Adventures of Ozzie and Harriet* eliminated the show business aspect of their fictional lives. Ozzie's job was not shown, and their house, a replica of their real house, was no longer in Hollywood, but in a nondescript suburban neighborhood in fictional Hillside (G. Jones 92). On the program, their former lives in show business were rarely mentioned. As Gerard Jones puts it in his seminal work *Honey, I'm Home!*, "The 'adventures' of the Nelsons were the thinnest comedy situations. . . . A mix-up with a furniture store . . . a quest for tutti-frutti ice cream . . . and David's first phone call from a girl. That's about as tough as the conflict ever got" (93). The two sons, David and Ricky, brought the only real life into the show. Jones characterizes them as "the most natural and authentic kid characters yet seen on a sitcom," and they were idolized by American kids and liked by their parents (93). As Ricky matured into a teenager, he began playing rock 'n' roll music. Many of his songs were featured within or tacked onto the end of shows and went on to become big hits (Brooks and Marsh 16).

Although one of the longest-running sitcoms, *The Adventures of Ozzie and Harriet* appeared in the top thirty shows only once during its fourteen years on television (Brooks and Marsh 1245–48). It started slow but built a large, loyal audience over the years, especially after Ricky began singing onscreen (G. Jones 95). Ozzie would make sure that the single record of the song Ricky was singing that week was in the stores the day of the show so that people, especially young girls, could buy it the very next day *(Ozzie and Harriet)*.

Ozzie's influence on the show and its market, however, was felt long before Ricky began singing. From the beginning, Ozzie maintained near total control on the program; he was the producer, director, and head writer. Although his initial goal may have been to keep from traveling so much (with the band) and to provide a stable atmosphere for his family, he also knew he had to support that family. One way to do that was to have first a radio and then a television show. Another way was to cast his actual family in the show.

Figure 5.1. David Nelson, Harriet Nelson, Ozzie Nelson, and Rick Nelson as themselves in *The Adventures of Ozzie and Harriet*, 1952–1966. Photo courtesy of Photofest. Used by permission.

Although the boys were not part of the cast in the beginning, they began to portray themselves on radio in 1949. They made the transition to television, but not before Ozzie tested them before a live audience *(Ozzie and Harriet)*.

After the upheaval and hard times of World War II, the Nelsons were both ideal and ordinary. Their comfortable, placid lifestyle was reassuring to the viewing public. Gerard Jones calls *The Adventures of Ozzie and Harriet* "one of the most determinedly bland programs ever broadcast" (92). Although this may be true, bland is exactly what the country wanted and needed after the tumultuous war years. We needed to feel secure about the way our daily lives and our country were heading. In pursuit of the American Dream (that the Nelsons were helping to define), more and more people were moving to the suburbs. Moms were supposed to stay at home and take care of the kids and the house; dads were supposed to go off to work and then come home and offer wise guidance. This is exactly what Ozzie and Harriet did, except that Ozzie did not go off to work. He was always hanging around. Ozzie justified his lack of a job on the show by saying, "by not designating the kind of work I did, people were able to identify with me more readily" (qtd. in G. Jones 92). He felt that it would seem insincere to pretend to have a job on the show, because everyone knew that he used to be a bandleader and actor.

The Nelsons provided a pattern for families in the suburbs to emulate. They showed us how a house should look (and what new appliances we should have), how to interact with our neighbors, and how to rear children. They showed us how to be moms, dads, and kids in postwar America. They showed us how to be consumers by introducing new products on their show. They showed us how to grow up. Their stories were small, their conflicts seemingly insignificant. This only made them seem more real, because for most of us, our lives and conflicts are small (although significant to us). Being able to watch the Nelsons every week helped us to know that we were doing okay, and that was just the reassurance we needed.

On the surface, the Osbournes are anything but reassuring. Bursting onto the television screen in 2002, fifty years after the Nelsons made their debut, the Osbournes are another entertainment family living their lives in front of the cameras. Ozzy Osbourne is an aging rock star. The former lead singer of Black Sabbath, a heavy metal rock group, he left the group for a solo career in 1978 (Hedegaard). His wife, Sharon, is both his business manager and, in many ways, the head of the family, which includes their three children. (Only two of the Osbourne kids chose to participate in the MTV show—Kelly and Jack, ages sixteen and fifteen, respectively, when the show began. The oldest daughter, eighteen-year-old Aimee, moved out of the house while they were filming to avoid being on the show.) Like *The Adventures of Ozzie and Harriet*, *The Osbournes* was an outgrowth of the family's appearance on another show, MTV's *Cribs*, in which a different musical celebrity's house is featured each week. The Osbournes were so much fun on the show, and the audience's

FIGURE 5.2. Ozzy Osbourne, Sharon Osbourne, Jack Osbourne, and Kelly Osbourne as themselves in *The Osbournes*, 2002–2005. Photo courtesy of Photofest. Used by permission.

response was so favorable, that MTV approached Sharon about doing a series (Stanley; Miller). Ozzy stated that "he wanted to showcase his version of family values" (Rutenberg), and Sharon agreed to do the show because she thought "that America needed to see what a normal family was really like" (Bentley). Of course, the primary reason was probably money. Although Ozzy's career has been long and fruitful, it has been on the wane in recent years.[1] His first album in six years was recorded in the fall of 2001 and included his first hit in ten years (Scully).

The Osbournes is a type of sitcom that has come to be known as a "reality-com" or "real-com."[2] For each season of the show, camera crews followed the family around for four months as they lived their lives, recording everything on tape. From each four months ten to twenty episodes were created (depending on the year). Packaged like a sitcom, the show features a very traditional opening with graphics and pictures reminiscent of the opening of *The Adventures of Ozzie and Harriet* (the final shot for both of the introductions shows the family standing in a row in front of their respective houses). *The Osbournes*'s theme song is a version of Ozzy's song "Crazy Train." The lyrics, "crazy, hey but that's how it goes; millions of people living as foes; maybe, it's not too late; to learn how to love and forget how to hate," take on a whole new meaning in this sitcom-style version, when compared to the heavy metal style in which it was originally recorded (James). This musical arrangement serves to place the show squarely in the 1950s sitcom genre.

The Osbournes are a show business family that seems very unconventional upon first glance. They all curse—incessantly—causing network censors to ride their beeper buttons. Everyone in the family dyes their hair: Mom a more conventional red coiffure; Dad a few red streaks in his long, dark-brown locks; and the kids sporting various styles and colors each season. Most family members have tattoos: Ozzie has many, Jack has several, and Kelly has at least one. Their many dogs walk on the furniture and the kitchen counters and poop and pee on the floors and rugs. Yet, despite these quirks, viewers find upon closer scrutiny that the Osbournes are remarkably conventional in their daily routines. Everyone cleans up dog poop, Dad takes out the trash and puts a new liner in the trashcan, Mom stacks the dishwasher and vacuums (after a hilarious struggle to figure out how to turn the machine on), and even the kids clean on occasion. Everyone helps, although there have been a few jokes about how Mom never cooks. The most remarkable thing about the Osbournes is that they talk to one another about everything. From cooking and cleaning to sex and drugs to gynecological visits and vaginas, no topic is off-limits for this family.

The Osbournes was wildly popular during its first season, averaging more than six million viewers and becoming the most popular show on cable television. It beat out professional wrestling (Bentley). The second season it reached at least half that many viewers (Chunovic, "Putting Some English").

The show won an Emmy Award for the best nonfiction alternative program in 2002. A third season aired during the summer of 2003, with the show ranking as the thirteenth most popular show on cable on July 15 ("Ratings"). A deal for a fourth season has been signed, with Ozzie saying, "this whole MTV thing has been just an incredible adventure and I didn't want the adventure to end so soon" (qtd. in Romano). Critics, scholars, and family therapists all laud the show for its traditional family values; at the same time some comment on the Osbourne's lifestyle in a critical way (James; Dempsey; Stanley; Chocano; Poniewozik, "Ozzy Knows"; Craig). Like the Nelsons, the Osbournes have had an enormous impact, in spite of the program's thin comedy situations, by making people think about what makes a family and what constitutes family values. Even the President of the United States (George W. Bush) professed to like the show and invited the Osbournes to the White House (Chocano).

On *The Osbournes*, Sharon is the one in control, while in *The Adventures of Ozzie and Harriet* Ozzie called all the shots. Sharon has been managing Ozzy's career for over twenty years, and it is she who manages the family, as well. Sharon actually negotiated the deal with MTV and is an executive producer of the show. Ultimately, all shows have to be cleared by her. The purpose for doing the show was not only to showcase their version of a family and family values, but also to be a marketing vehicle to develop the Osbournes "brand." It has succeeded beyond expectations in both cases. The first season, the family received $200 thousand for the ten episodes; the second and third seasons the figures were reported variously to be somewhere between $5 to $20 million dollars per season (Mermigas; Goodman; Lewis). Figures for the fourth season have not been released. Of course, these figures do not include any licensing agreements or other ancillary revenues. By early summer 2003, the Osbournes had signed fifty-five licenses for more than three hundred products, ranging from lunchboxes to plush bears that emit Ozzie's signature scream, "I'm the prince of fucking darkness!" (Lewis); Kelly had released her album *Shut Up!*, which includes the single "Papa, Don't Preach" that she had performed at the MTV awards show; Sharon had a deal with Telepictures for her own syndicated talk show (cancelled after the first season); and Ozzy and Kelly were planning two performances together in England—all money-making endeavors sparked by the television show (Lewis; Gliatto and Chiu; Chunovic, "Putting Some English"; Van Gelder). The economic ramifications of the show have been enormous for the Osbournes, collectively and individually, and for MTV.

At the same time *The Osbournes* brings a new reality-based dimension to the old faithful genre of the family situation comedy, it also offers a reassurance that the past is not forgotten and traditional values of family love and commitment endure. Situation comedies have been a staple of programming since the radio days, primarily because they offer us a view of idealized life and stability (Linder 51). In the era when divorce rates are over 50 percent and unemployment is at its highest level in over a decade, *The Osbournes* offer the reassurance that no matter how wacky, weird, and seemingly dysfunctional things may look on the surface, everything really is okay at the foundation because the family will prevail (Valletta 29).

Anna McCarthy, writing in *Time* magazine, says that *The Osbournes* takes the reality show genre and turns it on its ear. "Before we turned ordinary, real people into protagonists. Now we take celebrities and turn them into ordinary people" (qtd. in Stanley, E1). James Poniewozik, also writing in *Time*, describes *The Osbournes* as "Rock-'n'-roll fantasy meets take-out-the-trash reality" ("Ozzy Knows" 64). The Osbournes may not sound like the typical sitcom family. After all, these family members curse a blue streak and they look nothing like the television-generated image of the family next door—nor even what we think a family is supposed to look like. Yet, regardless of how we regard them, the Osbournes are a loving family.

On *The Osbournes*, life is fairly mundane. The Osbournes spend a lot of time talking to one another about fairly serious things, like obeying the law, doctor visits, drug use, breast implants, honesty, and, most of all, love. In more than one episode, Ozzy proclaims to one or all of his family members, "I love you more than life itself . . . but you're (all) fucking mad." He and Sharon hug and kiss each other and their kids frequently; and even though they fight all the time, a true affection is shown between Kelly and Jack. If the Nelsons showed us how to live in the postwar suburban world of the 1950s, the Osbournes show us how to love in the postmodern world of the turn of the century. In both instances, audiences are offered reassurance about the stability of the family as an enduring social institution.

The form and content of *The Adventures of Ozzie and Harriet* and *The Osbournes* are the same and they share a similar structure: they both are about celebrity, about musical families featuring mom, dad, and two children. Both shows utilize a half-hour format (including commercials), where a situation arises that is solved within that half-hour, and both are set in the family's own home (or close facsimile). Each show opens by introducing the characters one by one. In *The Adventures of Ozzie and Harriet*, Dad is introduced first, then Mom, David, and Ricky; in *The Osbournes*, Mom is introduced first, followed by Jack, Kelly, and then Dad. Although *The Adventures of Ozzie and Harriet* uses a male voiceover to introduce the family members, *The Osbournes* are introduced by having their names printed on the screen next to stop-action pictures of each in succession while the theme song plays in the background. Ozzy is introduced: "And Ozzy Osbourne as 'The Dad,'" a postmodern, self-reflexive wink and a nudge to all previous sitcom families.

Situation comedies are so named because of the situation that arises in each episode that must be resolved. For the Nelsons, it could be making more family time ("An Evening with Hamlet"), re-creating a missing photograph ("Wedding Picture"), or varying tastes in music ("Music Appreciation"). For the Osbournes it could be varying tastes in music ("Won't You Be My Neighbor"), how to survive the holidays ("A Very Ozzy Christmas"), or cleaning up after pets ("Bark at the Moon"). According to David Marc, noted media scholar, the basic structure of a sitcom is: the status quo is disrupted by an error made, a lesson is then learned, and finally there is a return to the status quo (*Comic* 190). Most older sitcoms follow this pattern, but most newer sitcoms are more complex and involve several plot lines. Scholar Michael Tueth notes that in most newer sitcoms a lesson is not necessarily learned and characters are left to make the same mistakes over and over (103). Both *The Adventures of Ozzie and Harriet* and *The Osbournes* follow the older structure. Little happens in either show; the plots are skimpy to nonexistent (especially for *The Osbournes*), but the value of family provides a frame to unify and support the episodes.

Although the form and content are the same, the styles of the two shows are different. *The Adventures of Ozzie and Harriet* is a scripted show and *The Osbournes* is not. Ozzie Nelson wrote or helped write all the episodes of that show, whereas the producers of *The Osbournes* viewed all the footage shot and then assembled shows around particular themes to create a coherency or story line (with final say by Sharon) (Dempsey). (Each day for four months the MTV crew would shoot for up to eighteen hours; from this, only ten episodes were produced, leaving a lot of footage unseen. Most of the remaining footage, it can be imagined, was irretrievably and unredeemingly boring—as most of our own lives would appear if they were filmed live.)

Another difference between the two families is the use of language. The Osbournes curse matter-of-factly and often, something the Nelsons would never do. The variance in language use between the two shows goes beyond that, however. Both feature a lot of discussion between family members, with the parents giving advice to the children as the kids fight with one another. But the Nelsons would never dream of discussing issues that the Osbournes talk about every week, such as sex, drugs, love, excrement, cancer, or tattoos. This difference is due to the coarsening of language in society over time and the relaxation of strictures against discussing subjects previously considered private or even taboo. Things are much more permissive now than they were in the 1950s and 1960s, and this is both negative and positive. We hear the Osbournes curse and scream, which we never hear from the Nelsons, but we also hear the Osbournes grapple with real issues, including Sharon's bout with colon cancer, and come out the other side saying they love each other, hugging and kissing. Such openness and emotion is implied but rarely demonstrated in the Nelson household. Sharon and Ozzy kiss frequently (on the mouth), much to the chagrin of their children, who think their parents are too old to be kissing. Ozzie and Harriet rarely kiss and when they do, the kiss is a peck on the cheek. Do they ever say they love each other or tell their sons how much they love them? Not onscreen, they don't.

On *The Adventures of Ozzie and Harriet*, Ozzie is respected as the patriarch, and Mom and the kids defer to him. Ozzie is somewhat bumbling, but he is still respected as the father. This was typical of sitcoms of the 1950s and 1960s. What was not typical for the era was the fact that Ozzie did not have a job. On *The Osbournes*, Ozzy is too bumbling to command respect most of the time, but he does have a job. Although his wife and kids often treat him as they would a child, he does go out and make a living (even if it is not your average, run-of-the-mill job). Ozzy is bumbling in the same way that Ozzie is, but he is far more befuddled. On *The Osbournes*, Sharon is the true head of the family. She is the glue that keeps everyone together; she is the voice of reason; and she is the person in charge. Harriet is never in charge on *The Adventures of Ozzie and Harriet*, although she is often the voice of reason. She spends most of her time cooking and cleaning (whereas Sharon rarely demonstrates domesticity), but Harriet is as much of a rock as Sharon is. In the evolution of the roles of mothers and fathers in sitcoms, the father has devolved into a less respected position and the mother has evolved toward a more respected position (Scharrer 1; Lichter, Lichter, and Rothman 47–48). The net result, perhaps, is that mothers and fathers demonstrate different interests and talents as they fulfill their family roles, but gender is no longer a signifier of uncontested power in the household; men and women are different, but no longer unequal in the sitcom world.

The Osbournes are celebrities on their show in a way that the Nelsons never are. This is partly because the Nelsons created a parallel, fictional world for their family, whereas the Osbournes are living their real lives on camera. Some might say that the Osbournes have no "real" life, that their life is purely a product of show business. The Nelsons's fictional lives were scripted. Their real jobs were as actors in a sitcom, but on-screen they did not play actors. On-screen, the Nelsons are a typical American family: mom, dad, two kids. Off-screen, they were Ozzie, bandleader and actor; Harriet, singer and actor; David, actor; and Ricky, actor and singer. Although Rick became a rock 'n' roll star in real life as the series progressed, he is not a rock star on the show; he remains forever Ozzie and Harriet's son, who happens to sing. (The music videos tacked onto the end of some episodes are of the real, rock star Rick Nelson, not the fictional, television character one.) On the other hand, Ozzy Osbourne is a rock star, and he plays one on television. Sharon is a wife, mother, and manager, and she plays these same roles on television. Kelly is a daughter and burgeoning rock singer, and she plays them on television; and Jack is a son and talent scout, and he plays them on television. They are not pretending. The Osbournes' celebrity status and their portrayal of it on the show are self-reflexive in a way that the Nelsons on *The Adventures of Ozzie and Harriet* never could be.

The family has been the mainstay of situation comedies since the form originated on radio. While many of the trappings of "family" have changed, a comparison of these two shows suggests that the changes may be more superficial than substantive. We still have parents, and we still have kids. We still have the mundane day-to-day events that all families go through. It is the manifestation of this day-to-dayness that makes *The Adventures of Ozzie and Harriet* and *The Osbournes* so appealing. In both of these shows, we see families dealing with issues that we all have to deal with—quarrels and neighbors, holidays and egos, cleaning and cooking. The two families each deal with them in ways that are fitting for their respective times. The 1950s was a simpler time; the 2000s are much more complicated and self-conscious. The Osbournes are the latest incarnation in the evolution of the sitcom family; they are direct descendants of the Nelsons. Both are products of their times, yet they share structural and thematic features. And both are part of the evolutionary fabric of the sitcom family. Some things do not evolve beyond recognition, but isn't that reassuring?

NOTES

1. Ozzy's career was somewhat revived by Ozzfest, a summer hard rock tour organized by Sharon and Ozzy that began in 1997 (Strauss).

2. The show has been variously termed a *vérité* adventure, a real-life version of *The Addams Family*, docu-series, docu-sitcom, reality-sitcom, situation reality, and a real-life distillation of *The Addams Family*, *The Simpsons*, and *The Beverly Hillbillies* (Walker; James; Tucker, Stanley; Poniewozik, "Ozzy Knows"; Leibrock; Gliatto and Chiu). Brooks and Marsh list it as a documentary in their 2003 edition of *The Complete Directory to Prime Time Network and Cable TV Shows*.

CHAPTER 6

Against the Organization Man

The Andy Griffith Show
and the Small-Town Family Ideal

John O'Leary and Rick Worland

From October 3, 1960, until September 16, 1968, *The Andy Griffith Show* was one of the highest-rated programs in the CBS line-up. The show never did worse than seventh in the Nielsen ratings and has been hugely successful in syndication ever since. Designed as a vehicle for Griffith, the show starred the down-home actor and stand-up comic as the sheriff of Mayberry, North Carolina, and revolved around his home and work life as the small town's unofficial leader. Sheriff Andy Taylor was spontaneous and wise, put-upon and shrewd, and the voice of rationality and common sense in a town often lacking both. Sharp writing and a devotion to characters both familiar and eccentric made Mayberry come alive as an ideal of traditional family and civic life in a period when both institutions were increasingly strained by the social and political upheavals of the 1960s. *The Andy Griffith Show* debuted at a time when America was reacting to a fear of what a popular book of the 1950s called the rise of "the Organization Man" (Whyte). As an increasingly tumultuous decade wore on, this influential show's comedy soothed fears of a loss of

FIGURE 6.1. Andy Griffith as Andy Taylor, Ronny Howard as Opie Taylor, Don Knotts as Barney Fife, and Jim Nabors as Gomer Pyle in *The Andy Griffith Show*, 1960–1968. Photo courtesy of Movie Star NewsFair.

individualism through a rehabilitation of character and story conventions found in character-centered comedy and an innovative use of setting. Its rural-wisdom versus urban-sophistication theme worked to assuage widespread fears concerning changing American values that for some were changing far too fast.

From 1960 through 1965, the regular cast of the series included Frances Bavier as Aunt Bee, the mother figure of Andy's household and symbol of a multigenerational, extended family; Ronny Howard as his young son, Opie Taylor; multiple Emmy-winner Don Knotts as Andy's cousin, Deputy Barney Fife; and Howard McNear as Floyd, the barber. Later, Jack Dodson appeared as the county clerk, Howard Sprague, a middle-aged bachelor still living with his clinging mother. A number of actors played recurring roles that helped sketch-in the community of rustic stereotypes, such as Jim Nabors as the dumb but earnest mechanic Gomer Pyle and Hal Smith as Otis, the town drunk. Moreover, as critic Richard Kelly points out, the show's social mosaic was enriched by characters often referred to but never seen, such as Juanita, a waitress at the diner, and Sarah, the local telephone operator (Kelly 9). Mayberry itself was an extended family of relatives and neighbors where the relations between home and community—growing ever more rigid and conflicted in mid-century America—were still open and mutually dependent. The show's easy reconciliation of family and public life and of work and leisure is displayed each week in its opening title sequence in which Andy Taylor, still clad in his sheriff's uniform, strolls down a wooded lane with Opie, bound for a lake with fishing poles over their shoulders, as the jaunty but laid-back theme song is whistled with acoustic guitar accompaniment. No hurry, no pressing obligations. Mayberry is a place where there is still plenty of time for dad to hold an important job in the community and go fishing with his young son.

THE RURAL SITCOM

In *Nervous Laughter: Television Situation Comedy and Liberal Democratic Ideology*, Hamamoto reminds us that "Rural situation comedies were not created with the intention of offering critiques of the excesses of urbanism and consumer culture. . . [. T]he overriding motive was to tap the growing audience in rural areas of the country" (Hamamoto 54). The influence of media institutions on popular texts is great but often indirect. While it is clear that the profit-driven networks were interested in appealing to a new audience (one that they would almost totally dismiss some ten years later), the resulting shows did offer a critical assessment of the changing folkways and mores of the culture at large.

In *The Complete Directory to Prime Time Network and Cable TV Shows*, Brooks and Marsh divide television history into seven eras (ix–xx). By 1957, the television industry was migrating to Hollywood and beginning to produce episodic series over the anthology dramas and variety series of the early 1950s. *The Andy Griffith Show* appeared during what Brooks and Marsh term the "Adult Western" era, lasting from 1957 through the mid-1960s. During the 1958–59 season, for example, thirty-one westerns aired in prime time. This was followed by the "Idiot Sitcom" era, which Brooks and Marsh date from the early to late 1960s, that featured gimmicks to drive the comedy in which the characters are cartoonish and plots are "restricted to farce" (Marc, *Demographic* 56). Shows such as *Mr. Ed, My Favorite Martian, Gilligan's Island, The Flying Nun*, and *My Mother the Car* would seem to affirm Brooks and Marsh's derisive designation. Rather than being built on gimmicks, however, *The Andy Griffith Show* harkens back to the affectionate and incisive rural humor identified with Mark Twain and Will Rogers.

Notably, perhaps the most successful producer of this period was Paul Henning, who placed three hit "gimmick" shows on CBS: *The Beverly Hillbillies, Petticoat Junction*, and *Green Acres*. Similar to *The Andy Griffith Show*, Henning's programs featured farm families or rural settings, and, as such, were a departure from the ethnic urban and WASP suburban family sitcoms that filled American television screens in the 1950s. It may be said that the most immediate sitcom influence on *The Andy Griffith Show* was *The Real McCoys*. Unlike *The Andy Griffith Show*, however, *The Real McCoys* centered on rural characters and culture without explicitly stressing this setting in opposition to modern industrial America. Rather than simply offering fantastic escapism, *The Andy Griffith Show* skillfully negotiated these currents of programming popularity, carving out a niche in which it thrived as strained gimmicks passed. Although spanning most of Brooks and Marsh's third period, *The Andy Griffith Show* does not adhere to the "Idiot Sitcom" model, but can be seen as a bridge between the eras of the "Adult Western" and the "Idiot Sitcom." It features a crucial western convention (a small-town sheriff tries to maintain order in the face of corrupting outside influences) filtered through a comic sensibility. Narrative conflicts emphasize the wisdom of the rural mindset and the folly, or more often the confusion, of urban thinking.

In "Bailey's Bad Boy," Ron Bailey, a nineteen-year-old spoiled, rich kid comes tearing through Mayberry in his fancy convertible en route to Miami. He sideswipes a farmer's truck and Andy puts him in the jail, even though the young man informs the sheriff that his father is a millionaire who "can have just about anything he wants in this state, including that Junior G-man badge of yours." Later the young criminal goes fishing with Andy and Opie and then to the Taylor house for dinner and homemade ice cream. His father's powerful attorney fixes things so that Ron can be released, but he learns a lesson when he hears Andy calmly lecture and punish Opie for breaking a window. He realizes that he too wants to "stand on his own two legs." The sheriff has seen that justice is done, and American values have been upheld in the face of wealth and corruption. In a classic Hollywood western, he would have done this with a gun; here he does it with his gentle folk wisdom.

Marc, who devotes a chapter of his book *Demographic Vistas* to an auteur study of Paul Henning, describes the theme of the rural sitcoms as "folk culture versus modern culture" (62). The pilot of *Petticoat Junction*, which opens in a big city corporate boardroom, reveals this clearly. A group of railroad executives bemoan the fact that one little section of the line is not cost-effective. An executive is sent out to rural Hooterville to shut down the train. Once there, he is befuddled by the simple values of the eccentric locals in a place where the train makes unscheduled stops so that a woman can do her grocery shopping. Eventually, he sees the value of the simple way of life in Hooterville and the crucial role that the antique train plays in the maintenance of that life. This is the central conflict to be worked out by the narrative of the rural sitcom: modern, urban America must uphold and respect the value of individual people, even in the face of inevitable "progress."

In some ways the plot of *Petticoat Junction*'s pilot could have been done on *The Andy Griffith Show*. Many of its early episodes feature an outsider who comes to Mayberry and looks with disdain upon its people. The 1963 episode "Man in a Hurry" is illustrative. It is "a variation on the theme in which an outsider gets 'stuck' in Mayberry and is transformed by the experience" (Brower 90). When a corporate magnate's Lincoln breaks down in Mayberry on a Sunday afternoon, the blustery tycoon is constantly frustrated in his attempts to get his car repaired and get on to his important appointment in a big city. At one point he is trying to use the phone, but the whole town has tacitly agreed to let two elderly sisters talk to each other uninterrupted (there is only one line) for three hours each Sunday afternoon. They seem to spend most of the time discussing various problems with their feet. Tucker, the businessman, explodes and berates Andy, Barney, Aunt Bee, and Opie as they sit down to Sunday dinner:

> TUCKER: Outrageous! Sheer idiocy! I can't believe a public utility is being tied up like this! You people are living in another world.
>
> ANDY: Now, easy Mr. Tucker . . .
>
> TUCKER: This is the twentieth century. Don't you realize that? The whole world is living in a desperate space age! Men are orbiting the earth! International television has been developed! And here, a whole town is standing still because two old women's feet fall asleep!
>
> BARNEY (looking at Andy): I wonder what causes that?

At this, Tucker walks away flinging his hands in a futile gesture. Yet, by the time his car is repaired, Tucker decides to linger in Mayberry a bit longer. As happens with the railroad tycoon in *Petticoat Junction*, the wisdom and charm of the townsfolk convince him that his fast-paced, modern life lacks something important. But these examples also demonstrate the crucial differences between the two shows. *Petticoat Junction* has its roots in farcical comedy in which the characters never face any real crisis. *The Andy Griffith Show* comes from a tradition of American comedy in which the characters must wrestle with opposing values in order to establish and maintain their identities.

The sets for situation comedies are a crucial reflection of its thematic concerns. Each week viewers must return, not just to familiar characters, but also to a welcoming space. *The Andy Griffith Show* used sets creatively to strengthen the show's thematic ideal that community—both at home and work—must become family. There are four central sets: the court house (work space); the Taylor home (domestic space); Floyd's barber shop (community space); and Myer's Lake (natural space). Rather than being distinct and isolated, these spaces often switch functions. The home can become a place of business, as when the summit meeting comes to town or Andy brings prisoners home. The home is also a natural space, as it is when Opie sets his birds free or the Taylor family and Barney sit out on the porch after supper. The court house is often featured as domestic space, as in some episodes when Barney actually sleeps there. It is a home for Otis the drunk and many other prisoners. The postwar Organization Man of city and suburbs comes home to escape his work world. The message of *The Andy Griffith Show* is that Americans must meld their worlds in order to achieve an authentic life.

MAYBERRY VS. THE "REAL WORLD"

Unlike the broad, satiric caricatures peopling *Petticoat Junction* and *Green Acres*, the citizens of Mayberry are both aware of, and recognizably a part of, the world at large, as signaled by frequent discussion and curiosity about the fast life in the urban center of Raleigh. The ongoing exchanges between the little town and the outside world often in episode plots but pay off significantly in several shows in which mass media representatives "discover" Mayberry and seek to turn its easy way of life into an exhibit and its people into semi-willing celebrities. In "Mayberry Goes Hollywood," the citizens and their friendly, relaxed ways captivate a movie producer passing through town. His plans to make a film about Mayberry's unspoiled traditions almost bring about their destruction. Led by the mayor, the town begins to refine and reshape itself for the possibility of fame. Shops change, people put on new and different clothes, and they adopt false personalities. All work to create what they perceive as a fancier, more modern image of the town. Andy, of course, resists this foolishness and in the climax, he and the producer are barely able to stop the citizens, who now look something like a well-dressed lynch mob, from cutting down the town's most ancient oak because they think it is spoiling the appearance of the main street. The lesson is that Mayberry is perfect just the way it is, and the people need to celebrate and enjoy their unique life.

"Mayberry Goes Hollywood" was the first suggestion of a note of sly self-consciousness that ran throughout the series. Recall that Disneyland, opening in 1955, was designed around a nostalgic vision of just such a small-town main street from the early part of the century. This script gently acknowledges that Mayberry, too, was already a kind of fantasy that might easily be packaged and sold to an eager public. In the 1965 episode "TV or Not TV," a Hollywood screenwriter wants to produce a TV series based on Andy Taylor called "Sheriff Without a Gun."[1] In the 1967–68 season, this turned into a three-episode journey to Hollywood where Andy, Opie, and Aunt Bee observe the filming of a movie version of the story—one in which a vain and hammy actor (Gavin MacLeod) played Andy and Aunt Bee was cast as a blonde bombshell. Stories had to be highly embellished if Mayberry were going to be a setting for sex and violence—the joke being that the Hollywood distortion only reemphasized the placidity of the "real" Mayberry.

But if not "the happiest place on earth," Mayberry was still too good to be true. As Americans grew increasingly anxious about crime and civil unrest in the 1960s, Mayberry remained an idyllic realm where the sheriff rarely carried a weapon, and his bumbling deputy was only allowed a single bullet (kept in his shirt pocket) for his pistol because it invariably discharged accidentally whenever loaded. In the interest of both public safety and common sense, the drunken Otis locked himself into a jail cell each evening to sleep off his bender, and released himself the next morning with the key kept handily in reach of the cell door. (Furthering the connection of family and workplace, Aunt Bee usually provides home-cooked meals for Otis or other prisoners in Andy's jail.) Crime in Mayberry would almost invariably come from the outside, its source a generalized modern city.

As an ideology, American populism championed the supposed purity and authenticity of small-town and rural life over the dangers and anomie of the big city; its essentially Jacksonian democratic vision extolled the superior virtues of the "common man" over the urban "sophisticate," usually depicted as an elitist and ultimately proven to be foolish or corrupt. On *The Andy Griffith Show* urban con men and bank robbers frequently landed in Mayberry, fruitlessly pursued by state policemen, city detectives, or FBI agents. Cops and criminals were often united in their condescension toward Andy and Barney, whom they dismiss as incompetent hicks. Yet as in the populist vision celebrated by Capra and others, it is the wily, seemingly unassuming local lawman, Sheriff Taylor, who always gets his man. In "The Big House," two bank robbers are temporarily held in Mayberry while detectives hunt for other members of the gang. Contemptuous of the rubes and their cracker box jail, the robbers scheme to escape. Their confidence grows when Barney tries to intimidate them. Sniffing and strutting, the deputy delivers what he hopes they will consider a hard-nosed introduction to the brutal life they must now endure in the Mayberry jail: "Now men . . . here at 'The Rock,' we have two basic rules. Memorize them so you can say them in your sleep. The first rule is: Obey all rules! The second rule is, do not write on the walls, as it takes a lot of hard work to erase writing off of walls!" With deft comic timing, Don Knotts sketches Barney's failed attempt to mimic the macho ideal of movie tough guys like James Cagney or Glenn Ford—stars often mentioned specifically by the Mayberry characters. The criminals indeed trick Barney and escape, but as usual, Andy recaptures them and their accomplices while making it look like his jittery deputy was the hero.

Knotts left the show in 1965 to make feature films but returned several times to reprise the role of Barney Fife. As Richard Kelly laments, though, these episodes unwittingly reveal the fragile underpinnings of the series as a place of timeless fantasy, because they prove Barney is no match for the vicissitudes of modern life (Kelly 98–99). In "A Visit to Barney Fife," Andy travels to Raleigh to visit his old friend, who has finally achieved his dream of becoming a detective on the big-city police force. But Andy is embarrassed to find that Barney is treated as a flunky and laughed at by the "real" detectives. Poor Barney has become a petty Organization Man himself, a minor cog in an impersonal bureaucracy riding a humiliatingly tiny desk set apart from the real activity of the department. Once more, Andy must crack a case and make it appear that Barney is the master detective. But Barney's humiliation is so palpable in the first part of the story that the wry ending that always worked before now sticks in the throat. Andy makes Barney a hero again, but now, stripped of the support and acceptance of the Mayberry family, how long will it last? Like Shangri-La in *Lost Horizon* (1937), a work often considered atypical in discussions of Capra's Depression comedies, Mayberry is a changeless place that once departed can never be regained.

The "Man in a Hurry" episode was one of many in which an outsider begins to appreciate the charms of Mayberry after enjoying one of Aunt Bee's home-cooked meals. This may have reached its apotheosis in "Barney Hosts a Summit Meeting," where a United States–Soviet negotiating session, improbably held in Andy's home to avoid media attention, is deadlocked until the diplomats meet informally at midnight in the Taylor kitchen, and are brought to an accommodation through their mutual enjoyment of Aunt Bee's cooking. This was one of the rare times that *The Andy Griffith Show* acknowledged the increasingly dangerous world of national and international politics in the 1960s. During the years in which Andy Taylor was the most popular southern sheriff in the country, at least as measured by the Nielsen ratings, network news also presented the most infamous one, "Bull" Connor, the commissioner of public safety in Birmingham, Alabama. Connor's deputies, no Barney Fifes, used clubs, attack dogs, and fire hoses to assault peaceful civil rights demonstrators. These diametrically opposing visions illustrate the medium's schizophrenia in the 1960s. In the years 1962 to 1964, especially, many network shows aired their own particular meditations on the sad state of American racial relations or added Black characters to the regular casts. Yet throughout the most ominous and violent years of the civil rights struggle, Mayberry remained a southern town without Black citizens. Though it is unlikely that the producers intended to capitalize on the absence of Blacks in Mayberry, it might be suggested that for conservative White viewers, in the South especially, this was a subconscious appeal of the program's vision, despite its many other strengths. The fact that relaxation over a matronly aunt's lovingly prepared food followed by a drowsy sit on the front porch swing might indirectly fix any problem, from high blood pressure to racial conflict or the nuclear standoff, showed how deeply *The Andy Griffith Show* spoke to millions of Americans in a society growing increasingly polarized and uncertain about the future.

THE CAPRA INFLUENCE

In *A Certain Tendency of the Hollywood Cinema, 1930–1980*, Ray posits that, "The dominant tradition of American cinema consistently found ways to overcome dichotomies," and that the most salient dichotomy was that of "individual and community" (58). He links these two values to two types of American heroes: the outlaw hero, who stands for "self-determination and freedom from entanglements," and the official hero, who stands for "collective action and the objective legal process." Sometimes, Ray argues, the character-istics of the two types are embodied in one character. It seems clear that Andy Taylor is just such a figure. He shows a fierce independence and unwillingness to bow to the demands of interloping outsiders and yet uses his independent streak to pull the community together to avoid the corrupt influences of the greater society.

The Andy Griffith Show writer Harvey Bullock once remarked, "I always regarded the show as set in the thirties, even though it played in the sixties" (Brower 140). Indeed, Andy's cinematic ancestors are some of the heroes found in the films of Frank Capra, especially in *Mr. Deeds Goes to Town* (1936) and *Mr. Smith Goes to Washington* (1939). Like Andy Taylor, Longfellow Deeds and Jefferson Smith are strong individuals who do not fit easily into an urban landscape. All three attempt to uphold small-town ideals and convince a larger populace to put its faith in "rural-agrarian folk wisdom" (Schatz, *Hollywood Genres* 180). In these two Capra films, the eponymous main characters move from a small town to the big city where the elite take advantage of them. (If we try to imagine what Deeds and Smith would have been like if they had never left town, we conjure up Andy Taylor.) The hero is accused of being insane or corrupt because he tries to do the right thing and must then use a folksy but eloquent speech to convince officials and "the people" that he has tried to uphold true, American ideals in the face of greed and dishonesty. When the literati mockingly praise Mr. Deeds's greeting card poetry or Mr. Smith is duped by the Washington press corps into doing ridiculous bird calls, we see the clash of the two value systems. The elite can make Deeds and Smith look foolish because both newcomers to the urban milieu are temporarily overwhelmed by its lifestyle: Deeds spends money wildly and gets drunk, and Smith falls for a senator's daughter and her conniving ways. But the Capra hero soon realizes that he must hold onto the values he brought to the city.

Finally, each hero uses his power of speech to, as Deeds says, get in his "two cents worth," and justice and order are reestablished by the victory of nineteenth-century American ideals. Deeds's speech to the courtroom and Smith's speech to the Senate serve to reveal the cynicism at the heart of their accusers' attempts to discredit them. Smith tells the Senate (and, he hopes, the nation), "I wouldn't give you two cents for all your fancy rules, if behind them they didn't have a little bit of plain ordinary, everyday kindness, and a little looking out for the other fellow, too. . . . It's just the bone and blood and sinew of this democracy." Rules are fine, but they must be backed by traditional American values. This demonstrates Smith's possession of the characteristics of both the outlaw and the official hero. Like Deeds, he is fiercely independent and yet must work within the corrupt system in order to reform it. The goal of the Capra narrative is to force the hero to reclaim small-town values for the good of the greater community.

In *The Andy Griffith Show*, this narrative pattern is filtered through the conventions of the family sitcom. Andy's role is to be the father of the town, and so in many episodes, the victim of greed and "modern" thinking is not Sheriff Andy, but a marginalized citizen of Mayberry. Andy's task is not to expose the corruption of the powerful but to change their hearts. A prime example is "The Christmas Story." Wealthy Ben Weaver, who owns Weaver's Department Store, forces Andy to evict a young family on Christmas Eve and put them in jail because of the back rent they owe. Weaver is obviously modeled after Dickens's Scrooge, but he also embodies certain characteristics of the Organization Man, such as valuing strict adherence to rules and laws over individual assessments of morality. When Andy, Barney, Opie, Aunt Bee, and Ellie, Andy's girlfriend and the town pharmacist (Elinor Donahue), decide to celebrate Christmas in the jail with the dispossessed family, Weaver sees the error of his ways and joins in the celebration. Andy has saved Mayberry from the dangers of the Organization Man, but has done so by using "good old-fashioned moral persuasion" (Hamamoto 53). While the Capra hero had to bring the antagonist down, Andy has to win him over. Jefferson Smith and Andy Taylor both use a combination of the methods of the outlaw hero and the official hero, but since family sitcom conventions establish Andy as the father of the community, his task is not to rid the town of an evil mogul but to bring him fully into the ethical community that is Mayberry.

"The Christmas Story" parallels another popular Capra film, *It's a Wonderful Life* (1946). The protagonist of that movie, George Bailey, is the victim of the Scrooge-like character, in contrast to Andy who serves as protector of the victim. A comparison of a scene from *It's a Wonderful Life* to a scene from another *Andy Griffith Show* episode is illuminating, however. George Bailey must convince the board of his deceased father's building and loan company not to close the business because it is important to the community. In "Mayberry Goes Bankrupt," the town council decides to evict an old man from his dilapidated home. Andy protests but eventually resolves that he must do his duty, no matter how distasteful. The comic twist comes when Andy discovers that the old man holds a one-hundred-year-old municipal bond and that the town actually owes him a fortune. The bond is eventually found to be worthless but not before the council members have worked to fix up the old house. At this point Andy convinces the council they have done a good thing for the community. Unlike George Bailey, Andy's role is not to do battle with the evils of capitalism, but to humanize it. The sitcom did not lend itself to the depiction of the battle between two kinds of capitalism but to the possibility of a capitalism that recedes when human values are at stake. If George Bailey's nightmare sequence in *It's a Wonderful Life* is capitalism as dystopia, Andy's Mayberry is capitalism as utopia.

CONCLUSION

Many influential twentieth-century American narratives have lamented the loss of passing values. The novel *The Great Gatsby* and the film *Citizen Kane* both feature heroes who try in vain to recapture the principles of individualism and innocence they enjoyed when they lived in the free and open West, before they were corrupted by eastern values. Mayberry is an American dream town where those principles are challenged but ultimately prevail.

In the 1967–68 season, *The Andy Griffith Show* was the number-one rated program in the country. Upon this high note, Griffith decided to leave the series. The show was so popular, however, it continued in a revised format. With most of the regular cast remaining, Ken Berry became the central figure of the new version, called *Mayberry, RFD*, playing Sam Jones, a farmer and town councilman. Devoted fans of *The Andy Griffith Show* usually dismiss *Mayberry, RFD* as the faint echo of a classic and a failure, though the latter assessment is not borne out by its rating success over the next three years. Indeed, *Mayberry, RFD* was still a top-rated show when strategically cancelled by CBS in 1971, along with other rural-based programs, as the network moved to court younger, more affluent urban viewers. The success of sitcoms such as *The Mary Tyler Moore Show*, *All in the Family*, and *M*A*S*H* would define the network in the decade of the 1970s by exploring contemporary social issues and anxieties pertinent to this demographic group. Young, single protagonists, childless couples, and workplace "families" would replace the small-town family ideal celebrated on *The Andy Griffith Show*, with its emphasis on the extended family and its interdependence with a small community. (When domestic sitcoms returned substantially in the 1980s, they would focus almost exclusively on isolated, suburban nuclear families.) If the world of Mayberry were already a mythic ideal in the 1960s, it became a nearly unimaginable one in prime time only a few years later.

NOTE

1. Perhaps the whole notion of Andy as a sheriff who did not wear a gun came from Griffith's earlier portrayal of a good-natured sheriff on Broadway in the 1950s western musical comedy, *Destry Rides Again*.

PART THREE

Gender Represented

CHAPTER 7

I Love Lucy

Television and Gender in Postwar Domestic Ideology

Lori Landay

"Lu—cy! You've got some 'splainin' to do!" Ricky Ricardo exclaims, demanding an explanation for yet another of Lucy's tricky schemes to get into the act, make money, outdo the "girls" in her women's club, or in some other way escape being just a housewife. *I Love Lucy* ran Monday nights on CBS as a half-hour situation comedy from October 1951 to May 1957 and as monthly hour-long specials from November 1957 until April 1961. It is the show in which the conventions, structure, and style of the sitcom genre were codified, and it may well be the most popular situation comedy ever. Of course, the genre of the television sitcom has antecedents, and *I Love Lucy* was not only based on conventions of comedy established in romantic comedy, vaudeville, film, radio, and the earliest television shows in general, but also reworked material from Ball's hit radio show, *My Favorite Husband* (1948–1951). *I Love Lucy* was innovative, however, in both its sense of the *situation* and the *comedy*; the situation was based in a comic tension between everyday life and comic exaggeration, and the comedy was based on the unrivaled comedic talents of Lucille Ball and the excellent supporting cast. At its height, *I Love Lucy* redefined what it meant for a television show to be popular; it was the first television show to be seen in over ten million American homes and it set many new ratings records. Not only did the show help develop the situation comedy into a genre, it contributed to the construction of postwar domestic ideology.

I Love Lucy could be this influential because it was created when television was inventing itself and its place in American culture. Recorded on black-and-white 35mm film before a live studio audience, edited, and then broadcast, the show set the standard for television aesthetics. The flat lighting style invented by legendary cinematographer Karl Freund gave depth and realism to the studio sets. Stylistically, the show set a new standard for the broadcast audiovisual medium by incorporating key aspects of both radio and film—a live studio audience and continuity editing, respectively. The live studio audience enabled the actors to play off and to their audience and helped blur the boundaries between the worlds of the home and the television screen. Viewers at home laughed along with the unseen studio audience. The editing between shots captured with three cameras running simultaneously facilitated the style of classical Hollywood cinema, establishing intimacy and identification through use of the close-up.[1] Moreover, when these spectatorial practices of classical Hollywood cinema were combined with the domestic exhibition of television, the sense of intimacy and closeness was even more pronounced. The medium of television had an immediacy and sense of presence that far outstripped radio and film. Whether live or, like *I Love Lucy*, filmed "live," the discursive patterns of early television encouraged viewers to feel as if they were actually present at the event or performance. As the 1946 book *Here Is Television, Your Window on the World* suggests, founding discourses represented television as both transparent and magical in that it not only extended the home but brought the world into the family living room.

The genre of situation comedy was at a crucial stage in its development. *I Love Lucy* and *My Favorite Husband* producer and writer Jess Oppenheimer explained that he and writers Madelyn Pugh and Bob Carroll, Jr., had broken new ground with their radio sitcom: "We just weren't writing what was then considered the 'in' kind of radio comedy show, where you have a series of comedy characters, each of whom comes in, does his own shtick, and then exits. Instead, we did whole stories—*situation* comedy" ("Laughs" 127–28). Indeed, each episode of *I Love Lucy* has a rational setup, and the emphasis on storytelling rather than shtick focused the show's content on cultural discourses of home and family life. The *situation* of *I Love Lucy* was the domestic life of Lucy and Ricky Ricardo, who were not stars but ordinary people (although in later seasons Ricky's career takes the gang to Hollywood and Europe). When the writers wrote the initial scripts for the series, they based the everyday details of the Ricardo marriage on the Arnaz's marriage, and many scenes set in the Ricardo bedroom as the characters wake up, get dressed, or get ready for bed have an intimacy that is grounded in the mundane details of everyday life and in the audience's knowledge that the actors were really married.

FIGURE 7.1. Lucille Ball as Lucy Ricardo and Desi Arnaz as Ricky Ricardo in *I Love Lucy*, 1951–1961. Photo courtesy of Movie Star NewsFair.

In portraying everyday domesticity grounded in realism, *I Love Lucy* brought a representation of home life into American homes at a time when many families were buying televisions and working out their own versions of domestic life. After World War II, Americans were, to use Elaine Tyler May's phrase, "homeward bound," both moving towards domesticity and also restrained by domesticity. The boundaries between home and the world, long a demarcator of gender, were in flux. The ideology of domesticity—an idealization of marriage, family, and the home prescribed, albeit differently, to both men and women—was an inherently unstable one (like the other postwar ideologies of containment) that tried to legitimate traditional definitions of gender and the separation of spheres at a time when those divisions were breaking down. At the core of the ideological construct of femininity in the postwar era were women's roles as housewives. High marriage rates, the explosion of suburban housing, the baby boom, emphasis on traditional gender roles, and a renewed belief in the importance of the home all bolstered a domestic revival in the 1950s. This revival informed the cultural context in which *I Love Lucy* struck such a chord, though with a twist that evolved from the real lives of Ball and Arnaz.

The origin of the series would have been well known to most television watchers, because it was repeated relentlessly in the popular publications of the time from *Life, Newsweek*, and *Look* to women's magazines and daily newspapers. The series originated in Ball and Arnaz's desire to work together so they could stop the work-caused separations that had characterized their marriage. CBS was interested in making a television version of Ball's radio show, *My Favorite Husband*, but balked at the idea of casting Arnaz as the husband because his Cuban ethnicity did not fit into the successful formula centered around the radio show's Midwestern family. Ball and Arnaz took matters into their own hands with a vaudeville tour intended to prove to CBS that they could find and please an audience.

The pilot and then the series kept the dizzy housewife character and the older couple foils relatively intact, but changed the setting to New York and the husband's profession from banker to bandleader. In shifting the situation from middle-class domesticity to the world of show business, *I Love Lucy* tapped into the television trend of stars playing versions of themselves (George Burns and Gracie Allen, and Ozzie and Harriett Nelson) and enabled musical numbers to be performed. The pilot centered on Larry Lopez, a bandleader who wanted as normal a life as possible, and his wacky wife, Lucy, who wanted to get into show business. In the pilot, Larry laments, "I want a wife who's just a wife." And so a major conflict of *I Love Lucy* was articulated: the dissatisfied housewife eager to escape the home versus the world-weary husband who wants his wife to provide him the comforts of home—characters clearly not based on Ball and Arnaz's real-life image or experience, although perhaps on some fantasy of the domestic bliss that postwar discourses promised would come from a conventional home life based on polarized gender roles.

How typical was the restlessness and frustration that Lucy embodied? According to Betty Friedan's *The Feminine Mystique*, "the problem that has no name" was unspoken yet widespread, and the comic treatment of women's desires for a life outside the home is more a precursor of 1960s–70s feminism than typical of the 1950s. It might be that Ball and Arnaz (and their writers) were continuing to perform the cultural work suggested by a 1938 *Photoplay* magazine poll of Hollywood stars, which found that 93 percent of female stars and 78 percent of male stars believed in women having careers after marriage, in contrast to the general population that disapproved of wives having jobs (May 41). *I Love Lucy* gives us both the actors' vanguard perspective, which obviously Ball and Arnaz shared, and the more conventional perspective of the population at large, which the show mimicked. Ball and Arnaz and the writers, including Madelyn Pugh, one of very few women television writers, based their work on their experiences as gendered people in the postwar era; they were surrounded by the domestic revival sweeping America, yet separate from it as part of Hollywood's more egalitarian culture.

Seen in this light, *I Love Lucy* resonated so loudly in the early 1950s because the show suggested the failure of the domestic ideal—based on the rigid gender roles portrayed in popular culture—to match up with people's real experiences of everyday life. The gap between domestic ideology and social experience was larger in the 1950s than in the earlier half of the twentieth century. Historian William Chafe summarizes some evidence to support this: "The poll data showed that most citizens preferred to retain traditional definitions of masculine and feminine spheres, even while modifying the content of those spheres in practice" (171). When Lucille Ball is quoted as saying, "I'm just a typical housewife at heart" in an article on "America's top saleswomen" (Morehead 19), she is indeed holding a traditional definition of femininity while in practice having an unconventional career excelling in the physical comedy that had been the province of men.

Of course, *I Love Lucy* was not a social realist critique of gender roles. It was comedy. But, comedy in American culture in general and in television sitcoms in particular is a major forum for reflecting and shaping cultural ideals; it is a testing ground for social formations from the simplest performance of mannerisms to the *situation* that gives the comedy its premise. In order for a sitcom to be popular, it does not have to depict how life really is, but it does have to portray a life that the audience likes.

Audiences not only liked *I Love Lucy*, they *loved* it and embraced not only the series but a range of Lucy and Ricky commodities, including his and hers matching pajamas, jewelry, nursery sets, aprons, smoking jackets, dolls, diaper bags, and furniture for every room. As Ball explains in her autobiography, "It was possible to furnish a house and dress a whole family with items carrying

our *I Love Lucy* label" (224). One ad proclaiming "Live like Lucy!" indicates
how television brought the world into the home and the home into the world
with commodities. Clearly the vision of domesticity enacted in the Ricardo's
apartment was, for Lucy, a commodified one, with many episodes centering
on Lucy's struggle to get the money to buy something for herself or the home,
perhaps most hilariously exemplified in the episode "The Freezer." Although
Ball and Arnaz were in a far different financial situation than the Ricardos or
most of their middle-class viewers, the show's emphasis on love—on emotions, marriage, friendship, and the pleasures of domestic life—outweighed
the dissonance between Ball-Arnaz and the Ricardos. At no point was this
more apparent than when the offscreen and onscreen lives of Ball and Arnaz
were at their closest: when the writers worked Ball's real-life pregnancy into
the show by making Lucy Ricardo pregnant, too.

On January 19, 1953, two babies were born—in the morning, Ball and
Arnaz had a son, and in the evening, Lucy and Ricky Ricardo also had a son.
"Lucy Goes to the Hospital" hit an all-time high rating, with an estimate of
more than 44 million viewers. In blurring the line between reality and artifice
with the synchronic "real-life" and "fictional" births, *I Love Lucy* was a
metaphor for what television as an institution and apparatus was doing anyway: making more permeable the traditional demarcations between public and
private, truth and artifice, and representation and social experience.

The seven pregnancy shows, culminating in "Lucy Goes to the Hospital"
(which barely had Lucy in it at all) built on the previous season and a half
when *I Love Lucy* established itself as a phenomenon. Many of the most bril-
liant episodes are from this early period, including "Job Switching," with the
hilarious candy factory conveyor belt scene, and "Lucy Does a TV Commercial" with the Vitameatavegamin scene. These episodes and many more lesser-
known ones followed the successful formula of building up to comic climaxes
that showcased the comedic talents of Ball and her co-stars. *New York Times
Magazine* writer Jack Gould explained the appeal in March 1953:

> "I Love Lucy" is as much a phenomenon as an attraction. Fundamentally,
> it is a piece of hilarious theatre put together with deceptively brilliant
> know-how, but it also is many other things. In part it is a fusion of the
> make-believe of the footlights and the real-life existence of a glamorous
> "name." In part it is the product of inspired press agentry which has made
> a national legend of a couple which two years ago was on the Hollywood
> side-lines.

The "inspired" publicity machine to which Gould refers was indeed indus-
trious and effective. By February 1952, just four months after *I Love Lucy*
premiered, the show was not only number one but also hit all the major
newspapers and magazines, which made connections between the real-life

actors and their onscreen characters and intertwined their personal and professional stories. Of the hundreds of magazine and newspaper articles and features that I have researched, hardly any stray from the Desilu publicity machine's story of how television saved their marriage. The story goes like this: After their 1940 marriage, they were so busy with their careers that they barely saw each other, and they tried to find a vehicle in which they could work together. Even though producers would not develop projects for them because of Arnaz's Cuban ethnicity and strong accent, Ball and Arnaz were convinced they could be a success. The vaudeville act they took on the road was well received, but they canceled the second half because of thirty-nine-year-old Ball's pregnancy. That pregnancy ended in a miscarriage, but soon she was pregnant again and they filmed the pilot episode when she was six months pregnant. CBS and sponsor cigarette company Philip Morris picked up the show, and they began production one month after their daughter Lucie was born. The innovations of the production context figure largely in the articles—that Ball and Arnaz owned the show through their company Desilu Productions and filmed it before a live audience in Hollywood—but the articles always stress the love story. As a March 1952 *Chicago Sunday Tribune* article put it, "Desi and Lucille are particularly grateful to TV because it has given them an opportunity to live a normal family life" (Wolters). An April 6, 1952, *L.A. Examiner* article ran a picture of the couple smooching in bed with the caption, "When Desi and Lucille do scenes like this in their TV show, they aren't just play-acting—they really mean it" (Albert). Or as "a friend" of Ball's explained in a June 1952 *Look* article, "The trouble with Lucy is that her real life is so much like her reel life" (Silvian 7).

Of course, despite the PR copy that the show was based on the Ball and Arnaz marriage, clearly it was not. In particular, the divergence between talented, successful, and famous Lucille Ball and thwarted, unfulfilled, unknown Lucy Ricardo is huge, and although the actors had a daughter, the Ricardos were childless. But it allowed Ball and Arnaz a bizarre public fantasy of a private life closer to traditional gender roles than their real-life partnership.

The situation of *I Love Lucy* articulated the contradictions of marriage, gender, the battle of the sexes, and middle-class life—concerns of the majority of television watchers and buyers. Ball attributed the series' success to identification:

> We had a great identification with millions of people. People identified with the Ricardos because we had the same problems they had. Desi and I weren't your ordinary Hollywood couple on TV. We lived in a brownstone apartment somewhere in Manhattan, and paying the rent, getting a new dress, getting a stale fur collar on an old cloth coat, or buying a piece of furniture were all worth a story. (qtd. in Andrews 225–26)

Note that the things Ball lists as ordinary problems all deal with domestic, private life; the problem solving leads back to the core of the show, the "love" between the couple. The actors' collaborative marriage filters through the comic representation of the demands of the companionate marriage, the postwar ideal that imagined the husband and wife as a team supporting the husband's work in the public sphere with the wife stationed in the private sphere.

This aspect of the conflation of Ball-Arnaz and the Ricardos emerged even more when the show incorporated Lucille Ball's real-life pregnancy into the fictional world of the series. When Ball and Arnaz revealed her pregnancy to the show's producer, they transformed what could have been the end of the series into a new arena for comedy; not only had television "saved" their marriage, but it enabled Ball to maintain her career and have a family. Moreover, Ball performed the cultural work of a trickster in mainstream America by being the first openly pregnant woman to perform on television, which challenged accepted ideas about the impropriety of public representations of pregnancy. For example, even though the censors would not allow anyone to say the word "pregnant" on the show (the French *enceinte* was used instead), Arnaz refused when Philip Morris wanted Lucy's pregnant body hidden behind furniture. Instead of hiding Ball's pregnancy, they made comedy from Lucy's cravings and mood swings, aspirations for the baby's future, Ricky's sympathetic morning sickness and important role as father, and cute maternity clothes (available at a store near you).

The intertwining of fictionality and reality in the pregnancy episodes resulted in an emotional intensity that allowed the viewer to participate in a highly mediated but nevertheless moving enactment of expecting a baby. Throughout these reality-based episodes, the audience is privy to a re-enactment of personal events, or rather, Ball and Arnaz turned their private experience into a public representation that reflected and shaped the popular pursuit of marriage and family.

The episode in which Lucy tells Ricky she is expecting was foreshadowed by media coverage of Ball's pregnancy and reports that the baby would be incorporated into the show. In the episode, Lucy tries to tell Ricky the news, things interfere, and the dramatic irony builds because the viewer knows what Ricky does not. The climax of the show occurs in Ricky's nightclub, and Ball and Arnaz were understandably emotional as they filmed the scene. Ricky gets an anonymous note that a woman wants to tell her husband they are expecting a "blessed event" and Ricky goes from table to table looking for the couple as he sings "Rockabye Baby." He finally comes to a table where Lucy is seated. After an emotional moment of realization, Ricky sings "We're Having a Baby" as he walks around the stage with a tearful Lucy, and he flubs the lyrics of the song. The episode ends with a close-up of the couple crying and laughing. Producer Oppenheimer recalls that they did another take and filmed a more upbeat scene as had been originally scripted, but they decided to use the first one.

This moment is significant because it is Lucille Ball and Desi Arnaz we are watching, not the characters. The fiction of the television series becomes, for a moment, transparent. Most striking, however, is the intimacy of this scene, a familiarity felt by the audience for the people on the screen that had been forged in a television series that revolved around the intimate moments of marriage and everyday life. In order for the creative team to choose the take in which the actors are choked up and have it work, there had to have been a long setup to this moment, paved with a hybrid of fictionality and reality that transcends both.

The scene itself plays with the line between reality and artifice and between public and private. As Ricky goes from table to table in search of the parents-to-be, the camera is positioned in the audience, encouraging our identification as a live audience member (reinforced by the laughter of the studio audience that blurs with the diegetic laughter of the club audience). The *mise en scène* of the nightclub stage and incorporation of musical performance into the plot is typical of how early television oscillated between domestic and theatrical space in shows like *The George Burns and Gracie Allen Show*, *The Adventures of Ozzie and Harriet*, and *Make Room for Daddy*, as well as *I Love Lucy*. As Lynn Spigel explains, "By acknowledging its own artifice and theatricality, the family comedy encouraged viewers to feel as if they had been let in on a joke, while at the same time allowing them to take that joke seriously" (165). The strategy of letting the audience in on both the joke and the seriousness runs through the pregnancy episodes and makes comedy out of reality— including Ball's pregnant body and what it could and could not do. Although there is not a great deal of Ball's trademark physical comedy in the episodes filmed while she was six and seven months pregnant, there are scattered moments. Not only is Ball a pregnant woman seen in public and continuing to work, but also in the scenes that showcase her pregnant body, Lucy is competent and resourceful in getting around its limitations.

The convergence of reality and fictionality suggested by Ball's physical comedy peaked on January 19, 1953, when the two babies were born. The *Newsweek* cover story of the same date, "Desilu Formula for Top TV: Brains, Beauty, Now a Baby," describes the schedule of the blessed events, "If all goes well, newspaper readers all over the country will be treated on Jan. 20 to the story of Mrs. Arnaz having a baby—the morning after they see Mrs. Ricardo go to the hospital on TV. All this may come under the heading of how duplicated in life and television *can* you get" (56). Because no one knew the sex of the Ball-Arnaz baby, they could not duplicate that piece of reality for the November filming of the episode "Lucy Goes to the Hospital," and it was kept secret that the Ricardo baby would be a boy. The pregnancy episodes play on this uncertainty, and the sex became a topic of popular speculation, culminating in the dual births. Examples of the headlines reporting the births foreground the collision of reality and fictionality—with fictionality winning out over reality: "Lucy Sticks to Script: A Boy It Is!" (*New York Daily Mirror*, January 20, 1953); "TV Was Right: A Boy for Lucille" (*Daily News*, January 20, 1953); and "What the Script Ordered" (*Life*, February 2, 1953).

Unlike the celebratory melding of real life and fiction in the babies, other real-life events were kept carefully away from the television text. Although *I Love Lucy* was subversive about domestic containment, Ball, Arnaz, the producers, and CBS downplayed the red scare accusation that Lucille Ball was a Communist. A full discussion of the media representations of how Ball had, in fact, registered as a Communist in 1938 in order, she insisted, to please her grandfather, is beyond the scope of this chapter, but Ball's red hair almost had a very different—and career-ending—connotation. The news of Ball's 1953 hearings before the House Un-American Activities Committee leaked out, leading to a *Los Angeles–Herald Express* headline, in three-inch red letters: "LUCILLE BALL NAMED RED." That night, before the filming of the 1953–54 season premiere, Arnaz gave a serious speech denouncing communism and labeling the rumors lies. The crowd cheered. He ended as he always did, with, "And now, I want you to meet my favorite wife," but then he continued, "my favorite redhead—in fact, that's the only thing red about her, and even that's not legitimate—Lucille Ball!" (Sanders and Gilbert 81) Not surprisingly the television series also eschewed the real-life unrest in the Ball-Arnaz marriage, which ended in divorce in 1960, about when the series ended. It seems that television could not really save their, or anyone's, marriage.

"There's no dream she wouldn't reach for, and no fall she wouldn't take." This is how Walter Matthau described the universal appeal and comedic genius of Lucille Ball, and indeed Lucille Ball's comic genius continues to entertain and amaze in its embrace of both hopeful aspiration and often-subsequent plummet (Sanders and Gilbert 368). In the role of Lucy, Ball and her collaborators created one of the most beloved and central kinds of cultural figures: a trickster, a subversive, paradoxical fantasy figure who does what we cannot or dare not by moving between social spaces, roles, and categories that the culture has deemed oppositional (Landay, *Madcaps*). When faced with a situation that appears to have only two choices, the trickster is the kind of hero/ine who creates a third possibility. But the trickster's schemes often backfire, and then the trickster becomes the dupe. Lucy is specifically a female trickster because her attempts to circumvent the limitations of postwar domesticity oscillate between "masculine" and "feminine" social roles, spaces, practices, and metaphors.

By calling attention to the power relations of the sexes in everyday domestic life, *I Love Lucy* participated in a proto-feminist current building in American culture. The continued appeal of *I Love Lucy* in reruns is not only due to comic brilliance, but also to how it offers contemporary audiences a fitting precursor to the women's movement of the 1960s and 1970s. Scholar George Lipsitz's term "memory as misappropriation" suggests a show can be popular because it represents the past as people wish it had been. *I Love Lucy* recasts the domestic prison of the 1950s into the easily escapable terrain of the female trickster. Lucy's daring pursuit of her desires and her irrepressible insistence that Ricky—and everyone else—acknowledge her as a talented individual provide a model that may be radically different from our impressions of our mothers, grandmothers, and great-grandmothers. Moreover, by wiggling under, vaulting over, and sneaking past the boundary between reality and fictionality, by playing fast and loose with the various windows between the world and the home that television promised and failed to be, Lucy the trickster delighted postwar Americans, and *I Love Lucy* shaped situation comedy forever.

NOTES

Thanks to my husband, Richard Cownie, for editing help, as well as seeing the humor in things.

1. Despite the myth it started, Desilu did not invent the three-camera system still used in television today. Arnaz and cinematographer Karl Freund (who shot the German expressionist *Metropolis* in 1926 and was Ball's cinematographer on the 1943 MGM musical *DuBarry Was a Lady*) adapted the system pioneered by Jerry Fairbanks but kept all three cameras rolling simultaneously. See Christopher Anderson, *Hollywood TV: The Studio System in the Fifties*, 53–56 and 65–68.

CHAPTER 8

Our Miss Brooks
Situating Gender in Teacher Sitcoms

Mary M. Dalton

INTRODUCTION

I never set out to become a teacher, and it certainly never occurred to me that I might eventually be considered an expert on the media portrayals of teachers. But this is exactly the position in which I find myself now as a professor actively engaged in scholarship that includes critical analyses of teacher characters in film and television. At times it has been a tough job, slogging through abysmal movies like *The Teacher* (a soft-core, serial killer flick that is painfully dull) and *The Class of 1984* (high camp that can be fun if one is in the mood for it and not under deadline), but somebody has to do it. Besides, there are wonderful stories about teachers, too (my personal favorite is *Conrack*), and that, along with the cultural significance of the narratives, has motivated me to extend my scholarship to include teachers on television. In the process of this research, television situation comedies like *Welcome Back, Kotter* and *Head of the Class* have summoned latent memories and helped to make this work more delight than drudge. *Our Miss Brooks*, a situation comedy that began on radio in 1948 and enjoyed a successful run there through 1957 that overlapped with its television run of 1952 to 1956, was a discovery rather than a revisitation for me. I had heard of it but had never actually seen an episode until I began researching teacher sitcoms.[1]

This research on mass media portrayals of teachers began with an examination of movies in which teachers are either cast as the central character or play prominent roles. *The Hollywood Curriculum: Teachers in the Movies* examines 116 films of various genres distributed widely in the United States over nearly seventy-five years. That research reveals that there are striking differences in almost every case between men and women teachers in the movies, but only in their personal lives outside the classroom.

This chapter will discuss identification of the gender patterns found in teacher movies, compare those patterns to similar ones evident in teacher situation comedies, and then will look more closely at *Our Miss Brooks*, the only teacher sitcom featuring a woman as the main character to land in the top thirty rated programs during its broadcast. The chapter will conclude with an analysis of the motion picture of the same title based on the series, a film released in 1956, which is the same year *Our Miss Brooks* ended its television run. This teacher feature and the sitcom of the same name stars the inimitable Eve Arden as Connie Brooks. Other regulars from the sitcom cast also appear in the movie, but there is a sharp divergence from the series in terms of the completely implausible coupling of Miss Brooks with the biology teacher. Miss Brooks had relentlessly pursued him for years and across mediums from radio to television to motion picture.

THE DIVIDED LIVES OF
WOMEN TEACHERS IN THE MOVIES

The first element that became clear in surveying motion pictures featuring teachers is that relatively fewer of these films star women than men as the central character. Aside from the number of films featuring women, there is a marked difference in the film narrative depending on the gender of the character who plays the lead role; women teachers are forced into divided lives in which they must focus solely on the welfare of their students to be considered "good" teachers, and these characters are not allowed to have rich personal lives that include a sexual component without being punished in some way.[2] It seems that this bifurcation of the public and private worlds of women—a condition that is not the case for male teachers in the movies or in television comedies—is played out in films with "unmarriedness," "childlessness," and a litany of other "maladies" acting as metaphors for the ways in which women teachers are forced to alternately draw upon and deny their femaleness. This is manifested in their being asked to nurture but not to mother the children they teach and to maintain a chaste domestic life.[3] There is a range of portrayals of women teachers in Hollywood films that is not carried over to the situation comedy, but the overarching pattern for "good" women teachers stretches across mediums.

In films, most women teachers are single and childless, or their marital and maternal status is not revealed to the audience. While many of the male teachers portrayed in films are also single, some are not, and the issues are different. In the movies male teachers are allowed to have happy, full lives outside of the classroom and to be heroes at school. They are also allowed a range of moral ambiguity or ambivalence that is not open to female teachers. In most of these films, the male protagonist is either happily married to a supportive spouse or a love interest emerges—almost always younger and more attractive—as a complication developed in a secondary story line. This pattern was established before teacher characters moved from the big screen to the small screen, and television sitcoms have reinforced these familiar images of teachers and have subtly shaped our expectations for real teachers.

We know that media texts never exist separate from contexts, including a reader's own lived experience, and that lived experience is similarly informed by many other media texts and personal narratives. The texts under consideration, in this case teacher sitcoms, are incorporated into the reader's everyday life at the same time the reader's everyday life becomes part of the construction of the text. "Because of their incompleteness, all popular texts have leaky boundaries; they flow into each other, they flow into everyday life. Distinctions among texts are as invalid as the distinctions between text and life," argues John Fiske. "Popular culture can be studied only intertextually, for it exists only in this intertextual circulation. The interrelationships between primary and secondary texts cross all boundaries between them; equally, those between tertiary and other texts cross the boundaries between text and life" (*Understanding* 126). According to their gender and other elements of their lived experience, viewers will read these texts from their particular perspectives. For me, women teachers represented in mass media are inevitably filtered through my own experience as a woman teacher, a divorced woman, a scholar studying representations of teachers in film and television, the mother of a son who attends a public school, the daughter of educators, and so on, and this set of personal experiences informs my critical analysis of the narratives I encounter, just as others will have their own preferred readings of the texts they encounter.

TV TEACHERS CONTINUE THE PATTERN

In my preliminary survey of teacher sitcoms, eighty-two sitcoms with teacher characters featured were considered.[4] Many of the series on the initial list included characters identified as teachers but never shown in the classroom (like Bob's wife Emily on *The Bob Newhart Show*) or characters who are peripheral to the main story line and just happen to be educators. Sixteen sitcoms regularly featured teachers as main characters and included some classroom scenes.[5] The intersection of media and culture is a complex and compelling space. Because I believe that the stories we see in mass media give us "scripts" that shape the possibilities and limitations for our lived experience—the narratives of our daily lives—I decided to view the most popular and enduring of the teacher sitcoms and selected those that had landed in the top thirty shows for the season during some point in their network run. This choice left five programs for consideration: *The Bill Cosby Show, Hangin' with Mr. Cooper, Head of the Class, Our Miss Brooks*, and *Welcome Back, Kotter.*[6] Most of these programs have enjoyed extended runs in syndication, and some representative episodes of all of them were available for review.

Consider first the male teachers who are protagonists in their respective series. Each of them clearly fits the "Hollywood model" of the "good" teacher set forth in my research on teachers in the movies. In the films, the good teacher is something of an outsider. In teacher sitcoms, there is less of this animosity among teachers, which is probably due to the necessity of focusing on fewer characters within the limited time slot and the general tone of sitcoms. One of the other elements common to the films remains fully intact, however: the good teacher does not usually fare well with administrators. Mr. Woodman is a nasty vice principal on *Welcome Back, Kotter*, Dr. Samuels is a self-serving principal on *Head of the Class*, Geneva is "Cousin Principal" on *Hangin' with Mr. Cooper*, and all of these antagonists fall neatly into the pattern established twenty years before in *Our Miss Brooks* by Mr. Conklin, the bumbling, self-absorbed, blustery principal at Madison High School, who is a perpetual thorn in the side of Connie Brooks. In both films and television sitcoms, the good teacher gets involved with students on a personal level (though we generally see more types of interaction outside of the classroom in films because they typically use a greater number of sets and locations) and learns lessons from those students. Sometimes these good teachers have a ready sense of humor, and Eve Arden's wise-cracking and wry Connie Brooks holds her own with the male teachers, several of whom were stand-up comics before they became sitcom teachers. Good teachers on TV match their counterparts in the movies by personalizing the curriculum to meet the everyday needs in their students' lives and extending lessons taught to transcend the boundaries of the classroom. Although only half of the films surveyed feature a "good" teacher as the main character, all of the teacher sitcoms are centered around a main character who generally conforms to the characteristics of the "Hollywood model," which suggests the influence of one set of narratives upon the other despite the considerable differences between the two forms.

Todd Gitlin advances a set of conventions for popular entertainment that have effectively reassured network executives and stood the test of time (many of the same conventions were set forth by Aristotle in the *Poetics* as elements of effective dramatic structure): "Heroes should be agreeable, villains clear, 'jeopardy' definite, outcomes pleasing, story lines simple, climaxes frequent,

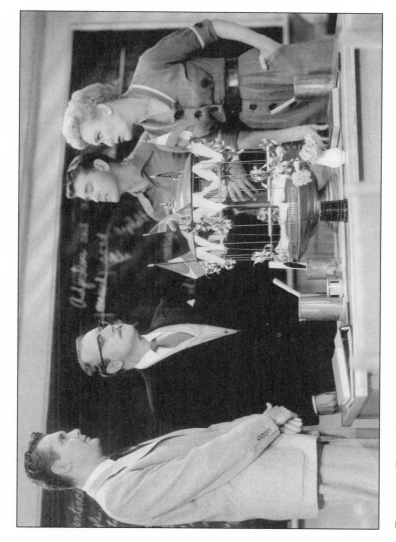

FIGURE 8.1. Robert Rockwell as Philip Boynton, Gale Gordon as Osgood Conklin, Richard Crenna as Walter Denton, and Eve Arden as Connie Brooks in *Our Miss Brooks*, 1952–1956. Photo courtesy of Photofest. Used by permission.

jokes flagrant" (*Inside Prime* 29). Gitlin writes later that sitcoms are designed to propel the audience from one crisis to another, many conveniently cropping up just before a commercial break, but that the audience can count on an easy, upbeat solution (*Inside Prime* 92). Not all genres are suitable for television. Some become tired and must be replaced, but the sitcom genre has both evolved and endured. "New genres spring up, like the situation comedy, descendant of radio, which in turn drew on vaudeville sketches," says Gitlin. "Sitcoms, with their incessant skein of personal problems in a family-like setting, seem peculiarly tailored to the small screen, to its living room locations, and to advertisers' desire for captive audiences whose commercials must be studded, like gems, in suitable settings" (*Inside Prime* 29). Teacher sitcoms draw on the established tradition and conventions of the "good" teacher in the movies and fold that model into the sitcom format, which was a relatively new format when *Our Miss Brooks* hit the airwaves but was fully established by the time the other most popular of the teacher sitcoms went on the air.

Part of that evolution can been seen in the changes from *Our Miss Brooks* and the visual style of 1950s programming (black-and-white film, a stagey look to the sets and the direction of the actors, and scripts that don't take particular advantage of the visual elements of the medium) to the other teacher sitcom hits beginning about twenty years later (color images, more detailed sets, larger casts of regular characters, more complicated story lines, and complex characters that develop over time).[7] To more closely examine the role gender plays in the teacher sitcom, it is useful to spend a little time looking at *Welcome Back, Kotter*, which, of the programs considered here featuring male teachers, is the most analogous to *Our Miss Brooks*. Both of these sitcoms aired for four years, and *Our Miss Brooks* peaked at number fourteen in its second season while *Welcome Back, Kotter* landed the number thirteen slot, also its highest season rating, the second year it aired. Both of the programs also divide time between sets representing the work environment and the private sphere of home. Both feature administrators as the irritating antagonist always questioning the good teacher and threatening his or her job over personal or inconsequential matters. Both are beloved teachers who show unflagging patience with "difficult" students; Miss Brooks is an English teacher trying to help a blundering student named Walter and a "dim" athlete named Stretch, and Gabe Kotter, played by Gabe Kaplan, teaches "sweathogs," a group of students with learning difficulties.

Despite the many similarities between Connie Brooks and Gabe Kotter, there is one major difference: she spends her days plotting, planning, and relentlessly tracking the shy biology teacher, Philip Boynton, without any success, while Gabe goes home to his cute, no-nonsense, very supportive wife, Julie. Over the years Gabe and Julie have some squabbles, some children, and marital problems—all situations common to the genre—but there is never a question about whether Gabe's having a spouse may preclude his ability to be a focused and effective teacher in the classroom. Similarly, Bill Cosby's Chet

Kincaid (in *The Bill Cosby Show*), Howard Hesseman's Charlie Moore (in *Head of the Class*), and Mark Curry's Mark Cooper (in *Hangin' with Mr. Cooper*) characters all have love interests or full-blown relationships in their series. The appropriateness of such couplings is never an issue either explicitly or implicitly. On the other hand, the closest we see Connie Brooks come to domestic bliss is her relationship with her nosy but well-meaning, elderly landlady, Mrs. Davis, who assists in Miss Brooks's efforts to snare the object of her affection, Mr. Boynton.

OUR MISS BROOKS ON SCREENS LARGE AND SMALL

Gerard Jones notes that a number of new shows were introduced in the early 1950s featuring "cute but dizzy" women in an attempt to replicate the success of *I Love Lucy* (79). Jones argues that women in these sitcoms generally caused trouble inadvertently in keeping with efforts to safeguard the best interests of their male superiors. In doing so, they backed away from the sexual conflict that distinguished *I Love Lucy* and "retreated instead to the level of wish fulfillment, comforting to female viewers who wanted to see themselves as helpful handmaidens and male viewers who wanted to view their women as exasperating but never threatening" (79). Some of these programs may have been ratings hits, but they were generally safe and bland. This was not quite the case for another Desilu endeavor, however. According to Jones, Lucille Ball and Desi Arnaz acted almost immediately to bring *Our Miss Brooks* over from radio to television as soon as *I Love Lucy* became a hit. Jones writes:

> Eve Arden, who played spinster schoolteacher Connie Brooks, was a movie and radio veteran of approximately Lucille Ball's vintage and celebrity. But Connie was no Lucy. Arden played her with a brassy, wisecracking self-assurance that made her more than a match for her three running battles: her power struggle with her pompous principal, her endless effort to drum knowledge into the head of a dim-witted student named Walter, and her battle to snare the shy biology teacher who never seemed to pick up her amorous hints. No other TV woman was as combative. Says Walter to her; "I'd say you were in your late twenties or early thirties or—" And says she: "Quit now. Teeth become you." Connie was the only one of those dames of the depression mold to win a place in TV comedy. In keeping with the times, she worked at a nurturing, surrogate maternal job, and her prime goal was to get married and quit. Yet in her struggles the tension of changing American life was preserved. (85)

That's not all that was preserved; Connie Brooks's inability to get her man—or any man—may have been played broadly for laughs, but it also maintained the split between her public and private lives. Ella Taylor writes that situation comedies started out as comedic plots based on misunderstandings, absurd adventures, or stars delivering monologues or dialogues that were essentially a series of running jokes. They then became more character driven as audiences became more familiar with particular characters, and humor in these situations "hinged on the idiosyncrasies of the central characters, in particular on the relations between them" (25). Connie Brooks's relationships with her coworkers may not have been as emotionally complex as Mary Richards's would be a generation later in *The Mary Tyler Moore Show*, but there is certainly an undercurrent here of Miss Brooks's strength, independence, and individuality—traits that would later be associated with happily single Mary—that belies what is presented as Connie's single-minded focus on matrimony. This is reinforced by the fact that the man she pursues shows so little interest in her that viewers might elect to never take their supposed courtship seriously.

Consider the possibility—a reading that is compelling to me—that Connie Brooks is really putting one over on viewers. Perhaps her popularity is enhanced by some recognition that there is more complexity in the characters of *Our Miss Brooks* than appears on the surface. Miss Brooks plays the "good" teacher and obeys the rules circumscribing the behavior of a woman in her position, but she also gives lip service to what are supposed to be the primary goals of single women in her era: marriage, a home, and a family. She dresses the part with tight, feminine, but not revealing clothes. She wears makeup and has her hair done. She circumvents references to her age, which we assume to be late thirties. She talks incessantly about wanting to marry Mr. Boynton and even alludes to her sexual desire for the "frog boy," but something in her expression, an intractability perhaps, contradicts those words. She is strong and bold and irrepressible, and this is an image that does not meld with any vision of Connie Brooks as Connie Boynton. Is Miss Brooks openly dissembling for us because she knows that women teachers cannot, after all, "have it all"? Does she fit Lori Landay's description of the female trickster? Interpreting Connie Brooks's character in this context makes this sitcom a much richer text. Landay writes:

> Women, encouraged to manipulate their appearance and sublimate assertive impulses behind a mask of feminine behavior, are necessarily involved in duplicitous practices in everyday life. The emotional, sexual, and social machinations of the dating and marriage market, the self-objectification that presents an appealing façade, are achieved by employing the trickster tactics of deception, impersonation, disguise, duplicity, and subversion. Because the social practice of femininity is a form of trickery, characters in cultural texts who are female tricksters resonate with and expose a fundamental tenet of the social relations of the sexes in

American culture: The only way for women to survive given their subordinate position and limited opportunities for exercising overt power, is to
use the covert power of female trickery. (*Madcaps* 172–73)

Miss Brooks's effective use of such trickery—pretending to be the unwilling
spinster while living a life of relative independence that would not be available
to her if she were, in fact, married to Mr. Boynton—makes the series more
compelling than it might be otherwise. This alternative reading of the text and
the characters populating it resonates with me.

This reading of gender in the sitcom *Our Miss Brooks* also goes a long way
toward explaining why the movie of the same title is so dull and unengaging—
ironic since the film ends with Miss Brooks and Mr. Boynton (they are finally
beginning to call one another Connie and Philip) officially engaged to be
married and walking off hand in hand to look at the cottage she has long
dreamed of and he has just purchased and wallpapered. This ultimate, "happy"
ending breaks with the established pattern of bifurcating the public and private lives of women teachers (unless we assume that she will give up her teaching job forever and renounce the public sphere), follows a narrative that contradicts the entire premise of the sitcom on radio and television, and just
generally does not ring true with viewers. Not only is Miss Brooks pursued, if
ambivalently, by Mr. Boynton for most of the movie when anyone familiar
with the series knows that he has always deflected her advances, but she is also
pursued by a millionaire newspaperman whose son she teaches then tutors
after school in the family mansion. This pattern not only breaks completely
with the situations and characters established in the long-running series and
familiar to viewers, it also breaks irrevocably with stories we have been told
over and over again about women teachers, narratives built around the forced
bifurcation of the public, professional persona as teacher (that was made available untarnished only so long as these characters stayed focused on the classroom and denied themselves a personal life complete with a component of
sexual expression in their private lives) with the private, domestic persona as
wife or girlfriend or domestic partner. Surely, there will be revisionist teacher
films that give women teachers fulfilling personal and professional lives—and
hopefully we won't have to wait seventy-five more years for those stories to be
told—but the motion picture *Our Miss Brooks* does not deliver because it simply is not a credible narrative on any level.[8]

CONCLUSION

At the junctures of private and public, of self and culture, it becomes critical to
look at the various forces that influence the way we think about gender and
teaching. Certainly, one of these forces is popular culture. Commercial narratives

not only tell women teachers how other people construct them and rearticulate them as characters on movie and television screens, these films and episodic programs also shape the way students and parents respond to teachers and the way women teachers respond to public opinion in the construction of their own lives. *Our Miss Brooks* may seem dated and *Welcome Back, Kotter* may seem like a bit of nostalgic fluff, but these stories reproduce and reinforce larger, gendered patterns that cut across genre and era. This alone makes them meaningful and powerful narratives worthy of our consideration.

NOTES

1. As David Marc notes in his chapter, "Dying in its twenties and dead around thirty, prime-time radio was only beginning to define its generic texts when they were kidnapped by television." So it is interesting to note that *Our Miss Brooks* ran continuously on both mediums during the decline of radio serials and the ascendancy of television. While I do not know how many actual scripts were duplicated across the two mediums in the series, I did discover quite by accident that some were. When I was on a research trip to view teacher sitcoms at the Museum of Television and Radio in New York, I watched the four television episodes that are in the collection then used some free moments to listen to one of the radio shows out of general interest. It so happened that the radio program I chose randomly duplicated almost word for word the script used for the television episode "Model Teacher."

2. I have defined the "good" teacher in the "Hollywood model" as one who meets the following criteria: typically, he or she is an outsider who is usually not well liked by other teachers, who are typically bored by students, afraid of students, or eager to dominate students; the "good" teacher gets involved with students on a personal level, learns from those students, and does not usually fare very well with administrators; sometimes these "good" teachers have a ready sense of humor, and in movies it is usually the male teachers who fit this pattern; these teachers also frequently personalize the curriculum to meet everyday needs in their students' lives. About half of the films I surveyed feature a "good" teacher as the main character.

3. Women teachers who appear solely as a "love interest" for male teachers in the starring role are seen occasionally in films and fall outside of this paradigm.

4. This list was gleaned mainly from *The Complete Directory to Prime Time Network and Cable TV Shows 1946–Present* (Brooks and Marsh): *Anna and the King, Better Days, Between Brothers, The Bill Cosby Show, Bob Newhart Show, Boston Common, Boy Meets World, Bridget Loves Bernie, Brother's Keeper, Charlie and Co., Clueless, Dear John, Dear Phoebe, Delta House, A Different World, Doctor, Doctor, Dorothy, Drexell's Class, Evening Shade, Facts of Life, The Faculty, Fast Times, Ferris Bueller, Funny Face, George, Gertrude Berg Show, The Good Life, Halls of Ivy, Hangin' In, Hangin' with Mr. Cooper, Harper Valley PTA, Head of the Class, Homeroom, The Jimmy Stewart Show, The John Forsythe Show, Just the Ten of Us, Kelly Kelly, King of the Hill, Learning the Ropes, Leave It to Beaver, Making the Grade, The Many Loves of Dobie Gillis, McKeever and the*

Colonel, Mr. Peepers, Mr. Sunshine, Moesha, Nanny and the Professor, Nearly Departed, Nick Freno: Licensed Teacher, O.K. Crackerby, Our Miss Brooks, Out of This World, The Parent 'Hood, Parker Lewis Can't Lose, Pearl, Please Don't Eat the Daisies, The Preston Episodes, Pursuit of Happiness, The Ray Milland Show, Saved By the Bell: The College Years, Sibs, The Simpsons, Smart Guy, Something So Right, SouthPark, Spencer, Square Pegs, The Steve Harvey Show, Strangers with Candy, Struck By Lightning, The Stu Erwin Show, Teachers Only, Teech, 3rd Rock from the Sun, To Rome with Love, True Colors, Two of a Kind, The Waverly Wonders, Weird Science, Welcome Back, Kotter, Welcome Freshmen, What a Country, and *What About Joan.*

5. The following series meet that standard: *The Bill Cosby Show, Drexell's Class, Hangin' with Mr. Cooper, Head of the Class, Homeroom, Mr. Peepers, Nick Freno: Licensed Teacher, Our Miss Brooks, Pursuit of Happiness, The Ray Milland Show, The Steve Harvey Show, Teachers Only, Teech, The Waverly Wonders, Welcome Back, Kotter,* and *What a Country.*

6. According to *The Complete Directory to Prime Time Network and Cable TV Shows 1946–Present, The Bill Cosby Show* reached number eleven for 1969–70; *Hangin' with Mr. Cooper* reached number sixteen (a tie with *Fresh Prince of Bel Air* and *The Jackie Thomas Show*) for 1992–93; *Head of the Class* reached number thirty for 1986–87, number twenty-three (tied with NBC *Sunday Night Movie*) for 1987–88, number twenty for 1988–89, and number twenty-six for 1989–90 and 1990–91; *Our Miss Brooks* reached number twenty-two (tied with *The Big Story*) for 1952–53 and number fourteen for 1953–54; *Welcome Back, Kotter* reached number eighteen for 1975–76, number thirteen for 1976–77, and number twenty-six (a tie with *The Incredible Hulk* and *Family*) for 1977–78.

7. *Our Miss Brooks* (CBS) aired from 1952 to 1956, *The Bill Cosby Show* (NBC) aired from 1969 to 1971, *Welcome Back, Kotter* (ABC) aired from 1975 to 1979, *Head of the Class* (ABC) aired from 1986 to 1991, and *Hangin' with Mr. Cooper* (ABC) aired from 1992 to 1997.

8. The 1995 film *Dangerous Minds* might have been such a narrative. The film as originally shot included scenes with actor Andy Garcia playing a romantic interest for Pfeiffer's character. Including such a character might have helped expand on the typical portrayal of the "gendered" teacher. Those scenes, however, were cut before the film was released and ensured that the character of the woman teacher would conform to the stereotype prevalent in other films.

CHAPTER 9

Talking Sex

Comparison Shopping through Female Conversation in HBO's *Sex and the City*

Sharon Marie Ross

I know where my next orgasm is coming from. Who here can say that?

—Miranda, *Sex and the City*

INTRODUCTION

Mariana Valverde is frustrated with mainstream cultural representations of women's sexual desire. These representations depict women's desire as a "slippery slope": give her an inch of sexual agency, and she'll want a mile (150). Noting that women's sexual desires have been linked historically to a desire for consumable goods, and that such compounded desire has also been seen as an indicator of social illness in the form of decadence, Valverde argues that "it is consumerism [not erotic desire] which constructs our desire as limitless" (152). While this is an astute description of one of the primary motifs governing the representation of female sexual desire and agency in the United

States, as a feminist I wonder why "limitless desire" is problematic—however it might be constructed. The implication seems to be that a desire that has no end is somehow uncontrollable and ultimately self-destructive, and while this is often the direction that sexually active female characters in media "take," I believe that this is a patriarchal construction working to assuage fears of female power in society. A representation of sexual desire as limitless does not have to be framed in this manner; to position female sexual desire as preferably finite and comprehensible is incompatible with many of the goals of feminism as a political movement.

The HBO comedy series *Sex and the City* speaks to this concern, offering a direct examination of female sexual desire and its connection to other desires. The show elucidates women's desires through three motifs: women discussing with other women sexuality and their own sexual actions, women discussing with other women gender roles in modern-day society, and women discussing with other women their consumption of material goods.

It is important for feminism and media studies that scholars continue to examine sex and all its representations, particularly in a television era that increasingly (and with more sophistication) niche markets to women. *Sex and the City* is HBO's first attempt to niche market to an adult female audience, according to Chris Albrecht, president of Original Programming and Independent Production (Higgins 54). In this chapter, I focus on how *Sex and the City* works to situate female sexual desire and agency along a spectrum of choice—a spectrum that demands "comparison shopping" and "informed decisions." The show also works to present restrictions on decision making about sexuality and interpersonal relations active in a capitalistic and patriarchal society, and suggests that female friendship is a potential site of resistance to such restrictions. I focus primarily, however, on the connections between consumerism and female sexual desire as the show frames these concepts. Through discussion of sexual choices, gender role options, and literal material goods, the women of *Sex and the City* incorporate personal sexual desire into a consumerist framework that allows them to manage their own sexuality.

MY MOMMA TOLD ME . . .
YOU BETTER SHOP AROUND

Sex and the City first appeared in the summer of 1998 as a new addition to HBO's growing comedy line up. Based on a 1996 book of the same title by New York newspaper columnist Candace Bushnell, the show's scripts play with Bushnell's essays about the sexual and romantic escapades of wealthy Manhattanites. The show's executive producer, Darren Starr, thought that a focus on four female friends would allow the writers greater flexibility with the book's more circumscribed environment of the world of New York's cultural

FIGURE 9.1. Cynthia Nixon as Miranda Hobbs, Cristin Davis as Charlotte York McDougal, Kim Catrall as Samantha Jones, and Sarah Jessica Parker as Carrie Bradshaw in *Sex and the City*, 1998–2004. Photo courtesy of Larry Edmunds BooksFair.

elite (Cornwell). Many early critics of the show argued, however, that the show's emphasis on shopping, dining, and meeting at exclusive New York establishments lacks realism for the viewers being targeted, and that the combination of sex and consumerism is created in part to garner high bids from foreign countries and companies seeking product-placement in the show (Bone; Gilbert, "Sex in City"; Higgins; Jacobs, "Let's Talk").

In a standard episode of the show, the narrative links a specific sexual issue to larger sociocultural issues of concern for (primarily, but not exclusively) heterosexual women. A recurring motif of consumerism emerges as one of the primary connections between female sexual agency and desire, sometimes positioning the purchase of consumable goods as analogous and substitutable for sexual fulfillment and at other times positioning the same as the site of power relations. Episodes feature the four friends coming together to exchange their points of view as a way of working through this quagmire of female sexuality and consumerism. Several examples can be provided from the first season of *Sex and the City* to demonstrate this consumerist motif and its conjunction with a motif of female desire.

In "The Turtle and the Hare," the narrative asks what single women will settle for in terms of their desire for sexual fulfillment. After the four friends attend the wedding of a former friend whom they thought would never marry due to her past pleasure in sexual variety, they meet for lunch to ponder why this woman would settle for marrying someone who loves her more than she loves him. Charlotte argues that their friend made a wise "investment" (she gets to take out more than she has to put in), but Miranda challenges her, arguing that the investment is only wise if sexual fulfillment is not lost in the deal. Charlotte argues in turn that sex is not important to a relationship if love is present, and Miranda challenges her to think about whether or not she could live the rest of her life without orgasms.

A subplot emerges in which Charlotte becomes addicted to a vibrator called the Rabbit—a $92 investment that Miranda says could make men and marriage obsolete. Eventually, Charlotte becomes so obsessed with her orgasms that Miranda and Carrie perform a "Rabbit intervention," triggered by the fact that Charlotte has been ignoring their friendship. A corollary subplot involves Carrie discovering that her boyfriend, "Mr. Big," does not wish to ever marry. She decides to invest in a marriage with her gay friend Stanford, so that he can receive an inheritance and she can receive the benefits of being married while retaining sexual fulfillment with her boyfriend. Eventually, Carrie decides that she will forego the marriage and settle for living in the present, wryly noting that Charlotte will not "settle for herself" in terms of sexual fulfillment.

These simultaneous stories resonate with the consumerist trajectory of the Sexual Revolution for women in the United States (Ehrenreich, Hess, and Jacobs). By the 1980s, a market strategy arose targeting women as sexually active and desirable consumers; group outings to see male strippers and group home-shopping parties for sexual aids (modeled on the format of Tupperware parties) were common in middle-class America. Ehrenreich, Hess, and Jacobs argue that the commodified activities of the 1980s emphasized female plea-sure in the actual group experience of purchasing *together*, which parallels the behavior of the friends in "The Turtle and the Hare." When Charlotte bought the Rabbit, her friends each bought one also. When the Rabbit threatened the primary group experience of the female friendship, though, the Rabbit had to go. Bonding beat out buying.

The parallel story lines in this episode speak to a late 1980s backlash trend against increased expressions of female sexual desire in the 1970s and 1980s (Ehrenreich, Hess, and Jacobs; Faludi). This backlash took the form of a cul-tural emphasis on single women's supposed loss of love and commitment—on sexual desire run amok. Carrie's initial willingness to split her sexual life from her married life, to also split love from commitment, reveals an ideological con-testation over such issues, specifically about what realms love, marriage, and sexual pleasure "belong" in and, indeed, whether love and commitment must be equated with each other. Stanford's dilemma also incorporates a current ideo-logical battle over gay marriages, highlighting the economic benefits of mar-riage in our culture. While Stanford has the high income associated with many White, gay males in our niche-marketing culture, he still stands to miss out economically on the investment of sanctioned marriage because his grand-mother will only give money to her legally married grandchildren. The bottom line is that even though the consumerist-driven ideology of capitalism is pleased to acknowledge Stanford as a "sexual citizen" when it comes to pur-chasing power, he does not have the same full body of rights that heterosexual citizens of the United States have (Evans, David T.).

In "The Baby Shower," the four women visit yet another friend who has left their single world to get married and raise children. Only Charlotte is excited about the baby shower; she is eager to visit the world she thinks of as wedded and maternal bliss. Sam only wants to see what her former rival looks like pregnant, and she even brings a bottle of scotch to drink in front of her. Miranda is disgusted with the entire concept of the shower, and she warns her friends that she has lost two sisters to "the cult of motherhood." Carrie attends the party with the fear that she, herself, may be pregnant—a fear exemplified by her ambivalence about even having a family.

The party ends up devastating Charlotte in particular; she discovers that their former friend has stolen her future baby's name. Charlotte is so upset that she later rips up the contents of her hope box: her dream man (a picture of John F. Kennedy, Jr.), her back-up dream man (an advertisement featuring a male model), her baby name pillow, and photos of her two dream homes in Manhattan and the Hamptons. Carrie, as she waits to find out if she is preg-nant, wonders about the mothers and wives she met at the party—what have they sacrificed and what have they gained? In direct-addresses to the camera, the mothers at the party recite a litany of sacrifices they made for their current lifestyles: a powerful position at work, time to one's self, a lesbian lover, sexual freedom, and sexual satisfaction.

Samantha decides that she is tired of married women looking at her and her friends as if they have nothing to live for without husbands and children in their lives; she throws an "I'm not having a baby" shower to celebrate the fact that her and her friends' lives have not been "squandered" on children and husbands. At the party, Miranda begins a sexual relationship with an accountant, noting her conviction that men will become obsolete does not matter when she can get her taxes done for free. Charlotte eventually decides that she does not need her dreams of marriage and a family to meet the consumerist ideals she had previously laid out for herself and that she will enjoy her life as it is. By the end of the episode, Carrie gets her period, and she feels both relieved and slightly sad. This episode's strategy of layering different and changing perspectives on motherhood and marriage results in a more complex representation of sexual fulfillment and self-fulfillment in general for women than TV typically offers. The stories told highlight the double bind still at work in American culture and society that often makes motherhood, career, and sexual agency mutually exclusive, even as they also highlight the legitimacy of women wanting marriage and children.

I am not attempting to argue that such ideological plurality serves as a thorough critique of the restrictions women in capitalism face. I agree with Robin Andersen that television shows in general ignore the world of work in the sense that the majority of series, including this one, follow a "logic of consumption" that focuses on consumerist activities rather than activities of production proper (71). The commodity is, indeed, attached seamlessly in *Sex and the City* to the fulfillment of social and emotional needs in a way that often obscures the failures of society, politics, and the capitalist economic system to support women's needs and desires. Certainly, we rarely see the four lead characters dealing with the demands of work or worrying about where their next meal is coming from. We do see women coming together in this series, however, whether it is to shop or try out different activities and ideas related to sex and gender. Ultimately, what can be seen in this show is an emphasis on the value of producing and maintaining female friendships as a source of information and support for making choices when "shopping" for sexuality.

SHOP TALK

Pat O'Connor argues that mainstream culture in the United States maintains "gender-role ideologies about romantic heterosexual love which depict friendships between women as very much second best" (91). Beginning in their teens, girls are trained to expect that their friendships with other girls will lessen in strength and importance as girls form romantic relationships with boys. The widespread denigration of women's collective activities culturally reinforces this ideological "given," and denigration of women's activities and desires extends to mainstream texts that offer representations of such activities and desires. Thus, for example, there exists a common ghettoization of such "subgenres" as the "chick flick" and "girl power" shows, as well as soap opera and melodramatic "women's films."

One of the motifs common to these denigrated representational venues is the focus on conversation among women—conversation most often coded as gossip. Many reviews of *Sex and the City* have focused on just this element, noting that the characters "jabber" and "reveal secrets" (Jacobs, "Let's Talk") and even that the show itself is an "empty diversion" akin to reading gossip columns (Kelleher). I came across only one critic (Hettie Judah of *The London Times*) who discussed gossiping about men and sex as supportive of the creation of a community that women can rely on to make informed decisions.

The predominance of discussions revolving around shopping in a text that also focuses on female friendship creates an intriguing intersection of female activities to examine. How is it that shopping can support the creation and maintenance of female friendships? Rachel Bowlby, in her research on the success of department stores in Western Europe during the 1800s, suggests that department stores structure a domestic space based on themes that position the female shopper as aware and educated about how best to choose. One might argue that shopping, over time, has consistently worked to interpolate female consumers as always "functionally," rather than "frivolously," shopping. Additionally, consumerist cultures tend to position shopping as a "feminine" activity that offers a gendered space for women to call their own, serving the consumerist culture's own ends but offering a site for the maintenance of female friendships and gendered bonding.

There is no doubt that *Sex and the City* positions shopping as a functional activity. Shopping goals may include the purchase of a gift to gain entrance to a social event or the purchase of a material object to enhance one's mood. And, of course, there is the kind of shopping that surrounds sex. These friends do not just *purchase* sexual goods. They shop also through discussions and gossiping—a sort of "comparison shopping by talking." In much the same way that department stores work to manage women's shopping through regular sales and competitive advertising, Carrie, Charlotte, Miranda, and Samantha manage their sexuality through regular comparison of sexual events and competitive perspectives on sexual issues.

Sex and the City's strategy of having each of the four friends talking about whatever the episode's topic of the evening may be emphasizes the value of women having access to multiple perspectives. The show seldom offers any definitive answer to the sexual questions raised. In fact, the four women often take divergent paths along the same sexual route. The talking that occurs in this show is an example of what Lorraine Code describes as affective knowing and epistemic negotiation—a knowledge building based on empathy and the ability to imagine other possibilities and perspectives. This motif of presenting equally valued perspectives on sexual issues and corresponding gender role issues is the source of much of the show's humor and emotional pull. The stories, or gossiping, that emerge in the conversations among of these four female friends allow these women to explore different possibilities in terms of their sexual desires and agency with the talk functioning as a mode of "window shopping," so to speak.

A specific episode near the conclusion of the first season exemplifies the function of gossip and the process of epistemic negotiation in *Sex and the City*. In "The Drought," the topic of the evening is that the women are not having sex as often as they want. Carrie's particular dilemma appears to her to have been brought on by her farting in bed with Mr. Big, an assessment she hesitatingly takes to her friends one by one. "There is a moment in every relationship when romance gives way to reality," Carrie notes in a voice-over. This is followed by a direct-address to the camera informing the viewer that she was "mortified." Sam tells Carrie that she is probably right about why her sex life has dropped off with Mr. Big because "men don't like women to be human." She advises Carrie to "just go fuck him and he'll forget." Miranda insists that Carrie's real problem is that she is trying to be someone she is not around her boyfriend and that she needs to emend that situation.

Miranda also points out to Carrie that she is not the only one of the four women who is not having her sexual desires fulfilled. Miranda herself is in the midst of a three-month "dry spell" that has led her to overindulge in Blockbuster movies, even though a group of construction workers harasses her every time she goes to the video store. Charlotte is out of the sex loop because Prozac has squelched her new boyfriend's sex drive; she, too, is watching a lot of Blockbuster movies. Samantha is currently depriving herself of sex, as she has become involved with a yoga instructor who deals in Tantric (read: no intercourse) sex. "Where have I been?" Carrie admonishes herself after she hears all of this. "Having sex," Miranda replies.

With all four women becoming increasingly sexually frustrated, the friends get together at Carrie's house to discuss the fact that Sam's advice to Carrie failed; Carrie went to seduce Mr. Big during a boxing match on pay-per-view, and he ignored her advances. The four friends discuss themselves as starving, and in Samantha's case "fasting," for sex. Carrie tells them that the research she has been doing on their topic (revealed to the audience in a series of "wo/man on the street" interviews) has revealed that no one in New York thinks they themselves are having enough sex. The exception might be the couple who lives across the alley from Carrie. Carrie has been watching them through her window and they have been having sex daily. Curious about this sexually sated couple, the women spend the remainder of their time together watching the "afternoon show" through Carrie's window, eating gummy bears, and discussing the marvel of the couple across the way—especially the fact that the man can stay hard for over an hour. Carrie describes their newfound activity as the 1990s version of ladies going to see a matinee.

After the show, the women decide to take matters into their own hands. Miranda, returning a movie to Blockbuster, confronts one of the construction workers who has been harassing her and announces that she does not think he can "give her what she wants" because she is looking for an awful lot of sex. She gets some satisfaction from seeing him back down and tell her he is married. Samantha, while in yoga class, begins randomly asking the men surrounding her if they want to fuck until someone acquiesces. Charlotte breaks up with her "Prozac lover." And Carrie tells Mr. Big that she is tired of trying to be perfect around him. The episode ends with Carrie and Mr. Big deciding that they can "do better" than the matinee couple who are having sex yet again. Carrie forgoes her "free show" and creates her own production instead.

This episode indicates the structural themes at work in many others. Unified by their outsider status in terms of sexual fulfillment, the women strategize about how to end their drought and simultaneously comparison shop by exploring what other men and women are doing. This is defined as a function of their friendship: to figure out how to achieve sexual fulfillment and to determine what the definitional boundaries of sexual fulfillment are. The episode highlights the friendship between the women, both when Miranda admonishes Carrie for slacking off on their friendship and when the women converge to offer advice to each other. Perspectives for coping are offered, all connected to consumerism either directly (Blockbuster movies and gummy bears) or indirectly (watching the show across the way). Through their talk and gossip, the women explore and confront larger cultural issues: Carrie and Samantha's belief that men demand perfection to the point of inhumanity from women is alternately given credence and denied, and Miranda's confrontation with the construction worker deconstructs the notion that such harassment is rooted in male sexual desire rather than gendered power relations. Via empathy, honesty, and "dishing the dirt," these four women not only work through individual dilemmas concerning sexual desire and agency, they also cement their friendship as inextricable from their ability to be sexually fulfilled. Their bonding activities help them make better choices.

CONCLUSION

I have only scratched the surface of the ways in which *Sex and the City* links consumerism with female sexual desire and agency. It is evident, however, that simply because the series focuses on economically privileged women, it does not follow that the high level of consumer activity in this text overpowers all other discourses at work. In fact, the focus on consumer activities to some extent strengthens other discourses at work in the show concerning gendered power relations in a capitalistic culture and society. In particular, the show offers female friendship as a potential site for contesting gender-role ideologies that are linked to sexuality. These women's friendships with each other serve to create and maintain healthy female sexual agency with the relationships between the women providing a space for conversation and gossip that encourages informed decision making guided by epistemic negotiation.

Since the first season, the show has maintained its focus on sexuality, consumerism, and female friendship, and some of the choices the women have had to make have intensified greatly. While episodes continue to make light of consumerist analogies (such as when Charlotte buys a puppy when she cannot find a suitable man or when Carrie writes an article for *Vogue* about men as the hot, new accessories for the fall fashion season), other choices have had more at stake. Charlotte gets married and eventually separates from her husband after she finds out that she cannot have a baby easily and that he does not want to try. Carrie ruins a relationship with a good man when she has an affair with a married Mr. Big. Samantha falls in love twice—first with a woman and then with a man who ends up cheating on her. And Miranda becomes pregnant and decides to have the baby but not get married.

The show has also begun to address issues of class and economy and how these dynamics interact with women's abilities to make choices and form bonds with other women. Miranda has emotional trouble when buying her own apartment because everyone she deals with financially looks at her askance when she tells them the apartment is "just for her" (that is, there is no man to live with her or buy for her). When Charlotte gets engaged to a wealthy man, she has to negotiate a prenuptial agreement that she feels underestimates her monetary value as a wife and possible mother. (In fact, the agreement states that she will receive more money in a divorce if she has a boy than if she has a girl.) When Carrie breaks off her engagement with her "good guy," he leaves her potentially homeless because he owned her apartment. Carrie finds out that she is "worth nothing" when she applies for a loan, and she and Charlotte actually have a big fight when Charlotte does not offer to loan her the money she needs. (Eventually, Charlotte gives Carrie her wedding ring, from her failed marriage, so that Carrie can sell it and buy her apartment.)

The availability of shows like *Sex and the City* is important in a society that continues to simplify representations of female sexuality and female friendship. Feminist scholarship needs to take its passion for discussing female sexual agency and desire in the "real" world and work more diligently to explore this area of representation in its contemporary media forms. There will need to be an exploration of the changing landscape of television as an industry and the complications this affords in terms of commercialism and censorship. It would be helpful to examine differences and similarities in representations of heterosexual and lesbian or bisexual agency and desire, given the complex links between the discouragement of the expression of such desires and the need for a consumer society to continually expand its market. We also need to examine the dynamics of race and ethnicity at work in texts that ideologically struggle over these issues, along with a more complete exploration of class than I was able to provide here. Representations of female sexuality, friendship, and consumerism are intimately connected to feminism's concern with female empowerment. We cannot afford not to invest in such research.

ADDENDUM: WHAT DO WOMEN WANT?

When I first began studying *Sex and the City*, the show was in the early years of its six-season run on HBO. Like millions of other viewers, I eagerly anticipated the end of the series because I was curious about how one of the few well-written shows that feature female friendship and female sexuality would conclude.

As a feminist scholar, I was intrigued by how the series explored the themes of consumerism, choice, sexuality, and female friendship in increasingly complex ways. Romantic relationships came and went, but these women privileged their friendship as a primary source of strength and knowledge. Carrie, Miranda, Charlotte, and Samantha kept on shopping, and talking, and talking about shopping, and shopping for and talking about sex. This framework stayed intact as richer story lines involving cancer, adoption, and even death wound their way into the mix. Toward the end of the series, the writers even revisited the season one episode "The Baby Shower" by having Carrie register for her wedding—to herself—so that she could get a pair of shoes back from a woman to whom she had given countless wedding and baby gifts over the years ("A Woman's Right to Shoes"). It was this commitment to exploring the range of what women want that kept me committed to the show.

I was disappointed, however, with the end result of the series; I felt that the narrative framework and theme of the finale moves away from the show's consumerist framework and its theme of female friendship. When Carrie faces her penultimate decision (Should she move to Paris to live with her new lover, a Russian artist?), the input of her female cohorts begins to fade in importance for her. She decides to move after little discussion (in contrast to past discussions about much smaller decisions). In fact, all of the women begin to turn more often to the men in their lives as they make major decisions, shifting the site of epistemic negotiation in the show's plots.

This shift was not absolute, nor am I suggesting that men should not be involved in women's lives and decision making. Rather, I am posing questions:

How powerful is the ending of a television series in defining it ideologically? Is this what women wanted from the show? Is this what women want from their lives? With regard to the first question, I must admit that I am stumped. In this chapter I argue that we cannot let the consumerist and elitist axes of this series overshadow its feminist rhetoric of choice and female friendship. Yet, I feet that Carrie's final choice overshadows the show's earlier thrust. Carrie dumps the negligent Russian lover just as Mr. Big—her "true love"—comes to Paris to reclaim her; she then makes a second choice to renew her romance with Mr. Big. Clearly, these are choices, but I was struck by the fact that Carrie's female friends, those women who stood by her through thick and thin, did not come to her rescue. Instead, they ask Mr. Big to "go get [their] girl" (as Miranda put it).

Generally, the pattern of the series is for the women to get together, talk and exchange perspectives, and then make informed decisions. The episodes featuring Carrie in Paris show her becoming progressively more depressed and angry as her lover abandons her, and she eventually realizes that what she is really missing are her three friends. I waited for what I thought was inevitable: certainly we would see "the girls" gathering over brunch, discussing a plan, slapping down their credit cards, and taking off for Paris in the final hour of the show. But, in the end, it appeared that all Carrie needed was the right man for the job.

Is this the ending women fans wanted? Responses from fans point to the need for continued research on this show, especially since it lives on in syndication and on DVD. It is striking that when the series first emerged on basic cable (WTBS) in spring of 2004, the promotional spots featured Carrie, Miranda, Charlotte, and Samantha *talking together as friends*: about heterosexual romance, about shopping and consumerism, and about sex. Across these spots, the most noticeable visual pattern involved the four women framed together talking as they worked through their issues and problems. Thus, while the final episode of *Sex and the City* may suggest (in regards to the final Freudian question I posed) that women ultimately want heterosexual coupling over and above female bonding, the cyclical nature of the series on television and DVD does not reinforce that theme because it continually revisits its dominant themes of female friendship, shopping, and sex through the glories of televisual repetition.

Doing what television does best, *Sex and the City* continues to fulfill different kinds of viewer needs and desire. For some fans writing in online fan sites, this is a show about romance and dating—a narrative emphasis that suits the finale of the show. For others, *Sex and the City* is about female bonding and lasting friendships. The battle continues over how to define "women's TV" and how to represent "what women want." Perhaps *Sex and the City*'s greatest success, and the key to its continued popularity after its initial run on cable, might be its refusal to answer this question in a clear-cut way and its ability to advance epistemic negotiations about its meanings outside of its own narrative boundaries.

PART FOUR

Race and Ethnicity

CHAPTER 10

The Hidden Truths in Black Sitcoms

Robin R. Means Coleman and Charlton D. McIlwain

George Bernard Shaw once said, "when a thing is funny, search it for a hidden truth." Such counsel becomes foreboding as we consider the "hidden truths," or messages, embedded in Black situation comedies. Shaw's charge, applied to the Black situation comedy as a form of cultural expression, leads us to consider the truths about Blackness that these programs offer, and the possible truths revealed about those who promote Black situation comedy programming.

Here, Black situation comedy describes programming that employs a core cast of African American characters and focuses on those characters' socio-cultural, political, and economic experiences (e.g., *Amos 'n' Andy*, *Good Times*, and *The Fresh Prince of Bel Air*). Black sitcoms are often cited for their additional and frequent reliance on negative, stereotypical characterizations of Blackness to promote humor (Gray; Hough; Means Coleman; Nelson). In this chapter, we discuss how the comedic mediation of Black identity impacts and informs African Americans' lives. We are concerned with the manner in which Blackness is defined within the symbolic, as well as how media as an industry and institution is guided by American society's own social, political, and ideological legacies. Toward these ends, we summarize the fifty-year history of the Black sitcom on network television, uncovering the purported "hidden truths" about Blackness these comedies propagate. To wrap up, we will consider the potential for those who consume media and care about its content to become agents of change through group activism and individual human agency.

BLACK AMERICA VIEWED

The 1984–85 television season brought the unexpected NBC smash hit *The Cosby Show*.[1] In the ensuing ratings wars, the networks created programming that sought to duplicate *The Cosby Show*'s popularity. *The Cosby Show* was important for its unique depiction of an upper middle-class American family, who just happened to be Black, without any of the expressions of deviance and deficiency traditionally attached to depictions of Blackness in past series (e.g., *Baby I'm Back, What's Happening!*[2]). The popularity of *The Cosby Show* spawned a number of network-run, Black sitcoms with noticeably more diverse depictions of the Black family. These new shows also elevated the personal creative worth of African American image-makers in the television industry (e.g., Debbie Allen, director of *A Different World*), and served as a catalyst for the crossover appeal of Black programming.

Beginning in 1985, the networks churned out a veritable stream of Black sitcoms. By 1990, over a dozen Black sitcoms aired, including *227, Amen, A Different World, Jackee, Family Matters, The Robert Guillaume Show, New Attitude, Sugar and Spice, You Take the Kids*, and *Fresh Prince of Bel Air*. Quantity did not necessarily bring quality, however, and the new influx of shows served as a reminder of how confining and problematic mediated, commercial Black imagery can be. One obvious truth, at least to African American viewers, was that African American participation in prime-time television continued to be relegated to the realm of the comedic. Even today, African Americans are rarely seen in dramas that focus primarily on Black culture.[3] Instead, ghettoized within the comedic, messages of inferiority, laziness, and de-centrality prevail (Staples and Jones). As Inniss and Feagin observe, "always seeing Blacks in situation comedies indicates that Black life and Black issues are not taken seriously" (200). Many of the series that premiered in 1989–90 failed to represent Black life and culture in a way that captured its diversity and complexity. For example, sassy, "Sapphire"-inspired characterizations were the norm in *New Attitude*, which featured a group of smart-mouthed, inept hairdressers.[4] The group presented itself in modernized "sambo" outfits, liberally engaged in physical comedy, and frequently fired off double entendre, sex-centered jokes.[5]

The networks gradually came to realize that series of this period were poorly conceived and inane. No one, Black or White, took these sitcoms seriously. With little in the way of an African American fan base, and absent a crossover audience, many Black sitcoms of the mid-to-late 1980s, the "Cosby Era," dropped off network schedules. *Charlie and Company*, *What's Happening Now!*, *He's the Mayor*, *Melba*, *Redd Foxx Show*, and *Frank's Place* were the first wave of Cosby-inspired hopefuls cancelled between 1984 and 1990. In a single year, 1989–1990, four additional Black situation comedies were cancelled, including: *227*, *The Robert Guillaume Show*, *New Attitude*, and *Sugar and Spice*. These departures introduced a perplexing dilemma: Given the troubling nature of African American representations in media generally, and in Black situation comedies (with few exceptions) specifically, were these cancellations-cum-absences a blessing in disguise? That is, what is worse for the mediation of Blackness, nonpresence or symbolic annihilation?

VIEWING THE SKEWING OF BLACKNESS

While the loss of Black sitcoms in the late 1980s and early 1990s was significant, the disappearance of Blackness on network television was not a new phenomenon, as African Americans faced virtual invisibility some three decades earlier during the "Nonrecognition Era" (C. Clark; Means Coleman, See). This era (1954 to 1967) marks a period when African American representations hit an all-time low on network television, with the Black presence on situation comedies relegated to cameo appearances on *Car 54, Where Are You?* and *Hogan's Heroes*. The Nonrecognition Era emerged during the rise of the civil rights movement as African Americans were fighting for equality and empowerment. The happy-go-lucky characterizations of Blackness in past television programming such as *Amos 'n' Andy* and *Beulah* seemed incompatible with the marches, church bombings, boycotts, police attacks, and assassinations that appeared on the nightly news. Afraid of alienating viewers on either side of the civil rights debate, "entertainment television chose not to choose sides, opting instead to ignore the crisis and [African Americans] altogether" (Means Coleman 82). Richard Jackson Harris describes it as a mode of representation in which Blackness "is not ridiculed, it is not caricatured, it is simply not there" (49).

The imagistic sacrifices that Black culture has had to endure are evidenced by over fifty years of a "racist regime of representations"[6] in Black situation comedy. The period immediately preceding the era of nonrecognition was the TV Minstrelsy Era, from 1950 to 1953. This era featured *Amos 'n' Andy* and *Beulah*, shows that originated on radio and which, in turn, evolved from nineteenth-century minstrel theater shows. Amos and Andy, nee Sam and Henry, were created by White blackface vaudevillian performers Freeman Gosden and Charles Correll. The Sam and Henry characters were doltish, southern Black men, speaking in blackvoice (caricatured Black dialect), heading north to find work. Gosden and Correll took their popular characters from the stage to radio in the 1920s. After some movement between radio stations, Gosden and Correll landed at WMAQ (NBC Red) in 1928, changing the name of their popular radio series from *Sam 'n' Henry* to *Amos 'n' Andy*. The impact of *Amos 'n' Andy* was significant in American popular culture as the radio program's format—its recurring characters and setting, program resolutions, and cliff-hangers—became the basis for future television series and serials. *Amos 'n' Andy* enjoyed a decade run and was phenomenally well-received by radio audiences, as MacDonald describes:

> Switchboards slowed to inactivity as few phone calls were placed; department stores piped in the broadcast so shoppers need not go home; and factories closed early to allow employees to listen. In 1931 a telephone survey by the Cooperative Analysis of Broadcasting gave Amos 'n' Andy an incredible rating of 53.4 percent of those listening. (*Don't Touch* 113)

Amos 'n' Andy was *The Cosby Show* of its day. Television broadcasters sought to amass viewers and profits by bringing the popular radio Black situation comedies to the little screen. Gosden and Correll wisely assumed that 1950s America would not tolerate White men performing sambo-coonish characterizations in blackface (as they had done on stage) and through blackvoice (as heard on radio). Consequently, the pair moved to the role of series consultants, and African Americans Alvin Childress and Spencer Williams, Jr., were cast to star in *Amos 'n' Andy*. Similarly, the Black situation comedy *Beulah* was first heard on radio with Beulah's blackvoice performed by the character's creator, White male actor Marlin Hurt. As with *Amos 'n' Andy*, *The Beulah Show* eliminated the White male in the starring role (here, a troubling racial and gender erasure), and replaced Hurt with Black singer and actress Ethel Waters.

These Minstrelsy Era series were marked by depictions of African Americans and Blackness as qualitatively different from, and inferior to, Whites and Whiteness. White was the norm; Black was the aberrant. "The" Black community was usually seen as a monolithic whole comprised of swindlers, incompetents, and buffoons. These comedies were political despite apolitical façades. The comical African American assuaged mainstream America as "the Black situation comedies of the 1950s reflected a racist American politics where African Americans . . . were looked upon with a nostalgic [antebellum] fondness," rather than as a group that was willing to fight against discrimination, exploitation, and inequality (Means Coleman 81).

When African Americans returned to television in 1968, they found television had little experience in creating sitcoms that represented a full range of Blackness. Having experienced the civil rights and Black power movements, television didn't dare return to the minstrelsy formula of *Amos 'n' Andy* and *Beulah*. Instead, the networks offered what scholars have termed

FIGURE 10.1. Spencer Williams Jr., as Andy Brown, Tim Moore as George "The Kingfish" Stevens, and Alvin Childress as Amos Jones in *Amos 'n' Andy*, 1951–1953. Photo courtesy of Movie Star NewsFair.

the "Assimilationist Era" (Dates; Gray; MacDonald, *Blacks*; Nelson; and Riggs). From 1968 to 1971, African Americans returned to television through Black situation comedies such as *Julia* and *The Bill Cosby Show*. *Julia* was blasted by viewers and critics in this period of Black empowerment for depicting Blackness that "evacuat[ed] as much ethnic and cultural difference as possible [and that] conformed to an unexamined White norm" (Bodroghkozy, "Color TV" 416). Indeed, *Julia* presented a world sans African American men, as well as racial, social, or political debates. This was an astonishing omission, given America's troubled climate of war protests, urban riots, and assassinations. *The Bill Cosby Show* likewise depicted a world that was wholly integrated and without conflict. It seemed to take its cues not only from *Julia*, but also from *I, Spy*, another Cosby series that featured the actor in an assimilationist role. Although the Assimilationist Era was an improvement over the minstrelsy-tinged depictions in *Amos 'n' Andy* and *Beulah*, it nevertheless offered a racist ideology that Black culture was most prized when it approached the norms and values of Whiteness. These series sent a placating message, presenting Blacks as accommodating, docile, and nonthreatening. For those invested in Blackness, these series carried a message of cultural abandonment and assimilation.

The period from 1972 to 1983, the era of "Social Relevancy and Ridiculed Black Subjectivity" (a.k.a. the Lear Era), was a dramatic departure from the Assimilationist Era. During this time Black sitcoms began to address the social and political experiences of the nation head on, in large part due to the efforts of Norman Lear (along with Bud Yorkin). Marc and Thompson write: "By consistently embedding authorial advocacy into plot and characterization on issues ranging from abortion and homosexuality to foreign policy and Watergate, Lear helped dispel the belief that situation comedy was an intrinsically superficial form that could only support its own status quo" (49–50). The Lear sitcoms, *Sanford and Son*, *Good Times*, and *The Jeffersons*, all attended directly to racism, public policy, and discrimination, as well as Black empowerment. For the first time, Black situation comedy presented African Americans as subjects rather than objects. Through Black-centered worlds and circumstances, America had an opportunity to see Blackness as canonical while African Americans went about surviving, thriving, and contributing to the citizenry without abandoning their culture. Still, the Black world that Lear and others created during this period was a segregated one; the White world was largely invisible and appeared to have little interest or regard for the Black world. The Black world of Fred Sanford *(Sanford and Son)* or the Evans family *(Good Times)* was one where citizens were largely distracted by their own poverty and disenfranchisement, thereby making their Blackness inaccessible and presenting Black circumstances as those to be pitied. In the case of George Jefferson *(The Jeffersons)*, Blackness was represented as sassy and rude, barely tolerable, and hardly useful. Unfortunately, the socially relevant

FIGURE 10.2. (top row, left to right) Tempestt Bledsoe as Vanessa Huxtable, Sabrina Le Beauf as Sondra Huxtable Tibideaux, and Malcolm Jamal-Warner as Theodore Huxtable. (bottom row, left to right) Lisa Bonet as Denise Huxtable Kendall, Bill Cosby as Dr. Cliff Huxtable, Keshia Knight Pulliam as Rudy Huxtable, and Phylicia Rashad as Clair Huxtable in *The Cosby Show*, 1984–1992. Photo courtesy of Larry Edmunds BooksFair.

Black situation comedies often fell back upon comedic clichés of trickery, buffoonery, and sambo-ism (i.e. J. J. Evans of *Good Times*) that recalled the Minstrelsy Era. Despite the increased social relevancy of Black situation comedies of the 1970s, there remained a clear and decipherable message about Blackness not only being socially irrelevant but deficient as well. Series such as *Diff'rent Strokes* and *Webster* emerged during this period with "White saviors," such as the Drummond *(Diff'rent Strokes)* and Papadapolis *(Webster)* families, bringing home African American boys who, through twists of fate, were unable to be raised in Black households. In this era of television programming, the hidden message was that African Americans operated in odd worlds marked by knavery and bigotry, and non-Blacks need not take part except to rescue African American youth from its deficient family peril.

The era of "Black Family and Diversity" (the Cosby years, 1984 to 1989) is one of the most promising five years that Black situation comedy has seen. *The Cosby Show* signaled a return to the Black subjectivity the Lear programming had promised but failed to deliver. The programming of the Black Family and Diversity Era was often focused on the family (as in *Charlie and Co.*, *Melba*, and *227*) and positioned African Americans within their own cultural center, though not wholly segregated from the rest of the world. Series such as Cosby spin-off *A Different World* and the critically acclaimed *Frank's Place* introduced Blackness as varied, sophisticated, and culturally relevant. Though *The Cosby Show* was criticized for its failure to attend to America's racial inequalities—including the struggles the Huxtable family would have faced to achieve their high level of professional success—much of this era of Black situation comedy showed Blackness as broadly diverse in its politics, economics, and cultural practices. The networks had trouble maintaining this trend, however, sacrificing quality and breadth for profits.

This abandonment resulted in one of the most notorious periods of Black situation comedy programming since the mammy/sambo characterizations of the 1950s. The Neo-Minstrelsy Era" (1990 to 1998), was a return to Black sitcoms popularized on the original minstrel stage. Sambos, coons, and Sapphires proliferated as racial separation and inequality returned.[7] The biggest culprits were the newer networks, FOX, UPN, and The WB, which had little experience producing Black sitcoms, and created series such as *Martin* (FOX), *Goode Behavior* (UPN), and *The Wayans Brothers* (The WB). Alvin Poussaint, Professor of Clinical Psychiatry and consultant to *The Cosby Show*, observes, "I don't think that *Martin* is a show that's projecting us forward. . . . Shucking and jiving is not representative of Black America" (Farley 81). Upstart UPN built its network around Black comedic programming. In 1996 alone, in addition to *Goode Behavior*, UPN premiered *Malcolm and Eddie*, *Sparks*, and *Homeboys in Outer Space*. According to television critic Robert Bianco, almost without exception, men in this UPN quartet are portrayed as sex-crazed idiots or stuffed shirts: women as shrews or sex-pots. Any behavior that borders on the intellectual is mocked; any sign of "uppity" aspiration is crushed. On *Malcolm [and Eddie]*, a man is ridiculed for reading poetry—and he's a fat man, which is supposed to make it twice as funny. On *Goode [Behavior]*, a college professor finds his tea party turned into a barbecue (ribs, of course). And so on. (4)

WB's *The Wayans Brothers* was considered so offensive that it became one of several comedies airing on the newer networks that a local NAACP chapter protested and boycotted. It was also during the Neo-Minstrelsy Era that Black sitcoms hit an all-time low when UPN premiered the "slave-com" (as it came to be called) *The Secret Diary of Desmond Pfeiffer* in 1998. A slave-era Black situation comedy set in the Lincoln White House, it featured the character Pfeiffer as a Brit who comes to America fleeing gambling debts and ends up as Lincoln's manservant. The series' pilot offered darky jokes, and in regular episodes, as L. Jones writes, "the South was remembered as a peaceful fairytale, largely absent racial animus, and a prime setting to revisit good-old fashioned racial humor . . . its bewildering supposition—that a Civil War story could be divorced from the atrocity of slavery, while treating race like a running gag" (32).

In recent years, inroads have been made on television toward presenting Blackness as relevant and necessary. Notable achievements include series such as *The Bernie Mac Show*, *The Hughleys*, and *My Wife and Kids*, in which Blackness is at the core of the cultural discourse and is a sociocultural experience against which all else is marked.[8] The representation of Blackness remains at risk, however. There is the obvious concern that Black life and culture remain relegated to the comedic on network television. Even more troubling, Black sitcoms continue to be further marginalized as this genre is limited to second-tier, upstart networks such as UPN (which has been colloquially termed "you people's network") and The WB. The impetus behind the major networks' rejection of Black programming likely rests in prejudices about the viewing market. Moss writes:

> All television programs live in the shadow of the ratings guillotine, but does the blade fall more quickly on a Black show? Ask any African American in the television business, and you'll get a long list of classic White sitcoms— *The Mary Tyler Moore Show*, *Seinfeld*, *The Drew Carey Show*—that had to be nurtured through difficult infancies by supportive networks. With Black shows, complains Mo'Nique, costar of [the Black sitcom] *The Parkers*, the same White-run establishment "puts us on and pulls us off." (19)

Although advances in representing Blackness have been made, marginalization and stereotyping continue.

Television is a mediated form, presenting images and narratives in short, often uncontextualized segments that are structurally unable to deal with the complexities of the human experience. Fundamentally, network television programming is incapable of representing the diversity of the Black experience. That is, while we must have some expectations in regards to content, we cannot anticipate that one or two shows will provide images that span the spectrum of the lived experience of the Black diaspora. We can strive for shows that, in their plurality, explore a variety of experiences—from the person who lives in a world that is self-consciously Black to the African American who does not see himself or herself as particularly invested in Blackness. We should expect shows that present Black characters' lived experience in Black-centered worlds, as well as those in which they interact with non-Black counterparts.

A second problem is a common perception of television viewers that a dualistic, subject/object relationship exists between them and the television screen. That is, we often get the feeling that the enterprise of television viewing is one that separates actors from audiences, doers from viewers, watchers from the watched. The experience of television viewing, however, is an interactive enterprise, a reciprocal process in which viewers' lived experiences intersect and overlap with the screen narrations. The reason we have the perception of television viewing as a separate, rather than interactive, experience, is because there is a vast disconnect between viewers and producers. This disconnect explains how stereotypical images of Blackness continue to dominate network programming and overshadow wider views of Black life. In order to work, Black actors are often forced to play limited roles and are themselves shut out of the creative process of writing and directing television programs. Few, if any, Blacks have access to corporate boardrooms or capital.

Three factors combine to foster a culture of powerlessness: the inherent failures of television to represent the diversity and complexity of Black life; our perception that a vast gulf separates us (the TV audience) from them (those controlling the television production process); and the barriers of wealth and power that restrict access to decision making regarding the presentation of Black images. We live in a culture that makes it difficult for the average media consumer to influence the production process and become agents of our own experiences.

CONCLUSION

By revealing the hidden truths expressed in Black sitcoms and other television programming, we identify problems that can only be addressed by human action. Though problematic, it is possible for those outside the television entertainment industry to turn the experience of television viewing from a one-directional, transmission experience to a more open and democratic model.

As individuals, we have the prerogative of choice. As an option of expressing favor or disfavor, the remote control is a powerful method in the aggregate of saying to network executives that their productions are farcical. While tuning out seems simplistic, there is some complexity here. Audiences can reject the overall message of the show and its social/political implications despite the fact that it makes them laugh and is entertaining. This would require viewers to be educated—to look beyond the surface of images in order to see the hidden truths in these expressions—and vigilant (that is, "resistant spectators").

Our individual efforts can be solidified through collective action that includes, but goes beyond, educating others regarding the demerits of a given show and urging them to collectively exercise the power of their choice in viewing. Options include collective actions such as boycotts, not only of the television shows themselves but also actions that influence industry profits. If it is true that, as NBC West Coast President Scott Sassa quipped, "NBC is the place to buy [advertising time] if you're selling to people who actually shop, not shoplift," (qtd. in Flint, "How NBC" A1), then African Americans, for example, can flex their collective muscles as the largest consumer segment in the country by refusing to purchase products advertised on offending networks (McIlwain and Johnson). Even the threat of withdrawing millions of dollars from advertisers who support network programs has proven to be an effective tool for assuring that other voices are heard in the decision-making process.

To effect change, viewers must utilize new communication media that allow greater access and interactivity between individuals with shared goals and objectives. The Internet has shown itself to be a powerful facilitator of political and social action. Henry Jenkins notes that the Internet has become a way to gain access to the creative process of television and other forms of entertainment production. One way this is happening is through the emergence of fan communities surrounding particular programs and individual actors. Often initiated by networks to further promote their shows (and their advertisers) and get instant, mass feedback regarding particular shows and episodes, such community forums allow those invested in Black televised images to share opinions, suggest alternative plots or characters, and convince decision makers that alternative content may translate into greater viewership-cum-profitability. Such individual and collective activities can inform a process through which more diverse images of Blackness are created rather than sambo/Sapphire stereotypes. The hidden truths expressed in Black situation comedies would then be apparent for all to see, debate, and change.

NOTES

1. *The Cosby Show* was rejected by ABC and CBS before being picked up by NBC.

2. *Baby I'm Back* told the story of Raymond Ellis, a husband (to Olivia Ellis) who deserts his wife and two children, because kids and marriage just weren't his thing. Raymond re-enters Olivia's life (hence, 'I'm back'), only to wreak havoc on the family. *What's Happening!*'s focal family, the Thomas family, consisted of two children, Raj and Dee, and their mother, Mama. One season into the series' run, viewers discover that the family patriarch, Bill, is no good and that the family's better off without him.

3. *Under One Roof* is the first (and, to date, only) African American, nuclear and extended family drama ever to air on network television. In 1995 the Langston family graced the airwaves offering one of the most whole, complex, and realistic depictions of a family (Black or non-Black) that we have ever seen. The series featured a seasoned cast in James Earl Jones, Joe Morton, and Vanessa Bell Calloway. The series barely lasted one month on CBS, as it aired from March 14 to April 18, 1995. Since *Under One Roof*, networks have attempted to offer up Black-centered workplace dramas such as *City of Angels* and *Gideon's Crossing*, both medical dramas. Each was a fast failure. *Homicide, Life on the Street* may be viewed as a Black drama due to its setting (Baltimore) and, over the run of the series, its increasingly African American core cast. We believe *Homicide* exemplifies what television, at its best, can do with the depiction of race: privilege its presence and diversity while not reducing it to the single focal theme, gag, or cliché.

4. Recurring African American stereotypes are, at times, described based on the characterization in popular culture that first popularized the stereotype (such as the Uncle Tom or the sambo). We can credit *Amos 'n' Andy* for naming the frequent depiction of African American women as smart-alecky, emasculating, nagging shrews as "Sapphire."

5. The sambo characterization is a negative, Black stereotype that originated in minstrel theater. The sambo was a male simpleton who sang, danced, sometimes strummed a banjo, and spoke in a caricatured Black dialect. Modern-day sambos can be seen in J. J. from *Good Times* and in Steve Urkel from *Family Matters*. During the minstrel era, audiences loved the sambo for his adoration and unabashed loyalty for the slave master, his docility, and outrageous costuming. Decoding the sambo phenomenon, Boskin says it "was an extraordinary type of social control, at once extremely subtle, devious, and encompassing. To exercise a high degree of control meant also to be able to manipulate the full range of humor; to create, ultimately, an insidious type of buffoon. To make the Black male into an object of laughter . . ." (13–14).

6. Stuart Hall describes racial stereotypes as a "racialized regime of representations" ("Representation" 245). When considering the treatment of Blackness in Black situation comedies over the past five decades, I have long felt the term "racialized" too subtle. As I elaborate in my book, *African American Viewers and the Black Situation Comedy: Situating Racial Humor*, any programming can be racialized, and that racialization does not always mean racist. More, Black situation comedy is obviously racialized with its focus on Blackness. Black sitcoms, however, often encompass a racist

regime of representations because of their frequent negative stereotyping of Blacks and recurring abhorrent characterizations.

7. Exceptions to the dreck of the 1990s included *Sister, Sister* and *The Parent'hood*. Tim Reid and Robert Townsend, respectively, produced and starred in these family-centered series. It is not surprising that these series stood out in their depiction of Black family life (though they hardly stood out in the ratings) since Reid and Townsend, like Bill Cosby, have spent much of their careers talking about and promoting the need for improved Black imagery. During this period, the networks all but abandoned Black sitcoms. For example, CBS aired no Black situation comedies in 1992 or 1993, and offered only two in 1996. NBC introduced no new Black situation comedy in 1993. In 1994, as FOX began to move from upstart to mainstream, it abandoned Black viewers by greatly decreasing the number of Black situation comedies it offered.

8. None of these shows air on the Big Three networks.

CHAPTER 11

Segregated Sitcoms

Institutional Causes of Disparity among Black and White Comedy Images and Audiences

Amanda Dyanne Lotz

Throughout U.S. television history, comedy has been the narrative form to first offer representations of those aspects of society outside of the hegemonic norm. Situation comedies offered some of the first portrayals of working women, gay and lesbian characters, and non-White characters, because sitcoms could both introduce and contain content and ideas within their twenty-three minutes of narrative time and because laughter softens difficult issues. By the end of television's first fifty years, women had achieved diverse and complex representation in a variety of genres, and sophisticated gay and lesbian characters began to find a presence in dramas as well as comedies; yet, stories about people of color, particularly Asian Americans and Latino/as, mostly remained limited to comedic fare.

African American characters have been somewhat plentiful in various eras of sitcom history, yet fairly monolithic in their characterization, with clear trends emerging in certain periods. Some argue the Black sitcom exists as a distinctive subgeneric form, although defining features of the Black sitcom beyond the presence of Black actors remain contested and varied (Means Coleman).

Much of the debate and controversy about the form has resulted from the need for these sitcoms to address both White and African American audiences throughout most of U.S. television history, forcing Black sitcoms to "walk a thin line to attract White Americans while not alienating African Americans" (Havens 37). Many scholars have delimited and analyzed the complicated history of the Black sitcom, and while their analysis is too extensive to recount here, their critical perspectives greatly inform the situation of the late 1990s that I consider (see Bogle; Gray; Hamamoto; Havens; Means Coleman; Riggs).

The multiplication of distribution outlets, beginning with cable in the 1980s and later broadcast networks such as FOX (1986), The WB (1996), and UPN (1996), reduced the imperative for Black sitcoms to appeal to both African American and White audiences. The spread of audience share from three broadcast networks to a multitude of cable networks allowed the development of series specifically hailing the Black audience, a strategy particularly viable for emerging broadcast networks in their first years, such as FOX in the late 1980s and early 1990s, and The WB and UPN in the late 1990s. As a result of this more particularized address, the more established networks (NBC, CBS, ABC) gradually reduced their use of series designed to attract an ethnically mixed audience and instead developed comedy series with overwhelmingly White casts *(Seinfeld, Friends, Frasier)*. As reports of "segregation" in comedy audiences became increasingly frequent, these competitive industrial practices had clear effects on comedy audiences, (Freeman; "Gap Between"; Poniewozik; "Study Shows"; "Who's Watching").

This chapter explores the institutional and formal causes of comedic audience segregation in the 1990s and examines one series as a case study in order to expose the industrial practices that lead to ethnically bifurcated series and audiences. The case of *For Your Love* is an anomaly in many aspects, but it illustrates how ironclad the rules may be. *For Your Love* premiered as a midseason replacement on NBC in March 1998. In the series' eight episode run it slipped from a 9.3 rating/15 share, to a 6.7 rating/11 share and fell from placing second in its time slot and twenty-fifth for the week, to fourth in the time slot and sixty-third for the week.[1] This ratings performance ended its run on NBC, but emerging network The WB (owned by Warner Bros., the company that produced *For Your Love*) purchased the series for the 1998–99 season and continued it through the spring of 2002. *For Your Love* is not only atypical in its two-network history, it is also one of the few recent sitcoms to feature Black and White characters in lead roles. The series depicts three couples at different stages of "couplehood." The multiethnic ensemble includes: Dean and Sheri, a White couple, married five years, who were childhood sweethearts; Mel and Malena, African American newlyweds who are friends with Dean and Sheri and move in next door in a Chicago suburb; and Reggie (Mel's brother) and Bobbi, both African American, as a somewhat commitment-phobic dating couple, who marry, then divorce in the series' last season.

FIGURE 11.1. (top row, left to right) Tamala Jones as Bobbi Seawright, Dedee Pfeiffer as Sheri Winston, D. W. Moffett as Dean Winston, and James Lesure as Mel Ellis. (bottom row, left to right) Edafe Blackmon as Reggie Ellis and Holly Robinson Peete as Malena Ellis in *For Your Love*, 1998–2002. Photo courtesy of Photofest. Used by permission.

Considering *For Your Love* as a case study creates a complex context for analyzing the institutional causes of segregated viewing, as the ethnically integrated cast defines the series as different from most comedy series. The disparate promotional and scheduling strategies used by NBC and The WB reveal the process through which programmers define the intended audience for television programs. The underlying goal of this chapter, then, is to explore how institutional practices, such as scheduling, promotion, executive corps, demographic imperatives, and the competitive environment, lead to dichotomous audience segregation in sitcom viewing.

BLACK SITCOMS AND THE 1990s

The sitcom emerges as the primary location for studying African American representation because the few predominately Black dramas—such as *Under One Roof* (CBS 1995), *413 Hope Street* (FOX 1997), and *City of Angels* (CBS 2000–01)—have had brief and relatively unheralded runs on network television. The Black sitcom has a long history in U.S. broadcasting, dating back to radio. Means Coleman argues the Black sitcom is a category all its own; its subgeneric distinction results from "its regular core cast of African American characters that works to illuminate Black cultural, artistic, political and economic experiences" (72). She also notes other aspects that define the Black sitcom: African American producers, directors, and writers; Black characters with limited contact with other races or ethnic groups; characters that employ Black language and verbal forms; a focus on Black issues; and the use of stereotypical characterization to promote humor (72).

In the 1990s, upstart networks added a new chapter to the already complicated history of Black sitcoms as their need to attract audiences led them to seek out groups underserved by ABC, CBS, and NBC. Targeting a Black niche audience yielded success for FOX with sitcoms and variety-comedies that offered a diversity of series dominated by Black actors and performers—*The Preston Episodes* (1993); *Townsend Television* (1993); *The Sinbad Show* (1993–94); *South Central* (1994); *House of Buggin'* (1995); *The Show* (1996)—and long-running successes—*In Living Color* (1990–94); *Roc* (1991–94); *Martin* (1992–97); and *Living Single* (1993–98). The representations of African American characters in these series have been the source of extensive academic debate (Bogle; Gray; Means Coleman; Zook), yet from an institutional standpoint, FOX's mid-1990s strategy of intentionally counter-programming ethnically diverse representations against a successful slate of programming that neglected non-White audiences was quite successful.[2] As the network gained in its competitive position, however, its programming shifted to target White audiences, particularly young males, some of whom had been among the viewers attracted to the Black sitcoms. Where FOX once courted an African American niche on Thursday evenings with a lineup of *Living Single*, *Between Brothers*, and *New York Undercover*, by fall of 1998, the network featured "reality programming" such as *World's Wildest Police Videos* and *FOX Files*. These programs drew the male eighteen to thirty-four demographic, allowing FOX to "trade up" for a demographic advertisers valued for its perceived cultural capital and buying power, while abandoning the Black viewers who helped the network compete with the Big Three. The purge was not limited to FOX, as broadcast networks canceled thirteen dramas and sitcoms featuring Black casts at the end of the 1997–98 season, with only one new comedy added the next fall *(What's Back)*.

At the same time FOX whittled away its Black sitcoms, emerging networks The WB and UPN gained in nationwide penetration, increasingly reaching enough homes to affect the audiences of other networks. Both of these networks applied FOX's preliminary strategy, and included a night of Black sitcom programming early in their network histories. Like FOX, these networks created series that succeeded in finding audiences, evident in The WB's *Sister, Sister* (1995–99);[3] *The Parent'hood* (1995–99); *The Wayans Brothers* (1995–99); *The Jamie Foxx Show* (1996–2001); *The Steve Harvey Show* (1996–2002); *Smart Guy* (1997–99); and *For Your Love* (1998–2002); and UPN's *In the House* (1995–98); *Malcolm and Eddie* (1996–2000); *Sparks* (1996–98); and *Moesha* (1996–2001). UPN also offered less successful series: *Goode Behavior* (1996–97); *Homeboys in Outer Space* (1996–97); *Good News* (1997–98); and the controversial *The Secret Diary of Desmond Pfeiffer* (1998). The WB and UPN continued to follow the FOX model, steadily decreasing their series featuring Black actors, and by the fall of 2001, The WB eliminated its night of comedies featuring African American characters with only *The Steve Harvey Show* finishing its run and a few episodes of *For Your Love* appearing in midseason. Only UPN maintained its Monday night comedies with *The Hughleys* (ABC, 1998–2000; UPN (2000–02), *The Parkers* (1999–), *Girlfriends* (2000–), *One on One* (2001–), and *Half and Half* (2002–).

With some notable exceptions, Black actors were absent from comedic series airing on the Big Three broadcast networks during this time. NBC's *The Cosby Show* (1984–92) embodied the high-water mark in terms of integrated audience success and made possible *227* (NBC, 1985–90), *Amen* (NBC, 1986–90), *A Different World* (NBC, 1987–93), *Family Matters* (ABC, 1989–97; CBS, 1997–1998), *The Fresh Prince of Bel Air* (NBC, 1990–1996), *Hangin' with Mr. Cooper* (ABC, 1992–97), *Cosby* (1996–99), and the critically acclaimed *Frank's Place* (CBS, 1987–88). The Big Three tried many other series modeled after those successful on FOX, but a combination of institutional reasons and poor artistic quality resulted in many short-lived and critically panned attempts—*Out All Night* (NBC, 1992), *Built to Last* (NBC, 1997), and *Arsenio* (ABC, 1997). Comedies with Black casts did not return to the primary networks with significant success until *My Wife and Kids* appeared on ABC in the spring of 2001, followed by *The Bernie Mac Show* on FOX that fall.[4] These shows have little in common except that African American actors primarily comprise their casts. Indeed, series such as *Family Matters*, *Frank's Place*, *Martin*, and *My Wife and Kids* are exceptionally disparate, indicating the questionable utility of "Black sitcom" as a narrative or generic category.

AUDIENCE SEGREGATION AND ITS CAUSES

The multiplicity of Black sitcoms in the 1990s, in combination with their tendency to appear on upstart networks, inaugurated a shift toward viewing of network television by ethnicity that had not previously existed. During the network era of U.S. television (approximately 1952 to 1985), each of the three networks needed to attract a minimum of 30 percent of the viewing audience (a 30 share) to remain commercially viable. Some network branding did occur in this era, but the need for that niche to encompass at least 30 percent of viewers prevented networks from targeting groups as specific as African Americans. Consequently, sitcoms featuring Black actors during the network era (*Julia*, *Good Times*, *The Jeffersons*, and *The Cosby Show*) needed to attract both White and African American audiences, a commercial imperative that clearly affected artistic content.

When FOX began programming sitcoms with primarily African American casts in the early 1990s, it was not facing the necessity of 30 percent of the audience. Although the network achieved some success earlier than many predicted, it was still a real possibility that the network would fold. FOX sought a foothold with a regular audience of any size. This institutional situation made a niche audience composed primarily of African American viewers valuable, particularly because increasingly sophisticated audience demographics revealed that African Americans constituted an estimated 11 percent of U.S. television households but maintained a viewing index approximately 25 percent higher than non-Black households (Alligood). By 1999, this research indicated African American audiences viewed 42 percent more television yearly (Williams-Harold).

As a result of increasing segregation of sitcom cast composition, as well as the dichotomization of networks airing series with Black and White casts, viewership of series also became segregated. This trend was particularly pronounced among comedies, with non-comedic programs such as *ER* (NBC), *Monday Night Football* (ABC), *N.Y.P.D. Blue* (ABC), *60 Minutes* (CBS), *Touched by an Angel* (CBS), and *The CBS Sunday Movie* still ranking in the top twenty for both "Black" and "non-Black" households in 1999 (Mifflin "Shared Favorites").[5] Great disparity exists among sitcom audiences, where—as of fall 1998—the number one sitcom in Black households ranked 112th among

Whites, and the number one White sitcom ranked 91st among Black viewers (Sterngold). In 1999–2000, *The Parkers* was the most watched show in Black households (126th in White households) (Schneider, "TV Racial"), while *Friends* and *Frasier* were the highest ranked sitcoms among all households (ranking 64th and 65th among Black households) ("Who's Watching What").[6] Figures released in 2001 suggested little change, as the most watched sitcom among Blacks ranked 119th among Whites, and the sitcom most watched by Whites ranked 65th among Black viewers (de Moraes).

The exceptional segregation in viewing comedies can be explained in a variety of ways with no one determining factor. Both sociocultural and institutional reasons explain different interests and varied viewing patterns among some Blacks and Whites. The sociocultural argument often notes that Black humor has a long tradition of existing separately from that of Whites', and recognizes that what is perceived as funny results from one's personal position (Watkins). Todd Boyd notes, "certain types of humor appeal to people based upon their personal experience, their interests, their background. And race is not the only factor" (qtd. in Richmond 1). This explanation certainly should not be discounted but also should not be too unequivocally referenced, as it overlooks many of the institutional causes of segregated viewing. Further, it is assumptive to simply suggest that sitcoms featuring Black actors originate from a perspective rooted in African American culture and its comedic tradition. Regardless of cast, most comedies airing throughout the 1990s were produced by Whites, written by predominately White writing teams, who worked under the supervision of White network executives, who sold advertising time to White advertising agents, who represented corporations managed by Whites. Instead of negotiating the complex terrain of culturally based comedic preferences, I emphasize the institutional forces that contribute to the construction of segregated sitcom casts and, consequently, segregated audiences.

SITUATING THE ANOMALOUS SITCOM: THE CASE OF *FOR YOUR LOVE*

As referenced previously, the text for *For Your Love* deviates from most network programs. The series aired on two different networks, but more significantly, it straddled contemporary notions of ethnically specific sitcoms by using an ethnically diverse cast. This deviation from the norms of "White" and "Black" sitcoms placed *For Your Love* in a precarious position in terms of many institutional practices. Even the basic question of what it is was difficult to answer, as the series did not fit neatly into any subgeneric category.

Networks rely on the audience's knowledge of televisual conventions and genres in designing new series and in turn rely on the past performance of shows in determining how and to whom they should promote series. Examining how networks place and promote series makes apparent various institutional factors affecting audience composition that often seem culturally determined. First, scheduling plays a crucial role in creating an audience. Networks seek to air programming blocks likely to maintain audience viewing throughout the evening, leading to a strategy of scheduling similar shows in sequence. In relation to the issue of sitcom viewing, this scheduling of like with like becomes problematic when networks assume that similar ethnic identity among casts equates to similar content. Consider the varied scheduling of *For Your Love*. When the series aired on NBC, the network hammocked it between *Mad About You* and *Frasier*. *For Your Love* bears a strong resemblance to *Mad About You*, as both focused on the negotiations couples experience in developing and maintaining their relationship. When it moved to The WB, however, the network redefined the series in terms of its ethnic composition. During the 1998–99 season, The WB scheduled *For Your Love* at the end of its Thursday schedule, an evening composed of other sitcoms with Black casts including *The Wayans Brothers*, *The Jamie Foxx Show*, and *The Steve Harvey Show*. The only commonality among the four shows results from the predominately Black casts of the series. With this schedule position, The WB de-emphasizes the importance of varied couple relations, instead categorizing the show in terms of its inclusion of Black characters.

Many television and cultural critics have commented on this network strategy of placing the few sitcoms featuring Black casts together in programming blocks (referred to as a "ghettoization" of Black performers), as though the hue of skin color provides a greater determinant of series content (and consequently viewership) than plot, setting, or narrative (Bauder; Schneider, "Where"). Despite the lack of success some Black sitcoms may experience without other series with Black actors surrounding them, it is clear that the separation of these shows into certain periods on certain networks perpetuates a notion that Black shows are only for Black audiences, and that skin color is an overdetermining factor in comedy preference. These shows can be defined many other ways, as seen in the scheduling of "White" sitcoms. NBC defined *For Your Love* in terms of its representation of young married life, situating it among similar shows. Similarly, FOX first placed *The PJs*, an animated series about life in the housing projects, within a lineup of other animated shows, while ABC positioned *The Hughleys*, a domestic sitcom featuring a Black family, after the domestic sitcom *Home Improvement* (however, when ABC canceled the series and UPN purchased it, *The Hughleys* joined UPN's schedule of comedies about Black characters). By defining their comedies primarily as "African American," The WB and UPN reinforce the notion that skin color delimits style, aesthetics, and narrative interests, and that actors with Black skin are of no concern to White audiences.

This determinist categorization as a "Black" sitcom is crucial to series' promotion, the second institutional factor contributing to audience size and composition. Promotion is vital to the success of television shows—not only the amount of promotion, but how and where networks promote series contributes to what audiences they hail. The tendency of The WB and UPN to program one or two nights of sitcoms with Black actors amidst a schedule designed to appeal to White teen girls and boys, respectively, makes promotion through conventional practices difficult. On other nights, The WB featured back-to-back, hour-long dramas targeting the under-thirty demographic, with all of the series featuring overwhelmingly White casts *(Dawson's Creek, Gilmore Girls, Felicity, Smallville, 7th Heaven, Charmed)*. The singular audience addressed on these nights facilitates cross-promotion for the network; however, because this is not the likely audience for its comedies featuring Black actors, there is little promotion of the sitcoms outside of the night they air.

Yvette Lee Bowser, creator and executive producer of *For Your Love* and *Living Single*, argues that promotion can be essential to series performance because assumptions made by promotion departments about who will watch the show can result in a self-fulfilling prophecy. Arguing for the crossover potential of her shows, Bowser says, "I think we should not be so narrow-minded as to think that no one from a different race should watch those shows, or that they should be marketed just to that group. This industry should not make the assumption that because a show has a Black cast it is only for Black people, but they do" (qtd. in Sterngold A1). Using *For Your Love* and many of the other comedies featuring Black actors as examples, we can see Bowser's concerns borne out in practice. The WB and UPN tend not to promote shows such as *For Your Love*, *The Steve Harvey Show*, or *Girlfriends* during series such as *Dawson's Creek* and *Buffy the Vampire Slayer*, implicitly not inviting White audiences to the series. In concert with the scheduling structure, promotion can effectively renounce the White audience, further explaining segregated viewing.

Another way programming attracts specific audiences results from the critical reviews and the "hype" or "buzz" surrounding the premiere of a show. In the case of *For Your Love*, reviews mainly fell into one of two categories.[7] Positive reviews acknowledged the series' ethnically mixed cast, and generally lauded NBC's move to introduce ethnic diversity into its "Nothing But Caucasians" comedic landscape (Grahnke; McFadden; Perigard).[8] Reviews panning the show largely ignored the significance of the presence of African American characters on the show and gave no mention to the anomaly of an ethnically mixed cast (Feran; Gilbert, "For Your"; Kaltenback).[9] In most cases, someone reading the review would have no idea the series brought any contrast to the lily-white programming dominating the comedy fare of the Big Three networks in March 1998 (*Cosby* providing the only exception). Promotion plays an essential role in an environment of six broadcast networks and a multitude of cable channels. In any context, a program is unlikely to "find" an audience without promotion, and the systematic promotion of series with

Black casts in spaces likely to have drawn Black audiences completes Bowser's "self-fulfilling prophecy."

Bowser also believes the segregation is "in large part a reflection of the executive landscape in TV. They are mostly White, and they are more likely to gravitate toward a show and an ensemble that they can relate to. The overwhelmingly White composition of network executive corps provides the third institutional factor contributing to sitcom audience segregation" (Richmond). Network programming executives decide what series will air and when and provide series' producers with notes, recommendations, and mandates. Issues of "representation" traditionally have been the site for examining the status of African Americans in U.S. television, primarily because this is the aspect of the industry to which most have access. Recent artistic commentary, evident in the films *Bamboozled* (Spike Lee, 2000) and *Dancing in September* (Reggie Rock Bythewood, 2000), and campaigns by the NAACP and other ethnic-based action groups have emphasized the relative insignificance of gains in diversity in front of the camera if similar gains are not made in the creative decision-making and executive structure.

The television industry's awareness of the limited options Black audiences possess is occasionally evident in comments made by industry insiders. Sharon Johnson, a Black writer who worked on a number of sitcoms featuring Black actors, became tired of creating Black stereotypes and told her agent that "she refused on principle to work for UPN or The WB" (Lopez 30). Of the difficulty she experienced finding work, Johnson said, "The attitude is let's just put anything with Black faces up there because we know Black people will watch" (Lopez 30). Although the 1990s saw some industry-based concern for reaching the African American viewer as a valuable consumer, the pervading logic appears to be that the audience can be reached simply by offering Black representations without much concern about show quality.

Despite the varied causes of audience segregation, those with the most power to change the institutional structures creating ethnic division appear the least concerned about the contemporary landscape. Critic James Sterngold acknowledges, "As much as they might prefer a different dynamic, a number of television executives, all White, said they were business people, not social reformers, and they maintained that there was generally little resistance from audiences to the trend of racial polarization, and thus little incentive to fight it" (A1). Executives also quickly shift blame to advertisers. An anonymous network president explains, "Black shows aren't viable today because advertisers want White, 18–to–49–year-old viewers—in other words the people who watch *Friends*" (Flint, "Fade" 9). This illustrates the assumption of some network executives that White audiences will not watch series with Black faces (proven false by *The Cosby Show*), as well as a total disregard for the power of the Black consumer.

Perhaps this executive is confusing some advertisers with all advertisers. Based on the overwhelmingly multiethnic casts of contemporary commercials, it is difficult to believe advertisers are so disinterested in Black consumers. And how can audiences express "resistance" to the state of audience segregation? Few alternatives exist as a result of the consolidation of media ownership, and it is impossible for audiences to support a product not currently available. But it is also shortsighted to blame all on a commercial media system. As the histories of African American representation indicate, depictions of Blackness and Black characters can and do evolve, all within a commercial media system. It may be easy to blame a few media moguls, but what audiences see on television is often a reflection of the society at large. Despite changes in the past fifty years, American society remains very segregated. Some of the language of the debate has changed, but White privilege still affords substantial economic and cultural power.

Finally, a question of basic economics enters in, as the post-network competitive environment changed industrial practices for all networks, demographics, and programming. The realization of niche programming as a profitable venture fuels the ability of programmers to seek only Black audiences and makes alteration from the present status quo of segregation difficult. NBC, ABC, CBS, and FOX can make a profit without actively courting the Black audience, while The WB and UPN can target that demographic and slowly prosper. In the late 1990s, with six broadcast networks (even if audiences were split inequitably among them) at least one network could have created sophisticated representations of Black and White characters and been profitable based on a niche of viewers who seek such depiction. Just a few years later, this seems an unlikely possibility, as The WB and UPN have continued to follow FOX's model and have steadily eliminated series featuring Black actors. Instead, PBS and pay cable network Showtime offer some of the most sophisticated depictions of non-White characters with *American Family* (PBS, 2002–2004), *Soul Food* (Showtime, 2000–2004), and *Resurrection Blvd.* (Showtime, 2000–2002). As long as network executives believe White audiences have no interest in Black representations, programming representing African Americans will remain targeted only to Black audiences. Although executives quickly pass blame to advertisers and the racism of the White audience, the limited vision of a predominately White executive corps has created and "broadcast" such restrictive views of Blackness, in effect mandating ethnically segregated audiences. Networks preordain audience segregation through the promotion and scheduling of shows and perpetuate a cycle of blame over who is responsible.

In a panel discussion about African Americans and television sponsored by the Museum of Television and Radio in 2001, Tim Reid, an actor, writer, producer, and director who has spent twenty-five years in the television and film industries, suggested that the answer regarding problems of diversity in Hollywood—problems he says result from one culture controlling media output— might best be found in the creation of a network (or networks) unconcerned with attracting a White audience. Reid suggests that the interests of Black audiences are broader than the liberal journalistic discourses expressing concern about what divergent viewing patterns might acknowledge. In order for the development of sophisticated stories about the complexities and variations of Black experience to occur, it may be necessary to create a separate space targeted toward Black viewers, either through subscription or through targeting advertisers who will allow the network to maintain its vision. Certainly, this need for a separate cultural sphere depicting Blackness should be considered with sustained theoretical analysis for both what it accomplishes and what it indicates about U.S. society and its purported multicultural aims. Similar concerns are clearly relevant with regard to Asian Americans and Latino/as. We may prefer to think of ourselves as a society whose integrated cultural texts indicate that racism has been conquered, but as deployed thus far, these depictions continue to shortchange those audiences who already have been offered the fewest options.

NOTES

1. Figures according to Nielsen Media Research, published in *Broadcasting & Cable* 30 Mar. 1998 and 18 May 1998.

2. The closest comparison is the renaissance sitcom form of the 1970s, but the audience economics of the 1970s network era demanded that these series be targeted at a White as well as non-White audience.

3. First aired on ABC, 1994–95.

4. By this point FOX had established itself, and although it draws audiences smaller than NBC and CBS, it ranks as a primary broadcast network.

5. "Black" and "non-Black" are Nielsen designations.

6. Also see Mifflin "Of Race and Roles"; Richmond.

7. The show received widespread review when it first premiered on NBC. Even though the show was new to The WB in the fall of 1998, few critics revisited the show in its new context.

8. Exception: Horst is a positive review that ignores race.

9. Exception: Both Mietkiewicz and Fretts offer negative reviews that note race.

CHAPTER 12

Negotiated Boundaries

Production Practices and the Making of Representation in *Julia*

Demetria Rougeaux Shabazz

Julia, a television situation comedy that first aired in 1968, signaled a major shift in the broadcast industry. For many media scholars, *Julia* marks the arrival of industry interest in the Black cast sitcom (Stroman, Merrit, and Matabane 44–56). Featuring Diahann Carroll, a popular Black stage and film entertainer, the show's creators thought they had the right formula for television's first consistently presented image of a Black family. For many African Americans, however, the series failed to satisfy demands that the industry "integrate" itself and show positive Black images (Peters 140–42). Nonetheless, *Julia*'s three broadcast seasons have had an enduring impact and are foundational to later, more successful programs like *All In the Family*, *Good Times*, and *The Mary Tyler Moore Show*, that claim to be socially relevant, gender sensitive, and ethnically diverse. *Julia* offers an important opportunity for the study of how television production practices shaped the representation of identity, particularly Black identity, during a period of social unrest and changing political views.

Through a multiphased creative process, television manufactures messages. Industry professionals, such as camera operators, lighting technicians, and directors, have a shared language in which they discuss their craft and how to achieve both the technical and aesthetic goals of production. This language, with all its norms and assumptions, shapes not only how they do what they do, but also the end product of their labor. Television's standardized language has its own grammar of race and way of encoding racial bias that developed over time within the racially segregated industry. *Julia* both disrupted the color-coded language at the same time its staging techniques and genre repetition reinforced racist stereotypes.

GENRE CONVENTIONS

As with other genres, the situation comedy reflects hegemonic values and dominant aesthetic conventions. It is a recognizable narrative form consisting of a familiar stock of plot lines that centered most often on the family. Barry Putterman, in *On Television and Comedy*, observes how built-in narrative "hierarchies" for specific genres constrain the modes of expression at different phases of production. He argues that such constraining elements demonstrate "fixed moral and utilitarian positions for audience identity and identification" of characters (117). In creating *Julia*, Hal Kanter, NBC executives, and publicity agents faced distinct positions regarding Black family life that ranged from the uninformed and the ill-informed to the decidedly negative (Shayon "*Julia* Symposium"). Knowingly or not, they confronted a monumental task of harmonizing their ideological intention with the established hierarchies of the sitcom genre. The instant producers chose to cast African Americans in the lead roles of *Julia*, the show encountered problems. Reality and affinity are both important ingredients for sitcom success and are a driving force behind the "mobilization of identification" between audience and sitcom characters (Taylor 39).

As the widow of a helicopter pilot shot down over Vietnam, Julia Baker could not represent the idealized notion of the two-parent nuclear family common to the genre. Yet, in contemporaneous shows such as *The Lucy Show* (1962–74) and *The Doris Day Show* (1968–73), commercial sponsors supported female-headed sitcoms. Single-parent shows were among the highest-rated programs during the period. The vice president of nighttime programming at ABC explained that the absence of one parent left the "remaining parent" free to "either embark on romantic endeavors" or to "attend to the children" (Weinberg 174). Corporations like General Foods and Mattel, however, were hesitant about supporting *Julia* despite its very conventional content ("Program and Production Report"). The show followed a popular trend with one key difference: race.

The expectation prevailed that if the series came close to portraying the actual Black experience, then middle-class consumers were certain to tune out. Many commercial sponsors believed that urban poverty and African American discontent were the only credible representations of Black life in the United States. Likewise, industry executives were chastened by what they perceived as the unfair accusation that their television programs inflamed Blacks to urban uprisings. Arguably, when it came to sitcoms such as *Julia*, the industry downplayed social realism and relevancy. Despite their conservative attitudes, NBC executives made a full-blown media event for the debut of *Julia*, hailing it as a watershed in the history of television and socially responsible entertainment.

In an interview in *Variety*, Kanter vowed to "show it like it is" (qtd. in Shayon, "*Julia* Symposium"). The network's pre-broadcast hype also suggested *Julia* would offer a realistic portrayal of a widowed African American nurse and her son. After viewing the pilot episode, one critic questioned Kanter about the contradiction between his advanced press statements and the "degree of lavishness of Julia's apartment." NBC's vice president of press and publicity, M. S. Rukeyser, Jr., and the publicity agent for the program, Dan Jenkins, responded to the criticism, "It is not, and never has been, the function of a commercial series to 'show it as it is, baby.' On those rare occasions when the medium has taken a stab at limning the unhappy reality of what goes on in much of the world, the public has quickly tuned out" (qtd. in Shayon, "*Julia* Symposium").

Julia, like other sitcoms of the 1950s and 1960s, relies upon a formula that focused on superficial familial interaction at home or at the workplace. With regards to commercial viability, *Julia* held the most promise as a sitcom. Because of its power to gain a sizable portion of female and young viewers and its overall popularity as a genre, NBC executives saw in the sitcom the best means available to introduce controversial subjects and non-mainstream characters. Such economic considerations may have influenced the elevated class status evident in the set design of the series. Like other single television parents of the period, such as part-time bank secretary and widow Lucy in *The Lucy Show*, Julia Baker lives well beyond her means (Weinberg 175). A critic noted that the "upscale" apartment of the Baker household was too "posh" for a nurse's salary ("Julia"), and Carroll's portrayal of a glamorous single mother remained a highly contested aspect of the show, despite its similarities to other programs.

The series most often features Julia and Corey in the kitchen and living room areas of their apartment. During this period of consolidation within the television industry, sitcoms became a primary means of commercial revenue for networks, particularly those where consumerism was a main feature of the set (Taylor 23). As a narrative device, the design of the set helps identify the class status of the family and reflects the tastes and sensibilities of the central female character. Programs that maintained a large female audience at the time keenly appealed to corporate sponsors, who held to the belief that American women made most of the purchasing decisions for the home.

Although the series may have wooed commercial advertisers with its middle-class, "posh" decor, it limits the cues available regarding the character's

African American culture and identity. Many Black viewers felt little affinity with Julia's middle-class lifestyle and decided that Carroll herself somehow had turned away from the Black community (See 27–30). The middle-class status of the main character, however, represents a common theme in sitcom narratives where the families portrayed are typically wealthy, White, and suburban dwellers. Set details, prior to 1968, operate mainly to define the gendered and socioeconomic class identity of the main character and her family, but with the introduction of Julia Baker the matter of African American identity required equal expression.

Designed by art directors Smith and Roth, and decorated by set decorators Scott and Wickman, the modern high-rise apartment where Julia and Corey reside differs little from mainstream sitcoms featuring White, middle-class characters. Through Smith and Roth's choices in costuming, set design, and lighting composition, they literally framed the Black female character as a wholly conflicted and contradictory subject. The set of *Julia* expresses little difference from that of her televisual neighbors, the Waggerdorns, or her prime-time competitor on *The Doris Day Show*. Only two African carvings sitting on a bare buffet in the Baker home convey the possibility of an Africa-positive aesthetic sensibility, perhaps a nod to the African-centered values that the Black arts movement and cultural nationalists had pushed for across America. The statues are sometimes visible in head to shoulder shots and, occasionally, Carroll is framed between them. Against this solitary, quasi-cultural cue, set decorators furnished the apartment with a brownish tan couch with green pillows, pastel green curtains and lamps, floral prints, and two prominently displayed photographs of Julia's dead husband. Interestingly, the picture of the absent father was first placed on a shelf in Corey's bedroom. In later seasons, the picture appears near the carved African figures (Kanter). The attention of show personnel to small details of decor and placement on the set help identify Julia Baker as Black, but not too Black, and as the consummate bourgeois woman.

Class values and set design communicate a bourgeois consumer culture in the series, one that was available to Blacks as well as Whites if the necessary income were present. The mandates of television as an advertising medium that Kanter negotiated and the set decor of Scott and Wickman combine to signify a racially pluralistic vision of democratic capitalism. Far from telling it like it is, the show tells a story of how the United States could be if Blacks and Whites simply behaved the way they did on television.

CINEMATIC STYLE AND STAGING CONVENTIONS

Camera angles and lighting operate symbolically and literally within the series to strengthen the constructed identity of the character, Julia Baker. Codified aesthetic and technical practices operate to frame her subjectivity in ways at once similar to and dissimilar from the set design. Camera angles and editing styles work to suggest a specific point of view or subject positioning (Messaris 183). In "Visual Pleasure and Narrative Cinema," Laura Mulvey argues that narrative structure offers a "masculine subject position" for the cinematic "male gaze." As she suggests, camera operators generally take a point of view that objectifies the female body, while placing men in the position of the spectator, although many modes of spectator identity are potentially available. Thus, interrelated and infused with the masculine, Eurocentric values inherent to the visual and narrative language of television are the identities of the producers to their own production practices. *Julia* offers a complex example of how devices such as editing and camera work function as traditional narrative mechanisms.

The series incorporates a single-camera mode of production into the usual television sitcom form creating unconventional camera angles and edited sequences that differed stylistically from shows of the period. Single-camera and multiple-camera are the two main modes of production used for broadcast television. "Mode of production" means the certain technological and economic conventions that govern the aesthetic style of a program. Although multiple-camera shows are less costly and more efficient to produce, programs using single-camera mode are thought to be qualitatively superior to those made in multiple-camera mode (Butler 175). Such devices grew out of a confluence of aesthetic styles from cinema and television. As film-trained technicians worked on studio productions for television, the style of representation began to change (Taylor 44). The style had yet to adjust, however, in any relevant way to the inclusion of people of color and other non-mainstream images in television.

Many of the scenes in *Julia* are highly orchestrated and shot in such a way as to position the viewer in a participative role rather than as a remote or passive observer. The ultimate point of view that lurks in the background is definitively male (Metallinos 225). This presentational style brings the viewer into the scene, unlike old modes of televisual cinematography that were restricted by one or two camera shots of the entire set. The visual style of *Julia* demonstrates a shift wherein lighter-weight cameras and cinéma vérité techniques borrowed from the big screen join to bring intimate shooting and segmented editing to the small screen (Caldwell 53). Although critics looking at the artistic value of such innovations on television praised the new techniques, the change resulted in literally segmenting Carroll's body into parts, a visual mode routinely used in media to objectify and festishize the female form. Nowhere is this more evident than in the first episode of the series, entitled "Mama's Man."

Demonstrating a reconciliation to racial and gender inclusion on the part of the production crew, "Mama's Man" employs shots and an editing technique that emphasizes the bouncy and percussive rhythm in *Julia's* introductory theme song. The opening scene has Corey making juice and toast for his mother, who is asleep on the foldout couch in the living room. The shots begin as a series of closeups on an orange that Corey is in the process of slicing in two. Instead of a slow pull out to the larger room, several views of the orange, Corey, the knife, and the sleeping mother are edited in montage and cut to the beat of the music. The narrative of the vignette and the punctuated rhythmic edits build suspense and tension that, as an opening to a sitcom, comments ironically on the light and airy themes of middle-class domestic life common to the genre. More appropriate for drama, the tense opening is diffused when Julia opens her eyes to see Corey at her bedside holding a tray with breakfast. John Caldwell suggests in *Televisuality* that the sequence "abruptly cuts in from a wide shot to a closeup without moving to another angle, thereby challenging Hollywood's artificially sacred 30–degree cutting rule" (Caldwell 54). The unorthodox editing of the sequence is stylistically risky for a formulaic genre. Nonetheless, the choppy introduction calls attention to the series' underlying discourse on difference.

Segmentation runs throughout the pilot episode of the series, bisecting Carroll's body. Gazed at in almost every episode, her legs signify Julia Baker's femininity (Carroll and Firestone 137). The objectification of Baker was intentional and specific. Male pleasure through spectatorship did not play a significant role in any 1950s sitcom that featured an African American woman. In *Beulah*, for example, Louise Beavers's femininity and sexual attractiveness are downplayed in favor of her maternal and nurturing qualities. Julia's physical appearance and haute couture clothing become an important part of the narrative so as to advance an ideological position of racial advancement. By portraying Baker as more glamorous than her White female counterparts, the producers normalize her television image.

Suzanna Walters, in *Material Girls*, identifies one implication of Mulvey's theory of male spectatorship. She writes that "point of view" is "crucial" to "narrative structure and mise-en-scène" and that it "literally act[s] out the male gaze" (61). Visual narrative devices, specifically camera angles and stylized, edited sequences, point to what becomes one of the most effective symbols of Julia's sexuality, Carroll's calves. In "Mama's Man," the camera angle rests just past her hemline as she walks into the Aerospace Industries Health Office to apply for the position of nurse. Dressed professionally in a dark woolen suit, pantyhose, and heels, the camera angle and costuming draws attention to Carroll's legs. The viewer participates in the scene voyeuristically, and the inclusion of a male spectator smiling at the sight of Julia ascending the stairs to the space center cues the viewer to join in the pleasure. A similar angle is used in the 1969 episode, "The Eve of Adam." As the romantic lead in the episode, artist Adam Spencer provides the added point of view, watching Baker's legs from behind. Walking forward, Baker bends slightly and places a portrait of Corey that Spencer painted against a wall and walks away.

In the scene, the image of Carroll's legs is visually constructed in such a way as to suggest an omnipresent sexuality framed like the portrait Spencer has stopped by to deliver.

Prior to *Julia*, Black women cast as servants and maids in familial comedies had little sexual appeal. As a rule, the series shies away from images of Julia that portray her as wild, aggressive, or hypersexualized (MacDonald, *One Nation* 12). Again, the normalizing goal of *Julia* results in the series taking on many of the common modes of female objectification in media, such as the visual segmentation of the female body. Up until 1968, this is used primarily to fetishize White women in television and cinema. Hence, Kanter normalizes the content of *Julia* by adhering to dominant modes of representation that had been developed for White women in television. The normalization of Julia Baker resulted in critical comparisons of Carroll to other well-known television widows of the time, placing her in the unfair position of seeming less Black to many viewers ("Did Diahann Carroll 'Sell Out' to Television?" 56; See 27).

By the 1950s, lighting for sitcoms had become an important aspect of staging. Like camera angles, lighting arrangement and design have a signifying function. Byrne, in *Production Design for Television*, states that in the days before color television, the intensity of the lighting was the major visual cue as to the seriousness or frivolity of the piece—a comic piece would be lit flat and bright, a serious one darker and more sculpturally (51). These conventions still persist. Soaps and some prime-time dramas are often lit with strong shadows and strong back lights while comedies are lit brightly and indiscriminately (Byrne 51). The traditional mode of lighting, however, operated differently for Black actors as compared to White ones. The narrative content for *Julia* coincides with the typical high-key lighting design for sitcoms. The lighting used routinely to frame White female characters in domestic sitcoms, however, did not work the same for Carroll. When used on her, the high-key lighting whitened her already light-brown complexion. Without adjusting to Carroll's particular production needs, her image signifies Black dilution. Byrne confirms this effect when he observes that a "dark-complected person will be lit more intensely and may have a stronger backlight" to "frame the face and hair and provide more reflective highlights from the cheeks, forehead, and chin" than White or lighter-complexioned actors (Byrne 52).

Lack of attention to racial difference in this case produces a washing-out visually of an important aspect of racial difference, skin tone. Traditional sitcom lighting in this particular context suggests Caldwell showcased Carroll "with a rather conventional sitcom style, that is with effaced direction and flattering high-key studio lighting that made her seem both very elegant and very white" (54). Important to Caldwell's analysis is how the lighting affects not only the representation of race in the series but the image of idealized womanhood, crucial to domestic sitcoms and Carroll's own star image.

FIGURE 12.1. Diahann Carroll as Julia Baker, Lloyd Nelson as Dr. Morton Chegley, and Marc Copage as Corey Baker in *Julia*, 1968–1971. Photo courtesy of Larry Edmunds BooksFair.

CASTING CONVENTIONS

Prior to her role in *Julia*, Carroll's image in popular media signified the attainment of bourgeois refinement, "sweet" sensuality, glamor, and femininity ("Hands and Song" 57–58; "Nightclubs: Bottom of the Top" 48). Kanter cast her with the hope that the discourse inherited from her stage and film performances prior to 1968 might ensure the show's crossover appeal. As an actress connected to both White and Black communities, Carroll's presence communicated a pluralist discourse on race while reifying White over Black cultural norms. As with many other producers, public perceptions of Carroll guided Kanter's casting choice for the lead role. Initially, he did not envision Carroll's image as matching the role of Julia Baker. He changed his mind, however, when she arrived at the interview "simple and understated" in a "black wool" suit "with a short skirt" (Carroll and Firestone 137). Once in production, his choice of Carroll appeared to undermine the concept of Julia and drew criticism that her sophisticated image hurt her "believability" in the role of mother and nurse. Carroll's detractors likened her inappropriateness for the part of Julia to that of White female icons such as Jackie Kennedy or Doris Day (See 27–30; Shayon, "*Julia* Symposium"). How she compared to an African American woman such as Merlie Evers (Evers 60) or the fact that she was herself a mother did not matter (See 27). Commenting critically in *Time* on the Julia breakthrough, Black entertainer Harry Belafonte notes how "for the shuffling, simple minded Amos-and-Andy type of Negro, television has substituted a new, one-dimensional Negro without reality" ("Blacks on the Channels" 74). Kanter seems to confirm Belafonte's critique when he states that a goal of the series was to feature "Black characters as people first" and "Black only incidentally" (Kanter 254). Thanks to Carroll's offscreen persona and performance background, the innovative character of Julia Baker begins to construct a new "standard of recognition" for Black women on television.

Julia follows the conventions of the genre that place White female leads at the center of the narrative, maintaining a tradition of actresses who are "well-dressed" and fashionable, but who lack depth (Mellencamp, *Logics* 66). Carroll is always shown in fashionable attire. The haute couture designs of fashion designer William Travilla both appear in the series and are mentioned in editorials on the show. In the episode "Tanks for the Memories," Julia answers a knock at her door in a peach-colored pantsuit trimmed at the collar with cream-colored feathers. This delights her male guests, who comment approvingly on her appearance. Her highly publicized wardrobe includes designer gowns featured in magazines such as *Ebony* and *Good Housekeeping* and was later duplicated as a line of clothes for Mattel's *Julia* doll ("Diahann Carroll Presents the *Julia* Dolls"). The character's identification with White middle-class housewives, fictional and real, and the heightening of her idealized feminine Eurocentric features displace her racial "otherness."

As with her costuming in *Julia*, Carroll's body itself engenders elements that place her within the boundaries of the dominant culture and signify an affinity with the status quo and a tangential relationship to African American phenotypic norms. As a legacy of slavery, African Americans with light skin tones often have been able to achieve greater social and economic mobility because of a perceived connection to their owners and ability to assimilate within the dominant culture (Omi and Winant 13–18). Such ideas have given way to aesthetic and class perceptions that influence how Black women are perceived historically, both inside and outside of mainstream American culture.

Throughout Carroll's career, her ability to succeed in the entertainment industry, particularly in leading roles, depended substantially on the lightness of her complexion. As with her predecessors Fredi Washington, Dorothy Dandridge, and Lena Horne, Carroll's light skin tone gave her an advantage over darker women, who, as with Louise Beavers, found no other roles in Hollywood except as servants (Bogle, *Toms, Coons* 59). Although lighter-complexioned actresses played more romantic leads than darker ones, such roles were not free of racist stereotyping (Anderson 18; Bogle, *Toms, Coons* 58). In the discourse on *Julia*, Carroll's image is "whitened" through frequent comparisons to White, female icons like former first lady Jackie [Kennedy] Onassis and the static idealized girl/woman image of Barbie (Simonds 917). Such whitening of Carroll proved devastating to her career after Black cultural nationalism successfully critiqued Hollywood biases and color-coded practices as anti-Black. One historian compares Carroll's "pert and proper" image to that of Onassis, and declares that she had "far more in common with Doris Day than Angela Davis" (Van Deburg 251). Similarly, Donald Bogle, in *Toms, Coons, Mulattoes, Mammies, and Bucks*, writes that Carroll's portrayal in *Julia* resembled a "black-face Doris Day" due to her poised mannerisms, glamorous image, and light-complexioned skin (Bogle 211). Other critics charge the producers of *Julia* with creating an "assimilationist" discourse at a time when African Americans were accelerating their demands for self-determination and celebrating their distinctive qualities. Herman Gray makes this point in *Watching Race*, arguing that programs such as *Julia* "celebrated racial invisibility and color blindness" (Gray 85). He contends that such programs had a "normalizing" effect that configured racism as an individualized experience and reduced the possibility of collective resistance against the savage inequities that persisted in the United States (84–85). The lessening of Julia's Black identity maintained a televisual status quo in that it caused White women to identify with her, while estranging African Americans from one of the few Black female characters on television (Bodroghkozy, "Is This" 415). Writing for *Good Housekeeping* in 1969, Rollie Hochstein offers a slightly critical assessment of Carroll's image in popular culture. She writes, "after starring roles in movies and television dramas as well as musical specials, after the ending of her own interracial marriage, after a famous and serious romance with superstar Sidney Poitier, *Julia* returned her [Carroll] to the sweetness-and-light department" (47). Contemporary and recent criticism of Carroll's physical appearance and performance in *Julia* stresses how television gatekeepers suppressed more radical identities, especially ones with the markers of Black nationalism. Carroll's image in the series has come to mean Black erasure and an elision of racial tensions through an idealized assimilation of people of color within the mainstream. It is not surprising, therefore, that the show was "originally scripted for a White actress" (Shayon, "Julia: Breakthrough").

Carroll performs as if unaware of her sexuality, although she was well aware of her own media image. She knew how the series utilized her body and her overall public image as a means to attract viewers, a standard device of representing sexuality that she chose to exploit and capitalize on. In her biography, Carroll reveals that the sexuality her character's legs signified was part of the initial crafting of the subjectivity of Julia Baker. She confesses that:

> By the time, I finished the script, I had gone beyond understanding Julia's character—I saw her actual physical presence. I knew exactly how she should look . . . I hunted through my closet and found exactly the right dress: black wool with a short skirt, simple and understated. (The script had made a point about Julia's great legs. If mine aren't spectacular, they ain't half bad, and I figured that was bound to help). (Carroll and Firestone 136–37)

The exploitation of Carroll's sexual image facilitates a whitening process in which Julia becomes a representation of Black assimilation. To "whiten" oneself in the United States refers to the accentuating of Eurocentric values and aesthetics as part of an overall process of assimilation into mainstream culture. Carroll's physical and cultural integration results in a perception that the struggle to assimilate into mainstream culture, workplaces, and neighborhoods is attainable for all African Americans. The representation system in *Julia* leads to Bodroghkozy's suggestion that Carroll's character communicates that "'Black people were just people' to the extent that they conformed to an unexamined White norm of representation," or normalization through Black erasure ("Is This" 416).

By design, *Julia* is a carbon copy of the "affable family comedies" of the mid-to-late 1950s (Taylor 29). Because attention to set decor, color, and lighting, the genre traditions and practices in the industry from the 1950s continued to have an impact on shows produced in the 1960s. The makers of *Julia* worked to produce a show that had a well-established formula, but they added an ingredient that had never before been included—Black actors performing a version of Black life as the central concern of the series. The experiment disrupted the language of television. Production techniques were adjusted, however, because of a decision to make Carroll and other Blacks appear as mainstream as possible, as White as rice. The role of the productive forces that created *Julia* and television's capacity to respond to the political climate of the late 1960s flowed together into matrimony within the holy family of liberal integrationism, democratic capitalism, and Virginia Slims femininity. The series helped workers and managers in the television industry realize that a world in living color could be represented with a measure of artistry and commercial success. Also, it revealed that the grammar of television had greater fluidity than was commonly recognized; certainly it was fluid enough to represent non-mainstream facets of the American experience in a way that was viable and met recognized standards of production. Finally, it demonstrated, perhaps painfully for some, that audiences—popular as well as professional critics—could read, decode, appropriate, be influenced by, and contest shows (particularly their ideological content) in relation to their material, psychological, and cultural locations. *Julia* forever changed the face of television. How fitting it is that the character of a nurse at a military industrial complex would bring a new level of comfort, confidence, health, and healing to a television industry steeped in years of the disease of racism and the nervous ticks of racial hierarchy. The show in no way cured television of its ills, but it did inspire the negotiation of new boundaries.

PART FIVE

Situating
Sexual Orientation

CHAPTER 13

Ellen

Coming Out and Disappearing

Valerie V. Peterson

The "puppy episode" of the *Ellen* television situation comedy aired April 30, 1997, and depicted the coming out of Ellen, a character played by actress and comedian Ellen DeGeneres. While the episode portrayed the lead character coming out of the closet to millions of viewers on television, the person playing the part was doing the same thing in real life. The coming out of Ellen the person lent authenticity to the coming out of Ellen the character. As the first television show to depict the coming out of a lead character, the episode was viewed and discussed by many people outside the show's usual audience. This combination of subject matter, authenticity, and popularity made Ellen's coming-out episode a media event with the potential to persuade many viewers.

How did *Ellen* characterize coming out to viewers? How did this characterization appeal to and shape understandings of lesbianism and/or homosexuality? In this chapter I argue that the *Ellen* coming-out episode failed to challenge mainstream biases against gays and achieve its imagined persuasive potential because it offered viewers a simplistic process of coming out and an essentialist version of lesbianism. By essentialism, I mean "belief in the real, true essence of things, the invariable and fixed properties which define the 'whatness' of a given entity" (Fuss, *Essentially* xi). I will show how Ellen Morgan (the character in the show) proceeds smoothly through four discrete stages of coming out, from shared meaning to self-labeling to confiding to announcing. This process, drawn inductively from the episode itself but reminiscent of other descriptions, implies and normalizes a latent, preexistent, natural, and essential lesbianism. As a consequence, viewers are invited to fortify rather than blur boundaries of sexual identity and to privilege one kind of lesbianism over others.

Critics in and of mass media have denounced limited and stereotyped portrayals of gays and lesbians. McDowell lamented the growing number of explicitly gay but oddly "libido restricted" characters, the consequence of "bizarre rules surrounding gay sexuality on TV" (116). *Newsweek* also criticized the sexual blandness of lead television characters but found "all the usual clichés" conveniently off-loaded to supporting cast members ("In or Out" 72). Because shows with gay and lesbian characters concern themselves most with the comfort and predicted responses of heterosexual viewers (Wilke 31), the performances of characters are limited accordingly.

In her 2001 study of television, the *Ellen* show, and the politics of gay and lesbian visibility, Dow charges mainstream media practices, a narrative of psychological autonomy, and strategies of personalization with constraining the possibilities of gay visibility. As a consequence, Dow says, Ellen became a token or "poster child" for lesbianism at the expense of more pressing political issues (such as, discrimination). Dow's study effectively shows how the coming-out episode was limited by regulatory discourses of self-determination and mass media but says less about what sort of lesbianism the show *did* offer viewers and how that might also be a problem.

Scholars, activists, therapists, and others have isolated and theorized important aspects of coming out. In their history of empowerment efforts in lesbian and gay communities, Garnets and D'Augelli offer a typical definition identifying key stages in the coming-out process. "Coming out is a complex sequence of events through which individuals acknowledge, recognize, and label their sexual orientation and then disclose it to others throughout their lives" (452). Some scholars (Fuss, Butler) have pointed to difficulties with coming out and its relationship to identity, power, and essentialism. They ask important questions such as: What or who is it that "comes out"? To whose advantage is "coming out"? Is it even possible to name (a) sexuality or to render (a) sexuality transparent? This chapter combines these concerns over identity and essence with the media portrayal of coming out as depicted in the *Ellen* coming-out episode.

CONTEXT OF *THE ELLEN SHOW*

The *Ellen* coming-out episode was embroiled in a larger web of advertising, interviews, and public discussion. Ellen DeGeneres, the focal point of the moment, granted three well-advertised interviews, one with Oprah Winfrey

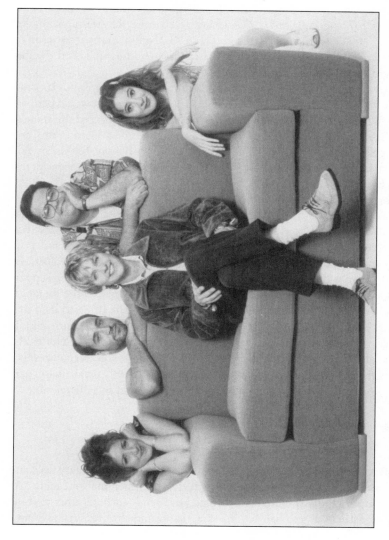

FIGURE 13.1. Joely Fisher as Paige Clark, Jeremy Piven as Spence Novak, Ellen DeGeneres as Ellen Morgan, David Anthony Higgins as Joe Farrell, and Clea Lewis as Audrey Penney in *Ellen*, 1994–1998. Photo courtesy of Photofest. Used by permission.

on the day of the show, one immediately after the show on *Primetime Live*, and one in *Time* magazine. These interviews, along with foreshadowing in *Ellen*, promotional commercials, news programs on television and the radio, Ellen's earlier appearances on talk shows, and other commentary, framed the coming-out episode as a momentous occasion. According to *US News and World Report*, more than thirty-six million people tuned in to watch it ("James Earl Ray" 16), and it earned a 23.4 rating/35 share in the overnight market according to Nielsen Media Research (Katz 4). Commentary afterwards on news, talk shows, and in the print media extended and complicated the discourses of sexuality begun in the show.

The coming-out episode was touted as a groundbreaking exemplar show (Handy 92). For the first time on television, a "real-life" lesbian would perform coming out. KCRG TV9 in eastern Iowa, for example, advertised the show as a "special" hour. Quoting *TV Guide*, KCRG called the show "A triumph!" and "THE episode!" David A. Neuman, president of Walt Disney Television, said of it "We have the rare opportunity to replicate something that happens in real life" (Cerone 53).

This alleged replication was controversial. "Not since *Maude* tackled abortion in 1972 [had] a sitcom served as a lightning rod for such intense emotions" (Cerone 50). Religious groups threatened ABC advertisers with boycotts and criticized Disney for supporting the show. Chrysler and J. C. Penney pulled their sponsorship. At the same time, Demi Moore, Melissa Etheridge, Billy Bob Thornton, and other celebrities showed their support and added to the hype by doing cameos. Oprah Winfrey played the therapist. As one of her executive producers, Dava Savel, put it, "She [Oprah] is so well liked . . . it was perfect to have someone like her who connects with middle America, where if Oprah said it was OK, then it was OK" (Cerone 51). Because of the extended commentary, the many viewers, and the controversy, what might otherwise have been overlooked as just another plot twist, personal quirk, or vehicle for laughs appeared politically and socially relevant.

STAGES OF COMING OUT

Compressing the process of coming out into sixty minutes is no easy task, and the *Ellen* show starts off reflexively by playing the dilemma for laughs. As Ellen primps in the bathroom before a date, her friends encourage her to come out. As one friend says to her, "Quit jerking us around already and come out." Ellen responds, "What is the big deal? I've got a whole hour."

This joke acknowledges the challenge of portraying the complicated process of coming out in such a short time span and suggests viewers consume the one-hour capsule with a healthy skepticism. But the depiction of coming out—the clear progression of disclosure, the speed, and the relative ease of the process—encourages viewers to see coming out in a particular way. Like disclaimers before a powerful statement, Ellen's joke is easily forgotten. More memorable is the cumulative effect of the story—the big picture of the process of coming out.

In the *Ellen* episode, coming out is accomplished in four stages: "shared meaning"—coming to a mutual understanding with one other person that one is gay; "self-labeling"—saying "I'm gay" (or lesbian) to that person or someone else; "confiding"—telling other important confidantes; and "announcing"— telling important communities. Because coming out in *Ellen* follows this simple trajectory, procedural issues are highlighted (such as, When should I tell? How should I tell?) while complexities of homosexuality as a concept and as an identity (What does it mean to say I am lesbian? What are the implications of embracing this label?) are ignored.

In the first stage of coming out, shared meaning, Ellen arrives at a mutual understanding with her therapist, and later with her love-interest, that she is gay. At the start of the show, Ellen meets a woman named Susan, and they hit it off. Susan is gay and thinks Ellen is gay, but Ellen denies this and is disturbed by the attribution. To prove her heterosexuality to her friends, Ellen lies about her exploits with a male friend, Richard. When she confides to her therapist about the lie, talk proceeds to issues of relationship and sexuality. When the therapist asks, "Has there ever been anyone you felt you clicked with?" Ellen says, "Yes." Then the therapist asks, "What was his name?" Ellen answers, "Susan." The two look at each other and smile. At this moment, Ellen and her therapist have come to a shared meaning; both recognize she is gay but without saying so. This recognition is as much an achievement for Ellen as it is for the therapist. It is not just that the therapist figures out Ellen is gay but that Ellen figures out Ellen is gay. Ellen succeeds in thinking of herself as gay and becomes comfortable with someone else thinking of her as gay.

Soon after this exchange, Ellen heads to the airport. This time, she wants to let Susan know she is gay. Encouraged by her friends who think her purpose is to express feelings for Richard, Ellen finds Susan and tries to tell her she is gay. When she cannot bring herself to actually say the words "gay" or "lesbian," she says, "I *did* get the joke about the toaster oven." Susan had made the joke about a toaster oven earlier in the show, before Ellen had begun to acknowledge homosexuality as a possibility for herself. Ellen had become upset when Susan called her gay and had accused Susan of recruiting. Susan had responded by lamenting how close she was to winning a toaster oven, and that National (Gay) Headquarters would be disappointed. At the time, Ellen had called the joke "gay humor" and said she did not get it. Now, by saying she does get the joke, Ellen identifies herself as gay to Susan (but again without actually speaking it).

In this stage of coming out, Ellen comes to terms with thinking of herself as gay and having a few others acknowledge her as gay. It is the beginning stage of embracing identity, depicted as something first rejected and then accepted as real. Susan acts as the toggle, enabled by the therapist, to throw Ellen's switch from one sexual identity, heterosexual, to another, gay.

Once Ellen becomes comfortable thinking of herself as gay and having a few others think of her that way, she enters the next stage of coming out: self-labeling. In this stage, Ellen goes from concept (thought) to signification (naming). She goes from thinking of herself as gay to calling herself gay, and from being thought of as gay to being called gay. This is the point where language, terms, and labeling become crucial. Will she call herself gay? Will she call herself lesbian? Will she call herself both? Will she call herself bisexual? Will she refuse to be labeled?

In the coming-out episode, Ellen begins by using the most general label of sexual identity available. By calling herself gay instead of lesbian, Ellen gives both male and female homosexual viewers the opportunity to live vicariously through her coming out, at least at the level of terms. Other people call her either gay or lesbian. The term bisexual never comes up, and there is no discussion of resisting or existing without a sexual label.

Ellen enters the self-labeling stage soon after she and Susan come to a mutual understanding about her sexuality. Once she admits to getting the toaster joke, Ellen struggles with the self-identifying words she wants to say. She tries to get Susan to speak them, but Susan says she does not want to be wrong again. For Susan, as for most people, it is not an "authentic" coming out unless it is the person herself or himself who says, "I'm gay/lesbian/homosexual." After much agonizing, Ellen finally says, "I'm gay." The comic twist to this scene is the intercom. When Ellen says she is gay, she accidentally speaks into a working microphone, and her announcement is broadcast to the all the people waiting in the airport for departing flight 368 to Pittsburgh.

This comic twist seems to usefully complicate the easy progression of the four stages of coming out. Once words are uttered, they can take on a life of their own. Speakers do not always have control over the way information travels once a statement is articulated, and sometimes even before it has been articulated. That is, coming out can easily jump to the announcing stage. The scene with the intercom suggests this. In this episode, however, the integrity and progression of coming out proceeds in an orderly fashion and without complication. At the self-labeling stage, Susan refuses to skip to the announcing stage and to "out" Ellen. To "out" a person (discursively) is to label/name/identify that person as gay against his or her wishes. Outing also suggests some "truth" to the attribution. Susan wants to avoid this, so she makes Ellen articulate for herself that she is gay, and Susan also insists that Ellen make the declaration first.

The integrity and progression of coming out are also maintained by the context of the show. Ellen's coming out is (accidentally) announced to the people in the airport terminal, but they are strangers and do not particularly care about Ellen or her sexuality. Because the public forum she addresses is not personally significant, she avoids skipping to the announcing stage, even though real people's coming-out experiences sometimes do skip directly to this stage.

After Ellen successfully labels herself gay, she continues to have anxiety-filled dreams where her lesbianism is the featured issue. She shares these dreams with her therapist, who encourages her to begin confiding in important others about her sexual orientation. Given the choice of talking to family or friends, Ellen chooses her close friends and invites them over.

The first friend she confides in, Pete, is a gay character on the show. Ellen has Pete come over early, ostensibly to help her prepare for her other guests. When Ellen tells Pete she is gay, his reaction to the news is warm, excited, and positive. When the rest of the group arrives, Ellen tries to confide in them, but she is tongue-tied. Pete cannot contain himself and tells them for her.

Audrey is the first straight friend to react. She, like Pete, is warm and supportive. The other three appear a little less comfortable, and a bit confused, but they pledge support. Overall, Ellen's confiding stage goes smoothly, as confirmed by the end of the scene. After some discussion, Joe asks Ellen, "Are you sure this is what you want?" When Ellen replies in the affirmative, Joe turns to the others to collect on a bet. That they have made a bet and could all so quickly focus on the wager rather than on Ellen's announcement displays how little Ellen's sexual orientation matters to her friends and what little shock or surprise it engenders.

In the final stage of coming out, announcing, people identify themselves as gay to important communities. With so little time, announcing gets the least illustration in this episode, but subsequent shows take the process further. In the last two episodes of the season, for instance, Ellen comes out to family (her parents) and at work (to her new boss at the bookstore). The scene at the lesbian bar, however, does show Ellen coming out to one important group, other lesbians.

In the scene, Ellen's straight friends have her meet them at a lesbian coffeehouse to cheer her up after Susan leaves town. Ellen does not know the bar is a gay bar but has no problem with it when she finds out. Neither does she seem disturbed by the way her presence at the bar might announce her lesbianism to its patrons. Though Ellen hardly announces her lesbianism actively, neither is she outed. As in the earlier scene with Pete, Ellen's friends participate in realizing her lesbianism by enabling rather than overriding or defying her wishes. Significantly, the community of Ellen's straight friends encourages her entrance into this particular lesbian group, bridging her initial trip to this new territory with familiar faces and personalities.

IMPLICATIONS

Coming out in *Ellen* is characterized as quick, orderly, and easy. Ellen is never outed and stages of coming out in the show flow smoothly from shared meaning to self-labeling to confiding to announcing. This depiction of coming out suggests a few things about lesbianism. First, the show suggests lesbianism is part of a gay/straight binary. As De Cecco and Shively have noted, in binary understandings of sexual identity:

> sexual identity is conceived as an essence, interiorly lodged within the individual, one which determines whether the individual has only female or only male sexual partners. . . . If the partners are of the opposite biological sex, the individual's identity is called heterosexual. If partners are of the same biological sex, the identity is designated homosexual. (2)

This understanding of sexual identity permeates the *Ellen* episode. At first, Ellen is assumed to be straight and vehemently rejects being gay. Later, she embraces the thought of being gay, being thought of as gay by someone else, and finally the label "gay" itself. Once named, Ellen's lesbianism exists and any heterosexuality she may be assumed to have had vanishes. She cannot be both gay and not gay. Ellen illustrates this in an exchange with her therapist. The therapist asks Ellen when she first might have known she was gay. Ellen responds by reading back into her memory and finding that she has been gay all along. Things that did not make sense before, read through straight lenses, are reread though gay lenses and make sense. Being both gay and straight or neither gay nor straight is impossible; such ideas do not fit the binary. As a consequence, gay and straight become intelligible and mutually exclusive.

Second, the lesbian sexual identity made intelligible by the show is latent, preexistent, and natural. Jokes throughout emphasize Ellen's always-gay self. On a date with Richard, Ellen comments about work, saying, "It's amazing, we are all doing what we always wanted to do. Well, . . . except for me." The laughs come because the viewer imagines Ellen is talking about her sexuality rather than her occupation. Lesbianism is something she has wanted to do "all along."

Ellen is so naturally gay that she shows no attraction to Richard. Richard is described as a "perfect guy," a guy any straight woman would want to sleep with. This description dichotomizes sexual desire by body type (and implies that heterosexual women have no diversity of taste). In keeping with this, Ellen sees Richard as just a friend and is completely numb to his apparent heterosexual sex appeal. When she fabricates a story about her date with Richard for her friends, she makes up stupid details; she cannot even fake heterosexual desire. Things she claims to have said—such as "Show me the money!" and "I love man/woman sex!"—suggest to her friends and the viewer that this is not the sexuality for her. She even says she is on a different "vibe."

Ellen shares her history of latent lesbianism with her therapist. She recalls reading Gertrude Stein in freshman English and the girl she sat next to. Before that, there was the girl at the junior high school snack bar. In another session with the therapist, Ellen says, "I feel like this weight has been lifted off of me" and "For the first time in my life I feel comfortable with myself." In all these cases, the lesbianism was there all along. This way of thinking about lesbianism explains why Joe's comment, "It's very fashionable to be lesbian now," gets laughs. Ellen's lesbianism in the coming-out episode is not a style or fad, nor is it a consequence of external or supernatural forces. In the show, Ellen is gay to and from the core.

The notion of a core gay identity is reinforced by both fictional and real-life others. In the show, Pete talks to Ellen about his experience coming out, saying he told his parents he was gay as soon as he knew. "Then," he says, "the next year when I entered kindergarten they were 100 percent behind me." Despite and perhaps also due to comic effect, Pete's comments support the idea that being gay is a preexistent, natural, and internally derived way of being. Ellen's real-life mother made statements with similar implications. In a *People* magazine interview, she commented on the effect of Ellen's coming out saying "people . . . could just see the difference in Ellen. She was blossoming" ("Speaking Out" 208). This attractive metaphor of the unfolding flower suggests, among other things, the natural fruition of an essential nature.

Third, the smooth progression of coming-out stages, the absence of any outing, and the warm reception Ellen receives from supporting characters imply lesbianism is a largely nonthreatening sexual identity. Compared to commentary and controversy *surrounding* the episode, the way lesbianism is received *on Ellen* overstates its public acceptance. Overstatement may encourage viewers to accept lesbianism and to use characters in the show as models for their own reactions and behavior, but it also leaves viewers blind to persistent and pervasive injustices against gays and lesbians writ large in American law, politics, and society.

There are other kinds of lesbianism besides the essential, latent, preexistent, and natural lesbianism featured in the episode, kinds that are potentially more threatening to heterosexual ideology. One kind was described by Anne Heche, Ellen's real-life partner at the time, in their interview on *Oprah*. In the interview, Heche described how she saw Ellen from across a crowded room and just knew they were meant to be together. Heche said her affections were driven not by an innate nature, but by spiritual forces and a love somewhere beyond her control.

The way of being Heche described does not require a sexual orientation. Instead, it foregrounds a polymorphous sexuality and displays a fluid attitude towards sexual identity, one more like the lesbian continuum described by Adrienne Rich. Rich suggests considering the possibility that all women exist on a lesbian continuum and can see themselves as moving in and out of this continuum whether they identify themselves as lesbian or not (130). This understanding of lesbianism appeared to confuse and disturb Oprah and members of her audience. Had Heche always been bisexual? No. Had she been heterosexual before? Well, she'd had boyfriends. Was she lesbian? Yes and no. Heche's comments could not explain what looked to the audience like either an apparent lack of identity or a sudden and unexplainable shift from straight to gay. That DeGeneres and Heche have since broken up seems to confirm the volatility of celebrity love relationships. Such news, however, also bolsters mainstream faith in the importance of clearly labeled, easily recognized, and fully articulated sexual identity to help cement two people in relationship.

Another kind of lesbianism not featured in *Ellen* is radical feminist lesbianism. As Kitzinger notes, "Constructions of lesbians from within liberal humanistic ideology are incompatible with radical feminist and lesbian separatist constructions" (vii). Unlike liberal constructions of lesbianism—as innate sexual preference, alternative lifestyle, way of loving, route to personal fulfillment, and/or form of self-actualization—radical lesbianism is "fundamentally a political statement representing the bonding of women against male supremacy" (vii).

Radical lesbian feminists see compulsory heterosexuality as fundamental to the patriarchal oppression of women and consider heterosexuality a political regime that must be overthrown (Turcotte ix). Because radical feminist lesbianism is a conscious and overt political act in the face of women's oppression, it threatens those who are invested in patriarchy and some who are invested in heterosexuality. Considering the investments of many viewers of the episode, silence on this kind of lesbianism is no surprise.

This episode suggests lesbianism is part of a gay/straight binary and presents a latent, preexistent, natural, and nonthreatening sexuality. Lesbianism as performance, as love's outcome, as a political decision, as the result of trauma or abuse, or as a possibility latent in any one of a number of women are not discussed in *Ellen*, and are rarely discussed in surrounding commentary. When the topic of these other kinds of lesbianism does arise, confusion and anxiety reveal the limits of tolerance for deviating from the dominant sexual ideology.

CONCLUSION

The coming-out episode of *Ellen* presents lesbianism and the coming-out process in a way that depoliticizes homosexual identity and makes lesbianism more acceptable to a mainstream audience. Because Ellen is a lead character and because so many people watched the show, this presentation matters. Close analysis shows how this episode depicts coming out in four stages. As Ellen progresses through these stages, viewers are invited to fortify boundaries of sexual identity and privilege and normalize a particular kind of essential, latent, preexistent, and natural lesbianism.

Privileging an essential lesbianism does serve the goal of visibility. As Bullough notes, "The equation of homosexuality with sexual identity has facilitated the appearance of a militant gay movement emphasizing this identity" (4). Lesbians with a high investment in gay power benefit from maintaining and reinforcing strict boundaries between gay and straight. As Fuss suggests,

> adherence to essentialism is a measure of the degree to which a particular political group has been culturally oppressed . . . the stronger lesbian endorsement of identity politics may well indicate that lesbians inhabit a more precarious and less secure subject position than gay men. Lesbians, in other words, simply may have more to lose by failing to subscribe to an essentialist philosophy. (*Essentially* 98–99)

By coming together, forming a minority, and rallying behind a common quality or essence, lesbians can achieve critical mass and start working to have their concerns heard.

On the other hand, heterosexuals with a high investment in the dominance of their (own) sexual identity also benefit from this move. "The very existence of the queer," Andrew Sullivan argues, "depends on the majority's refusal to accept, on their intolerance, disdain, titillation, or discomfort" (89). In this way, lesbianism becomes a "necessary evil" maintaining the intelligibility of heterosexuality. As Wittig puts it, "[s]traight society is based on the necessity of the different/other at every level. It cannot work economically, symbolically, linguistically, or politically without this concept. . . . But what is the different/other if not the dominated?" (28–29). Privileging an essential lesbianism reinforces a gay/straight dichotomy and the minority status of lesbians in the face of heterosexual ideology. It also positions lesbians against each other as they try to approximate or resist expectations of identity. To complicate matters, when queer identity is largely based on difference from heterosexuals, fighting for equality becomes harder to do without undermining that difference (Gamson). As Sullivan argues, by aligning queer cultural revolt with a politics of equality and acceptance, "queer politics subverts itself. It seeks the means of its own abolition" (89).

Privileging essential lesbianism also poses problems for people who are not invested in or served by rigid categories and definitions of sexuality. People who cut across boundaries of sexual identity and defy common definitions and expectations risk being perceived as a threat to those who more closely fit the dominant ideology. Without an identity to rally behind, these individuals may be more easily discriminated against. Without a critical mass, they have little recourse against injustice.

Essentialist lesbianism of the sort depicted in the *Ellen* coming-out episode ultimately fails to challenge much in the social order. Despite its liberating potential for those who fit its rather narrow parameters, the "alternative" sexuality offered is limited by the same essentialist boundaries it outlines in order to legitimate itself. The Catch-22 of identity politics is that identities grounded in "essences" as a means to political legitimacy often lash back against the interests of the people who invest in them. While we may draw a number of conclusions from this observation, one from this analysis is clear: mainstream television shows trafficking in this sort of identity, even shows touted as "groundbreaking," are unlikely to contribute much to social or political change.

CHAPTER 14

Sealed with a Kiss

Heteronormative Narrative Strategies in NBC's *Will & Grace*

Denis M. Provencher

> Heterosexual desire and romance are thought to be the very core
> of humanity. . . . It is the one thing celebrated in every film plot,
> every sitcom, every advertisement.
>
> —Warner, *The Trouble with Normal*

AN INTRODUCTION TO *WILL & GRACE*: (HETEROSEXUAL) PAIRINGS AND THE ONSCREEN KISS

NBC's situation comedy *Will & Grace* is the most recent prime-time television effort since ABC's *Ellen* to deal with lavender issues in a significant way. In fact, Andrew Holleran refers to *Will & Grace* as the first "gay sitcom" and describes its content as "not merely gay, but hard-edged, LA circuit-queen gay. . . . Nothing of the gay content has been held back, nothing homogenized" (65). Indeed, weekly episodes of *Will & Grace* incorporate many elements of gay experience as depicted through various story lines, themes, and the characters' use of gay English (Leap). Thus, this sitcom, linguistically, subverts many norms related to gender and sexuality in pioneering ways.

Will & Grace has been recognized for its creative and innovative efforts. In September 2000, this show won three Emmy awards, including best situation comedy, best supporting actor, and best supporting actress. In November 2001, Eric McCormack won the Emmy award for best male actor. Moreover, NBC producers moved the sitcom into their Thursday night "Must See television" prime-time lineup during the 2000–01 season. In addition, in the spring of 2001, the Gay and Lesbian Alliance Against Defamation (GLAAD) presented a media award to the show's producers for their commitment to dealing with gay issues on commercial television. In a sense, *Will & Grace* attempts to present fresh and positive images of homosexuality and gay men in everyday situations, analogous to how *The Cosby Show* normalized African Americans on television during the 1980s.

Nonetheless, in its attempt to mainstream homosexuality on commercial television in the United States, *Will & Grace* still falls short in its visual representations of homosexuality and gay experiences. If we examine the narrative structure of this situation comedy, we see how it resembles many other successful network sitcoms with its use of male-female character couplings. In fact, from the very beginning, this show suggests a heteronormative trap with its title, which implies "the codependent relationship between a man and a woman who can do everything but sleep with each other" (Holleran 65). The show's use of character duos certainly reinforces this notion. Several examples underscore this point.

During the sitcom's first four years (with the exception of season two), the eponymous characters, Will Truman (a gay lawyer) and Grace Adler (a straight interior designer) share a Manhattan apartment, which visually reinforces a heteronormative story line and "codependent relationship." In addition, throughout the show, they share evenings in front of the television, eat meals together at home and in restaurants, exchange heart-to-heart conversations, and share numerous affectionate moments. These include walking down the street together, holding hands, sitting close together on the couch and in the bedroom, calling each other at work to make "dates," sharing financial expenses, escorting each other to weddings, and kissing on a regular basis (often under the pretense of a wedding ceremony).

Moreover, the show's supporting cast follows a similar narrative path. Jack McFarland (an "actor-singer-dancer" and generally unemployed gay character) and Karen Walker (Grace's "office assistant," married to a wealthy business man) hang out together, go shopping, recount outrageous stories, support each other through their respective addictions and character flaws, touch each other inappropriately, share hugs, and exchange tongue-filled kisses. In a similar manner, Jack and Rosario (Karen Walker's straight San Salvadorian maid) get married to keep her in the country, watch television together in bed, share living quarters in Karen's uptown penthouse (during the first and second seasons), and lock lips to convince immigration officers of their long-time commitment.

FIGURE 14.1. Sean Hayes as Jack McFarland, Megan Mullally as Karen Walker, Debra Messing as Grace Adler, and Eric McCormack as Will Truman in *Will & Grace*, 1998–. Photo courtesy of Movie Star NewsFair.

Hence, this sitcom provides a series of affectionate visual moments for its male-female couplings, many of which take place in domestic settings that suggest "family" values. Moreover, each of these three "couples" engages in some act of kissing during the first four years. Television viewers also regularly observe expressions of affection, kissing, and sexual activity between Grace and her various boyfriends who come and go (Danny, Josh, Ben, Nathan, etc.). In contrast, the show's two gay characters, Will and Jack, never appear in affectionate (or sexual) pairings—neither with each other nor with any other gay male character who drifts in and out of the sitcom. In fact, in many episodes, Will and Jack do not even appear together. Jack often conveniently forgets to meet Will for a prearranged rendezvous. Furthermore, Will regularly appears annoyed by Jack and occasionally ditches him to spend time with his best friend, Grace. In addition, Will rarely goes out on dates, and Jack often complains about Will's "antigay" behavior with such remarks as: "Do you *ever* touch men?" Although Jack complains about having to juggle several of his own boyfriends, little visual evidence of this occurs on-screen. In essence, virtually no visual display of same-sex affection takes place and certainly no suggestive hugging or kissing appears on the small screen for either of the show's two "gay" characters.

Indeed, the history of same-sex affection and kissing on commercial television is quite precarious. Of course, same-sex affection has found a place on public television in such PBS miniseries as *Tales of the City* and on cable series such as *Queer as Folk* and *Six Feet Under*. Moreover, network television episodes of such series as *thirtysomething*, *L.A. Law*, *Roseanne*, and, most recently, *ER* and *Dawson's Creek* have included suggestions or expressions of same-sex desire (Bruni 327–28). Some major networks, however, have subsequently retracted from syndication of many of these particular episodes. As Bruni points out, "Seeing a same-sex couple kiss makes it impossible for an observer to think about homosexuality only as an abstraction or to interpret warm interaction between two men or two women as something else—something less disturbing" (328). Hence, major commercial networks aim to minimize overt representations of same-sex affection and kissing on prime-time U.S. television so as not to offend the "viewing American majority" or commercial television sponsors (Hantzis and Lehr 119–20; Hubert 35; Moritz 140–41).

The characters on *Will & Grace* are squarely situated in this same "kissing" tradition. The fact that *Will & Grace* represents the "first gay sitcom" yet includes virtually no visual evidence of gay affection or kissing is quite remarkable. In the remainder of this chapter, I analyze the use of the onscreen kiss for both opposite-sex and same-sex couples in *Will & Grace*. I compare and contrast a representative episode that presents an opposite-sex kiss (between Will and Grace) with the *only* episode to include a same-sex kiss between two men (Will and Jack) during the show's first four years. The one-time occurrence of an unsentimental gay kiss, in contrast with the continual recurrence of the straight kiss between male-female couplings, on this "gay sitcom" merits some critical attention and explanation.

YOU MAY KISS THE BRIDE: SAME-SEX CIVIL UNION OR STRAIGHT LOVERS' QUARREL?

I begin my study of the "semantic smooch" on *Will & Grace* with an examination of the episode "Coffee and Commitment" from the third season. Although a whole chain of other quasi-romantic kisses—that imply Will and Grace's semi-married status—occur during many other episodes, this particular embrace represents perhaps the most problematic example of the opposite-sex kiss and its heteronormative undertones as they emerge on the small screen. In fact, this episode most closely resembles an exchange between husband and wife (or groom and bride) of any story line during the show's first four years.

In "Coffee and Commitment," Will and Grace drive to Vermont with Jack and Karen to attend Joe and Larry's same-sex civil union, the first ceremony of its kind to be depicted on prime-time television since the state law's inception in December 1999. As the civil union ceremony begins, the female justice of the peace introduces the same-sex couple (Joe and Larry), however, she never utters the names of the two men who participate in this union: "What a wonderful day, and what a wonderful couple." The fact that the justice never verbally recognizes the couple in a direct manner leaves the text open for interpretation as to who actually ties the knot. Directly following this opening greeting, the camera cuts away to Will and Grace, who sit as attendants and continue an argument that ensued between them earlier in the day. During the argument, Will expresses his discontent, associated with always having to pay for and take care of their common expenses (dinner, bills, dry cleaning, wedding gifts, and cards). He also admits his desire to be invited to such events with a male guest and wonders why his invitations are always marked "Will and Grace" instead of "Will and guest."

As both the argument and the ceremony unfold, the justice of the peace calls upon friends and family members (of Joe and Larry) to share their readings. Again, she never specifies the names of the two people who stand at the altar: "And now I'd like to call upon your friends here who have some words they'd like to share with you." In turn both Jack McFarland and Joe's sister Joan offer their individual readings. Again, during Joan's reading, the camera cuts away to focus on the ongoing argument between Will and Grace. In the midst of this "lovers' quarrel," the justice of the peace interrupts Will and Grace and calls upon them to stand and do their reading.[1] It is important to note here that both Jack and Joan have been asked to do individual readings.

The fact that Will and Grace do a joint reading is exceptional because at most American weddings, while a song may be sung in duet, a reading is usually done individually. Thus, considering the circumstances, this narrative situation seems extraordinary as it foregrounds Will and Grace, who must stand side by side in a wedding-like pose while they read from a printed card:

WILL: When I'm feeling like there's no love coming to me . . .

GRACE: And I have no love to give . . .

WILL: When I'm feeling separated from the world . . .

GRACE: And cut off from myself . . .

WILL: When I'm feeling annoyed by every little thing . . .

GRACE: Because I'm not getting what I want . . . I'll remember that there is an infinite amount of love available to me.

WILL: And I'll see it in you.

GRACE: I'll remember that I am complete within myself . . .

WILL: So I'll never have to look to you to complete me.

WILL AND GRACE: And most of all, I'll remember that everything that I really need I already have, and whatever I don't have will come to me when I'm ready to receive it.

WILL: (To Grace) Oh, my God. I am so sorry.

GRACE: Me, too.

WILL: I love you. You know that, right?

GRACE: I know.

(Joe and Larry glance nervously at each other.)

WILL: Don't you?

GRACE: I do. And you know I love you, right?

WILL: I do. (Will and Grace kiss and hug)

(Everyone claps. Will and Grace hold hands and walk down the aisle.)

GRACE: Thanks for coming!

JOE: Guys? Hey, guys! Guys! We're not really done here.

(Embarrassed, Will and Grace quickly sit back down.)

As Will and Grace do the reading, little by little they turn toward each other; by the end of the recitation, they are actually facing each other and pronouncing the words in unison. Once the reading is complete, Will and Grace remain standing and proceed to share their feelings for each other in a public display that is not unlike exchanging marriage vows. Each one confirms a commitment to the other with the traditionally scripted wedding phrase, "I do." Moreover, when Will and Grace exchange their mutual remarks about "love," the camera cuts away to the nervous same-sex couple (Joe and Larry), and the television laugh track intervenes, suggesting that viewers take notice of this narrative twist. In addition, they consummate this "relationship" by sealing the narrative with a kiss and proceeding to leave the chapel in the traditional chain of matrimonial events. Finally, the wedding attendants acknowledge this consummation by clapping.

It is important to note that the civil union between Joe and Larry is never visually consummated on-screen. There is no exchange of vows or any physical display of affection between the two of them during the ceremony. The only exchange that ensues involves a worried look that subtly suggests their frustration with Will and Grace, who take over, or "steal the spotlight," at their civil union ceremony. The justice of the peace never delivers any sort of performative declaration or final proclamation ("I now pronounce you . . .") that could consecrate this union or authenticate, naturalize, or normalize such an event for television viewers. The congregation never has the opportunity to recognize the couple as bound in any kind of union. After the ceremony, the camera cuts to Joe and Larry who unwrap various wedding gifts and thank their attendants for their kindness. This image is balanced and to some degree neutralized, however, by the image of Will and Grace, who sit nestled in a corner sharing a single piece of wedding cake. Finally, the fact that Will and Grace have offered a single wedding gift with a card signed "from Will and Grace" reconfirms Will and Grace's relationship for both the characters and viewers.

The writers of *Will & Grace* recycle many elements of a marriage narrative in several episodes throughout the sitcom's first four seasons. Moreover, the kiss is often recycled to situate their relationship into a heteronormative framework. I would like to stress that it is not one individual episode or occurrence, per se, that makes the straight kiss so problematic on a "gay sitcom." On the contrary, it is the ceaseless repetition of such visual acts throughout the four seasons, not only between Will and Grace, but also between Jack and Rosario and Jack and Karen, that allows a narrative of heteronormativity to emerge. Indeed, to some extent *Will & Grace* parodies both gay and straight relationships. This is certainly the case with Grace and her boyfriend Josh (with her constant neglect of him and his annoying forehead kisses), as well as with the superficial relationship between Karen and her unseen husband Stanley. Moreover, Karen's character regularly challenges family values through her unapologetic use of alcohol and drugs, disinterest in her children, and her allusions to adulterous acts. Some scholars even argue that Karen represents the "queerest" (most non-normative) character on the show (Holleran 66; Kanner 34–35). Nevertheless, it is important to remember the power of the visual message and the repetition of such messages on actors that makes characters appear "believable," "natural," and "realistic" in both their gendered and sexually oriented roles.

Judith Butler reminds us that the body is but "a passive medium that is signified by an inscription from a cultural source figured as 'external' to the body" (*Gender Trouble* 129). Indeed, an individual's (gender or sexual) identity becomes inscribed on the surface of the body through carefully crafted artifice (136). Butler adds that "the action of gender requires a performance that is *repeated* . . . gender is an identity tenuously constituted in time, instituted in an exterior space through a *stylized repetition of acts*" (emphasis in original) (140). Similarly, sexual orientation, as it appears on the small and big screens, is created through a stylized repetition of acts, through visualized production and reproduction. Will and Grace's repeated affection and exchange of kisses (across multiple episodes) allow Will to emerge as a "straight character," and Will and Grace to "come out" as the palatable "straight couple" for television viewers. Similarly, I believe it is Jack's visual coupling with Karen and Rosario that allows him to "pass" on prime-time television despite his outrageously flaming comments and behavior. The repeated acts of kissing that take place between Will and Grace (as well as between Jack and his assorted female side-kicks and between Grace and her assorted boyfriends) authenticates and normalizes straight relationships and negates or nullifies the signs of a homosexual narrative. Indeed, verbal or linguistic parody takes place regularly on the show. Nevertheless, it is the visual message that works with, and at times against, these verbal messages to create meaning for television viewers.

YOU MAY KISS THE . . . NOT YOUR BOYFRIEND, MY ASS!

In comparison to the opposite-sex kisses that regularly take place between characters on *Will & Grace*, the same-sex (male-male) kiss only emerges once during the show's first four years, and television viewers must wait until halfway through the second season to see such a display. In this episode, "Acting Out," Will, Grace, and Jack all become television spectators as they settle in to watch "the first ever prime-time kiss between two men" on their new favorite television sitcom, *Along Came You*. The three characters sit on the couch and hold hands (Grace sits between Will and Jack) as they await the lip lock between the two male characters. The kiss never comes.

At the end of this scene, both Jack and Grace express their shared disappointment with the show while Will reinforces the heteronormative narrative and conservative (middle-class) values with his voice of homophobic reason: "Clearly, nobody wants to see two men kissing on television. Not the network, not the viewers, not the advertiser." This spectatorial disappointment provokes

Jack to take matters into his own hands by filing an official complaint at NBC headquarters. Will eventually follows Jack down to the NBC studios where they meet NBC's executive vice president in charge of public relations, who tells them: "But you will never see two gay men kissing on network television." Jack responds: "Wha—It's a gay network, for God's sake! The symbol is a peacock!" Indeed, there is room for some queer linguistic maneuver in this episode as Jack mocks the network that produces the very sitcom in which he appears. Nonetheless, Jack does not see any resolution to his complaint from the television executives.

After leaving the NBC headquarters, Jack and Will spot weatherman Al Roker in the street hosting NBC's *The Today Show*. After getting Roker's attention and following a bit of idle conversation with the weatherman, Jack proceeds to make his plea "on national television" to see "two hotties get it on."

> JACK: . . . the reason we're here. Um, I don't know if you're aware, but on this week's episode of *Along Came You*, there was supposed to be a kiss and there wasn't.
>
> AL ROKER: You know, Jack, sometimes a kiss is just not a kiss. Do we have any annivers—
>
> JACK: Whoa, whoa, back to Jack. We went to complain, and this closet case upstairs—cute, in an offbeat way, got his number—totally gave us the brush off. And I just want to know how long I'm going to have to wait until I can see two gay men kiss on network television.
>
> WILL: Not as long as you'd think.
>
> (Will grabs Jack and kisses him. The crowd cheers.)

At first glance, it appears that the gay kiss (between Will and Jack) has finally emerged on a major network sitcom. The writers have made the attempt to authenticate the characters of Will and Jack by depicting them going into the NBC studios. This is not unlike the effect of the "live camera" on *Late Night with Jay Leno* or *Saturday Night Live* (or any of the other voyeuristic shows including *MTV Real World, Survivor,* and *Big Brother*) that presents seemingly "real" or "live" situations. This episode, however, becomes sanctified or "authenticated" with the use of Al Roker and *The Today Show* label because the weatherman is a "real-life" figure who may listen to Jack and broadcast his message on "live" television. Jack also attempts to make this experience as real as possible for the viewers of *Will & Grace* when he says, "We need to get the message out there . . . I know! I'll write an epic poem and post it on my web site—www.justjack. com. . . ." In fact, this Web site did exist when this episode first aired. Subsequently, the "justjack" Web site has been updated and has moved to http://www.nbci.com/willandgrace.

Finally, the writers of this episode have tried to authenticate this gay kiss by placing Jack and Will on the street with hundreds of other "real" spectators. Indeed, the event is well strategized; it cannot be missed, and all of New York City is there to see it. In Holleran's words: "[the characters] seemed so free, so believable all of a sudden, out in the open air. There was spaciousness about their world, and suddenly the possibility of their interaction with real life, the real city, and real emotions, rose up" (66). Like many of the kisses that appear on *Will & Grace*, the "gay kiss" is recognized and encouraged by the roar of the onlooking spectators.

This particular episode clearly illustrates a lack of affection, a situation that persists between same-sex characters on prime-time commercial television. First, Will kisses Jack in a "read my lips" fashion to make a political statement about gay representations in the media. It is done out of the blue and is not "passionate" per se. Will admits, "four seconds before we did it, I didn't know I was going to do it. And then . . . I just did it." Moreover, Jack's reaction does not indicate any passion directed for Will: "I just pray none of my boyfriends saw that tragic display. 'Cause that's like five serious long-term relationships down the tube." Neither character can explain the precise goal of the kiss or be hopeful of a positive outcome from it.

It is important to remember that at the very moment the kiss occurs, Will and Jack have become actors in a television broadcast *(The Today Show)* within another television show *(Will & Grace)*. This is a production within a production, or in theatrical terms, a play within a play (Forestier). So many layers of artifice now exist between the spectator of *Will & Grace* and the two characters (Will and Jack) that the kiss remains virtually impossible to read as an authentic form of expression between two gay men. They are no longer the weekly characters in the first-level text (Will and Jack in *Will & Grace*) but are now characters in the second-level text (Will and Jack in *Will & Grace* in *The Today Show*) involved in the theatrics of this new layer. The other characters from *Will & Grace* have become the spectator-characters of the first-level text who watch Will and Jack on the small screen of the second-level text.

By tuning in to *The Today Show* and watching Will and Jack perform their gay identity, everyone else on *Will & Grace* has become a spectator-character, and in turn this first layer of text has become more "real" and closer to the television audience's lived experience than what transpires between Will and Jack on the set of *The Today Show*. In a sense, the *Will & Grace* set has dissolved as spectator-characters emerge; moreover, as television spectators we are drawn into the "realness" of this first level of text. For example, Grace and her boyfriend, Josh, watch *The Today Show* from bed. Karen and her husband, Stan, watch it from the tub. Mrs. Freeman (the assistant to Will's boss, Ben Doucette) watches from the law firm. One would think that this would authenticate the kiss between Will and Jack. As television viewers, however, we become as interested, if not more interested, in the point of view of the spectator-characters who appear almost as real as we are, watching NBC television. It is also worth noting that the laugh track intervenes here to draw our attention to the reaction of the spectator-characters and detract us from the kissing event itself. Karen gasps at the sight of the two men kissing and sinks into the tub. Mrs. Freeman shares her own acrimonious opinion of Will and Jack's act: "Not your boyfriend, my ass." Finally, Grace freaks out since she has been trying to break up with Josh by convincing him that she is in love with Will. In fact, it is her reaction to this lip event that is the most extreme, as she later storms into Will's apartment and exclaims, "Well, thank you very much! Because of your little on-air lip lock, I am going to spend the next week in an *ashram* with no heat with my undumped boyfriend Josh . . . some big queen on *The Today Show* blew my alibi."

The television audience becomes separated from the gay kiss—not only through the multiple layers of action that take place, but also through the displacement of viewing pleasure. As viewers, we are diverted by the reaction of the new spectators (Grace, Josh, Karen, and Mrs. Freeman), and it is at least in portion from their reactions during this narrative game that we draw our viewing pleasure. Grace's words serve as a reminder that Will and Grace should be together in principle, and it is her reaction coupled with her word choice that counteract, or help to negate, the "homosexual act" that has just occurred. Grace's use of the word "queen" emphasizes how this attempted act of same-sex affection on television was an unusual, if not derogatory, homosexual act. In a sense, her voice of reason intervenes at the end of this episode and acts as a deus ex machina to bring the heteronormative narrative back where it belongs.

CONCLUDING REMARKS: IN SEARCH OF HOMONORMATIVE NARRATIVES

In this chapter, I have emphasized the absence of the "gay kiss" and the problematic recurrence of the "straight kiss" on a gay sitcom. We could argue that *Will & Grace* is just a sitcom, and viewers should not expect more from this show than a few laughs. The fact remains, however, that a limited range of (straight) signifiers, story lines, and plots are recycled on this sitcom and throughout a whole range of commercial television shows that include gay and lesbian characters. It is worth noting that in the fall of 2001, CBS began airing the new sitcom *The Ellen Show*. In a July 2001 interview, Ellen DeGeneres admitted that her former show *(Ellen)* "got to be too issue-oriented" and promised that her new show would be "all about funny this time" (hence, less political) (Keveney 3D). In *The Ellen Show*, DeGeneres plays a gay character who returns to her small hometown after having just left a relationship.[2] This is the same premise on which *Will & Grace* began in 1998. Hence, in parallel

to *Will & Grace* (and their relationship), many commercial prime-time television series still continue to avoid the candid treatment of gay characters and
their stories by portraying them as "de-sexed" and "uncoupled" second-class
citizens who must participate in heteronormative settings to find a sense of
"normalcy" or "belonging." It should come as no surprise that *Will & Grace* has
received overwhelming support from (straight) "middle America," since the
show produces and reproduces gay characters (and their female counterparts)
in multiple heteronormative situations.

Indeed, we must be thankful to NBC, the producers, writers, and actors
of *Will & Grace* for tackling such a touchy subject and bringing it to the small
screen. This show has certainly begun to lead American television out of the
closet by putting gay male characters on prime-time commercial television.
Nonetheless, as *Will & Grace* still foregrounds heterosexuality, heteronormativity, and family values, especially on the visual level, these gay male characters still remain closeted—with reference to same-sex affection and intimacy.
These gay representations obscure the "lived reality" of many gays and lesbians
by suggesting that only "good" sexual citizens (those who subscribe to heterosexuality or heteronormativity) are allowed access to "healthy" and "positive"
relationships in which they can care for each other and live together (Bell and
Binnie 26). We must ask commercial television producers and scriptwriters to
rethink the old dominant narratives that depict only long-term, monogamous,
heteronormative pairings. The production and reproduction of queer images
is truly the only means by which to neutralize compulsory heterosexuality and
to create narrative spaces in which gay and lesbian characters and their
lifestyles can emerge on the small screen as desirable alternatives.

As this chapter goes to press, *Will & Grace* has completed its seventh year
on NBC. In 2002–2003, Grace marries Leo (a Jewish doctor played by Harry
Connick, Jr.) and they move across town into a Brooklyn apartment.
Nonetheless, this heterosexual coupling does not prevent the two eponymous
characters from continuing to spend most of their time together. Furthermore,
in 2003–2004, Grace and Leo separate after she discovers that the doctor has
slept with another woman wile on assignment with Doctors Without Borders.
During the same season (spring 2004), the sitcom also tempts television viewers with a poential same-sex relationship for Will with the introduction of
Vince (a New York City police officer played by Bobby Cannavale). In less
than one complete television season, however, this gay couple splits when
Vince loses his job and becomes too burdensome on a professionally successful Will. Hence, a full-fledged, recurring same-sex relationship still remains
strikingly absent on the show while the heteronormative coupling of Will and
Grace returns full and center when she moves back in after her separation.
Indeed, faithful sitcom viewers watch patiently to see how NBC (and the
other major television companies) will negotiate either a same-sex kiss or relationship that is both passionate and persistent. We can only hope that the

"next generation" of commercial television shows that follows *Will & Grace* will attempt to open new doors and "boldly go where no 'gay' sitcom has gone before" by representing same-sex narratives in more visible ways.

NOTES

I would like to thank both Van Cagle and the Center for the Study of Media and Society at GLAAD for providing the financial support during this research project. An earlier version of this chapter was presented as part of the plenary session on *Will & Grace* at the Eighth Annual Conference on Lavender Languages and Linguistics held in September 2000 at the American University in Washington, D.C. Several colleagues have read various drafts and offered helpful suggestions during both the conceptualization and rewriting of this chapter. In particular, I would like to thank Bill Leap, Melinda Kanner, Susan Crutchfield, Betsy Morgan, and Carmen Wilson.

1. This scene is hauntingly similar to the first-year season finale in which Jack and Rosario get married and Will and Grace argue while sitting in attendance.

2. Since the completion of this piece, CBS has canceled *The Ellen Show*, due to lack of viewer interest.

CHAPTER 15

Poofs—Cheesy and Other

Identity Politics as Commodity in *South Park*

Karen Anijar, Hsueh-hua Vivian Chen, and Thomas E. Walker

Do we need some one, some thing to believe in? A hero perhaps? From the dank reaches of the frozen West here come cowboys. Albeit cartoon cowboys.

> *South Park* . . . is, simply, the most clever show on TV. Its wry social commentary mixed with surrealistic, sophomoric humor has reached just about every demographic. Think: Man Ray does Peanuts.
> —David S. Evans in http://gaytoday.badpuppy.com

> Every now and then there comes a show everyone is talking about: . . . *South Park* . . . There is no doubt that this show is either the funniest show out there or the sign of the next apocalypse.
> —Jay Leno on *The Tonight Show* (in Cartmanfan)

South Park is described as the "most extraordinary television cult since *The X Files* went mainstream" (Clark C8). *South Park* is a half-hour (deliberately poorly) animated cartoon. Shown on Comedy Central, the cable program is touted for describing (disparagingly) the prejudices and preoccupations of small-town America. It is a satire that is "an Ecstasy tab set [in] a story in dysfunctional America" (Clark C8); "Peanuts on acid . . . whose intelligent wit overshadows the simplicity of its drawings" (Millar 11); "the most sophisticated show on television" (Jay Leno, qtd. in Cartmanfan); or a program whose crudeness and lewdness makes it a dangerous subversion (perversion) for young people. A cartoon that engenders so many accolades and so much disdain must really mean something.

In contemporary media parlance, this also means that it is worth quite a bit. Beyond the literal self-referential merchandising, what else might this phenomenon be pushing? In this chapter we explore identity commerce and related concerns surrounding the problematic commodification of gay identity as demonstrated in *South Park*.

THEY SAY QUITE A BIT, BUT WHAT DO THEY *SAY*?

> "You can't teach a gay dog straight tricks."
> —Chef in *South Park*

TOWNSMAN: Speech!

FRANK: Stan, what do you want to tell the world about this stunning almost victory?

STAN: It's really cool that we beat the spread against the Cowboys.

CROWD: Woooo!

STAN: And it's OK to be gay!

Silence.

JIMBO: What?!?

STAN: Being gay is just part of nature, and a beautiful thing.

MR. GARRISON: What the hell is he talking about?

For a long period of time *South Park* was the thing to watch. It struck a chord with many young people, who are a "generation [. . .] conceived in the sights and sounds of media culture, weaned on it, socialized by the glass teat of television used as pacifier, baby sitter, and educator by a generation of parents for whom media culture, especially television, was a natural background and constitutive part of everyday life" (Kellner 143). We all create meaning out of the texts that inform our everyday lives. *South Park* is just one text that speaks to and interanimates the terrain of contemporary adolescence with an

FIGURE 15.1. Big Gay Al in *South Park*, 1997– . Photo courtesy of Photofest. Used by permission.

explicit inclusion of and discussion on homosexuality best exemplified by Big Gay Al, an occasionally recurring character introduced in the early episode entitled "Big Gay Al's Big Gay Boatride." What does *South Park* say about homosexuality? Perhaps more importantly, how are homosexual images that appear in popular television texts translated and interpreted?

THROWN TO THE MARKET

The malls of America are filled to the brim with hot-selling *South Park* items, ranging from plush dolls to boxer shorts to empty boxes of cheesy poofs (Cartman's favorite snack food). You simply cannot have a phenomenon without a marketing strategy.

Beyond the literal merchandising of the show, within the popular imaginary, a histrionic (albeit ahistorical) notion of causality occurs. The presumption is that "impressionable youth" emulate or imitate and ultimately become (or are made into) mindless copies (automatons) of what they see in this or other programs. Mathews *(Global Culture)* suggests cultural identity involves a "cultural supermarket"—a social world in which subject-consumers exist and interact, shopping for a variety of possible options surrounding identity. We purchase our identities in the same manner we purchase plush dolls and snack food. You are what you wear, eat, and own; identities (even seemingly objectionable ones) sit on store shelves—a social space (the mall is above all a social space)—while contemporary marketers attempt to hawk identities (such as the hip, cool, and "with it" personae). The President of the United States tells us that it is our patriotic duty to consume. Advertisers hawk, kids shop, parents spend and fret, and political pundits promise (re)action. *South Park* models and glorifies identity shopping through the character of Eric Cartman, who regularly seeks to remake himself as bodybuilder ("Beefcake. BEEFCAKE!"), as apprentice police officer ("Respect my authori-tay") and as troubled teen/talk show guest ("Whatever! I'll do what I want").

Within this overly determined causal model, if a child finds *South Park* irresistible will he or she turn into a cartoon character? Will he or she use words like "fart" or "bitch"? Will she or he bring home a gay dog? Will she or he start dressing in drag? Why is what is irresistible (read as interesting) seen as a pejorative? Further, what is *South Park* saying that is so transgressive or transformative as to engender the wrath of the scions of public morality? How can something that sells well be a transgressive space? Or, does *South Park*'s apparent transgressive status make it more appealing to the market, therefore buying into the very forces it presumably attempts to castigate?

PARTY-TIME: AREN'T YOU GLAAD YOU CHOSE GAY?

A Big Gay Al float participated in the 1997 Greenwich Village Halloween Parade (if you can make it there you can make it anywhere, as the song goes). The following announcement was proudly placed on Comedy Central's Web site: "Come aboard . . . we're expecting you on the *South Park* 'Big Gay Al's Big Gay Float' at the 24th Annual Village Halloween Parade in New York's Greenwich Village . . . join the Halloween festivities by dressing up as your favorite *South Park* character . . . receive a free *South Park* T-shirt!" (www.comedycentral.com). Comedy Central as a corporate entity would not sponsor a float in a parade unless it helped their corporate profit interests. And yet, we wonder, can *South Park* really be that mainstream? Has gay, too, become mainstream? How do the forces of commodification and globalization normalize countercultural and insurgent cultural artifacts, appropriating and rearticulating everything back into the mainstream center?

Awards given by the Gay and Lesbian Alliance Against Defamation (GLAAD) have been sponsored by Absolut vodka, American Airlines, Sony, Wells Fargo Bank, ABC Entertainment, *Entertainment Weekly*, Norman Lear, and Sid Steinberg. In a world of intensified consumerism, everything is thrown into the marketplace and appropriated for consumption. Marketers initially can sell "gay," for example, to those who already identify with the identity: "gay" is sold to gays. This plays, in part, on the erroneous notion that gays' disposable incomes are higher than heterosexuals' disposable incomes. The gay market is positioned as an upper-income market, paralleling Foucault's theorizing in relation to economy and sexuality. Even if universally true, this market is numerically small, and successful marketing would, at some finite point, saturate the market. Given the nature of capitalism, this would be deadly, since all markets continually need to expand.

Limited consumer niches (that is, small identity categories) are economically insufficient. To maximize the "product," the product's appeal needs to increase in an ever-expanding base. Advertisers seek to optimize their products' profitability by seeking elements that appeal to everybody. Homosexuality, therefore, needs to be liberated as controversial identity from the "backroom" of society (the restricted area where good people do not shop) and then with a good spin, thrust as a "fresh new look" to spotlighted areas, making it the latest fad (for example, lesbian chic, the homoeroticism of Abercrombie and Fitch ads, and the irresistibly gay characters on *Will & Grace*). Nicely packaged "queer" identity is served up with gusto for all (identity) shoppers. Economic agendas thereby create criteria of normality. Difference is leveled into a chicken-in-every-pot, mall-in-every-town sameness.

While seemingly "progressive" in normalizing marginal nonheterosexual identity, we worry that such an offering of the gay and lesbian communities (as consumable object-subject) weakens, erases, and undermines the significant political aspects of identity. This is definitely a bit ironic because identities are socially constructed, the category of identity itself is also socially constructed, and we organize the political around the socially created categorical. The erroneous (right wing) reactionary discourse disguised as progressive political base is embedded in the notion that one can "choose" to be gay; that "gay" is a fashion statement for purchase. Fashion and style may well invite people to be part of a consuming "in" crowd, but style and fashion have nothing to do with the political aspects of coming out, staying out, and living gay. Equal market share cannot be conflated with equal rights. In order to gain a modicum of respectability in the marketplace, homosexuality is painted as a variation of heterosexuality (it sells better that way). The effects are so pervasive and profound that it even becomes difficult to distinguish gay magazines from straight magazines; oftentimes sexuality remains an unmarked identifier. In this one-dimensional, unmarked version of sexuality, homosexuality is reduced to good cultural exemplars of gay men trying to adopt children, Will and Grace trying to have a baby, and Big Gay Al caring for the unwanted animals and children of South Park. Marketing forces paint homosexuality as fashionable, as an advertisement. Advertising transforms homosexuality into a rather exclusive club of the White and bourgeoisie and privileged. Thus, we have benevolent White gay depictions that are marketed for kind consumption, such as Jack on *Will & Grace*, Smithers in *The Simpsons*, and Big Gay Al in *South Park*. But the characters are devoid of political agency. Other identities on *South Park* (and other programs) can also be seen as essentializing or stereotyping identities into stock characters. For example, the hypersexual Black male of *South Park*'s Chef, the modern mammy of *Gimme a Break*, and the ubiquitous prime-time dumb blond or slow-witted jock. We find that rather disturbing. Indeed, we find any form of essentializing rather disturbing. But, we find essentialisms defined by the locus of capitalism the most disturbing of all.

CATEGORICAL ESSENTIALISMS— EPISTEMIC ESSENTIALISM

Categorical social conceptual constructs are based on modernist, positivist either/or binaries of distinction. Categories help map a dichotomous, albeit efficient, mode of playing out or framing a social order. The use of the categorical as a tool in the service of social differentiation is rife with evaluation and esoteric criteria of belonging. Although the categorical professes to be a mapping tool, it is an aggressive, annihilating strategy that neutralizes difference by positing the category and naming parameters of the category itself. The categorical essentializes, framing and focusing on what is believed to be fundamental biological, emotional, and cognitive structures, further "objecti-fying" what is subjective, and constructing a plethora of processes as the (only) absolute thing. The myopic morality, a peculiar framework, is seen as a higher order by many who cling to modernist notions like a buoy in a tempestuous sea of change.

Yet, this scaffolding of knowledge does have profound political implica-tions in its perversion. Face it, some bodies are valued more than others; and some people are more valuable than others. Mr. Garrison, the teacher on *South Park*, explains in the following scene from "Big Gay Al's Big Gay Boatride":

MR. GARRISON: Who should we call on next Mr. Hat?

MR. HAT: Well, how about Stan, our little South Park quarterback star?

MR. GARRISON: Oh, good idea. Ok Stanley, you're next.

STAN: Um, I'm not really prepared either.

MR. GARRISON: Well, just make something up, like Eric did.

STAN: Ok, uh. Asian culture has plagued our fragile earth for many years. We must end it—

MR. GARRISON: Excellent. A minus.

CARTMAN: Eh.

STAN: Wow, cool!

CARTMAN: Wait a minute, why the hell does he get an A minus?

MR. GARRISON: Eric, Stanley just might lead our team to victory against the Middlepark Cowboys for the first time in decades. And we treat star athletes better 'cause they're better people.

CARTMAN: That's not fair!

MR. HAT: Life isn't fair kiddo, get used to it.

In this example, star athletes are essentialized, and we all have to get used to it.

FAIRNESS BY WALK AND BY TALK?

BULLY 2: Hey Stan, your dog been to any Pride marches lately?

BULLY 1: Huh huh, yeh, maybe you should take him to a Barbra Streisand concert.

Contemporary gay pride marches commemorate the Stonewall riots of 1969, which represented a historically and socially significant moment within the gay and lesbian communities. Swept up in the liberatory movements of the 1960s, the patrons of the New York City gay bar Stonewall resisted a police raid, which they felt demonstrated unfair police (and larger social) discrimination. As the symbolic birth of the gay rights movement, Stonewall was a clarion call for freedom. The banners proclaimed, "We Are Everywhere and We Are Free" (Bronski 90). The spirit of Stonewall insisted that a gay identity existed as a political and cultural formation. And then came queer theory.

Queer theory deliberates and contemplates concerns surrounding discourses of power that operate along lines of gender, sex, and sexuality. In some ways, queer theory and feminist theory share several notions. Both have tended to neglect class, racial, and ethnic exigencies. We sense queer theory far too often seems to overlook interanimating processes, maintaining a bourgeoisie position, oftentimes a voguish postmodern posturing. In other words, it is one more identifier in a game of static-location-identity politics. Depoliticizing what must be both theoretically rich and connected, queer theories are often far too conceptual and opaquely abstract, resisting piercing and penetration. In doing so, queer theory enters into a hermeneutic circle jerk of politicized apoliticalness. In queer theory's effort to do away with essentialisms, it tends to essentialize.

The experiences of gay and lesbian communities cannot be reduced to kitsch superlatives. The biggest thermometer in the world is in California, also home of the best homosexuality. Lives cannot be reduced to the pornographic postmodern that seeks to queer America, by making queerness something normal, something centrist, something everyday, something banal. "Shopping" is not a "substitute for change" (Allen 283). We are asking for, begging for, some more Stonewall effect, some different Stonewall effect, some gay Stonewall effect. We want to see political action, not semiotic rearticulation.

But, when suburbanites come to watch the Los Angeles gay pride parade are they coming for a show? Are they proclaiming their solidarity with the gay and lesbian community? Or are they engaging in a fashion statement? When the Big Gay Al float leads the Greenwich Village parade and is mainlined on Comedy Central's site for middle America to see ("Hey there, Mom and Dad, let's go to NYC to see the Empire State Building and the Big Gay Al float!") are we speaking about gay pride and rights anymore, or are we speaking about homosexuality "brought to you by Frito's corn chips?"

REPRODUCING GAYNESS

In "Tom's Rhinoplasty" Kyle, Stan, and Cartman vie for the affections of a pretty substitute teacher who wears bare-midriff outfits. After they discover that she is a lesbian, they decide that the way to her heart is to become lesbians, too. There is one problem—they do not know what a lesbian is. When

Kyle and Stan later encounter Cartman in his living room eating a cardboard box, he explains, "My mom said if I chow enough box, I can be a lesbian." Crude, but (in many ways) honest in articulating the presumed gay-ing and gay-ability of *Will & Grace*'s United States.

Discussing this chapter with several colleagues in other areas of the country, we were told "many people pose as gays and lesbians because *it* is *in*" and that "the neighbors all visited the gay couple when they moved in across the street . . . but nobody bothered to visit us." This colleague theorized that he and his wife were just not that fashionable or that the neighborhood reaction also signified "how far gay rights had come." But there is homophobia embedded in his comments: the erasure of difference, and a leveling effect when lives are reduced to a fashion statement. Would our contemporaries say the same thing about African Americans, Latinos, or even Marxists? What do the creators of *South Park* mean when they say "Everybody is just a little bit gay." Maybe they mean "everybody" wants to be gay. Of course, what "they" mean is a particular gay(ness) depicted in the advertisements of hip, witty, cosmopolitan, sophisticated, rich, and White—this construction neglects oppression, power formations, and the day-to-day struggles of gays and lesbians attempting to negotiate an inhospitable straight terrain.

Queer theory shares with much of contemporary postmodernism an emphasis on representation as an aesthetic rather than a political problem, a desire to deconstruct all fixed points in the interests of "destabilizing" and "decentering" our preconceptions. Given the arcane language within which a sizable amount of such theory is written, theory is almost totally ignored by the vast majority of people whose lives it purports to describe (Altman). Or transform. And what good is queer theory if there are no queers in the center?

IDENTITY-AS-PRODUCT VS. IDENTITY-AS-PROCESS

So, we have advertisers attempting to commodify, normalize, and sell gayness (and other marginal/objectionable identities), and the dual concerns that youth will buy into these products (parental worry) and that the marginal groups will be homogenized and erased in the process (our worry). Even if we accept the identity-as-product idea, the undesirable/marginal identity is made desirable, is centered, by the commodification process. Bart Simpson, for example, has lost much of his "forbidden fruit" intrigue of the early 1990s because his marketers were so successful in centering him in the marketplace. Part of the allure of *South Park* to teens is its resistance appeal; they like it in part because authority figures do not. Tastes change. The once forbidden, once fashionable, becomes relegated to bland normalcy among all the other identities on the warehouse store shelves, and the next, latest "thing" becomes all the rage . . . and nothing changes.

Avoiding all this, a communicative perspective sees identities as formed, changed, and negotiated through social interaction. These identities are enacted or performed through communication and relationships, and constitutive of social pattern (Gergen). From this perspective, the self is not only created through and in social interaction, but interaction is an enactment of self (Carbaugh). Hecht argues that "identity is inherently a communicative process and must be understood as a transaction," extending the concept of identity beyond the individual to interactions and relationships (78). Harris and Hall similarly stress that identity is more a process than a product, is about "becoming" rather than about "being." Hedge agrees with Hall that we should think of identity "as a production which is never complete, always in process, and always constituted from within, not outside, representation" (qtd. in Hall, "Cultural" 222). Seen in this way, the identity-as-product metaphor breaks down. Identity cannot sit on shelves, be imposed by advertisers/entertainers/educators or be swallowed whole by our impressionable youth—there is no finite, static, essential commodity to begin with. Instead, identity is in the process—the interpretation and negotiation with others, which may be initiated by the show.

IS EVERYTHING QUEER?
OUGHT AMERICA BE QUEERED?

Sparky, trekking through the snow, comes to Big Gay Al's Big Gay Animal Sanctuary.

BIG GAY AL: Hello there little pup, I'm Big Gay Al.

Sparky looks at him.

BIG GAY AL: Have you been outcast?

Sparky pants an affirmative.

BIG GAY AL: Well then, I'm so glad you found my Big Gay Animal Sanctuary. We're all big gay friends here. Would you like to live with us?

Sparky pants an affirmative.

BIG GAY AL: Come on in little fellow. Nobody will ever oppress you here.

—"Big Gay Al's Big Gay Boatride"

We all are part of several processes-positions, but never something that is static. All things, all subjects, are not equal; some things are marked, others are not.

The question becomes one of becoming conscious of our subject position in a peculiar semiotic stew of signification. BUT, and we capitalize the word for a reason, are all things so relative that they fall into a solipsistic relativism that renders them meaningless? Can there be a brick in the bricolage? Are gender and sexuality merely performances that can be manipulated? Are they codes and costumes without a core? In the pornographic postmodern, politics, power, and polemics become poetic, and criticism becomes an exercise in thematic lavender hazes of just-oh-so-marvelous metaphors. The auto-erotic-academic sleight of hand and twist of tongue takes precedence over the political. Once the political is obscured it all descends into unmercifully vapid vacuousness.

VIVE LA DIFFÉRENCE? OR VIVE LA MARKET? OR IS THIS ALL A CRUEL JOKE?

MR. GARRISON: Oh, stop filling his head with that queer-loving propaganda.

CHEF: Say what?!? You of all people should be sympathetic.

MR. GARRISON: What do you mean?

CHEF: Well, you're gay aren't you?

MR. GARRISON: What?!? What the hell are you talking about?!? I am not gay.

CHEF: Well, you sure do act like it.

MR. GARRISON: I just act that way to get chicks, dumb ass.

Chef looks puzzled but seems to wonder.

—"Big Gay Al's Big Gay Boatride"

Somewhere between the liberatory moment of Stonewall and the horrors of the AIDS crisis, a transformation of gayness occurred. This fundamentally Western reconceptualization transpired in conditions and in a time that also signaled the triumph of capitalism and a retreat from any notions surrounding egalitarian social justice and democracy. The fantasy becomes an illusion of a unitary whole. So, democracy couples with capitalism, liberalism dabbles with change, and the whole process is posited as natural and logical and whole. It argues that homosexuality, like jean jackets and nose piercings, can and will be spread through (identity) market forces; this is called political and purchase progress (it is acceptance!), and it is called good. It is, in fact, a giant drag performance. Change comes through struggle not through a natural, spontaneous production of capitalist expansion. Change is not ahistorical; equal market share is not actual political equity. That we are "all" objectified does not make any us of equal.

We must not lose sight of this discursive struggle simply because we see images of gay characters on the screen. It is not sufficient that "we have never had it so queer" (Edge and Lyttle 20). "In the twilight," to quote Anna Deavere Smith, "it is important that we sharpen our vision. We might not like what we see," she says, but in order to change it, we have to see it clearly (xii). Identity rights cannot be reduced to theory divorced from practice or practice divorced from theory or cartoon caricatures of human beings or parades for capitalist consumption.

PART SIX

Work and Social Class

Women, Love, and Work

The Doris Day Show as Cultural Dialogue

Phyllis Scrocco Zrzavy

A culturally inscribed perspective on the analysis of popular culture focuses on the functions of entertainment as a social construction and negotiation of reality (Newcomb and Hirsch 563). As John Belton has observed, the American comedy genre "endorses change as a positive feature of history, unlike tragedy, which conceives of change negatively" (Belton 145). The televised situation comedy, in particular, operates as "a site of negotiation of cultural change and difference" (Neale and Krutnik 237), and the genre occupies a subjunctive space, a liminal realm in which cultural mediation can occur through the explorations of "supposition, desire, hypothesis, [and] possibility" (Turner, *Drums* 82).

Even the most cursory look at the history of broadcasting confirms that the situation comedy has a long-standing tradition of mediating tensions and ambiguities in American culture, and women and their changing roles in society have found particularly pertinent representations in the genre. Media critics and scholars have recognized the cultural significance of series as varied as *Sex and the City* (Hensley), *Ellen* (DeCaro; Goldstein), *Murphy Brown* (Alley and Brown), *The Golden Girls* (Kaler), *Roseanne* (Rowe), and *Laverne &*

Shirley (Staiger). *Maude* has been lauded for its boundary-breaking treatment of women's issues, as have been *The Mary Tyler Moore Show* (Alley and Brown, *Love*; Dow, *Prime-Time*) and *That Girl* (Cole).

Typically absent from this canon of breakthrough, women-centered television programs is *The Doris Day Show*. The series aired from September 24, 1968, to September 10, 1973; this places the premiere of *The Doris Day Show* some two years after the first episode of *That Girl*, and its last episode two seasons after the first run of *The Mary Tyler Moore Show*. It was in this crucial interstitial period that many nuances of the cultural dialogue regarding women, their changing attitudes toward love and work norms, and the corresponding representations of these were negotiated and expressed in the media. On the following pages, I will situate *The Doris Day Show* in its historical and cultural contexts, deconstruct some of its televisual texts as the show progressed from conservative values affirmation to sociocultural liberation, and conclude with an interpretation of the series' value as a chronicler of changing gender expectations toward work and intimate relations.

THE MAKING OF *THE DORIS DAY SHOW*

The Doris Day Show was clearly a television series *malgré lui*. Conceived by CBS executives as a light situation comedy that could counter the ever-increasing salary demands of Lucille Ball and her perennial audience favorite *The Lucy Show*, the show was the brainchild of Doris Day's third husband, who was also her agent, Marty Melcher. Without her knowledge, Melcher signed her to a five-year contract as she completed work on *Where Were You When the Lights Went Out?*, her last major film for MGM, and was filming *With Six You Get Eggroll* with Brian Keith for Warner Pathé. Melcher did not live to see his project come to fruition; after a short bout with bacterial endocarditis, he died unexpectedly in April of 1968.

For Doris Day, Melcher's sudden death coincided with two shocking revelations. The first was her discovery of the series' pilot scripts: "'The whole nature of television is wrong for me,' I had said [to Marty]. 'Under no circumstance do I want to do television.' Now here, on top of his dresser, were two shooting scripts for what looked like a series that was all ready to go" (Hotchner 228). To make matters worse, the contract committed her to a situation comedy, whose very format she loathed:

> It was bad enough that I had been forced into television against my will, but what made it doubly repulsive was the nature of the setting that had been chosen for my weekly series. A farm. A widow with a couple of little kids living on a farm. With grandpa, naturally. Whatever reputation I

had made in films, it certainly wasn't bucolic. . . . In my wildest night-mares I would never have done scripts like those handed to me. But I was too enervated . . . to care. (Hotchner 239)

Her husband's death also exposed that he had squandered all the money she had earned as a big band singer and major Hollywood film star in risky invest-ments; an audit revealed that Day owed the government nearly half a million dollars in back taxes (Gelb 145).

Given this confluence of personal tragedy, grief, and the imminent threat of bankruptcy, the lines of *The Doris Day Show*'s opening song, "Que será, será / Whatever will be, will be / The future's not ours to see / Que será, será," take on special meaning. The song, which had originated with her perfor-mance in Alfred Hitchcock's 1956 masterpiece *The Man Who Knew Too Much*, now came to express Doris Day's personal history—a recent widow's resigned acceptance of fate and an unsure stance concerning the future.

The romantic, heavily backlit visuals that accompanied the signature song in the opening montage introduced the show's geographic setting and its main characters: Doris Martin (Doris Day) walking hand-in-hand with two young sons, Toby (Todd Starke) and Billy (Philip Brown), in an elysian California landscape filled with lush grass and tall flowers. We find Doris spending qual-ity time with her boys and Lord Nelson, the family's Old English sheepdog. An extreme closeup of a butterfly on a flower dissolves into the smiling face of Doris, and she is identified in a caption as the show's main star.

Except for the absence of a father (here, instead, is the wise grandfather, Buck Webb, played by Denver Pyle), the show's opener represented the tele-visual family myth of a decade earlier: an attractive and stylish mother who chooses not to work outside the home, a number of sincere but fun-loving children, and the typically shaggy dog—all indicators of what David Marc has aptly termed the "suburban ecstasy period" (Marc, *Comic* 43). The constella-tion of characters and their placement in the opening sequence also followed the representation of cultural types in the domestic situation comedy (Butsch 390). Both Doris Martin and Buck Webb were identified as members of the successful White middle class, communing with nature in neo-Jeffersonian yeomanry. While Doris Martin was often depicted doing farm work alongside her father or the hired hand, her portrayal as a "working woman" on the farm remained circumstantial, improbable, and even awkward at times.

A comparison between the series pilot and the last episode in the 1968–69 season will demonstrate the ambivalence with which Doris Martin's role as a working woman was handled during the show's first season. The pilot, entitled "The Job," reveals that Doris had a career in New York City in the publishing field; her husband's sudden death precipitated her move back to the farm. Her former employer, the editor for *Ladies' World Magazine*, wants her to return to the big city and to her position. In the end, however,

Doris rejects the offer in favor of keeping her children on the farm and so validates motherhood over career. Conversely, the season's closing episode, "The Relatives," has Doris Martin and her housekeeper, Juanita, setting out to prove their ability to do "man's work" by painting and wallpapering a part of the house; in the end, however, they have to rely on the help of relatives, who show up to complete the job. The *mise-en-scène* of the series' first season is thus unambiguous: the work-family dichotomy is discussed openly but somewhat clumsily, and any temptations of serious employment revert or are made subservient to her more valued role as mother and caregiver.

The character's sexuality is equally conflicted. Doris Martin is continuously spoken of as Buck's "daughter," and visual representations reaffirm her position as "daddy's little girl," vulnerable and innocent, not as the sexually mature mother of two. Yet Doris Martin is also represented as a resourceful facilitator of other characters' romances, as in the episode "The Date." The romantically inclined but sexually abstinent ambivalence of the main character in matters of intimacy was particularly affirmed in the episode "The Flyboy," which aired midseason. The show's coy treatment of female sexuality harkened back to the double-bind messages of classic Doris Day–type movies like *Pillow Talk*, and it appeared hopelessly out of step with the much edgier contemporary treatment of sexual intimacy on shows such as *Rowan and Martin's Laugh-In*, the 1968 season's ratings leader.

The Doris Day Show's first season was "certainly no blockbuster" (Gelb 145). Some industry trade publications found it praiseworthy for its quaintness and escapist nature: "When the show finally hit the air last September, it was everything you knew it would be—pure, unadulterated, wall-to-wall freckle, Doris-Daysies-in-my-garden-type Doris Day, a real throwback to the good old days when there was no problem that goodness couldn't solve" (Whitney 2). Some critics panned the show as outdated and plain silly: "Everything about this show is so icky-poo sweet and jim dandy confectionary you might know the sponsor would be Duncan Hines cake mix" (Reed 91). Others criticized the filming style: "[Doris Day] is photographed through so many filters that you feel she is not on TV but on your radio—but never mind. If she's too far away to think of her as the girl next door, think of her as the girl next to the girl next door" (Amory 42). "Doris is an enormously natural and personable performer, but she's neither old nor ugly, so why . . . must all of her close-ups be shot with so many filters over the camera that she looks like she's being photographed through Vaseline?" (Reed 91).

Perhaps the harshest critique came from *TV Guide*: "Not only is this show no more interesting than anyone's everyday life, it's a good deal less so. You can prove it. Tonight, instead of tuning in on the show, don't. Just sit around your kitchen with your family and friends. Ask whether anyone would like a glass of milk. If someone says either yes or no—terrific. You've got your dialogue." The show was judged as irrelevant:

In the first place, take the idea. And whatever you do, don't lose it, because the producers of this show sure did—if indeed they ever had one. . . . There are plots in this series. We realize people will challenge this statement, but there are. However, they are buried under so many layers of cotton-candy writing, not to mention the thunderous laugh track, that they deserve better. (Amory 42)

Not only was this show out of touch with contemporary culture, it was even more out of touch than other television programs of the era.

Clearly, the blithe first season of *The Doris Day Show* was ill-timed, falling during one of the most turbulent periods since World War II. Foreign policy crises coupled with widespread domestic violence that resulted from the arrest of the Black Panther leadership, the assassinations of Martin Luther King, Jr., and Robert Kennedy, and the protests at the Chicago Democratic National Convention had turned 1968 into *The Year of the Barricades* (Caute). Thematically inoculated from such political concerns, the series also appeared to be blind to the country's changing social realities, particularly with regard to women's issues. Following the publication of Betty Friedan's *The Feminine Mystique* in 1963, women had been stirred by "the problem that has no name" and questioned the proscriptive norms of domesticity and ideal womanhood. More than half of the nation's single women and more than 40 percent of married women had claimed emancipation by entering the work force (G. Matthews, "Housewife" 267). Women had started to establish their own periodicals, which multiplied exponentially, from two in 1968 to sixty-one in 1972, and began to give voice to social reform movements. They formed organizations such as the National Organization for Women (NOW) and the Women's Equity Action League (Wandersee 4).

While the show's pilot, "The Job," had made cursory reference to this social reality in mentioning Doris Martin's previous career in publishing, during the first season the theme of the working woman evaporated in favor of simpering affirmations of traditional values. Doris Day herself was unhappy with the way things had turned out: "I should have worked on the scripts but I couldn't. I didn't have the energy or the desire. I simply didn't care. . . . My resignation to mediocrity was strange, since by nature I am a perfectionist and I am normally concerned about every aspect of a role I am performing." And she recognized that the show had to change if it was to succeed:

By the end of my first year in television I came to realize that . . . it was up to me to take over *The Doris Day Show* and turn it around. I had always left production and management to Marty and others, but now I would have to acquaint myself with every aspect of the show and make my own decisions. I hired new producers and new scriptwriters and worked out a new locale for the show. It was removed from the farm and relocated in San Francisco. . . . I worked with the writers, set designers, costume designers, makeup, music—there wasn't an aspect of the show that I didn't get into. For the first time in my career I saw all the daily rushes and even involved myself in editing. (Hotchner 239, 249)

The new sense of woman-centered control was first expressed in the new opening montage for the show. While the song "Que será, será" was retained, the opening sequence now showed Doris Martin leaving the farm in a large red convertible, being waved off by grandpa and the boys. As she drives into the city, she is bathed in sunshine. After a crosscut, we find her coming out of a dark tunnel and driving onto the Golden Gate Bridge, crossing the bridge with a view of the city, driving over the hilly streets in the city, and ending up at the harbor. Smelling flowers at a flower stand, she is reminded of her family, and Buck—smiling, turning, looking hopefully upwards at the sun—and Billy and Toby are introduced as they play with a frog. The montage shifts back to Doris in the city, who steps off a streetcar in the Chinatown section and skips across the road. An upward pan of a large downtown office building evokes the image of Doris Martin's workplace, an image that is confirmed by the introduction of her boss, Mr. Michael Nicholson (McLean Stevenson) and her coworker Myrna Gibbons, played by Rose Marie of *The Dick Van Dyke Show* fame. The opening sequence ends with a pre–Mary Richards hat scene as Doris scurries across the sidewalk and runs into her office building.

The opening sequence visually separates the home sphere from the work sphere, both in terms of geographic locales and also in the use of color symbolism. The farm is associated with red, including Buck Webb's red kerchief around his neck, while the city is evoked by the colors yellow and white. Significantly, Doris Martin is shown wearing mostly yellow and white. This is interspersed with the tractor-red of the car, which got Doris from the farm to the city, and a closeup of her red shoes as she steps off the streetcar—symbolically, Doris is not in Kansas anymore. The geographic separation of home and work spheres was duplicated in the show's dominant scenarios. Episodes alternated between narratives that played on the farm on weekends ("The Chocolate Bar War" and "Togetherness") and those that were set in the office in the city ("Doris, the Model" and "The Office Troubleshooter"). On occasion, the locations would be bridged, typically with invitations from Doris for office staff to spend a weekend on the ranch ("A Two-Family Christmas" and "*Today's World* Catches Measles"), but there remained an indisputable Parsonian separation of occupational and private spheres.

Plots were firmed up to take on the tensions between work and family more directly. In the very first episode of the second season, "Doris Gets a Job," Doris vies for the job as secretary to the managing editor of *Today's World Magazine*. She is advised to hide in the application process the fact that she has children at home; the resulting complications fill the episode. In another

FIGURE 16.1. Rose Marie as Myrna Gibbons and Doris Day as Doris Martin in *The Doris Day Show*, 1968–1973. Photo courtesy of Photofest. Used by permission.

episode, "A Frog Called Harold," the escape of Toby's favorite frog from Doris's purse causes *Today's World Magazine* to lose a needed bank loan when the search for the amphibian disrupts a tour by bank officials.

The reconceptualization of the Doris Martin character as a working woman in the process of emancipating herself entailed a revealing differentiation of conduct. In the public sphere, Doris Martin was portrayed as strong, wearing male-style hats, even taking on gangsters and bullies that frighten her male colleagues, as she does in the episode "Kidnapped." Even though she is a strong character at the office, Doris knows better than to be adversarial and continues to act demure and to defer to her male colleagues. In a typical scene from the two-part episode "Doris Hires a Millionaire," Doris is neglected and interrupted no less than four times, both by her male colleague and her superior, before she can finally submit a winning story idea, a human interest story about a local drifter. When the drifter reveals himself to be William Tyler, a multimillionaire hiding from the press, Doris feels compelled to reverse herself. Unjournalistically, she argues vehemently for Tyler's right to privacy and meets with Mr. Nicholson to suppress the publication of the photograph that Ron Harvey had taken of Mr. Tyler.

This process of negotiated insertion into, and subsequent retraction from, the male work domain could be interpreted as harking back to the disconfirming discourse of Lucy's harebrained work schemes on *I Love Lucy*, but its denouement reveals a crucial difference: Doris is not represented as stereotypically inept but as a woman eager to probe the limitations of the status assignments in the traditional office roles by convincing her editor of the correctness of her viewpoint—twice. Besides the uneasy navigations of the stratified order of office politics, romantic encounters remained a favorite theme, but special complications of intra-office relations were added to the topic of normal sexual attractions of a widow and mother. Coworker Ron Harvey consistently makes advances towards Doris, and on several occasions, there are insinuated relations between Mr. Nicholson and Doris.

Throughout the second season, Doris Martin's restrained sexuality is counterpointed by Myrna Gibbons's more overt interest in men. Many of the story lines involve innuendos and subplots that explored Myrna's man-hunting activities, and one entire episode, "Singles Only," is devoted to her sexual aggressiveness, while the episode "The Woman Hater" squarely takes on the issue of the liberated woman. The season's finale revolved around uncaring technocrats taking over the magazine to improve efficiency. This plot, which foreshadowed the final episode of *The Mary Tyler Moore Show* seven years later, left viewers wondering if *The Doris Day Show* would come back the next season and in what form.

While the critics were kinder to the series during the second season, the fact that the show had used no less than ten writers and nine different directors did not enhance its dramatic coherence nor its visual integrity. But despite the unsettled production schedule, the series' new format managed to garner the number ten spot in the year's Nielsen ratings; by comparison, Lucille Ball's *Here's Lucy*, ninth the year before, scored the sixth position in the 1969–70 season (Brooks and Marsh 969). *The Doris Day Show* was on the way to becoming culturally relevant.

The third season, in the fall of 1970, saw the third wholesale format change of the show. Doris Martin progressed from secretary to magazine writer and relocated with her sons and dog to an apartment in San Francisco. Her father and his handyman continued to operate the ranch, but their characters became tangential to the show's continued narrative. The main emphasis was now on Doris Martin as an aspiring career woman, albeit with a latent family component. In the second episode of the season, "The Feminist," Doris is given an assignment to get the magazine rights to a militant feminist's book since the author refuses to deal with the men in the office. An obvious inversion of "The Woman Hater" from the previous season, the narrative structure of "The Feminist" is an example of how Doris's character was realigned to cultural relevance and brought to maturity. In the two-part "Doris Leaves *Today's World*," which aired during sweeps in October 1970, multimillionaire Mr. Tyler returns to hire Doris away from her position at the magazine, but she returns because she feels more needed at *Today's World*.

While the prior seasons had been devoid of any political references, the show now ventured into the realm of politically inspired comedy. With a nod to the fears of leftist infiltration, Doris is taken into custody as a foreign spy after accidentally exchanging an attaché case with an agent in "Doris, the Spy." In "Doris vs. Pollution," Doris takes on Colonel Fairburn, the paper's owner, in her own environmental initiative to curb pollution, and in "Colonel Fairburn, Jr.," Doris mediates a conflict between the colonel and his hippie son, who is left in charge of the magazine while the colonel and Mr. Nicholson attend a convention.

The pervasive portrayal of the work sphere was periodically interspersed with episodes that showed Doris Martin as a grounded mother engaged in familial affairs. In "Billy's First Date," her son has gotten the prettiest girl in school to agree to be his date for a dance, and Doris's attempts to chaperone them create occasions for comedic confusion. In the episode "Young Love," Doris mediates skillfully a marital conflict involving her niece, a recent bride, and her husband, who feels he is not ready to take on the responsibilities of fatherhood.

By its third season, the show had become a critical success. *TV Guide's* cover featured Doris Martin with derby hat and with hands self-confidently stuffed in her coat pockets. Another issue contained an elaborate pictorial of the sound stage that served as Doris Martin's apartment, and a third *TV Guide* issue featured the show and its producer-star in an extensive interview. Critics noted the marked improvement of the show's thematic treatments and overall orientation over the previous years: "Whereas the old Doris rarely spoke of anything more controversial than her love for daisies and the color yellow, she now discourses boldly and emphatically on such subjects as Vietnam, ecology and consumerism" (Davidson 32). Clearly, the show had gained in relevance and cultural currency, and Doris Day knew it: "This TV show of mine, we really got it on the track this year" (ibid. 34).

Even though the show's fourth season brought yet another complete change in its *mise-en-scène*—gone were the characters of her father, farmhand Leroy, her sons, and even the shaggy dog—the underlying premise built on and completed the leitmotif of previous seasons. Doris Martin is now depicted strictly as a career woman, free to pursue romantic interests ranging from an Italian art connoisseur ("When in Rome, Don't") to a man selected by a computer dating service ("A Fine Romance") to an airline pilot ("Have I Got a Fellow For You") to a doctor played by Peter Lawford ("Doris and the Doctor" and "Doris at Sea"). This format was retained for the show's fifth and final season, with Doris further rising in rank to the position of editor-in-chief in the episode "The New Boss." As a successful career woman, her dating options multiply, and her romantic engagements are split between Peter (Peter Lawford) and Jonathan (Patrick O'Neal). The show's last episode, "Byline . . . Alias Doris," deals with a reporter who has taken credit for Doris's writing. The show thus came full circle in its denouement in the form of an anagnorisis of sorts. Doris Martin, the magazine's successful editor-in-chief, is finally given full credit for her work, a theme that was foreshadowed in the show's pilot five years earlier.

DECONSTRUCTING *DORIS*:
THE PROGRESS TOWARDS CULTURAL RELEVANCE

Although *The Doris Day Show* is typically overlooked in interpretive analyses that examine prime-time television texts as documents of sociocultural history of the late 1960s and early 1970s, the contribution of the character of Doris Martin to the shifting imagery of women in televisual texts merits a serious reevaluation. The show's four major format changes in five broadcast seasons were obvious attempts to calibrate the series to the contemporaneous social discourse and to gain relevance in the cultural dialogue.

It is precisely in these self-conscious negotiations that the cultural and subcultural codes that structured the discourse reveal themselves. While contemporary counterparts were conceptually more stable than *The Doris Day Show*, they were consistently based on the postulate that series episodes ought to be formulaic declensions relying on developmentally quiescent characters. By contrast, *The Doris Day Show* emphasized the processual aspect of female identity formation and the articulation of complementary, polyvalent identity iterations in response to variable conditions. In particular, the show chronicled shifts in the cultural expectations of women, both in personal relations and in the workplace. Early episodes portrayed Doris Martin simultaneously in terms of filial innocence and of widowed asexuality, but as the series progressed, the heroine was granted different aspects of mature sexuality, including negotiations of workplace-related liaisons. In the show's final two seasons, Doris Martin had multiple competing romantic interests, but she narrowed her choices to two, and eventually one as she accepted Jonathan's wedding proposal ("Meant for Each Other"). The development of the character of Doris Martin thus chronicled the progression of what Ella Taylor has called "prime-time feminism," the transition of the typical portrayal of the single woman from that of sexless widow *(The Lucy Show)*, husband-hungry spinster *(Our Miss Brooks)*, or unmarriageable career woman (Sally in *The Dick Van Dyke Show*) to a "popular feminist" representation that allowed "the viewer to identify with the 'new woman' while hanging on to older ideals of femininity" (Taylor 85, 89).

A similar developmental progression took place with regard to Doris Martin's career. From the awkward beginnings of Doris's "working woman" image on the farm, the character gained autonomy in the second season by accepting a commuting job in San Francisco. Like Mary Richards of *The Mary Tyler Moore Show*, she found employment in the media industry, but unlike Mary Richards, she started lower, as a secretary, and ended up higher on the corporate scale, as the editor-in-chief of *Today's World*. Doris Martin's meteoric rise was not without conflict, and on the way she encountered numerous examples of what Acker has termed "gendered hierarchies." Clearly, Doris Martin's occupational world mimicked the real-world workplace as a site for the creation and reproduction of gender difference and gender inequality. But what set the series apart was the added dimension of the notion of "comparative worth." On several occasions, Doris Martin was courted by different organizations and executives, starting with her former employer at *Ladies' World Magazine* in the episode "Doris Leaves *Today's World*" in season three, to "The Great Talent Raid" in season five, in which Doris, in a nod to contemporary culture, was temporarily lured away to *NOW Magazine*. Other episodes ("The Press Secretary" and "Just a Miss Understanding") showed Doris going to work as press secretary and all-night radio talk-show host, respectively, thus underscoring the multidimensionality of the character's talents and ability to handle diverse work assignments.

In a similar vein, her supervisory and managerial capabilities were depicted as developing over time. These qualities were only hinted at in "Doris Hires a Millionaire" and were challenged in the fourth-season episode "Cover Girl," in which she hires her Italian artist friend to paint the cover illustration for the magazine; but with the episode "The New Boss" during season five, Doris Martin is firmly entrusted with managing the daily operations of *Today's World Magazine*, so her leadership qualities are no longer contested.

Doris Martin's ritualistic reconnaissance of the shifting geographies of love and work in a changing cultural environment place the show squarely into the category of a narrative *à thèse*. In its perennial examination and reexamination of the choices that are open to the characters that were placed in a particular plot or that affected society at large, viewers of this episodic media narrative were treated to weekly explorations of how fluctuant social roles could be negotiated, contested, or affirmed with variations over the course of time.

The Doris Day Show raised pertinent questions about the nature of individual identification and social participation in altering the received norms of gender stratification, about the power of agency and the resilience of structure, about the liminoid space of hyperreality and the mediated simulacra of lived experience. In Felicia Hughes-Freeland's words, media and rituals "become means to being: sites for the generation of action and meaning which are both the cause and effect of identity" (Hughes-Freeland 45). As such, the series' weekly engagement in the discourse about women served as an important social ritual, as a "stage," in Turner's formulation, "on which roles are enacted and the conflicts of the secular drama are reflected in symbol, mime, and precept" (Turner 274–75). If Caldarola is correct in asserting that "the simulacra of mass media" are "forms of representation encoded in ritual activity" and that "change is increasingly the product of altered representations" (68, 66), then *The Doris Day Show* is certainly due for a reassessment in the way that it dramatized and facilitated the cultural dialogue about the women's movement during the second wave of feminism in the 1960s and 1970s.

CHAPTER 17

Liberated Women and New Sensitive Men

Reconstructing Gender in the 1970s Workplace Comedies

Judy Kutulas

In the early days of television, paid work was an afterthought on situation comedies, but one almost exclusively reserved for men. Home and family were the essence of Americanism in the 1950s, and home and family were at the center of the sitcom (May 11). Representations of television women demonstrated what Betty Friedan described as a feminine mystique, the valuing of women's relationships to others (husband, children, parents) over their own independent identities. Television housewives helped soothe postwar social anxieties about gender roles by "naturaliz[ing] woman's place in the home instead of the factory or office" (Haralovich 112). A clear sense of gender differentiation prevailed in the 1950s, on television and in real life. But following the sweeping set of late 1960s social changes, women were no longer content to stay invisibly at home doing for others. Although domestic sitcoms addressed the changes, the better venue for exploring gender issues was in the new genre of the workplace comedy. The audience encountered a mainstreamed version of new gender ideals in 1970s workplace comedies, one that emphasized liberation while containing feminism.

Television does not create gender norms, but it is a vital part of any cultural conversation about them, providing both a frame of reference and a forum where social contradictions can be explored. Television representations of 1950s women as invisible housewives were market driven; they were reactive to social trends because advertisers valued women as *family* consumers. Women have always been disproportionate watchers of sitcoms, and their self-images must be reflected in successful programming (Press 18). Once women chafed at their traditional roles, networks needed to find safe ways to accommodate their rebellions. They had to readapt the traditional sitcom formula to changing norms.

The family sitcoms reinforced the strict gender roles of the 1950s, providing visual compensation for the housewives' roles with their lush renderings of suburban life. Women provided "moral backup" to fathers who knew best, but also often challenged the family hierarchy, venturing into the workplace or forcing their husbands to do housework (Leibman 118). Sitcoms, like other forms of popular culture, provided safe opportunities for rebellion but ultimately reinforced the status quo. Thus, women's challenges on television inevitably ended in amusing failure, although, as Janine Basinger has argued about women's films, female viewers probably enjoyed the rebellion more than the lessons at the end of the show (21). Only rarely did women venture beyond the domestic television scene and into the television workplace.

When they did, the experience was distinctly gendered. Theirs, unlike men's, was an either-or proposition, jobs or families, but not both. Their jobs, moreover, were not glamorous; they were teachers and secretaries, echoing the reality of a gender-segregated workplace that limited real women's employment possibilities. Consequently, they were denied access to the consumer pleasures television housewives had. They lived in small apartments, wore tweedy skirts, sensible shoes, and sometimes, black framed glasses; they did not have handsome husbands or cute kids. And it was clear, on shows like *Our Miss Brooks* and *Private Secretary*, that they were frustrated. Eve Arden's Connie Brooks, for example, was snippy and snide, irritated yet capable. What television's frustrated working girls lacked most were husbands because, as in real life, a television husband was "the base of the pyramid on which she would pile washer-dryers and refrigerator-freezers and sterling and fine china" (Bailey 75). The very qualities that made working girls fun to watch—sarcasm and wit—made them poor marriage material. They were a little too mouthy and too masculine, like Sally Rogers on *The Dick Van Dyke Show*. Often characterized as one of the guys, Sally had a successful comedy-writing career, lots of Jackie Kennedy suits, and a cool Manhattan apartment; however, she could not get her mama's boy boyfriend to propose. Her story offered female viewers the chance to vicariously experience independence and career achievement while reassuring everyone that staying home was the more rewarding choice a woman could make.

The networks did not voluntarily alter such programming, but were pushed into change for a variety of reasons. By 1968 or 1969, there was no cultural consensus in the United States. The generation gap, political fights, lifestyle changes, and various empowerment movements forced the networks to rethink their strategies. A television gap existed, too; baby boomers, those most affected by the 1960s, did not watch much television, something network executives discovered when they began to segment and study the audience. And boomers particularly did not like domestic sitcoms (Bodroghkozy, *Groove* 64). In part because they rejected their parents' paths—choosing instead to get more education, marry later, and have fewer children—they were attractive targets for advertisers; yet their rejection of traditional domesticity also meant they did not find family sitcoms compelling.

Television responded with what have been called relevancy programs, like *All in the Family*, that moved beyond the bland unreality of the traditional family sitcom (Gitlin, *Inside* 203–20). Relevancy television championed a new liberal perspective on politics, lifestyle, and gender, but feminism was trickier because the young target audience did not automatically embrace it. Consequently, when a feminist appeared on relevancy television, she was safely flawed. *Maude*, an *All in the Family* spin-off, had a feminist as its title character, but a feminist with an angry foghorn voice, a middle-aged body, no visible means of support, and a milquetoast husband she could boss. Maude symbolized the stereotype of the angry, emasculating feminist, who was represented even less favorably on the news and more traditional sitcoms, like *The Beverly Hillbillies* or *Green Acres*, although some audience members might read her as strong and independent (Douglas 196–202). But if feminism was too contested a value to be fully endorsed by sitcoms, the women's movement altered women's roles as consumers in ways that influenced the sitcom and forced changes. Where once women's value was a function of her familial role, doing (and shopping) for others, by the early 1970s, "a more independently minded female generation was coming of age," and they had money to spend (Rabinovitz 145). Female viewers could no longer be counted on to watch programs (and commercials) that centered them in the home as wives and mothers. The workplace sitcom became one place where their new desires and possibilities could be represented.

The beauty of the workplace sitcom was its versatility. It did not disturb the traditional gender roles that persisted in the next generation of family sitcoms because most of its workers were single. It was not as confrontational as relevancy television. It featured ensemble casts, appealing to a lot of different audiences simultaneously. Such shows were attractive to baby boomers because they focused on people like themselves, making their way in a world they could not control and did not fully support (Taylor 111–12). The first 1970s workplace comedy was *The Mary Tyler Moore Show*. It was successful because it spoke specifically to young women without alienating the rest of its audience (like *Maude* might). Its protagonist, Mary Richards, left her hometown and fiancé for a career in television news in Minneapolis, liberating herself from the wife-and-mother trajectory (Dow, *Prime-Time* 25). Mary is liberated, but not a feminist. The difference was crucial, for liberation was gender-neutral, consumer-friendly, and built community, while television feminism was inimical to all those things. Liberation, thus, was safe enough for television, while feminism was not.

To accommodate Mary and other women, representations of the workplace had to change. Previously, popular culture portrayed it as hostile, hierarchical, and exploitative. In 1970s workplace comedies, coworkers became family, a metaphor that suited baby boomers' desire for community on their own terms. In the final episode of *The Mary Tyler Moore Show*, Mary asserted that what defined a family was "people who make you feel less alone and really loved." Her claim that the family was a construct rather than a biological entity mainstreamed an idea from the hippie counterculture by situating it within the capitalist system and rendering it compatible with biological family. The workplace family facilitated television women's entrance into the workplace by implying its dynamic was cozy, familiar, and gendered.

Indeed, men were in charge of the sitcom workplace, and television's workplace women held mainly service or clerical jobs, which was true of the real world as well. Few, however, performed those jobs without complaint. Their protests against the menial nature of their work and, especially, the expectation that they serve men provided a cultural reference for the women's movement and modeled a new workplace etiquette. Receptionist Jennifer Marlowe *(WKRP in Cincinnati)* would not get coffee or take dictation. Carol Kester *(The Bob Newhart Show)* balked at having to collect her boss's dry cleaning. Despite the seemingly conservative family dynamic, viewers saw women who took their jobs seriously and refused to be as servile as their sitcom ancestors.

Workplace women expected to be treated as people rather than women, a concept that, unlike most feminist ideas, quickly found broad popular acceptance because it was a variant of traditional American beliefs about fairness and mobility. Audiences watched as Mary Richards applied for a secretary's job at WJM-television, was hired as associate producer of the six o'clock news (which paid less), and was promoted to producer several years later. A number of episodes showcased her struggles to be taken seriously and her developing sense of professional expertise. Bailey Quarters of *WKRP in Cincinnati* joined the radio family with a degree in journalism and moved from creating promotions to writing news copy to broadcasting the news. Except for chauvinists, who could quibble with this view of the work world? It confirmed that hard work and talent would be rewarded while it also reinforced 1960s' values like diversity and equality. For female viewers, there was the added reassurance of seeing both a friendly, supportive workplace and female characters struggling to be assertive. Mary's voice cracked and Bailey was shy, but they managed anyway, largely because their coworkers respected them.

For younger female viewers, who had few meaningful models of the workplace, images of strong, competent working women were particularly revelatory. Workplace women were not marking time until marriage and were not sadly desperate for men, like earlier television working women. Mary Richards was not a bitter spinster or one of the guys. She made a big difference for a generation of women coming of age in the 1970s, a generation *sui generis*. "Mary was my role model, pure and simple," one recalled. "She showed me how to pursue a career, how to keep romance in perspective, how to suffer fools, how to face my own foolishness" (Ode E3). As Andrea Press has concluded after studying middle-class women's television watching habits, characters like Mary Richards "captured middle-class women's imaginations at the time these shows were on, particularly for young women imagining and making plans for their future lives" (77). So too did they educate other viewers about the single working woman's life, helping parents understand how their single daughters lived or teaching men how to treat their new female colleagues. Mary Richards became a cultural symbol, like June Cleaver before her, a shorthand representation of what liberation meant for women.

But television liberation was different from feminism. Workplace television helped to stigmatize feminism as extremist and mean. Real women who worked for a living and had bad hair days and bad dates were liberated and not feminists. They wanted to be treated fairly, equally, respectfully, and they treated others with respect. Feminists, who shouted and carried picket signs and never wore skirts, were not respectful or fair. They were divisive, pitting men against women and women against each other (Douglas 221–44). They were not interested in equality, but in privileging women and demeaning men. On *The Bob Newhart Show*, for example, psychologist Bob Hartley organized a consciousness-raising group; but once empowered, the women in the group disrupted his marriage and excluded him because of his gender.

So when sexism reared its ugly head in the television workplace, feminists did not solve the crisis; instead, the workplace family protected its own. After a sleazy photographer took nude pictures of Jennifer, her WKRP colleagues invented a scam to get them back. When Elaine Nardo *(Taxi)* suspected that taxi dispatcher Louie DePalma was spying on her through a hole in the bathroom wall, her coworkers helped her catch him at it. In workplace sitcoms, portraits of feminism and female ambition were articulations of the "I am not a feminist, but . . ." mentality. They supported women's desire to compete with men in the workplace without alienating them, changing the rules, or otherwise disturbing the structure of the workplace. Television's liberated women managed what few real-world women could; their gains did not come at the expense of men, except perhaps greedy, sexist, undeserving men.

In fact, it was precisely their ability to get along with men that helped broaden the workplace sitcom's audience. While young women might tune in to watch their television counterparts succeed in the office, they, like male viewers, also enjoyed the vicarious pleasures of another kind of liberation, sexual liberation. Sexual freedom was a value enthusiastically embraced by a whole generation (Weiss 171). It freed women from the cult of virginity that had consigned them to early marriage or prolonged sexual longing while it made more willing partners available to men. The 1960s definition of sex as a joyous, spontaneous, physical act not limited to the marriage bed informed the 1970s workplace comedy. Television feminists, by contrast, were as asexual as 1950s television working women because there were not, as one explained, "here to have fun." Television's liberated working women explored their sexuality, albeit with the same charming nervousness as they approached the workplace. And with good reason, since the double standard never quite disappeared.

On *M*A*S*H*, for instance, male characters, married or not, pursued all sorts of sexual relationships and none of them worried about their reputations. But *M*A*S*H*'s head nurse, Margaret "Hot Lips" Houlihan's sexuality was constantly judged. What the audience saw was not how Margaret felt about her choices, but how the men around her perceived her, whether they thought her too promiscuous, too emasculating, or too clingy. The male gaze and attendant male judgments about female sexuality prevailed, but the woman's perspective was also present, minus either sugarcoating or moralizing. When Mary's friend Rhoda repeated the old saw about men respecting virtuous women, Mary asked if she thought it was true. "No," Rhoda replied, "but my mother does." Her rueful comment captured a generational identity and a gendered one, a recognition of both possibilities and limits. The workplace sitcom offered the vicarious pleasure of female sexuality and its complex containment within a sexual dynamic still controlled by men.

On workplace sitcoms, as elsewhere in the popular culture, sexual liberation became the less-threatening substitute for other kinds of power because it reinforced women's traditional role as consumers. Liberation became a commodity, fanned by Virginia Slims cigarette advertisements exhorting "You've come a long way, baby." Herbal Essence shampoo and Candies shoes were touted as tools to help women be sexy and free. While 1950s television wives dressed in housedresses and looked comfortably middle-aged, 1970s working women wore clingy dresses, Farrah Fawcett hair, and slender figures that served as markers of their independent, modern status. The evolution began earlier, but by the end of the 1970s the television women who garnered the biggest audience were on *Charlie's Angels*, known as "jiggle television" because its stars "often went braless" (McNeil 156). Going braless became the symbol of television's liberated women, different from feminists' bra burning, with its evocations of anger. But, once the bras came off, the audience's understanding of female competence changed. Receptionist Jennifer Marlowe *(WKRP)* lacked ambition but had power thanks to her long platinum hair and skin-tight dresses. While Loni Anderson, who played Jennifer, did not want her seen as a dumb blonde, it was not Jennifer's brain that got her places (Kassel 24). By the end of the decade, the media's objectification of women and its concomitant emphasis on youth, slenderness, and sexuality was already having its impact on workplace sitcoms.

Female characters were supposed to be all things to all people—sexy (but not too sexual), competent, sweet, kind, and nurturing. They brought culture and class to the workplace, like the flowers on Mary Richards's desk or the paintings Elaine Nardo helped her fellow cabbies buy. Their apartments were impeccable; they went to concerts; they knew how to cook. They exemplified the super woman of the perfume ad, who could "bring home the bacon, fry it up in the pan, and never let him forget he's a man." Liberated status required its own set of goods, a theme that advertisers cultivated. Meanwhile, the shows themselves offered visual reassurance that liberated women had more attractive lives than their married housewife sisters. Liberated consumerism was about personal care, convenience, and gratification, unlike the purchases of the saintly June Cleaver mom. It proved, to cite another popular commercial, that liberated women were "worth it," that they had enough self-respect (and money) to buy what they wanted. Workplace comedies, like the ads embedded within them, showed their female audiences what clothes they might wear, how they might wear their hair, and what their apartments might look like. By commodifying the image of the liberated woman, they mainstreamed it and further distinguished it from the feminist, who did not wear nice clothes or shave her legs, who did not, in short, use the kinds of products television sold.

Another accoutrement to the liberated lifestyle was less purchasable, the new sensitive man, who complemented the working woman in the office and dated her outside of it (Kimmel 293). He was a media creation, a man himself liberated from gender stereotypes and open to his feelings, genuinely interested in women as people, nurturing and warm, a man not afraid to cry. Alan Alda and talk show host Phil Donahue were prototypical sensitive men (Sterns 6–8, 125). Andy Travis *(WKRP)* and Alex Reiger *(Taxi)* were sitcom representatives of the type, and the character Alda played on *M*A*S*H* came close, except that he was too much of a womanizer. In the workplace, the new sensitive man facilitated the liberated woman's achievements because she did not threaten him. Off the job, other new sensitive men treated liberated women respectfully, cooked them dinner, and cuddled. The new sensitive man stood between the liberated woman and what television suggested were two unattractive extremes, spinsterhood and feminism. He was as much a part of the consumerist dream as the studio apartment, the platform shoes, and the feathery hairdo: the handsome man who supported both the liberated workplace woman's ambitions and her sexuality off the job.

The new sensitive man added the final critical touch to the portrait of the liberated woman. He provided the legitimacy that separated her from the feminist. He modeled sensitivity for male viewers, reassuring them that there was still a place for them in liberated women's lives and teaching them how to treat female coworkers as friends and equals. Perhaps more importantly, off the job, the new sensitive man found his sensitivity rewarded in sexual ways not available to earlier television working singles. More than the cute apartment, new job, and stylish clothes, he promised that being liberated had its own set of payoffs; payoffs that could cycle a working woman into traditional domesticity or, like Mary Richards, keep her proudly careerist.

Together, the liberated woman and the new sensitive man carefully separated the most palatable aspects of feminism and packaged them into a neat consumer-friendly ideal. From the start, television's notion of liberation was fraught with contradictions, but a lot of its appeal was its complexity, which signified its realism. That complexity expressed the frustrations and pleasures of real women's lived experiences—their uncertainty, their sense of being trapped between ideologies, their objectification, and their new consumer identities. That same complexity also provided ample space to accommodate other viewer perspectives and values, whether they looked at Mary and Bailey and Elaine as friends, sisters, daughters, or merely sexy office babes.

By the early 1980s, workplace television began to lose steam as family sitcoms revived (Waldron 466–67). The next big workplace comedy, *Cheers*, premiered in 1982. Gender was more fixed in *Cheers*. Sam, the proprietor of the title bar, was not a sensitive male, but a self-identified "babe hound," which altered the essential gender dynamic in significant ways. Without the anchor of a new sensitive man to support the aspirations of the female characters, they floundered. Workplace equality gave way to a kind of Mars and Venus scenario where men and women were essentially different. Frasier, the new sensitive man in the piece, was rejected by Diane and dumped by his wife, Lilith. The women in *Cheers* poured less energy into their careers than their romances, and the men that attracted them were what Lilith characterized as "bad boys" like Sam rather than supportive co-equals like Frasier. Their choices often seemed foolish and their career competence declined.

Further undermining their workplace status in 1980s workplace comedies was the emphasis on lifestyle over career, a reflection of Reagan-era yuppie self-indulgence. What Robert Goldman labeled commodity feminism, "an apparent détente between femininity and feminism" predicated on consumer choices, was very much in evidence (131). *Cheers*'s Diane was a waitress by trade, but her clothes were preppy and her tastes elevated. Stephanie Vanderkellen *(Newhart)* was a maid with designer duds, a dashing boyfriend, and a wealthy father. Even a character like Murphy Brown, whose self-identity was work related (and who, tellingly, also identified herself as a feminist), still had the perks that came with her network news magazine anchor status—the fancy car, designer clothes, and stylish Georgetown townhouse. It was a long way, baby, from Mary Richards's pitiful Minneapolis television station and studio apartment, a journey measured in commodities. More and more, the pleasures of being independent, but especially of being female, were presented in material terms rather than arising from meaningful work.

As liberation grew more commodified and sensitivity less privileged, the workplace became a site where barbs, insults, and sexual objectification occurred. One 1995 study found a lack of respect among characters and, particularly, sexual harassment of female characters was "routine" on modern sitcoms (Lorando E1). The workplace support men offered liberated women was replaced by a much more sexual combination of lust and loathing. Sam and Diane started the trend, but it has cropped up routinely on workplace sitcoms ever since. Such love-hate relationships take place against the backdrop of critical workplace commentary, most of it devoted to judging the women's looks and behavior and the men's machismo. In these workplaces, it is not hard work that pays off, but aggressiveness and cunning for men and sexuality for women. Mary Richards's allure, despite her perky good looks, was her ability to be a lot of things to a lot of people but, most particularly, to be a role model for women lacking in other models. Today's young women model their hair—not their character—on Rachel Green *(Friends)*. If they notice her workplace (in fashion, of course) at all, they see it as the site of the seduction of her younger, handsome, male assistant. Is Rachel liberated and, if so, from what?

But Rachel can only exist because Mary existed before her. As mass commercial entertainment, network television was never going to embrace feminism wholeheartedly for a lot of reasons, including its general anticommercial ethos. By choosing, instead, to promote liberation, which grafted aspects of feminism onto a more commercially viable set of values, workplace sitcoms mainstreamed the most centrist version of feminism possible. Liberation offered tangible psychological rewards for women along with a whole host of consumer goodies, from studio apartments to platform shoes. Achieving liberation on workplace comedies was within the comfort level of most women. It did not require them to stop shaving their legs, go to law school, or give up men. By modeling an attainable goal, one consistent with capitalism, one that modified but did not completely assault patriarchy, workplace sitcoms, with their mass-market definition of the liberated woman, provided millions of American women with a way of being modern. Simultaneously, the complement to the ambitious woman, the new sensitive man, at least briefly modeled an alternative way for men to be. His residue remains in characters like Frasier and Elliot *(Just Shoot Me)*. Although the character types have since lost a lot of the qualities that once served them well, the liberated woman and the new sensitive man continue to help shape our television-normalized sense of reality.

CHAPTER **18**

"Who's in Charge Here?"

Views of Media Ownership in Situation Comedies

Paul R. Kohl

In November 2002, I attended a faculty seminar organized by the Academy of Television Arts and Sciences. The seminar provided an invaluable opportunity to witness the behind the scenes workings of the television industry, from production meetings to program tapings, and to meet those whose job it is to bring America's most popular entertainment to our homes on a weekly basis. The few days I spent in that Hollywood environment impressed upon me what I had been aware of for years but could only imagine until I witnessed it directly: Television is an incredibly collaborative medium. Television writers work in committees to develop story lines and scripts that are then submitted to and commented on not only by the creative personnel involved in a particular program, such as directors and actors, but by production executives, network programmers, and representatives of the advertisers who sponsor the programs.

But perhaps the term "collaborative" is misleading here. Collaboration is generally regarded as working together towards a common goal. In television terms, that common goal is generally defined as attracting the largest audience. There is, however, division between the creators of television programs and the corporate executives who oversee their creations in terms of how best to attract viewers. While creators operate through artistry and instinct, corporate executives depend on ratings and demographics to make content decisions. This eternal tension is perhaps best described by Ben Stein in his 1979 book, *The View from Sunset Boulevard*: "The Hollywood television writer . . . is actually in a business, selling his labor to brutally callous businessmen. One actually has to go through the experience of writing for money in Hollywood or anywhere else to realize how unpleasant it is. Most of the pain comes from dealing with business people" (27). This is hardly a "collaborative" relationship between writers and executives that Stein is portraying. "Antagonistic" is a word that more quickly springs to mind. This antagonistic relationship is propounded in more theoretical terms in the work of Karl Marx.

The common reference to Marxist thought in critiques of the media is Marx's contention, according to Strinati, that: ". . . the predominant ideas common to a capitalist society, including its popular culture, are those of the ruling class. These ideas have to be produced and disseminated by the ruling class or its intellectual representatives, and they dominate the consciousness and actions of those classes outside the ruling class" (131). Marx's distinction between the ruling class, which owns and controls the means of production, and the working class, which provides the labor for production, begs the question of where "intellectual representatives" fit in.

Television writers are, as Stein states, selling labor. They are employees working for the owners of the production apparatus. As such, their interests are aligned more closely with the majority of viewers than with ownership, despite the fact that writers' wealth and position may far outweigh those of the common populace. As Gitlin writes, "However magnificently rewarded, writers and producers have ample reason to resent the power of the corporations they know best: television networks and major suppliers" (*Inside* 270). Television writers are part of the professional and managerial class, and as such, they are part of the same class as blue collar and manual workers.[1] As Fiske and Hartley state, "Managers and professionals may be relatively privileged in the premium they are able to set on their labour power. . . . But it remains the case that many of them are ultimately just as dependent on selling their labour power as blue-collar workers" (103).

The suggestion that the media speak with the voice of the ruling class presupposes that members of the working class must be trained to speak with that voice. Thus business people collaborate in suggesting to creators what is appropriate content. There is a long tradition of resistance, however, within the communities of the working class and oppressed, and despite their monetary and social success, television writers can still be defined as oppressed in Marxist terms. As Fiske and Hartley note, "Their lack of control over property, and hence the conditions of their own employment and production, results in an actual or potential insecurity which provides a basis for 'identity of interest'" (103). Thus, even successful television creators may be aligned with the oppressed members of society in the fact that they do not control or own their work.

Some of the dominant voices of resistance in history have been comic ones. In cataloguing cultural texts with the most potential for resistance, Scott, in *Domination and the Arts of Resistance*, includes "Rumor, gossip, folktales, jokes, songs, rituals, codes, and euphemisms . . ." (19). The modern television situation comedy, as the product of such a tension, should certainly show evidence of its potential for resistance.

What follows are analyses of three classic situation comedy texts that can be read as resistant, works in which the creators have planted seeds of commentary and dissension against those who control the means of production. The first text, an episode of *The Dick Van Dyke Show*, further expands Marx's concept of the alienated worker and comments on the situation of the television creator, whose work is controlled by the owners of production. The second text, the final episode of *The Mary Tyler Moore Show*, uses the potential for resistance of carnival to ridicule the corporate end of the media. Finally, a series of episodes from *Seinfeld*, in which the show's origins are self-reflexively parodied, uses the carnivalesque technique of the grotesque to comment on the owner-worker relationship.

It is important to note that the textual analyses provided here go beyond the boundaries of the programs themselves. An important part of any cultural text is its intertextuality, which may be defined as the relationships that exist between it and other texts or the real-life practices of its textual production. Fiske notes two types of intertextuality, horizontal and vertical, both of which come into play here. Horizontal intertextuality refers to relations "between primary texts that are more or less explicitly linked" while vertical intertextuality occurs between the primary text and the historical and cultural background of its production (*Understanding* 108).[2] In this way, forces from the real socioeconomic system in which the episodes were created can come to bear on their meanings.

ALIENATION OF THE WORKER:
THE DICK VAN DYKE SHOW

As previously mentioned, the creation of television texts involves inherent conflict between creative personnel and business interests. These conflicts are enhanced by the mysterious decision-making process at the network level. In his study of 1980s' programming practices, *Inside Prime Time*, Gitlin reports that those involved in the industry confess to ignorance when asked how television programming works. This, he suggests, is "a gesture of concealment, a way of protecting power from prying eyes" (22). The hidden nature of programming

FIGURE 18.1. Richard Deacon as Melvin Cooley, Rose Marie as Sally Rogers, Morey Amsterdam as Maurice "Buddy" Sorrell, Mary Tyler Moore as Laura Petrie, and Dick Van Dyke as Rob Petrie in *The Dick Van Dyke Show*, 1961–1966. Photo courtesy of Movie Star NewsFair.

decisions is one manifestation of how the television industry further reflects Marx's theories of conflict between owners and workers, a conflict leading to the objectification of labor and the alienation of the worker. As Marx writes in *Capital I*, "The laborer exists for the process of production, and not the process of production for the laborer" (536).

Erich Fromm's analysis of Marx highlights two points: "In the process of work . . . [, e]specially . . . under the conditions of capitalism, man is estranged from his own creative powers, and . . . the *objects* of his own work become alien beings" (48, emphasis in original). The gist of Marx's argument is that under capitalism, workers no longer control their own work nor are they rewarded accordingly for it. Although issues of monetary recompense would not appear to be an issue in the highly paid world of television, Fromm says that is beside the point. Marx, he notes, "is not concerned primarily with the equalization of income. He is concerned with the liberation of man from a kind of work which destroys his individuality, which transforms him into a thing, and which makes him into the slave of things" (48–49). The "Coast-to-Coast Big Mouth" episode of *The Dick Van Dyke Show* echoes Fromm's analysis in its own manner, revealing the alienation of the worker at the heart of capitalism.

This episode was written by Bill Persky and Sam Denoff and was first broadcast on CBS September 15, 1965; it subsequently won the best comedy script Emmy for that year. On the show, Van Dyke plays Rob Petrie, a writer on the fictional television program *The Alan Brady Show*. In this episode, Rob's wife, Laura, is tricked by a television game-show host into revealing that her husband's boss, Alan Brady, is really bald, a fact Brady has kept carefully hidden throughout his career. Laura attempts to apologize to a humiliated and furious Brady in order to save Rob's job. She finds Alan in his office, his various toupees lined up before him. As Laura enters, he introduces them: "Fellas! There's the little lady who put you out of business!" Alan ultimately reveals that he is relieved that his secret is out because it was hard to keep, and more people prefer him bald.

Alan Brady's baldness and his complex attempts to cover it up (he has seasonal toupees and toupees of different lengths) are symbolic of the character's alienation from his craft. Despite seeming to play himself on his variety show, Brady is actually playing a character, a situation revisited in the *Seinfeld* episodes to be discussed later in this chapter. Brady's alienation is suggested in a number of other ways throughout the episode. In his meeting with Laura, he is laid up with a sprained ankle. He has to remove his producer/brother-in-law, Mel Cooley, from his chair, part of a recurring situation in which Alan berates Mel at every opportunity. (Mel's own baldness suggests one possible reason for Alan's continued hostility toward the character.) We learn during the episode that not only has Alan been keeping his baldness secret, he has also had a nose job. Alan Brady's incompleteness as a character is echoed in Rob Petrie's character when the host of *Pay as You Go*, the game show on which Laura appears, believes initially she is the wife of television writer David Petrie, a misidentification of Rob. Since Rob is a writer on Alan's show, he is in a sense subject to the same alienation as Alan, an alienation that removes the individual's true self from his work. The misidentification of Rob signifies this alienation. It is also appropriate that Alan's secret is revealed in the service of winning commodities such as a grill and a vacuum cleaner on a game show, since his alienation is a consequence of working within a capitalist system.

"Coast-to-Coast Big Mouth" contains crucial elements of vertical intertextuality to emphasize its conflicts. The actor Carl Reiner, who appears as Alan Brady, is also the creator of *The Dick Van Dyke Show*. Reiner based the show on his own life as a writer/performer on Sid Caesar's *Your Show of Shows* and played Petrie in the original pilot of the series, entitled *Head of the Family*. Reiner's commitment to his show was so great he even went so far as to write thirteen episodes of the show before it was even picked up as a series, commenting that, "This would be a nucleus, a bible, for anybody who would help write after that. It would guard against supposition; everything would be spelled out" (Marc, *Comic Visions* 93).[3] Ironically, producer Sheldon Leonard had to tell Reiner "you're not right for what you wrote for yourself" (Weissman and Sanders 5). And so Reiner's Jewish Rob Petrie became Van Dyke's WASP Petrie, complete with a new background that reflected the new actor's own life. Marc even suggests that it was the original character's ethnicity that prompted Leonard to suggest the change, as performers like Sid Caesar and Milton Berle "had proved 'too Jewish' for the vastly expanded television audience of 1960" (98).[4]

Reiner's real-life predicament and that of Alan Brady is emblematic of Marx's alienated worker, despite the differing circumstances of their labor as opposed to Marx's industrial worker. As Fromm notes, "Marx did not foresee the extent to which alienation was to become the fate of the vast majority of people, especially of the ever-increasing segment of the population which manipulates symbols and men, rather than machines." These workers are even more alienated since they are forced to sell their personality, smile, and opinions (Fromm 57).[5] Alan Brady, like Reiner himself, is at the fulcrum of the conflict between the creative and business interests of television. He is the creator of his show yet does not own its property, a fact symbolized by outside pressures to cover his baldness and hire his brother-in-law. Reiner is not in control of the programming decisions of his network, but he does have the power to characterize his superiors, as do the writers of the next two programs to be discussed.

THE CARNIVAL WORLD:
THE MARY TYLER MOORE SHOW

The Mary Tyler Moore Show aired its last episode on CBS in 1977. Written by the show's highly successful staff of James L. Brooks, Allan Burns, Ed

FIGURE 18.2. (top row, left to right) Edward Asner as Lou Grant and Ted Knight as Ted Baxter. (middle row, left to right) Gavin MacLeod as Murray Slaughter, Mary Tyler Moore as Mary Richards, and Georgia Engel as Georgette Franklin Baxter. (bottom) Betty White as Sue Ann Nivens in *The Mary Tyler Moore Show*, 1970–1977. Photo courtesy of Photofest. Used by permission.

Weinberger, Stan Daniels, David Lloyd, and Bob Ellison, the episode went
on to win the Emmy for comedy script writing. In the episode, television station WJM is sold to a new owner, and its employees are marked for termi-
nation. In the show's ultimate irony, it is Ted Baxter, the incompetent
anchorman, who is kept on while hard-working professionals Mary
Richards, Lou Grant, and Murray Slaughter are let go.

The decision of the new ownership is obviously questionable to an audience familiar with the characters and made even more dubious by Ted's own
realization that he deserves to be fired. When Lou informs Ted that the new
owner wants to evaluate him, he adds, "I told him to watch the news and decide
for himself," to which Ted tearfully responds, "Oh my God!" As the final decision is made, the new owner announces that he must "get rid of anything that's
pulling you down," concluding with a phrase that echoes Gitlin's responses
from network executives: "It's not a science, but I have to go with my instincts."

The final episode of *The Mary Tyler Moore Show* is, in essence, a world
turned upside down. As Mary double-checks to make sure that she was truly
fired along with "the guys," she is informed "especially" her. This is a carnivalesque world in which the high are made low, and the low are exalted, and the
man in charge is made to look like a fool because all present, including the
audience, know that his instincts are uneducated and wrong.[6]

Russian literary critic Bakhtin applied the concept of carnival to those
medieval festivals and texts in which traditional hierarchies were toppled. As
Stallybrass and White note, "Carnival, for Bakhtin, is both a populist utopian
vision of the world seen from below and a festive critique, through the inversion of hierarchy, of the 'high' culture" (7). In this case the high culture is that
of the corporate decision makers who would valorize a Ted Baxter while fir-
ing a Mary Richards.

There is some irony in *The Mary Tyler Moore Show* making such a critique,
it being one of the most critically acclaimed series ever, and one of the few
allowed to end on its own terms.[7] Its production company, MTM, became syn-
onymous with quality television, prompting Zynda to comment in his essay
"*The Mary Tyler Moore Show* and the Transformation of Situation Comedy,"
"the MTM story is one of enlightened capitalism finally delivering the cultural
promise of television" (133). But even *The Mary Tyler Moore Show* faced issues
with network decision makers in its early stages of development. The original
intention of creators Brooks and Burns was to make Mary Richards a divorcée,
but network executives objected "because it would seem like she'd divorced
Dick Van Dyke, her television husband in *The Dick Van Dyke Show*" (Zynda
132). Marc reports that the head of CBS programming, Mike Dann, stated
that "his own research had conclusively proven that there were three types of
people Americans didn't want to see in situation comedy: people from New
York, people with mustaches, and people who were divorced" (167). The wisdom of those findings would be challenged in the 1990s by *Seinfeld*.

THE GROTESQUE: *SEINFELD*

The "wisdom" of network program executives is similarly portrayed in a series of 1992 episodes of *Seinfeld* in which Jerry is approached by NBC and offered the chance to make a pilot. This plot echoes the real situation in which stand-up comic Seinfeld was given the chance to create a show with writer/producer Larry David. As Seinfeld plays himself on the series, David's alter ego is George Costanza. In the episodes, George and Jerry come up with the idea for Jerry's sitcom to be based on incidents and characters from their own lives. George suggests that it be a "show about nothing," an appellation for which *Seinfeld* became famous. Jerry and George pitch their idea to NBC executives, who are dubious about the merits of a "show about nothing."

The self-reflexive nature of *Seinfeld* gives it an appropriately satirical bent while toying with reality in a carnivalesque manner. Part of the carnivalesque attitude is a celebration of the grotesque. According to Bakhtin, "The essential principle of grotesque realism is degradation, that is, the lowering of all that is high . . . [by] transfer to the material level, to the sphere of earth and body" (19).[8] *Seinfeld* was notable for its use of the grotesque, and in "The Pitch" episode, and its follow-ups, it is used considerably to comment on high/low relationships.

The first appearance of this relation occurs early on, as Kramer suggests that Jerry play the manager of a circus in his proposed show. As Stallybrass and White remind us, "The carnival, the circus, the gypsy . . . play a symbolic role in bourgeois culture out of all proportion to their actual social importance" (20). Or, as Kramer states, "The show isn't about the circus, it's about watching freaks." George articulates the high/low juxtaposition as he expresses anxiety in meeting with NBC executives, men who are quite unlike him with their "jobs, suits and ties, wives, secretaries." Ironically, it is at this meeting that George meets his future fiancée, Susan, a network executive, who will later die in the series from licking the cheap wedding announcement envelopes George buys. Susan is the high brought low as she becomes the victim of Kramer's vomiting attack while announcing to Jerry and George that their show idea has been accepted. Jerry, George, and Kramer are representatives of the low, who are given authority to bring down the high.

The main target of these carnivalesque practices is the character of NBC president Russell Dalrymple. George manages to convince Russell to back their pilot show about nothing, offering as his credentials a fake off-Broadway play titled *La Cosina*. His agreement to do the pilot is punctuated with another comment reminiscent of Gitlin's interviews: "I've got a feeling about you two." The joke here, that NBC executives are clueless enough to give the go-ahead to a show about nothing written by a stand-up comic and his terminally unemployed, no-talent best friend, is doubled by the fact that the real *Seinfeld* was eventually picked up and became the biggest hit of the decade despite the concerns of executives that the show was "too New York, too Jewish" (Jacobs, "Seinfeld" 11), echoing the opinion articulated earlier by Mike Dann. Russell is eventually brought down from his position of power through his infatuation with Elaine, who rejects his advances and refuses to take him seriously. This rejection makes Russell desperate, and he attempts to fire a stagehand for no reason. In an outburst, he screams, "Do you know who I am? Do you know how much money I make? . . . I can have any woman in this city I want." Believing that his job is keeping Elaine from him, Russell throws it all away, joins Greenpeace, and is lost at sea. Meanwhile, his replacement cancels the *Jerry* pilot two minutes after it is broadcast.

Several subplots in this narrative arc celebrate the body and the grotesque, including George's obsession with a growth on his lip and his conviction that his death is imminent, Elaine's attempt to file a discrimination lawsuit against a restaurant owner whose waitresses all have large breasts, and Kramer's incontinence. This last plot line allows for one of the more telling juxtapositions in the story. As the pilot for *Jerry* is about to be filmed in front of a studio audience and Jerry announces "Are you ready to meet our cast," the scene cuts to Kramer preparing to receive an enema to cure him of his ills. This joke is typical of the sophomoric humor that was prevalent on *Seinfeld*, causing Stark to reflect on its "evocation of early male adolescence." He notes that, "many psychologists consider that preteen stage of life, when one is acutely aware of being powerless, as the time when individuals are most subversive of society-at-large" (*Glued* 285). *Seinfeld* is ironic in its subversiveness, as evidenced by its self-reflexive portrayal in this series of episodes. For instance, Jerry states his insecurities about the show: "I can't act. I stink. I don't know what I'm doing." He confesses his belief that the show will ruin his career. While it was widely noted during the series' run that Seinfeld himself was not a great actor, the show obviously did not ruin his career.

Just as in the final episode of *The Mary Tyler Moore Show*, this series of *Seinfeld* episodes gave writer Larry David a forum for subversiveness, played out in his portrayal of broadcasting decision makers. While Russell Dalrymple okays the fictional *Jerry* despite George's incompetence, the pilot is ultimately rejected by his successor. The audience, however, knows that the real *Seinfeld*, using the same premise, became the most successful program of the 1990s.

CONCLUSION

As workers selling their labor to the owners of the production apparatus, television sitcom writers have to deal with the realities of the business world. Unless they have achieved uncommon power, they are subject to the decisions of corporate executives and others. Their words and characters may be changed and eventually taken away from them. With the product of their labor removed from their control, writers are subject to alienation. But writers, especially those who work in the comedic vein, are capable of instilling messages of resistance in their texts. They reclaim some power by creating a world where their oppressors are brought low, and in doing so, they speak for more than just themselves. As Fiske writes in *Understanding Popular Culture*, "What people in capitalist societies have in common is the dominant ideology and the experience of subordination or disempowerment" (28). The episodes discussed here reflect that subordination while providing renewed empowerment for both the viewers and the program's creators.

Television creators like Carl Reiner, James Brooks, Jerry Seinfeld, and Larry David may not appear to have much in common with average viewers settled into their living rooms ready to laugh at the latest installment of their favorite situation comedy. But in Marx's formulation of the classes, they have in common that neither writer nor viewer own the production apparatus. Though obviously more highly rewarded than most workers, television creators still work in an environment in which the product of their labor is not entirely within their control. When a show is as successful as *The Dick Van Dyke Show*, *The Mary Tyler Moore Show*, or *Seinfeld*, however, it is certainly given more power to control its own destiny, and the creators of the episodes discussed here have used that power to comment upon tensions and conflicts prevalent in the television industry beneath a veil of humor. Like all great comedy, there is a good deal of truth behind the laughter.

NOTES

1. Marx notes a distinction between class *in itself*, or the objective reality of social conditions of existence, and class *for itself*, in which classes respond to their situation through solidarity with other classes by creating a common identity (see Fiske and Hartley 101–102).

2. Secondary texts are publicity materials, journalistic, historical, or critical items produced by the professional media. Tertiary texts are produced by the fan audience through fan literature, water cooler discussions, etc. (see Fiske, *Television* 108).

3. Reiner also used his experiences as a young actor as the basis for his novel *Enter Laughing*, which later became a Broadway play and a 1967 film, which he directed.

4. In the early days of television, 40 percent of television sets were in the New York City area. As television spread across the rest of America, the popularity of Jewish vaudeville comedians like Berle and Caesar waned in favor of the situation comedy (see Marc, *Comic Visions* 98).

5. The final episode of *The Dick Van Dyke Show*, broadcast in 1966, brings the Reiner/Brady connection full circle as Rob Petrie's autobiography is bought by Alan so he can play Rob in a television series.

6. Other series that have shown media executives in a less than flattering light include *WKRP in Cincinnati* and *NewsRadio.*

7. It should be noted that the other two series discussed here also left the airwaves on their own terms rather than through cancellation.

8. For a discussion of Bakhtin's notion of carnival and the grotesque in relation to rock 'n' roll, see Kohl.

PART SEVEN

Implications of Ideology

Sex and the Sitcom

Gender and Genre in Millennial Television

Christine Scodari

As the twenty-first century loomed, the competitive climate of broadcast network television in the United States was characterized by increasing specialization and "narrowcasting" due to competition with syndication, cable, and satellite (Croteau and Hoynes 122–29). Commercial-free premium (pay) cable networks such as Showtime and HBO joined the fray with original situation comedy and drama series. The newest of the "big four" networks, FOX, had established itself by carving out younger niche audiences. This inspired its fledgling successors (The WB and UPN), cable, and pay cable networks to enter the demographic sweepstakes, often earmarking gender and/or ethnicity in their programming. The evolutionary trajectory for the big four and premium cable networks has been toward targeting many of their series to either male *or* female audiences exactingly and, to an unprecedented degree, dichotomizing narrative structure and other constituents accordingly. It should come as no surprise that situation comedies, normally associated with the feminine, have been in the forefront of this paradigm shift (Rowe, *Unruly* 103–04).

This chapter adopts a feminist perspective to examine the text and context of two such sitcoms, FOX's *Ally McBeal* and HBO's *Sex and the City*, within the framework of this larger evolution. Each, as an exemplar of an emergent subgenre referred to as the "sexcom" and in accordance with the parameters and commercial imperatives of its network, exhibits narrative and other textual elements that simultaneously privilege and trivialize concerns of the feminine, private sphere (as opposed to the masculine, public sphere). This focus further entrenches audience segmentation via a separate spheres doctrine, while purporting to celebrate the emancipated, multifaceted, millennial woman.

EMERGENCE OF THE "SEXCOM"

Ally McBeal premiered in 1997 after prolific creator/producer David E. Kelley was commissioned by FOX to develop a "series with a strong female lead, one who appeals to women, ages eighteen to thirty-four" and immediately challenged half-hour sitcom convention with its sixty-minute format (Chunovic, *Complete* 40). In fact, some have labeled the series a "dramedy" with similar tendencies to magical realism as ABC's *Moonlighting*, CBS's *Northern Exposure*, and another of Kelley's creations, CBS's *Picket Fences* (Peterson).

Sex and the City, created and produced by Aaron Spelling protégé Darren Starr and based on Candace Bushnell's *New York Observer* column and book of the same title, debuted on HBO in 1998. As a late spring/summer series, it offered fresh, thirty-minute episodes at a time when the majority of broadcast network programs were in reruns. Like most pay cable series, its season is abbreviated, comprising twelve to eighteen installments.

Differences exist between the commercial imperatives of pay cable and those of broadcast networks. Eric Kessler, HBO's executive vice president in charge of marketing, explains the distinction: "The brand itself is very critical. Most television networks promote a show so you will watch that show. We promote a show to help sell the network. That's a big difference" (qtd. in Ross 20). Consequently, offering something for all key consumers in a household affluent enough to afford premium cable is vital in the marketing of networks such as HBO, both to these consumers and to the cable companies through which they subscribe. The tendency to segment the audience, however, is so prevalent elsewhere that it cannot help but influence the decision making of pay cable programmers.

Each program features a female principal—Calista Flockhart as attorney Ally McBeal and Sarah Jessica Parker as *Sex and the City*'s sex columnist Carrie Bradshaw—and a slate of attractive, urban, professional women, most of whom are also single, White, and fit snugly into the twenty-five to thirty-four demographic grouping. Only *Ally McBeal* includes a minority of regularly appearing male characters. Both series deal almost exclusively with the feminine, private-sphere issues surrounding sexual and/or romantic relationships and can be considered prototypes for a subgenre called the "sexcom," evolving out of such "buddy" series as NBC's *Seinfeld* and *Friends*. It is the prevailing,

FIGURE 19.1. Calista Flockhart as Ally McBeal in *Ally McBeal*, 1997–2002. Photo courtesy of Larry Edmunds BooksFair.

de facto situation that both series not only target but feature women, although, hypothetically, the subgenre need not require it. Structurally, sexcoms extend what Newcomb labeled "cumulative narrative" traits, such as those seen in *The West Wing*, *ER* (both NBC), and *N.Y.P.D. Blue* (ABC), all of which feature multiple story arcs of varying duration. The evolutionary sexcom, however, appears to limit arcs longer than one episode to relational issues.

Ally McBeal's primary setting, a Boston law firm headed by John Cage (Peter MacNicol) and Richard Fish (Greg Germann), also places it within the subgenre of what Nochimson refers to as "workbuddy" shows, which "focus on the interconnecting lives of a group of professionally linked people that approximates the cohesion of a family despite the absence of actual blood ties" (26). Although dramatic workbuddy programs such as *ER* and *The West Wing* also focus on activities within a professional environment, work-related issues and conflicts drive many of the stories. On *Ally McBeal* legal cases are contained within a single episode and exist primarily to parallel the sexual politics of personal relationships played out within longer story arcs beyond the courtroom. This is not explained purely in terms of the comedy/drama differentiation, however, since earlier workbuddy sitcoms such as CBS's female-oriented *Mary Tyler Moore Show*, *Murphy Brown*, and *Designing Women* dealt more with work-related situations.

Symptomatic of *Ally McBeal*'s unrelenting intrusion of the private upon the public are the twenty-something title character's incessant daydream fantasies, including the notorious, computer-animated "dancing baby" that ludicrously signifies her ticking biological clock. Ally must also play colleague to her high school beau, Billy Thomas (Gil Bellows), for whom she still carries a torch, as well as his wife, Georgia (Courtney Thorne-Smith). The negotiation of relational matters between and among the sexes in the firm's "unisex restroom"—the most personal of spaces—as well as the coworkers' ritualistic revolving dalliances at the office cellar bistro, also accentuate the private domain while, particularly in the case of the former, trivializing it. Unlike the convivial, multi-topical repartee characteristic of the coffeehouse in *Friends* or the diner in *Seinfeld*, the sexcom's off-hour discourse is limited to the strictly and intensely personal.

Sex and the City's New York action proceeds from Bradshaw's narration as she conjures up angles for her newspaper column based on her own sexual/romantic escapades and those of her three gal pals, but the nod to the public sphere mostly begins and ends there. We know that Miranda Hobbes (Cynthia Nixon) is a lawyer, Samantha Jones (Kim Cattrall) is a publicist, and Charlotte York (Cristin Davis) runs an art gallery, but little interplay occurs within their workspaces or alongside their professional cohorts. The movable "girls' lunch" is *Sex and the City*'s answer to *Ally McBeal*'s unisex bathroom and happy hour ritual—a leisure setting in which the friends converge at least once an episode to discuss their primarily romantic/personal affairs. Interestingly,

Ally McBeal retorted in season four with a periodic "girls' sleepover," similarly excluding men from participation in personal chatter. Unlike in *Ally McBeal*, the relational story arcs that establish continuity from episode to episode are, in *Sex and the City*'s cumulative narrative, almost exclusively romantic entanglements between one of the featured women and a short-term or semi-regular male character. Thus, the duration of these arcs automatically manifests each heroine's monogamous or promiscuous propensities, and the program's focus on the (very) private sphere is woven into its very fabric.

Samantha is the eldest of the "girls" and the most sexually adventurous, with the bulk of her affairs and, consequently, her stories, contained within a single thirty-minute installment. Season four brings two exceptions—Samantha's fling with her boss, who halts the vacillation in her romantic cynicism by cheating on her, and a lesbian relationship that folds because of her stereotypically "masculine" inability to commit. Samantha's conservative flip side is Charlotte, whose single-minded quest for a husband serves to maximize her number of sexual liaisons and minimize her number of multiple episode tales until she lands one, albeit tentatively, in season three. Carrie is the most monogamous; her on again, off again relationships with recurring presences Mr. Big (Chris Noth) and Aidan Shaw (John Corbett) provide the most sustained story arcs of the series' first four seasons.

While Ally's parents have appeared intermittently, *Sex and the City*'s women are framed as one another's only true kin. Miranda's unseen mother dies in season four, and other relatives remain voiceless and backgrounded at the funeral as Miranda seeks solace with her friends. Beyond that, nary a relative appears onscreen or is even mentioned by the quartet—an omission that seems most conspicuous in episodes in which the family of Charlotte's fiancé, rather than her own, is integral to events surrounding her upscale, society nuptials. Although Bradshaw's narration and a few isolated plots in *Sex and the City* tout the profundity of female friendship, for both *Ally McBeal* and *Sex and the City* the bonds of such friendship appear, in the fullness of the narrative, to be fashioned of mostly flimsy stuff—the travails of twenty- and thirty-something singles seeking an elusive but supposedly transcendent romantic fantasy.

SITCOMS AND SEPARATE SPHERES

Both *Ally McBeal* and *Sex and the City* have been variously commended and denounced by scholars and the popular press for their gender representation. Ginia Bellafante uses the former and Wendy Shalit references the latter to condemn contemporary feminism, conveniently presuming, without much substantiation, that the feminist consensus has been to consider their heroines icons. In her much-debated, 1998 *Time* cover story, Bellafante observes:

"Fashion spectacle, paparazzi-jammed galas, mindless sex-talk—is this what the roadmap to greater female empowerment has become?" Stacey D'Erasmo probes the "new single-girl pathos" of both programs in the *New York Times*: "These characters really do just want to get married. . . . Who'd feel threatened by economically powerful, independent women as long as they're dissolving into tears?" (13). In *New Republic*, Ruth Shalit critiques the new crop of "postfeminist" television characters as "sophisticated women humbling themselves" in a "male producer's fantasy of feminism." She states that "Ally feels compelled to remind us again and again what a mess she is: the pain she feels takes the form of self-denigration bordering on self-hatred" (24). In *Vanity Fair*, James Wolcott concurs that *Sex and the City* pretends empowerment but is actually "spiked with self-loathing," proselytizing viewers into a "clique mentality" borne of a "sense of entitlement that underwrites the characters' existence" (69).

Certain scholarly analyses reflect, perhaps, a reason why some popular press critics rather simplistically assume these series to be feminist manifestos. Nochimson considers *Ally McBeal*'s postmodern style genuinely liberating, lauding the "many conflicting planes of existence" manifested in *Ally McBeal*'s character introspection and fantasy sequences (25), and condemning "puritanical feminist denunciations of the show for not justifying its fantasy by providing useful Aesopian feminist lessons" (30). Even she contends, however, that the series begins to exhibit sexist regression by the middle of its second season, interpreting this as a backlash against such orthodoxy (30). Similarly, Cooper lauds *Ally McBeal*'s feminine subjectivity and narrative reversal of the male gaze (see Mulvey) in the show's first season but still admits that this subversiveness was not adequately sustained in later episodes (429). As we shall see, there are problems with both Nochimson's and Cooper's claims of resistance, even with respect to the series' inaugural season. Shugart, Waggoner, and Hallstein are most critical of *Ally McBeal*, implicating the very postmodern style Nochimson extols by asserting that juxtaposition is employed to "recontextualize images and messages of resistance in a context in which those messages are reinscribed and consequently rendered insignificant or ineffective" (207).

Several of these commentaries allude to the issue spotlighted here—the sexcom's ample yet shallow treatment of the feminine, private domain in such as way as to hegemonically reinforce a separate spheres doctrine that encourages both men and women to suppress ambitions, desires, and qualities that do not harmonize with their culturally stipulated territory (Coontz 62–63). Female-oriented workbuddy sitcoms of the previous decade, such as CBS's *Murphy Brown* and *Designing Women*, dealt with friendship, family, and romance, but professional liaisons and work-related matters were just as frequently their grist, although Bonnie Dow argues that *Murphy Brown* ultimately reproduced the culture's tendency to discipline and tame the independent, working woman (*Prime-Time* 135–61). And, while male-oriented sit-coms such as NBC's *Seinfeld* and HBO's *The Larry Sanders Show* have also veered in the direction of the personal sphere, men's typical association with the public sphere and these shows' somewhat greater attention to work and the working environment in multiple episode arcs are a counterbalance when compared to the female-oriented sexcom.

Nochimson is correct that *Ally McBeal*'s narrative violation of the usually straightforward legal genre through its fantasy interludes can be considered, in isolation, counter-hegemonic (26). Laura Mumford, writing of soap opera, has challenged feminist critiques that celebrate as counter-hegemonic narra-tive structures and genres based primarily on their refusal of traditional, "mas-culine" conventions, arguing, "such an intervention would also have to occur at the level of content" (88). The previously mentioned content implications of *Ally McBeal*'s trademark dancing baby, for instance, can outweigh the implications of its innovative form.

Individual stories and vignettes in the two series illustrate the marginal-ization of the public sphere and backhanded ridicule of the private sphere per-vasive in the lives of the characters. If the women of *Sex and the City* and *Ally McBeal* are liberated, they are liberated in ways that tend to support, rather than challenge, patriarchal definitions of female sexuality. In a season-four sweeps episode of *Ally McBeal*, the svelte, attractive female attorneys at Cage and Fish discourage a woman from continuing a suit against a marriage guru who provided questionable advice; they collectively observe that the plaintiff is overweight and not particularly appealing and determine that her husband left her for reasons other than incompetent counseling. The lasting impression is that women should not chide men for judging women based on their appearance, since women judge one another based on such criteria.

A similarly slanted story premiering during third-season sweeps has the usually contentious colleagues Ally and Ling Woo (Lucy Liu) exploring same-sex desire with a date and a goodnight kiss, but the interludes play to a decidedly male gaze, as exemplified by a scene in which the two women dance together suggestively purely for the benefit of a gang of gawking men. In the end, they both decide that although their kiss was nice, what they "really want is a penis." Another tale finds John Cage eavesdropping on his girlfriend, attorney Nelle Porter (Portia de Rossi), as she confesses to Ling that she has fantasized about being spanked by her lover. When John attempts to grant Nelle that very fantasy, she is outraged and breaks off their romance. But her protest seems feigned and hypocritical, belied by the supposedly confidential revelation of her apparent need to feel dominated.

Other stories turn on purportedly emancipatory grounds but also validate masculine views of "acceptable" feminism. Ally gives women's rights lip ser-vice as she clashes with a male judge who forbids her to wear micro-miniskirts in the courtroom. The firm rallies to defend Ling from charges associated with her operation of an escort service. Partners in an all-female law firm founded by Ally's roommate, Renée Radick (Lisa Nicole Carson), require male applicants to remove their shirts during interviews. Although Cooper suggests that "when such behavior seems out of bounds for a woman, it suddenly becomes clear how unseemly it is for a man," there is another and more probable outcome (424). Given that "women do it, too" is often used in defense of such male behavior, it is likely that such reasoning would not summon condemnation of male employers who sexually objectify their female employees but, rather, reaffirmation that this behavior is a perk of power that anyone would embrace. While Cooper claims as resistive early stories involving the firm's representation of a newscaster who is fired because of her age and of a woman who breaks a prenuptial agreement after her husband leaves her for fresher quarry, these instances are few and far between, and their contents are simultaneously belied by the qualifications of youth and beauty upheld by the show's most visible female characters. Moreover, as Nochimson posits, the subversive desire previously manifested in fantasy transforms into hegemonic absurdity in later seasons (31).

Sex and the City, at least, exhibits no pretense in its meager attention to the professional sphere. Work-related incidents merely flesh out the women's prevailing personal issues, many of which involve aging, sexual performance or exhibition, and/or competition among women. Carrie uses her column to tell on her candidate boyfriend after he makes a rather unconventional sexual request and then rejects her because of the possible political ramifications of being linked to a sex columnist. Assuming conflict between married and single women, Miranda pretends to be a lesbian so that her male colleagues' wives, no longer considering her a threat, will invite her to dinner parties critical in her campaign to become partner. The double standard of aging is apparent in an episode in which Samantha, approaching forty, interprets vaguely menopausal symptoms as a sign that her sex life is over, and another in which Carrie and Samantha date younger men but ultimately decide, despite the many older man/younger woman couplings in evidence, that such an arrangement cannot work in reverse. Samantha's resentment of younger women intensifies when her youthful assistant hijacks her professional contacts. Charlotte works through her modesty when an artist asks to immortalize her vagina on canvas.

In fact, both programs are rife with sexual and commodity fetishization of the body and its adornments, with *Ally McBeal* emphasizing the female and *Sex and the City* appearing, on the surface, to be more evenhanded. The "equal opportunity nudity" of *Sex and the City*, in which exposed male derrières and female breasts (with the exception of Parker's, who has a no-nudity clause in her contract) are customary, sets the tone. Moreover, *Sex and the City*'s conversational consideration of the male member has fixated on size (too small for Samantha's exigencies in one instance, too large in another), its uncircum-

cised state, its inability to sustain an erection (troubling, most notably, Charlotte's short-lived marriage), right down to the unpleasant flavor of its ejacu-
late. Again, what may appear at first glance to be the resistive turning of patriarchal tables actually serves to ratify the legitimacy of similar criteria for
desirability in women. Do women gab about sex and the physical characteristics of their significant others? Yes, but not to the virtual exclusion of other
attributes and other topics—a reality that is not reflected in the show.

Women's bodies and their ornamentation are fetishized on *Sex and the
City* in the friends' deliberations concerning particular men's preferences.
Another mechanism is the pervasiveness of very posh and revealing fashion,
as reflective of the clandestine product and lifestyle advertising concocted by
premium cable networks distinguished by their upscale clientele and supposed
lack of overt commercial content. The show has run afoul of animal rights
groups critical of its unrepentant display of fur. Designer labels are habitually
name-dropped; Kate Spade and Fendi handbags, and Manolo Blahnik and
Jimmy Choo shoes have figured prominently in story lines. Fans interested in
identifying all the clothing and accessories sported by *Sex and the City*'s fashion mavens may do so by visiting the show's official Web site
(www.hbo.com/city). Thus, the female body is equated with conspicuous consumption, and the parade of fashion status symbols becomes a strategy by
which HBO promotes itself as a status symbol to be coveted by the prosper-
ous and chic.

On *Ally McBeal*, women's bodies, style, and fashion prevail under the
microscope. Ally's micro-miniskirts are not the only issue, as the firm's secretary, Elaine Vassal (Jane Krakowski), develops a sag-reducing "face bra" as a
moneymaking scheme and, somewhat later, a "vi-bra" that appears to maneuver the breasts by remote control. Richard Fish displays a fetish for the fleshy
undersides of older women's necks (their "wattles"). His abbreviated romance
with Judge Whipper Cone (Dyan Cannon), twenty years his senior, plays as a
testament to the male veneration of women's body fragments and the corresponding pressure for women to accumulate piecemeal surgical enhancements
as they age. Ally's unspoken attraction to men she encounters is evidenced by
a sudden lashing of her tongue in their direction—an elongated, lizard-like,
animated tongue. John Cage devises a gadget that releases his girlfriend
Nelle's long blonde locks from their proper updo, and another that raises and
lowers the heels of her pumps—both at his whim. Moreover, the only two
female characters on the show who are not exceptionally thin, Renée and
Elaine, also depart from the others in terms of their "colors"; Renée is the primary Black regular, and Elaine is the lone pink collar/working-class presence.
Predictably, these two, plus a second non-White heroine, Ling, are the most
sexually rapacious women on the show. On *Sex and the City* it is Samantha,
marginalized by virtue of being five years the senior of the other three, who is
granted that stereotypical distinction.

Once again, Cooper takes a more favorable view of some of these aspects of *Ally McBeal*, alleging via narrative analysis alone this text's reversal of the male gaze while neglecting the camera and the dominant visual imagery of the women's idealized, fetishized, and commodified bodies. For instance, the fact that Fish admires women's "wattles," and that this is a common feature in older women, is offered by Cooper as a counter-hegemonic element (425). The fact that most "real" aging women do not resemble his older love interest, Whipper Cone—that she is so obviously a creation of cosmetic surgery— is not considered. In a season-five episode, he fixates on a septuagenarian in an effort to "cure" himself of this fetish. The visual image of Fish fingering the elder lady's flaccid neck is meant to disabuse *us* of any notion that loose female skin can ever be considered attractive.

It seems as if women's professional success is at once utterly conspicuous and taken for granted in the female-oriented sexcom. There is little in the structure and content of these shows, especially with regard to the appearance and experience of the major female protagonists, to call attention to women's day-to-day struggles to achieve aspirations in the public arena, unless it's to sanction what Ruth Shalit considers that "male producer's fantasy" of the modern, liberated woman. To be sure, struggle endures in these texts, but mainly in terms of the heroines' picayune and highly individualistic romantic/sexual lives and the prerequisite currency of their commodified female forms, imperatively decorative (and decorated), youthful, and reproductive. Dancing baby fantasies notwithstanding, until Ally's biological daughter, the product of an egg donation, surfaces in season five (the series' last), and Miranda's unplanned pregnancy plays out in *Sex and the City*'s fourth go-round, actual children are seldom pertinent in either show. Whereas family sitcoms have been known to portray the feminine and the feminine sphere as mundane, the sexcom, while pretending to rescue women from such humdrum domestic pursuits, actually belittles and disparages the private arena even more by representing it as petty and self-indulgent (Dellinger-Pate and Aden 160).

CONCLUSION

Recent studies performed by this author (with Jenna Felder) dealing with romantic comedy, soap opera, and *The X-Files* have attempted to reclaim matters of the private domain such as sex and romance as valuable despite their hegemonic misappropriation and to argue that a sense of security in this sphere allows women to devote more of their energies to public endeavors. This perspective challenges that of cultural critics such as Gitlin. In his book *Inside Primetime*, Gitlin dismisses the private sphere as a site of wasteful personal excess that discourages fruitful public life (332–33). I would submit that this view arises, in part, from a sense of the private sphere constructed via the typical experiences of bourgeois males, as opposed to those of the working class, the poor, and many women who are neither. In fact, women of various economic strata may derive their greater concern for social issues, such as public health and education, from the compassion, nurturance, sacrifice, and/or hard labor *they* have traditionally offered within the domestic realm. The message of the sexcom, however, appears to be that if women cannot navigate their public lives as smoothly and stylishly as Ally, Carrie, and their cohorts navigate the mean streets of Boston and New York, whatever intellectual, emotional, and physical energy remains will not be sufficient to achieve success in their demanding and time-consuming private affairs. Here, it is not a situation of ease and succor in the realm of personal relationships allowing greater devotion to public aspirations—an arrangement which, in turn, permits the cultural devaluation of the private domain under a masculine model and gives rise to the feminist rallying cry: "The personal is political." Instead, *Sex and the City*, *Ally McBeal*, and their ilk endorse the notion that women who flourish professionally must, unlike most of their male counterparts, scrape, scrounge, and sacrifice for personal happiness measured in terms of narrow and frivolous criteria.

Certainly, one ought not anticipate that a show entitled *Sex and the City* would concern itself with much else, and this analysis does not claim that its content is altogether new, only that it has been further honed and shielded from challenge and revision in the last decade or so due to commercial catalysts. In his book *Breaking Up America*, Turow acknowledges that segmentation has provided previously marginalized groups with "audiovisual identities," but counsels that such representations should ideally be shared among diverse populations instead of being narrowly targeted (199). Both men and women can be addressed with material that conflates the public and private in credible and resistive ways, but this has mostly been the province of drama. As previously mentioned, cumulative narrative series such as NBC's *West Wing* and *ER* do succeed in seamlessly integrating masculine form and content with feminine, albeit with male characters predominating in number, age diversity, and/or status. Efforts have been made to interpolate women in the audience with primarily female characters while maintaining a public/private synthesis. In her book *Defining Women*, Julie D'Acci chronicles the disposition of CBS's *Cagney and Lacey*, a 1980s cop/buddy series targeted to working women. Although the network pressured the show's creators to make the female leads and their activities more traditionally feminine, the initial intent was otherwise. Some recent series, such as CBS's *Family Law* and *Judging Amy*, appear to grasp *Cagney and Lacey*'s original concept. The return to prominence of the family drama, however, exemplified by such recent series as NBC's *American Dreams* and The WB's *7th Heaven*, suggests that network executives still believe that the domestic arena must dominate in order to gather a female audience.

As for comedy, the work/buddy subgenre has increasingly shifted away from the "work" and toward the "buddy," especially in terms of those courting the younger female demographic. Along with family dramas, which aim for a somewhat older segment, sitcoms such as *Ally McBeal* and *Sex and the City* could become even more pervasive—the primary sites for "ghettoization" of the female audience, in much the same fashion as African Americans have been relegated to the comedy genres and emergent broadcast outlets such as The WB and UPN. Darren Starr's African American version of *Sex and the City*, *Girlfriends* (UPN), is but one example of such ghettoization. As mentioned earlier, the characteristics of the sexcom could, theoretically, apply to male-oriented vehicles. It is noteworthy that they do not—at least to the extent elaborated here.

Empirical audience investigation might supplement this analysis, particularly in order to assess Nochimson's assumption that postmodern form is resistive in and of itself; Shugart, Waggoner, and Hallstein's assertion that it can actually serve hegemonic ends; Mumford's view that content trumps form; and Cooper's claims about *Ally McBeal*'s resistive feminine subjectivity. It is also quite true that a male/female gender divide is not the only basis upon which to assess such programming. Observation of online bulletin boards reveals, particularly in the case of *Sex and the City*, a significant gay male following, and this might be investigated (see Wolcott 64–72). This chapter demonstrates, however, that the genesis and acceptance of the sexcom—exemplified by female-oriented *Ally McBeal* and *Sex and the City*, both accentuating and demeaning the private sphere to the virtual eradication of the professional domain as a generator of pivotal plot—warrant apprehension as they illustrate a commercially instigated trend to further dissociate the masculine from the feminine in audiences, narrative structure, content and, indeed, in the experience of everyday life.

CHAPTER 20

Cheers

Searching for the Ideal Public Sphere in the Ideal Public House

Robert S. Brown

The issue of representing the multiple voices of society that occur within the unified whole has been the subject of debate in education, politics, and entertainment. Making a place at the table for all members of a diverse society challenges its members to create an environment where all might participate in the sharing of knowledge and the crafting of culture. Jürgen Habermas is known for his theories on the ideal speech situation and further attempted to locate those situations in an ideal public sphere in *The Structural Transformation of the Public Sphere*. Searching through history, he found his ideal sphere in late-medieval Europe, yet failed to find it in the modern world, mainly due to his high, arguably elitist, standards. In a continuing effort to locate that elusive, ideal public sphere, I shall combine Habermas's ideas with those put forth by his critics and apply them to contemporary society to argue that a model for the modern ideal public sphere appeared on television every Thursday night for eleven years in a place called *Cheers*.

HABERMAS AND HIS CRITICS

Jürgen Habermas, sociologist, political scientist, and cultural critic, studied the problems of legitimation and communication in the creation of the ideal public sphere. In *The Structural Transformation*, Habermas argues that in this sphere, where a community of independent, educated people existed as equals between the state and the masses, opinions on matters of general interest were openly debated in the salons, reading rooms, and coffee houses of Europe. This realm of ideas, brought about by economic and historical circumstances, monitored the tensions of a changing society in the late seventeenth and early eighteenth century. According to Habermas, however, this ideal sphere was short-lived, failing to survive in its critical social role due to the intertwining of society and the state through democratization.

Keith Michael Baker offers multiple criticisms of Habermas's bourgeois public sphere. Baker questions Habermas's definition of the sphere's membership, arguing that from Habermas's description, only male property owners had any say in "the needs and interests of civil society in the political public sphere" (186). Baker continues this line of thinking, arguing that the public opinion formed by Habermas's public would represent a single class. Baker also argues that Habermas's public sphere was actually private, representing a select few opinions while leaving out the vast majority. Baker then applies these criticisms to pre-revolutionary French society, concluding that this public sphere was better than the British bourgeois public sphere because it was open to more people and had a special focus on the increased role of women (186–87).

David Zaret's major criticism is that Habermas is too focused on the role of economics in creating a public sphere. While Zaret admits that economics are important, one cannot understand the historical development of the public without taking into account the influence of religion, science, and printing. According to Zaret, these factors are key in the public sphere's interaction with the larger culture, and when included in Habermas's findings, the characteristics of the ideal public sphere are altered, for the better. First, the three new factors allow for more participants in the public sphere, whom Zaret describes as people of "a more popular social milieu than in the learned culture that is the focus of Habermas' account" (220). Next, Zaret points out that while Habermas does mention the role of the press in his study, he reduces its function to the dissemination of information. Zaret argues that the press had a much greater effect as "a causal factor that shaped new modes of thought" (214). These new ways of thinking still have the critical rational traits that Habermas idealizes, but they are not quite as rational or universal (Zaret 221, 223). Zaret also argues that by expanding the identification of the public sphere using his three criteria as well as economics, the public can be involved in "more critical, rational modes of reflection on matters of collective social interest . . . situated in their social context," rather than separated from civilization, as is the case in Habermas's description (215). This idea of a broader public using different styles of rational criticism to discuss cultural issues is important in thinking about the way a public, with an emphasis on diversity, must communicate.

Habermas's historically based study found the elusive ideal public sphere to be a small community of educated socialites practicing social criticism in late-seventeenth-century Europe. In order to find a modern equivalent—taking into account changes in society—it is necessary to expand on Habermas's original criteria. Employing Baker's requirement of a more representative community and Zaret's inclusion of multiple social influences and varying forms of criticism, allows us to look for contemporary models of the ideal public sphere.

LOCATING A CONTEMPORARY IDEAL PUBLIC SPHERE

The television show *Cheers*, an ensemble comedy based on the antics of patrons of a Boston bar, finished its eleven-year run on television in 1993. Its end was not due to a lack of viewers; it was still a highly rated program when it left the air. As is the case with many long-running programs, however, some members of the cast, most notably lead actor Ted Danson, decided to make career changes. Steven Stark, columnist for the *Boston Globe*, states that while many shows have good writing and acting, *Cheers* had something more. Stark credits the show's appeal to the idea that "the real message of 'Cheers' was an affirmation of the power of the group and of the community" (11). Rarely has any successful television show relied so heavily on dialogue alone. While other programs with ensemble casts may rely heavily upon one or two locations—regulars on *The Andy Griffith Show* in Mayberry's jail or Andy's home, the cast of *M*A*S*H* in a few tents, the characters of *Friends* and *Seinfeld* split between an apartment and a local eatery—the citizens of *Cheers* were rarely seen outside of the bar throughout the eleven-year run of the program. While outside lives were mentioned, the whole show was based upon how the elements of those lives were discussed from a series of barstools. In fact, most episodes opened with one of the characters, typically Norm, entering the bar and starting a conversation. Certainly, a key to the show's popularity was its tremendous writing, but by considering concepts of community, the program can be seen as demonstrating a higher, more inviting purpose. The environment of Cheers was very appealing to a huge audience because it appeared to be such a welcoming place to sit around and converse. This ideal discussion space, while basically reflecting Habermas's description of the salon, goes a step further by including the suggestions of both Baker and Zaret, which positions Cheers as a model for the modern ideal public sphere.

Both Baker and Zaret agree that Habermas's bourgeois public sphere was too narrow in its representation of the public, leading to public opinion based upon the conversations of a singular, literate strata of upper-class men. At Cheers, a wider spectrum of the public was represented, and all had equal voice in discussions. The cast of characters includes the highly literate, represented

FIGURE 20.1. (top row, left to right) John Ratzenberger as Cliff Gavin, Roger Rees as Robin Colcord, Ted Danson as Sam Malone, Woody Harrelson as Woody Boyd, and George Wendt as Norm Peterson. (middle row, left to right) Rhea Perlman as Carla Tortelli LeBec, Kirstie Alley as Rebecca Howe, and Shelley Long as Diane Chambers. (bottom row, left to right) Kelsey Grammar as Dr. Frasier Crane and Bebe Neuwirth as Dr. Lilith Sternin in *Cheers*, 1982–1993. Photo courtesy of Larry Edmunds BooksFair.

by Diane, Frasier, and Lilith, and a seemingly uneducated working class, represented by Coach, Woody, and Carla. Cliff fits the role of what Habermas and Goethe describe as the public person, a "servant of the state," who through dress and bearing purposefully tries to appear as a representative of their position (Habermas 13). Norm, spending most of the series as an uninspired or unemployed accountant, appears to represent the average person, the "norm." Sam Malone, a former major league pitcher for the beloved hometown Red Sox now serving drinks from the center of his four-walled castle, represents royalty, looked up to by most of the other characters.

While these characters represent many different levels of education, wealth, and social position in their individual lives, they all have an equal place at the bar once they enter Cheers. Their allegiances seem to shift with the topics, and even the core group of Sam, Cliff, Norm, and Carla is occasionally split by some issue. Yet, by the end of the day, issues have been fully discussed and a conclusion with which all are satisfied has been arrived at. All of the characters have their chance to shine, just as all are suitably insulted. Cliff appears to get the most constant abuse, perhaps because he exemplifies the tension existing between the public and the state.

The women of the show hold just as strong a position as the men and are rarely excluded from any debate. As Stark comments in his column, "'Cheers' presented a true cast of many equals" (11). It can be argued that the female characters reinforced very negative stereotypes: the pedantic, perky Diane; volatile, oft-unwed mother Carla; the intellectual, ice queen Lilith; and obtuse, gold-digging Rebecca. Yet, the men were portrayed with equally stereotypical characteristics: Sam, the dumb jock; Cliff, the braggart; Woody, the hick; Norm, the sloth; and Frasier, the elitist rounding out this cast of characters. They are at once perpetrators and victims of each other's jokes. They often suffer humiliation at the hands of social "superiors," such as the unscrupulous rival Gary, of Gary's Tavern, and the wealthy aristocrat Robin Colcord. Yet, the gang at Cheers always comes through. Gary loses his bar, and Colcord is bankrupted and jailed while the representatives of the larger culture situated at Cheers survive.

The forms of critical rational debate that occur in the bar represent much of what Zaret desires. Bar debates are not always of the high standard that Habermas demanded from his literate bourgeois but, instead, reflect the less rational mode that Zaret expects to exist when influenced by an expanded community. The debates are unstructured, the information often weak or confused, yet the characters take them very seriously and perform rational criticism that a diverse social group would be capable of attaining. The intellectuals—Diane and Frasier—are not granted superior status in this sphere, nor are Coach and Woody relegated to the margin. In the process of discussion, all of the voices are heard, alternately denigrated and respected, all contributing to the marketplace of ideas.

The subject matter of these debates is also not always at the level that Habermas idealizes. Instead, some critical debates fall under the category Zaret refers to as "collective social interest" (215). Sports, television, and movies make up the majority of the debate issues that occur around the bar— issues that should be expected of a society heavily influenced not by the theater, symphony, and literature of Habermas's elite culture, but by the popular press, television, and movies of Zaret's public sphere.

Michelle Hilmes, in her article "Where Everybody Knows Your Name: *Cheers* and the Mediation of Culture," argues that much of the show's appeal was based upon the merging of high and low cultures. Diane and Frasier represent the more intellectual ideals and act as foils for the rest of the bar characters. By having both qualities represented, Hilmes argues, the show fulfills multiple audience desires for both high- and low-culture entertainment without viewers being forced to choose (72). Hilmes recognizes that "meaningful critical interpretation is not limited to the high art," while lower standards "are often subtly reinforced through a demonstrated consensus, even when those attitudes are directly critical of such high culture totems" (70). Hilmes doesn't go so far as to examine the diversity of the topics discussed and the resulting consensus, although her argument seems to be moving toward that conclusion.

Besides the popular culture and highbrow versus lowbrow debate topics, the gang at Cheers also debates more serious social issues. Topics such as homosexuality, alcoholism, gender roles, and relationships often take center stage. Quite a few shows examine political issues, including an episode in the final season during which a discussion over the state of Boston politics leads to Frasier campaigning for Woody's election to Boston's city council. These bar debates can be seen as clear examples of Habermas's ideal, with the modifications supplied by his critics, as the characters bring their various backgrounds and experiences to the discussion. The issues are then discussed at length until a satisfactory conclusion is reached and a new, often very insightful, understanding is gained.

The social impact of the process of intellectual debate can actually be seen over the course of many seasons. Take, for example, the issue of homosexuality. In the show's first season, Tom Kenderson, one of Sam's old baseball buddies—his former catcher in fact—requests the use of Cheers as the site for the start of his book tour (in the episode "Boys in the Bar"). While the catcher urges Sam to read the book first, the less-than-well-read former pitcher schedules the event without even glancing at the volume. What Sam is unaware of is that his old buddy has come out and discusses his homosexual lifestyle in the book, a fact later pointed out to Sam by the erudite Diane. The bar debate then explodes. Some of the obviously homophobic bar patrons take the side that the reputation of the bar, and Sam, could be hurt by hosting the book signing. This would damage business and Sam's image as a ladies' man. Diane, representing a more open-minded opinion, argues that Sam should not throw away the friendship simply because the other man has announced his sexual preference. In the end, after discussing the potential outcomes for the length of the program, Sam joins his ex-teammate in the bar in front of the media to support his friend. Sam's reputation is not hurt; his bar business does not fall off; and perhaps more importantly, his friends at the bar change their attitudes about the issue.

The group learns by talking out the issues openly, and this discussion leads eventually to acceptance. By the seventh season, Norm is willing to pretend that he is gay in order to get an interior decorator job ("Norm, is that you?"). By the tenth season, the bar has come to a clear acceptance of the gay lifestyle ("Rebecca's Lover . . . Not"). It is Rebecca, a relative newcomer to the bar, who is unaware that her ideal man, an old high school friend in town for a visit, is gay. The community of the bar must work together to find a tactful way of telling Rebecca the news without crushing or embarrassing her. No longer is there any fear of homosexuality or how it will change their lives. The issue has been discussed openly and dealt with in a positive manner, sometimes intelligently and sometimes with base humor, without significant disruption of the community.

The cultural representation at Cheers is not without flaw. Although class and gender differences are clearly present, there is nary a minority. Few African American, Asian, Hispanic, or other minority group members appear as lead characters or even background customers in the show. What is worse is that when these characters do appear, they are very stereotypical. Sam hires an Asian man to fix his jukebox and supply a karaoke machine. During the show's second season, Cliff's constant chatter has drawn the ire of a bully ("Cliff's Rocky Moment"). Cliff brings a Black coworker named Lewis, a large, athletic male, to the bar as a bodyguard to protect him. While it could be argued that the writers have attempted to duplicate the racist reputation of Boston's Beacon Hill district, this should not be an excuse for the lack of minority representation. Because of this, the bar is not truly representational of all multicultural facets.

Cheers retained its popularity on television in the primetime schedule for eleven years and continues to do so in syndication. I have argued that this popularity is due in large part to its public accessibility. Cheers, as a physical location, invites the public to enter and take their place in the discussion. The banter runs from the most trivial of conversations to heavier dialogues in which contemporary social issues are debated to a peaceful conclusion. The show represents a model of the modern ideal public sphere, as suggested by Habermas and his critics, which fans have obviously found appealing. As a model, it serves as an example of what can be achieved through public discourse. As a popular television show, it invites viewers into the discussions as virtual patrons of the bar, viewer-participants in the discussion of the day. Hilmes points out that through series like *Cheers*, "television, rather than existing in a state of tension between high and low culture demands, becomes the very place where differences are not only mediated but celebrated" (71–72). The sphere, while not measuring up to the demands of Habermas's ideal, instead includes the suggestions of Baker and Zaret, creating a better public sphere where representatives of the state, royalty, literary, and working classes, male and female, poor and well-off, can participate in equal and open social criticism. It is public address at its best: a space where the conversations of the masses overlap with media reports, speeches, and other symbolic exchanges to provide a locus for serious discussion resulting in democratic outcomes. *Cheers* truly provides a place where "everyone knows your name."

CHAPTER 21

"It's Just a Bunch of Stuff That Happened"

The Simpsons and the Possibility of Postmodern Comedy

H. Peter Steeves

At the center of the finest episodes of *The Simpsons* there is absolutely nothing. ("Ummm . . . creamy nothing center. Aghghghgh. . . .") This should only be disappointing if we are thinking that something should be there, that we deserve something there. Part of the postmodern condition, of our condition, is such frustration of expectation—not just particular expectations, but the notion of expectation in general with its linear conception of cause and effect, its reliance on there being a stable and coherent self to do the expecting, its overall naive innocence about how the world operates. *The Simpsons*, hollow as it is, is anything but naive; and thus it demands a sophisticated conception of humor.

TRADITIONAL THEORIES OF COMEDY WORKED FOR MORE TRADITIONAL TIMES

Immanuel Kant's (very Kantian and thus very unfunny) description of what is funny—"the placing of heterogeneous notions under common genera"—

explains why jokes about rabbis, priests, and ministers who hang out together on golf courses can get laughs. But who tells these sorts of jokes anymore, at least unironically? Thomas Hobbes's insistence that all humor stems from a sudden sense of superiority—that jokes bring pleasure precisely because someone is in pain *and it is not me*—might explain why it is funny to watch the Three Stooges, why it is funny (for some) to tell ethnic jokes, or why it is hilarious to note that Hobbes is dead and you and I are not. But so much comedy today is about self-deprecation (think of David Letterman's late night incarnations or Larry David's HBO series *Curb Your Enthusiasm*) that Hobbes seems quaintly out of place—like Don Rickles guest-hosting *The Chris Rock Show*. Henri Bergson's claim that humor arises from involuntary actions, that we expect to find adaptability and pliability in human beings but when met with a stumbling block—literally or metaphorically—we often still stumble, speaks to the human condition. But in a world where stumbling has become the norm and the possibility of a universal human condition is continually under question, tripping is not as funny as it used to be.

Here, then, is the problem: a nice chapter of this book could be written on Kant and *Three's Company* ("Come and Knock on Our Door: Mr. Kant, Mr. Roper, and the Placing of Hetero/Homosexual Notions Under a Common Apartment Roof"), on Hobbes and *Saved by the Bell* ("The Importance of Not Being Screech"), or on Bergson and *The Dick Van Dyke Show* ("On Hassocks, Both Real and Metaphorical"). But who can speak to *The Simpsons*? Though we might laugh at the improbable coupling of Burns and Smithers, or with a sense of superiority when we watch Chief Wiggum, or with surprise at the eternal lack of adaptability in Homer, this sort of laughing does not seem to get at the heart of what is funny about the show. Springfield is located squarely in a newly postmodern world.

Of course, this is literally true. Springfield, the hometown of the Simpsons, is not in any particular American state but is, instead, an eclectic geographic mixture of places. Fans noted this early on, and the show has since made a coyly self-aware running joke out of it. This is as good a place as any to begin our investigation of postmodernity, for the way in which Springfield is (dis)located is telling.

Place, for the modern, is unimportant. Modernity's politics, metaphysics, and ethics rejected the importance of context and situation, the possible importance of being one place instead of another. Universal rights and universal conceptions of Being were the goals, and universal notions of the individual were thus assumed. From Hobbes's placeless state of nature to the placeless marketplace of capitalism to the American assumption that U.S. democracy is the finest form of government for everyone in the world, there is thus a long history of thinking that the specifics of place are unimportant to anything that really matters. The project of modernity can even be described in terms of the systematic destruction of place: the golden arches of

McDonald's look the same around the globe and a Big Mac tastes the same as well; cosmopolitanism destroys true difference even as it commodifies it; the liberal state would have us treated as generic, isolated, individual selves with generic, isolationist, and individual rights; and mass communications technologies trick us into thinking that we are near family and friends—and home—even when we are separated by untold miles. One of the myths of modernity, then, is that we can happily live dislocated.

Postmodernity becomes aware of such false assumptions but without resorting to melancholy over similarly false constructions of the "good old days" with their good old places. Springfield is an embodiment of this ideal. As an artistic representation, it is both generic and specific at the same time. It is not a particular place of this world, yet it is not placeless. Think of the importance of the town to the show; compare this to the seeming unimportance of "real" locations to other comedies. The New York City of *Friends* is essentially irrelevant to the identities of the characters and the nature of the action. If it does appear (like in the episode in which Ross's new girlfriend lives a long train ride away, or the one in which Jean-Claude Van Damme shows up to film a movie in the city), the plot seems contrived and the city is at most a backdrop, not nearly a character in itself. The Mayberry of *The Andy Griffith Show* falls into the melancholy category. The small town seems to have created the good-natured neighbors that populate the show, but the maudlin tone and utter lack of race- and sex-politics suggest a whitewashing of true Southern geographic embodiment.

Not so with Springfield. The town may flaunt its inability to be located squarely in one state, but this fluid positioning does not turn it into a placeless everyplace. Springfield is unique and rooted. Its history informs the characters, though that history is always ready for rewriting—see, for instance, Lisa's discovery that the town's pioneer founder and namesake, Jebediah Springfield, was in reality a terrible man, and her refusal in the end to announce this discovery when she realizes that "truth" is always up for grabs and the townspeople are legitimately constructing themselves and their history at every moment ("Lisa the Iconoclast"). Springfield, too, is self-sufficient in a way most towns are not but should be. Though there are moments of disruptive globalism, local products (such as Duff beer) are more prevalent than multinational corporate products (such as Mr. Sparkle). Even the local nuclear power plant is run by a local billionaire, whose mistake in one episode of selling the plant to "the Germans" (who are not all smiles and sunshine) is quickly righted ("Burns Verkaufen der Kraftwerk").

Critics have suggested that Springfield comes close to the classical polis, but that it unrealistically portrays modern local community. "[W]hat are authentic movie stars like Rainer Wolfcastle doing living in Springfield? And what about the fact that the world-famous Itchy and Scratchy cartoons are produced in Springfield?" (Cantor 744). In placing the stars and industries in

Springfield, though, an important point is being made. The distinction
between local culture and global culture is eroded, but not in the way in which
it is being eroded today in our world. In our "real" world (or at least, let us say,
"non-animated world"), homogenization of culture works in such a way as to
destroy what is local. Architecture, food, language, music, humor, and nearly
all customs embedded in local communities are giving way to mass-produced
artifacts and thinking. Hence the aforementioned ubiquitous golden arches
and Big Macs. *The Simpsons'* twist on this is to make the local culture the
dominant culture—to erode the distinction, but from the other end. That is,
Krusty Burger restaurants are not only a mockery of McDonald's, they are an
inversion of McDonald's. Krusty is a local celebrity, and his local business is
presented as if it were the homogenizing, corporate, distantly owned fast-food
franchise, as if the local were homogenizing the rest of the world. Itchy and
Scratchy are world-renowned cartoon characters enjoyed by kids everywhere,
but they are created and produced locally. What *The Simpsons* realizes is that
commercialization is caught up in webs of global production and consumption, and that the world the show presents—and even the show itself—is
complicit in this.

Let us be clear about how this is so. There are three sorts of (television)
comedy: traditionalist, modern, and postmodern. Though they tend to be
chronologically ordered (roughly: traditionalist television comedies range
from the 1950s to the 1960s, modernist comedies from the 1970s to the
1980s, and postmodernists from the 1990s on), there is nothing necessarily
chronological about this. Indeed, *Monty Python's Flying Circus* in the 1970s
was, perhaps, the first truly postmodern television comedy; *The Cosby Show* of
the 1980s was surely traditionalist; and very few twenty-first century programs are truly postmodern. Still, there is something to be said for such quaint
linear classification schemes. Regardless, the types can be defined in part by
their reaction to their own status in the culture and thus their relation to their
production.

All production is somehow complicit in the modern market, including
the production that makes television comedies possible. If a show does not
acknowledge this, and is even seemingly unaware of it, it would be traditionalist. Commercialization never was a theme for *The Donna Reed Show* (though
it was undoubtedly for Donna Reed). If a show realizes this and tries to find
a way out, it would be modernist. There are multiple modernist tricks toward
this end. Some modernist television naively attempts to create community by
showing local products being consumed as if they were the only products on
the shelf. Others cynically exhibit only mass-produced products (thereby
accepting their status) and lure us into false community with the characters by
naming these as products we all have in common. *Seinfeld*, for instance,
chooses this latter tactic. Realizing that brand names are everywhere, *Seinfeld*
refers to them explicitly, thus making the viewer think that he or she has

FIGURE 21.1. Marge, Maggie, Homer, Lisa, and Bart Simpson in *The Simpsons*, 1989– . Photo courtesy of Larry Edmunds BooksFair.

something in common with the characters ("I love Junior Mints, too!").
Acknowledging the nature of the commercial culture thus makes the show
modernist rather than traditionalist. It could have taken the postmodern turn,
though, if it had admitted its own complicity and immersion in this culture.[1]

And *The Simpsons* does just this. It acknowledges what it is and how it is
situated in the world. It exposes the artifice that holds it up. It admits its complicity in late capitalism. And it gives us a reason to smile that does not simultaneously demand bad faith, demand that we either ignore the complexities of
the world (as the traditionalist would have us do) or imagine that we can rise
above those complexities (as the modernist maintains we can). By making
local products and local culture in Springfield into the assumed mass culture
of the world, *The Simpsons* concedes the relation between the two but forces
us to think about that relation in a new way. It does not stand outside of that
relation but twists it from within. It is hard to do such topological maneuvers
when one is immersed in the medium being contorted, but it is the only
authentic stance to take in a postmodern world.

Consider, for instance, the Butterfinger candy bar. *The Simpsons*–Butterfinger alliance has been going strong since the late 1990s with Bart and
other Springfield residents appearing in various commercials both on television
and in print. A package of Butterfinger BBs (an incarnation of the candy consisting of little, round candy bar pieces) is decorated, for instance, with a picture of Bart laughing hysterically and Krusty the Klown saying, "I heartily
endorse this product and/or promotion." These are the moments in which *The
Simpsons* confesses its complicity. There are multiple levels to this text. Most
obviously, the presentation is different from other product tie-ins. The image
of the character or celebrity is typically what is meant to sell the product. It is
enough, then, to have a picture of the Church Lady on a T-shirt, or—more to
the point of the tie-in—images of Michael Jordan on the Wheaties box or
Jar Jar Binks on the Pepsi can (while Britney Spears gyrates in the Pepsi television commercial, of course, showing us her can). With Butterfinger, Krusty
speaks, acknowledging that he is pushing a product, not trying to rise above it.
Furthermore, he confesses that this is the norm; that he does so often enough
to need a generic pitch statement. The fact that he (and thus the Butterfinger
folks) feels comfortable keeping the pitch generic—not changing "this product
and/or promotion" for "these Butterfinger BBs"—indicates an assumed cynicism over such commercialism, as if there is no need to go out of the way to
point out what the product is since we all know it does not really matter to the
spokesperson. And the fact that Bart laughs at us on the wrapper for buying
into it seals the deal. Bart not only laughs because he is aware of his (and our)
complicity. He laughs because he knows what we know: He knows that Krusty
is famous on *The Simpsons* for endorsing terrible products, for having a line of
dangerous household appliances and children's toys with his likeness, for selling boxes of Krusty-O's cereal with a surprise jagged metal O in each box

("'Round Springfield"). Thus, to buy the Butterfinger endorsed by Krusty (who is, after all, not even interested in knowing what it is he is endorsing) is to buy a shoddy and potentially dangerous product. And we happily do so.

This does not mean that there is little reason to laugh at traditional and modernist comedy. None of this is to say that *Seinfeld* or *Friends* or *The Donna Reed Show* or even *Three's Company* are not funny. They are (though perhaps in decreasing order, and perhaps in exponentially decreasing order). Defining postmodern comedy is not the same as putting down modernist or traditional comedy. I have been doing quite modernist things throughout this chapter in the name of trying to be a little humorous. Mentioning moments from these sitcoms without explanation (such as an offhand reference to Mr. Roper) is a way of cheap inclusion: if you get the reference, you laugh; if you laugh, you are part of the "community." You and I most likely do not have much more in common, so I—the struggling philosopher—take what I can get. It would only turn postmodernly funny if I were to admit to you that I am doing this and you were to find this liberating and humorous. Neither, I fear, is likely to happen.

SO WE CANNOT RISE ABOVE THE WORLD.
THIS IS NOT TO BE LAMENTED. NOTHING RISES.

Language was once thought to rise above it all, or at least to ride on top of it. Language, before postmodernity, was about reflecting the world. Words had meaning because they reached out and denoted things. Propositions had meaning because they reached out and denoted states of affairs. Language magically floated above us, with words mirroring our reality back to us rather than creating it. But nothing really floats.

Words do not anchor themselves like labels stuck to things. Language does not work like the Post-its® in Ned Flanders's beach house, labeling the world around us and instructing us as to meaning ("Summer of 4 Ft. 2"). Words, instead, are linked in intricate webs of self-reference. They mean each other; they mean what we agree to allow them to mean. And with them, we carve up an ever-malleable world rather than reflect a rigid world. Thus, when I say "I love you," there is no stable and universal referent for each word. No necessary self, no Other, no Platonic relation of love to be instantiated in-between. "I love you" has meaning because each word means other words, and because when I speak it I am speaking an echo of every time the phrase has ever been uttered before: It means everything it has always meant. All language is metaphor.

There is, then, no way out, no rising above, no escaping language. But there is still a chance to speak "truthfully." Doing so requires quote marks; when truth is gone, "truth" is all we have left. And *The Simpsons* is masterful in its use of quotational discourse. Umberto Eco explains:

> I think of the postmodern attitude as that of a man who loves a very cul-
> tivated woman who knows he cannot say to her, "I love you madly,"
> because he knows that she knows (and that she knows that he knows)
> that these words have been written by Barbara Cartland. Still, there is a
> solution. He can say, "As Barbara Cartland would put it, I love you
> madly." At this point, having avoided false innocence, having said clearly
> that it is no longer possible to speak innocently, he will nevertheless have
> said what he wanted to say to the woman: that he loves her, but he loves
> her in an age of lost innocence. . . . [B]oth [the man and the woman] will
> consciously and with pleasure play the game of irony. . . . (67–68)

Eco is onto something here, but perhaps with a few caveats. Irony is not just a
game; it is the only game in town. It is the inescapable, foundational late-mod-
ern context of all meaning. Once we realize this—and we realize that our words
constantly ring with the echoes of all their past uses, that innocence is not only
lost but was never really there to begin with—we need not remain in silence for
fear of speaking naively. Instead, we must acknowledge our state and our complicity. One way of doing this is to usher in quotational discourse. It is not really
that the romance novelists have taken "I love you madly" away from us, making
it too cheesy for everyday use. It is that *all* words are simultaneously utterances
of other words and other past meanings, and thus, to speak at all is to risk
sounding trite and clichéd. Even Eco echoes. We cannot rise above this, but our
discourse can acknowledge it. Hence, we speak using quotation marks: "As they
have said in the romance novels and on soap operas and in Shakespeare and in
parked cars and everyplace everywhere throughout time, 'I love you madly.'"

Sometimes we do this explicitly. When I stub a toe or otherwise hurt
myself superficially, I will occasionally respond to a query about my condition
in a bad British accent, "It's just a flesh wound." Forced to excuse myself from
a room at an inopportune time—during a meal or a conversation, for
instance—I have once or twice muttered in a bad Austrian-German accent,
"I'll be back." My wife several years ago suggested that her older sister received
more adoration from their parents; my retort of "Marcia! Marcia! Marcia!" got
me in a bit of trouble ("D'oh!"). And I pity the fool who dares say to me
"Surely, you must be joking." Because I am seldom joking. And I do not like
to be called Shirley.[2]

I know that some people do such things to an annoying degree. I know
some people who do such things to an annoying degree. I consciously attempt
not to be one of them. It is just not funny after a very short while; one appears
a maladjusted showoff, aping every cultural moment of the past, never seeming to speak in one's own voice. But the point to remember is that we are all
doing this, whether we admit to it or not, all the time. And admitting to it is
the only authentic thing left to do. Still, a joke told every five minutes quickly
loses its luster.

The Simpsons admits to its involvement in quotational discourse on multiple levels, telling different jokes about the same thing every five seconds. In
the ultimate postmodern turn, it often quotes itself (which is another way of
understanding the self-references to its own commodification); but it also
quotes other art—linguistically, visually, and thematically. As such, it is a commentary not on the American family but on the American family's appearance
in television. Indeed, it could not be otherwise, for the meaning of the family
today is (in part) the meaning it has through television. On a more basic level,
the show, realizing that it is a visual art and that other works of art have come
before, will often conjure a scene in terms of scenes that have come before.

Season thirteen ended with an episode in which Homer is targeted by the
mob, and as Fat Tony and his crew drove to the Simpson's house, the opening
credits of *The Sopranos* were re-created with Springfield landmarks rather than
Jersey ones ("Poppa's Got a Brand New Badge"). Why? How can one authen-
tically make art about a mob hit today without quoting *The Sopranos* (which
itself is often [literally] quoting *The Godfather*)?

The sixth season cliff-hanger ("Who Shot Mr. Burns?") was, in its
entirety, a reference to *Dallas* and the ultimate cliff-hanger of "Who Shot
J. R.?" Why? How can one stage a non-naive cliff-hanger without admitting
that the ultimate cliff-hanger has already been done?

In the fourth season's "A Streetcar Named Marge," there are at least half
a dozen references to classic movies: Maggie attempts escape from the Ayn
Rand Daycare Center (!) in the style of *The Great Escape*; Homer, Bart, and
Lisa show up to the center to find the babies have taken over in the style of
The Birds (complete with pacified babies perched everywhere and a walk-on
cameo from an animated Hitchcock); and Homer expresses his initial boredom at Marge's performance by tearing his program into a fan and playing
with it in the same way that Joseph Cotten's character does in *Citizen Kane*
when he is forced to watch Kane's wife in her own terrible performance. Why,
why, why? How can one speak to the desire to escape unjust authority, the
creepiness of seeing the small and supposedly powerless suddenly take over,
and the boredom associated with bad live performance without quoting these
past moments of our collective experience? To have Homer say "I'm bored"—
which means, visually, drawing Homer looking bored—is to say "I love you
madly." To have Homer quote someone else in order to indicate his boredom—which means, visually, re-creating (quoting) a scene from *Citizen
Kane*—is to say, "As Barbara Cartland would put it 'I love you madly.'"

As the Comic Book Guy would say, this may be the worst . . . chapter . . .
ever. *The Simpsons*, it turns out, is not really hollow. And all that talk up front
about needing a new theory of comedy to deal with the show was just, well,
talk. We have talked a lot about talking, really. About words and language and
self-reference. And though we have taken some time to address the way in

which *The Simpsons* is postmodern art, we have not really touched on why it is so funny. There have been hints here and there as to what makes it all so successfully comedic, but no fully drawn theory of postmodern comedy has emerged.

Of course, this should only be disappointing if we were thinking that something should have been here, that we deserve something at the end. In uprooting modernity, *The Simpsons* uproots the trappings of modernity including linearity, narrative flow, and expectation in general. Sometimes the monster at the end of the book has been there all along; sometimes it is the lovable old narrator himself, and the end is thus the means—and always has been.

When Bart gave blood to a dying Mr. Burns only to get a thank you card in place of a reward, Homer responded by writing a nasty letter: "Dear Mr. Burns . . . I'm so *glad* you enjoyed my son's blood. And your *card* was *just great*. In case you can't tell, I'm being sarcastic" ("Blood Feud"). After considering having Homer beaten for his insolence, Burns relents and buys the Simpsons an extravagant gift—a gigantic $32,000 sacred Olmec carved-head statue. At the end of the episode, the Simpsons sit at home trying to figure out the meaning of it all:

HOMER: Save a guy's life and what do you get? Nothing. Worse than nothing. Just a big scary rock.

BART: Hey, man, don't bad-mouth the head.

MARGE: Homer, it's the thought that counts. The moral of the story is a good deed is its own reward.

BART: Hey, we got a reward. The head is cool.

MARGE: Then . . . I guess the moral is no good deed goes unrewarded.

HOMER: Wait a minute. If I hadn't written that nasty letter we wouldn't have gotten anything.

MARGE: Well . . . Then I guess the moral is the squeaky wheel gets the grease.

LISA: Perhaps there is no moral to this story.

HOMER: Exactly! It's just a bunch of stuff that happened.

MARGE: But it certainly was a memorable few days.

HOMER: Amen to that! [Everyone laughs.]

It is not, I suppose, that any one moral does not really fit. It is that they all fit. And in fitting, they draw attention to the plasticity of narrative itself and the clichéd manner in which narrative is necessarily understood.

And so we have the possibility that an episode—or a chapter—can be content to be aware that it is just a bunch of stuff that happens, headed only where one wants it to head, meaning exactly what it has always meant—itself and, simultaneously, everything else—avowing, especially, that even in questioning the possibility of an ending and a moral, the claim that "It's just a bunch of stuff that happened" becomes the moral and the ending. In our fallen era, it is thus that we can maintain and display what is most important to us: our lack of innocence. What, after all, is not to like about the fall? We have reclaimed it to be the time of season premieres rather than finales. And so we wear with pride our true achievements: the collection of scarlet letters that comprise our language; our giddy impurity; our proudly mongrel nature and culture; the knowledge that we know what *The Simpsons* knows and *The Simpsons* knows what we know and we all know that we love each other madly ad infinitum. This, then, is how we can maintain our lack of innocence and keep our cool. And it is, in the end, the only way to avoid the cliché, the moral, and the trite conclusion. Amen.

NOTES

1. There were attempts at this, especially in terms of the story line involving Jerry and George trying to sell a sitcom to NBC based on their lives—on "nothing"—but the show as a whole was decidedly modernist with postmodern moments (see chapter 18 for more on this episode).

2. Of course you do not need to be told, but the quotational discourse references are—in order—to *Monty Python and the Holy Grail*, *The Terminator*, *The Brady Bunch*, Mr. T on *The Simpsons*, and *Airplane!*.

Bibliography

Acker, Joan. "Hierarchies, Jobs, Bodies: A Theory of Gendered Organizations." *Gender and Society* 4 June 1990: 139–58.

Adler, Richard, ed. All in the Family: *A Critical Appraisal*. New York: Praeger, 1979.

Albert, Katherine. "Everybody Loves Lucy!" *L.A. Examiner* 6 April 1952: 6–7, 18.

Allen, Dennis. W. "The Marketing of Queer Theory." *College Literature* 25 (1998): 282–89.

Alley, Robert S., and Irby B. Brown. *Love Is All Around: The Making of* The Mary Tyler Moore Show. New York: Delta, 1989.

———. Murphy Brown: *Anatomy of a Sitcom*. New York: Delta, 1990.

Alligood, Doug. "Blacks 'Are Gravitating to Programs with Black Themes That Relate to Them.'" *Broadcasting & Cable* 26 Apr. 1993: 74.

Altman, Dennis. "On Global Queering." *Australian Humanities Review*. (July 1996). 27 July 2001. <http://alpha.lib.latrobe.edu.au/AHR/archive/Issue-July-1996/altman.html>

American National Biography Online at www.anb.com.

Amory, C. "The Doris Day Show." *TV Guide* 16 Nov. 1968: 42.

Andersen, Robin. *Consumer Culture and Television Programming*. Boulder, CO: Westview, 1995.

Anderson, Christopher. *Hollywood TV: The Studio System in the Fifties*. Austin: U of Texas P, 1994.

Anderson, Lisa. *Mammies No More: The Changing Image of Black Women on Stage and Screen*. Lanham, MD: Rowman, 1997.

Andrews, Bart. *The* I Love Lucy *Book*. New York: Doubleday, 1985.

Bailey, Beth. *From Front Porch to Back Seat: Courtship in Twentieth-Century America*. Baltimore: Johns Hopkins UP, 1988.

Baker, Keith Michael. "Defining the Public Sphere in Eighteenth-Century France." *Habermas and the Public Sphere*. Ed. Craig Calhoun. Cambridge: MIT P, 1992. 181–211.

Bakhtin, Mikhail. *Rabelais and His World*. Trans. Helene Iswolsky. Bloomington: Indiana UP, 1984.

Ball, Lucille, with Betty Hannah Hoffman. *Love, Lucy*. New York: Putnam, 1996.

Basinger, Janine. *A Woman's View: How Hollywood Spoke to Women, 1930–1960*. Hanover, NH: Wesleyan UP, 1993.

Bauder, David. "Night of All-Black Comedies Rankle Some of Their Stars." *The Associated Press*. 4 July 2000, BC Cycle.

"Beauty into Buffoon." *Life* 18 Feb. 1952: 93–97.

Bell, David, and Jon Binnie. *The Sexual Citizen: Queer Politics and Beyond*. Malden, MA: Blackwell, 2000.

Bellafante, Ginia. "Who Put the 'Me' in Feminism." *Time* 29 June 1998. 22 June 2001. <http://www.time.com/time/magazine/1998/dom/980629/cover1.html>.

Belton, John. *American Cinema/American Culture*. New York: McGraw, 1991.

Bentley, Ricky. "Not Your Average Family." *Fresno Bee* 7 May 2002: E1.

Bergson, Henri. *Laughter: An Essay on the Meaning of the Comic*. London: Macmillan, 1928.

Bianco, R. "For Shame! New UPN Sitcoms Dredge Up Old Racial Stereotypes." *Pittsburgh Post-Gazette TV Guide* 18 Aug. 1996: 4.

"Blacks on the Channels." *Time* 24 May 1968: 74.

Boddy, William. *Fifties Television: The Industry and Its Critics*. Urbana: U of Illinois P, 1990.

Bodroghkozy, Aniko. *Groove Tube: Sixties Television and the Youth Rebellion*. Durham: Duke UP, 2001.

———. Excerpt from "Is This What You Mean by Color Television? Race, Gender, and Contested Meanings in NBC's *Julia*." *Gender, Race and Class in Media*. Eds. Gail Dines, and Jean M. Humez. Thousand Oaks, CA: Sage, 1995. 413–23.

Bogle, Donald. *Blacks in American Films and Television: An Illustrated Encyclopedia*. New York: Garland, 1988.

———. *Primetime Blues: African Americans on Network Television*. New York: Farrar, 2001.

———. *Toms, Coons, Mulattoes, Mammies, and Bucks: An Interpretive History of Blacks in American Films*. New York: Continuum, 1994.

Bone, James. "Ladies Who Lunch and Lust." *The Times* (London) 25 July 1998.

Booth, Wayne C. "The Company We Keep: Self-Making in Imaginative Art, Old and New." *Television, the Critical View*. Ed. Horace Newcomb. New York: Oxford UP, 1987. 382–418.

Boskin, Joseph. *Sambo: The Rise and Demise of an American Jester.* New York: Oxford UP, 1986.

Bowlby, Rachel. "Modes of Modern Shopping: Mallarme at the Bon Marche." *The Ideology of Conduct: Essays on Literature and the History of Sexuality.* Ed. Nancy Armstrong and Leonard Tennenhouse. New York: Methuen, 1987. 185–205.

Boyd, Todd. *Am I Black Enough for You: Popular Culture from the 'Hood and Beyond.* Bloomington: Indiana UP, 1997.

Brady, Kathleen. *Lucille: The Life of Lucille Ball.* New York: Hyperion, 1994.

Breines, Wini. *Young, White, and Miserable: Growing Up Female in the 1950s.* Chicago: U of Chicago P, 1992.

Bronski, Michael. "Book Reviews." *Cinecaste* 21 (1995): 90.

Brooks, Tim, and Earle Marsh. *The Complete Directory to Prime Time Network and Cable TV Shows 1946–Present.* New York: Ballantine, 1999.

Brower, Neal. *Mayberry 101: Behind the Scenes of a TV Classic.* Winston-Salem, NC: Blair, 1998.

Bruce, Donald. *Topics of Restoration Comedy.* New York: St. Martin's, 1974.

Bruni, Frank. "Culture Stays Screen-Shy of Showing the Gay Kiss." *The Columbia Reader on Lesbian and Gay Men in Media, Society and Politics.* Ed. Larry Gross and James D. Wood. New York: Columbia UP, 1999. 327–29.

Bullough, Vern L. "Weighing the Shift from Sexual Identity to Sexual Relationships." *Journal of Homosexuality* 10 (1984): 3–5.

Bushnell, Candace. *Sex and the City.* New York: Warner, 1996.

Butler, Jeremy. *Television: Critical Methods and Applications.* Belmont, CA: Wadsworth, 1994.

Butler, Judith. *Gender Trouble: Feminism and the Subversion of Identity.* New York: Routledge, 1990.

———. "Imitation and Gender Insubordination." *Inside/Out: Lesbian Theories, Gay Theories.* Ed. Diana Fuss. New York: Routledge, 1991. 13–31.

Butsch, Richard. "Class and Gender in Four Decades of Television Situation Comedy: Plus Ça Change. . . ." *Critical Studies in Mass Communication* 9 (1992): 387–99.

Byrne, Terry. *Production Design for Television.* Boston: Focal, 1993.

Caldarola, V. "Embracing the Media Simulacrum." *Visual Anthroplogy Review* 10.1 (1994): 66–69.

Caldwell, John T. *Televisuality: Style, Crisis, and Authority in American Television.* New Brunswick, NJ: Rutgers UP, 1995.

Canfield, Douglas J. *Tricksters and Estates on the Ideology of Restoration Comedy.* Lexington: U of Kentucky P, 1997.

Cantor, Paul A. "The Simpsons: Atomistic Politics and the Nuclear Family." *Political Theory* 27.6 (1999): 734–49.

Carbaugh, Donal A. *Talking American: Cultural Discourses on Donahue.* Norwood, NJ: Ablex, 1988.

Carroll, Diahann, and Ross Firestone. *Diahann!: An Autobiography.* Boston: Little, 1986.

Cartier, Bill, and Lawrie Mifflin. "Mainstream TV Bets on 'Gross-Out' Humor." *New York Times* 19 July 1999: C1+.

Cartmanfan@aol.com. "Transcripts of *The Tonight Show* and *The Daily Show*." E-mail to Karen Anijar. 16 July 1998.

Caute, David. *The Year of the Barricades: A Journey Through 1968.* New York: Harper, 1988.

Cerone, Daniel Howard. "'Ellen' Finally Says . . . Yes, I Am." *TV Guide* 29 Mar. 1997: 49–53.

Chafe, William H. *The Paradox of Change: American Women in the Twentieth Century.* New York: Oxford UP, 1991.

Charles, Arthur L. "Now We Have Everything." *Modern Screen* Apr. 1953: 32, 84.

Chocano, Carina. "Herman Munster, Rock God." TV Diary. *Salon.com.* 11 Apr. 2002. http://www.salon.com/ent/tv/diary/2002/04/11/osbournes/index.html

Chunovic, Louis. *The Complete Guide to* "Ally McBeal." London: Macmillan, 1999.

———. "Putting Some English on *'The Osbournes'*; Ratings Monster of Sinking Sitcom." *Electronic Media* 3 Feb. 2003: 4.

Clark, C. "Television and Social Controls: Some Observations on the Portrayals of Ethnic Minorities." *Television Quarterly* 8 (1969): 18–22.

Clark, Steve. "It's As If Roald Dahl Had Dropped an Ecstasy Tab and Set a Story in Dysfunctional America. . . . A Coarse but Sharp-Witted Adult Cartoon Series Ridiculing Small-Town Living Is Taking US Television by Storm. And Now It's Coming Here." *The Guardian* [London] 16 March 1998: Media Page.

Code, Lorraine. *Rhetorical Spaces: Essays on Gendered Locations.* New York: Routledge, 1995.

Cole, Stephen. *That Book About That Girl.* Los Angeles: Renaissance, 1999.

Color Adjustment. Dir. Marlon Riggs. San Francisco: California Newsreel. 1991.

Coontz, Stephanie. *The Way We Never Were: American Families and the Nostalgia Trap.* New York: Basic, 1992.

Cooper, Brenda. "Unapologetic Women, 'Comic Men,' and Feminine Spectatorship in David E. Kelley's *Ally McBeal*." *Critical Studies in Mass Communication* 18 (2001): 416–35.

Core, Philip. *Camp: The Lie That Tells the Truth.* New York: Delilah, 1984.

Cornwell, Tim. "Is It Just Dirty Talk for Girls?" *The Times* (London) 15 Jan. 1999: 40.

Craig, Amanda. "Mad, Bad, and the Teenager's Perfect Dad." *Sunday Times* (London). 21 April 2002: 3.

Cripps, Thomas. *"Amos 'n Andy* and the Struggle for Racial Integration." *American History, American Television: Interpreting the Video Past.* Ed. John E. O'Connor. NY: Ungar, 1983. 33–54.

Croteau, David, and William Hoynes. *The Business of Media: Corporate Media and the Public Interest.* Thousand Oaks, CA: Pine Forge, 2001.

D'Acci, Julie. *Defining Women: Television and the Case of* "Cagney and Lacey." Chapel Hill: U of NC P, 1994.

Dalton, Mary M. *The Hollywood Curriculum: Teachers in the Movies.* New York: Lang, 2004.

"Danson 'Proud' of Racial Act at Roast." *Arizona Republic* Oct. 25, 1993: B8.

Dates, Jannette L. "Commercial Television." *Split Image: African-Americans in the Mass Media.* Ed. Jannette L. Dates and William Barlow. Washington, D.C.: Howard UP, 1990. 253–302.

Davidson, B. "The Change in Doris Day." *TV Guide* 20 Feb. 1971: 30–34.

DeCaro, Frank. "Finally Out, and Suddenly In." *Newsweek* 12 May 1997: 83.

De Cecco, John, and Michael G. Shively. "From Sexual Identity to Sexual Relationships: A Contextual Shift." *Journal of Homosexuality* 9 (1984): 1–26.

Dellinger-Pate, Charlene, and Roger C. Aden. "'More Power': Negotiating Masculinity and Femininity in *Home Improvement.*" *Mediated Women: Representations in Popular Culture.* Ed. Marian Meyers. Cresskill, NJ: Hampton, 1999. 153–64.

de Moraes, Lisa. "Black and White Viewers Are More In Tune on Top 20." *Washington Post* 13 Feb. 2001: C1.

Dempsey, John. "MTV Auds Go Gaga for Ozzy's Oddball Antics." *Variety* 1–7 Apr. 2002: 24.

D'Erasmo, Stacey. "The Way We Live Now." *New York Times* 29 Aug. 1999, late ed., sec. 6: 13.

"Desilu Formula for Top TV: Brains, Beauty, Now a Baby." *Newsweek* 19 Jan. 1953: cover, 56–59.

"Diahann Carroll Presents the *Julia* Dolls." *Ebony* Oct. 1969.

"Did Diahann Carroll 'Sell Out' to Television?" *Sepia* Aug. 1969: 56–57.

Doherty, Brian. "Interview with Matt Groening." *Mother Jones* 24 (Mar./Apr. 1999): 35–37.

Doty, Alexander. "The Cabinet of Lucy Ricardo: Lucille Ball's Star Image." *Cinema Journal* 29 (1990): 3–22.

Douglas, Susan. *Where the Girls Are: Growing Up Female with the Mass Media*. New York: Random, 1994.

Dow, Bonnie J. "*Ellen*, Television, and the Politics of Gay and Lesbian Visibility." *Critical Studies in Media Communication* 18 (2001): 123–40.

―――. *Prime-Time Feminism: Television, Media Culture, and the Women's Movement Since 1970*. Philadelphia: U of Pennsylvania P, 1996.

Eco, Umberto. *Postscript to the Name of the Rose*. Trans. William Weaver. New York: Harcourt, 1994.

Edge, Steve, and John Lyttle. "Are Homosexuals Gay?" *Independent* [London] 13 Dec. 1996: 20.

Ehrenreich, Barbara, Elizabeth Hess, and Gloria Jacobs. *Re-making Love: The Feminization of* Sex and the City. New York: Doubleday, 1986.

Ely, Melvin Patrick. *The Adventures of Amos 'n Andy: A Social History of an America Phenomenon*. New York: Free, 1991.

Evans, David Scott. "South Park: Comedy Central's Low-down-Hoe-down Created by Matt Stone & Trey Parker, Roomies." *Gay Today*. 29 Dec. 1997. 12 Sept. 2001 <http://gaytoday.badpuppy. com/garchive/entertain/122997en.htm>

Evans, David T. *Sexual Citizenship: The Material Construction of Sexualities*. New York: Routledge, 1993.

Evers, Merlie. "A Tale of Two Julias." *Ladies Home Journal* May 1970: 60–65.

Faludi, Susan. *Backlash: The Undeclared War Against American Women*. New York: Anchor, 1991.

Farley, Christopher John. "Black and Blue." 142:22 *Time* 22 Nov. 1993: 80–81.

Feran, Tim. "*For Your Love* a Shallow *Cosby*." *Columbus Dispatch* 17 Mar. 1998: 7E.

Fiske, John. *Television Culture*. New York: Routledge, 1987.

―――. *Understanding Popular Culture*. Boston: Unwin Hyman, 1989.

Fiske, John, and John Hartley. *Reading Television*. New York: Methuen, 1978.

Flint, Joe. "Fade to White." *Entertainment Weekly* 23 Apr. 1999: 9.

―――. "How NBC Defies Network Norms—To Its Advantage." *Wall Street Journal* 20 May 2002: A1+.

Forestier, Georges. *Le Théâtre Dans Le Théâtre Sur La Scène Française Du XVIIe Siècle*. Genève: Droz, 1981.

Freeman, Michael. "Black-Oriented Sitcoms Gaining White Viewers." *Electronic Media* 26 (Nov. 2001): 1A.

Fretts, Bruce. "Keep a Watch on TV Do Not Adjust Your Sets—These Three New Sitcoms Are Broadcast in Black and White." *Entertainment Weekly* 27 Mar. 1998: 54.

Freud, Sigmund. *Jokes and Their Relation to the Unconscious.* New York: Norton, 1960.

Friedan, Betty. *The Feminine Mystique.* New York: Dell, 1963.

Friend, Tad. "The Next Big Bet." *New Yorker* 14 May 2001: 83.

Fromm, Erich. *Marx's Concept of Man.* New York: Ungar, 1961.

Frum, David. *How We Got Here: The 70s, the Decade That Brought You Modern Life—For Better or Worse.* New York: Basic, 2000.

Fuss, Diana. *Essentially Speaking: Feminism, Nature and Difference.* New York: Routledge, 1989.

————, ed. *Inside/Out: Lesbian Theories, Gay Theories.* New York: Routledge, 1991.

Gamson, Joshua. "Must Identity Movements Self-Destruct: A Queer Dilemma." *Social Problems* 42 (1995): 390–408.

"Gap between Black and White TV Viewing Habits Narrows." *Jet* 17 May 1999: 65.

Garnets, Linda D., and Anthony R. D'Augelli. "Empowering Lesbian and Gay Communities: A Call for Collaboration with Community Psychology." *American Journal of Community Psychology* 22 (1994): 447–81.

Gelb, Alan. *The Doris Day Scrapbook.* New York: Grosset, 1977.

Gergen, Kenneth J. *Realities and Relationships: Soundings in Social Construction.* Cambridge: Harvard UP, 1994.

Gilbert, James. *A Cycle of Outrage: America's Reaction to the Juvenile Delinquent in the 1950s.* New York: Oxford, 1986.

Gilbert, Matthew. "*For Your Love* Retro and Stale." *Boston Globe* 17 Mar. 1998: B12.

————. "'Sex in the City' Is Savvy and Cynical." *Boston Globe* 6 June 1998, city ed.: C6.

Gitlin, Todd. *Inside Prime Time.* Berkeley: U of California P, 2000.

————. "Prime-Time Ideology: The Hegemonic Process in Television Entertainment." *Television: The Critical View.* Ed. Horace Newcomb. New York: Oxford UP, 1994 ed. 516–37.

Gliatto, Tom, and Alexis Chiu. "Daze of Their Lives." *People* 9 Dec. 2002: 66–71.

Goldman, Robert. *Reading Ads Socially.* New York: Routledge, 1992.

Goldstein, R. "Sitcom-ing Out." *Village Voice* 6 May 1997: 36–38.

Goodman, Tim. "'The Osbournes' Faces Reality; In Second Season, It's Neither Fresh Nor as Funny, and Sharon's Illness Raises Difficult Issues." *San Francisco Chronicle* 25 Nov. 2002, final ed.: D1.

Gould, Jack. "Why Millions Love Lucy." *New York Times Magazine* 1 Mar. 1953: 16.

Grahnke, Lon. "Living, Loving in Suburbia; NBC Sitcom Set in Oak Park Offers Up Slices of Life." *Chicago Sun-Times* 16 Mar. 1998: 39.

Gray, Herman. *Watching Race: Television and the Struggle for "Blackness."* Minneapolis: U of Minnesota P, 1995.

Greene, Alexis. "The New Comedy of Manners." *Theater* 23.3 (Summer 1992): 79–83.

Habermas, Jurgen. *The Structural Transformation of the Public Sphere: An Inquiry into a Category of Bourgeois Society.* Trans. Thomas Berger. Cambridge, MA: MIT P, 1992.

Halberstam, David. *The Fifties.* New York: Columbine, 1993.

Hall, Stuart. "Cultural Identity and Diaspora." *Identity: Community, Culture, Difference.* Ed. Jonathan Rutherford. London: Lawrence, 1990.

———. "Encoding/Decoding." *Media Studies: A Reader.* Ed. Paul Marris and Sue Thornham. Edinburgh: Edinburgh UP, 1996. 41–49.

———, ed. *Representation: Cultural Representations and Signifying Practices.* London, Thousand Oaks, New Delhi: SAGE Publications, 1997: 245.

Hamamoto, Darrell. *Nervous Laughter: Television Situation Comedy and Liberal Democratic Ideology.* New York: Praeger, 1989.

"Hands and Song." *Life* Dec. 1959: 57–58.

Handy, Bruce. "Roll Over, Ward Cleaver." *Time* 14 Apr. 1997: 80–85.

Hantzis, Darlene M., and Valerie Lehr. "Whose Desire? Lesbian (Non) Sexuality and Television's Perpetuation of Hetero/Sexism." *Queer Words, Queer Images: Communication and the Construction of Homosexuality.* Ed. R. Jeffrey Ringer. New York: New York UP, 1994.

Haralovich, Mary Beth. "Sit-coms and Suburbia: Positioning the 1950s Homemaker." *Private Screenings: Television and the Female Consumer.* Ed. Lynn Spigel and Denise Mann. Minneapolis: U of Minnesota P, 1992.

Harris, Angela. "Race and Essentialism in Feminist Legal Theory." *Feminist Legal Theory: Readings in Law and Gender.* Ed. Katharine T. Bartlett and Rosanne Kennedy. Boulder, CO: Westview, 1990.

Harris, Richard Jackson. *A Cognitive Psychology of Mass Communication.* Hillsdale, NJ: Erlbaum, 1994.

Havens, Timothy. "Globalizing Blackness: The International Distribution of African American Television Programming." PhD diss. Indiana U, 2000.

Hecht, Michael L. "2002–A Research Odyssey: Toward the Development of a Communication Theory of Identity." *Communication Monographs* 60 (1993): 76–82.

Hedegaard, Erik. "Ozzy." *Rolling Stone* 6 July 2000: 112.

Hedge, Radha S. "Swinging the Trapeze: The Negotiation of Identity among Asian Indian Immigrant Women in the United States." *Communication and Identity Across Cultures.* Ed. Delores V. Tanno and Alberto Gonzalez. Newbury Park, CA: Sage, 1998.

Henderson, Katherine, and Joseph A. Mazzeo, eds. *Meanings of the Medium*. New York: Praeger, 1990.

Henning, Paul. Personal interview with David Marc. Television History Collections of the Center for the Study of Popular Television, Syracuse U Library. 12 Sept. 1996.

Hensley, D. "Hooked on Sex." *Advocate* 23 Nov. 1999: 88–91.

Higgins, John M. "HBO Tries to Pick Up Women." *Broadcasting and Cable* 26 Oct. 1998: 54.

Hilmes, Michelle. "Where Everybody Knows Your Name: *Cheers* and the Mediation of Cultures." *Wide Angle: A Film Quarterly of Theory, Criticism, and Practice* 12.2 (Apr. 1990): 64–73.

Hirst, David L. *Comedy of Manners*. New York: Methuen, 1979.

Hobbes, Thomas. *Leviathan* (esp. Pt. 1, Ch. 6). New York: Penguin Classics, 1982.

Hochstein, Rollie. "Diahann Carroll's Juggling Act." *Good Housekeeping* May 1969: 38+.

Holleran, Andrew. "The Alpha Queen." *Gay and Lesbian Review* 7.3 (2000): 65–66.

Horst, Carole. *"For Your Love." Variety* 21 Sept. 1998: 47.

Hotchner, A. E. *Doris Day: Her Own Story*. New York: Morrow, 1976.

Hough, A. "Trials and Tribulations—Thirty Years of Sitcom." *Understanding Television: Essays on Television as Social and Cultural Force*. Ed. Richard Adler. New York: Praeger, 1981. 201–23.

Hubert, Susan J. "What's Wrong with This Picture? The Politics of Ellen's Coming Out Party." *Journal of Popular Culture* 33.2 (1999): 31–36.

Huff, Richard. "'South Park' Fuels Truth-in-Labeling Debate." *New York Daily News* 5 Mar. 1998: 103.

Hughes-Freeland, Felicia, and Mary M. Crain, eds. *Recasting Ritual: Performance, Media, Identity*. New York: Routledge, 1988.

Hustler Magazine v. Jerry Falwell, 485 US 46. US Supreme Court 1988.

"In or Out." *Newsweek*. 14 Sept. 1998: 72.

Inniss, Leslie B. & Feagin, Joe. "The Cosby Show: The View from the Middle Class," in *Say It Loud! African American Audiences, Identity and Media*, Robin Means Coleman (ed.). NY: Routledge, 2002: 187–204.

Jacobs, A. J. "Let's Talk About *Sex and the City*." *Entertainment Weekly* 5 June 1998: 32.

———. *"Seinfeld." The 100 Greatest Television Shows of All Time*. Special issue of *Entertainment Weekly* (1998): 10–11.

James, Caryn. "That Lovable Sitcom Dad Who Likes to Nibble Bats." *New York Times* 5 Mar. 2002: E8.

"James Earl Ray; Autumn Jackson; Amy Grossberg; Koko the Gorilla; Ellen DeGeneres." *US News & World Report* 4 May 1998: 16.

Jenkins, H. "Interactive Audiences? The Collective Intelligence of Media Fans." *The New Media Handbook*. Ed. D. Harries. London: British Film Institute, forthcoming.

Jones, Gerard. *Honey, I'm Home! Sitcoms: Selling the American Dream*. New York: St. Martin's, 1992.

Jones, Lisa. "Slave TV." *Village Voice* 10 Nov. 1998: 32.

Judah, Hettie. "Real Living." *The Independent* [London] 31 Jan. 1999: 4.

"Julia." *Variety* 25 Sept. 1968.

Kaler, A. K. "*Golden Girls:* Feminine Archetypal Patterns of the Complete Woman." *Journal of Popular Culture* 24.3 (1990): 49–61.

Kaltenbach, Chris. "*For Your Love* Tries for Three Times the Laughs." *Baltimore Sun* 17 Mar. 1998: 4E.

Kanner, Melinda. "Can *Will and Grace* Be 'Queered'?" *Gay and Lesbian Review* 10:4 (2003): 34–35.

Kant, Immanuel. *The Critique of Judgment*. Indianapolis: Hackett Publishing, 1987.

Kanter, Hal. *So Far So Funny: My Life in Show Business*. Jefferson, NC: McFarland, 1999.

Kassel, Michael B. *America's Favorite Radio Station: WKRP in Cincinnati*. Bowling Green, OH: Popular, 1993.

Katz, Richard. "'Ellen' Episode a Big Ratings Winner, Except in the South." *Media-Week* 5 May 1997: 4.

Kelleher, Terry. "Tube." *People* 8 June 1998: 31.

Kellner, Douglas. *Media Culture*. New York: Routledge, 1995.

Kelly, Richard. *The Andy Griffith Show*. Winston-Salem, NC: Blair, 1981.

Keveney, Bill. "'It's All About Funny This Time,' Ellen Says." *USA Today* July 26, 2001: 3D.

Kimmel, Michael. *Manhood in America: A Cultural History*. New York: Free, 1996.

Kitzinger, Celia. *The Social Construction of Lesbianism*. London: Sage, 1987.

Kohl, Paul R. "Looking Through a Glass Onion: Rock and Roll as a Modern Manifestation of Carnival." *Journal of Popular Culture* 27.1 (1993): 143–61.

Landay, Lori. *Madcaps, Screwballs, and Con Women: The Female Trickster in American Culture*. Philadelphia: U of Pennsylvania P, 1998.

———. "Millions Love Lucy: Commodification and the Lucy Phenomenon." *National Women's Studies Association Journal* 11.2 (Summer 1999): 25–47.

Leap, William. *Word's Out: Gay Men's English*. Minneapolis: U of Minnesota P, 1995.

Leibman, Nina C. *Living Room Lectures: The Fifties Family in Film and Television.* Austin: U of Texas P, 1995.

Leibrock, Rachel. "Who's Your Daddy? If Your Family Values Are Closer to the Osbournes than the Nelsons, TV Programmers Want You to Know—You're Not Alone." *Modesto Bee* [California] 19 May 2002: G1.

Lewis, Nick. "Osbournes Are a Smashing Success: But Their 'Madness' Is Tough to Duplicate." *Calgary Herald* [Alberta Canada] 2 June 2003, final ed.: B14.

Lichter, S. Robert, Linda S. Lichter, and Stanley Rothman. *Prime Time: How TV Portrays American Culture.* Washington, DC: Regency, 1994.

Life Magazine 24.2 (18 Sept. 1964), p. 24, as cited in the *Online Oxford English* Dictionary under "sitcom" <http://dictionary.oed.com/cgi/entry/00225799?query_type=word&queryword=situation+comedy&edition=2e&first=1&max_to_show=10&single=1&sort_type=alpha>

Linder, Laura R. "The Family as Portrayed in Television Situation Comedies." Thesis. U of NC at Greensboro, 1986.

Lipsitz, George. *Time Passages: Collective Memory and American Popular Culture.* Minneapolis: U of Minnesota P, 1990.

Lopez, Steve. "Death of the Sitcom." *Entertainment Weekly* 16 Apr. 1999: 30.

Lorando, Mark. "Sexual Harassment Played for Laughs on Television Sitcoms." *Times-Picayune* [New Orleans] 5 Jan. 1995: E1.

Lovell, T. "Writing Like a Woman: A Question of Politics." *The Politics of Theory.* Eds. Francis Barker, Peter Hulme, Margaret Iversen, and Diana Loxley. Colchester: U of Essex P, 1983.

"Lucille Ball: Love Is Her Favorite Career." *Quick* 27 Nov. 1950: cover, 51–53.

MacDonald, J. Fred. *Blacks and White TV: African-Americans in Television Since 1948.* Chicago: Nelson, 1992.

———. *Don't Touch That Dial: Radio Programming in American Life from 1920 to 1960.* Chicago: Nelson-Hall, 1979.

———. *One Nation Under Television: The Rise and Decline of Network Television.* Chicago: Nelson, 1994.

Marc, David. *Comic Visions: Television Comedy and American Culture.* Malden, MA: Blackwell, 1997.

———. *Demographic Vistas: Television in American Culture.* Philadelphia: U of Pennsylvania P, 1996.

Marc, David, and Robert J. Thompson. *Prime Time, Prime Movers: From I Love Lucy to L.A. Law—America's Greatest TV Shows and the People Who Created Them.* Boston: Little, 1992.

Marin, Rick. "The Rude Tube." *Newsweek* 23 Mar. 1998: 55–62.

Marx, Karl. *Capital I.* Chicago: Kerr, 1906.

Mathews, Gordon. *Global Culture/Individual Identity: Searching for Home in the Cultural Supermarket.* New York: Routledge, 2000.

Matthews, Glenna. *"Just a Housewife": The Rise and Fall of Domesticity in America.* New York: Oxford UP, 1987.

May, Elaine Tyler. *Homeward Bound: American Families in the Cold War Era.* New York: Basic, 1988.

McConnell, Frank. "How *Seinfeld* Was Born: Jane Austen Meets Woody Allen." *Commonweal* 123.3 (9 Feb. 1996): 19–20.

McDowell, Jeanne. "Television's Coming-Out Party: Gay Characters Have Quietly Become Hot. Can Their Love Lives?" *Time* 25 Oct. 1999: 116+.

McFadden, Kay. "New on TV—*Lateline*—*For Your Love.*" *Seattle Times* 17 Mar. 1998: E8.

McIlwain, Charlton D. & Lonnie Johnson Jr. "Headache and Heartbreak: Negotiating Model Minority Status among African Americans." *The Emerging Monoculture: Model Minorities and Benevolent Assimilationism.* Ed. E.M. Kramer. Westport, CT: Praeger, 2003: 110–123.

McInerney, Jay. "Is *Seinfeld* the Best Comedy Ever?" *TV Guide* 1 June 1996: 14–22.

McNeil, Alex. *Total Television.* New York: Penguin, 1996.

Means Coleman, Robin. *African American Viewers and the Black Situation Comedy: Situating Racial Humor.* New York: Garland, 2000.

Mellencamp, Patricia. *Logics of Television: Essays in Cultural Criticism.* Bloomington, IN: Indiana UP, 1992.

———. "Situation Comedy, Feminism, and Freud: Discourses of Gracie and Lucy." *Studies in Entertainment: Critical Approaches to Mass Culture.* Ed. Tania Modleski. Bloomington: Indiana UP, 1986. 80–95.

Mermigas, Diane. "Freston Swears by 'The Osbournes'." *Electronic Media* 10 June 2002: 2.

Messaris, Paul. "Visual Literacy vs. Visual Manipulation." *Critical Studies in Mass Communication* 11 (June 1994): 180–203.

Metallinos, Nikos. *Television Aesthetics: Perceptual, Cognitive, and Compositional Bases.* Mahwah, NJ: Erlbaum, 1996.

Mietkiewicz, Henry. "New Sitcom Flashes Its Own Death Knell." *Toronto Star* 18 Mar. 1998: D4.

Mifflin, Lawrie. "Of Race and Roles." *New York Times* 20 Jan. 1999: E9.

———. "Shared Favorites." *New York Times* 3 Feb. 1999: E7.

Millar, Steve. "'Peanuts on Acid' Bring Anal Probes Down to Earth on TV: American Cartoon Erudities Hit Terrestrial TV Screens." *The Guardian* [London] 1998: PSA-2139.

Miller, Douglas T., and Marion Nowak. *The Fifties: The Way We Really Were*. Garden City, NY: Doubleday, 1977.

Miller, Nancy. "American Goth." *Entertainment Weekly*. 19 April 2002: 22.

Mills, David. "What's So Funny?" *Washington Post* 26 Oct. 1993: 5.

Mink, Eric. "'South Park' Comes up a Hallo-winner." *New York Daily News* 29 Oct. 1997: 89.

Morehead, Albert. "'Lucy' Ball." *Cosmopolitan* Jan. 1953: cover, 15–19.

Morgenthau, Henry, III. Personal interview with David Marc. Television History Collections of the Center for the Study of Popular Television, Syracuse U Library. 6 May 1998.

Moritz, Marguerite J. "Old Strategies for New Texts: How American Television Is Creating and Treating Lesbian Characters." *Queer Words, Queer Images: Communication and the Construction of Homosexuality*. Ed. R. Jeffrey Ringer. New York: New York UP, 1994: 122–42.

Moss, R. "The Shrinking Life Span of the Black Sitcom." *New York Times* 25 Feb. 2001: 19+.

Mulvey, Laura. "Visual Pleasure and Narrative Cinema." *Screen* 16 (1975): 6–18. *Popular Television and Film*. Ed. T. Bennet, S. Boyd-Bowman, C. Mercer, and J. Woolcott. London: British Film Institute with the Open UP, 1981: 12–15.

Mumford, Laura. *Love and Ideology in the Afternoon: Soap Opera, Women, and Television Genre*. Bloomington: Indiana UP, 1995.

Neale, Steve, and Frank Krutnik. *Popular Film and Television Comedy*. London: Palmer, 1990.

Nelson, Angela M. S. *The Objectification of Julia: Text and Contexts of Black Women in American Television Comedies*. Paper presented at the Feminist Generations Conference, Bowling Green, OH, 1996.

Newcomb, Horace. "*Magnum:* The Champagne of Television?" *Channels of Communications* May/June 1985: 23–26.

Newcomb, Horace, and Paul M. Hirsch. "Television as a Cultural Forum." *Television: The Critical View*. Ed. Horace Newcomb. New York: Oxford UP, 2000 ed. 561–73.

Nielsen Ratings. *Broadcasting and Cable* 30 Mar 1998; 18 May 1998.

"Nightclubs: Bottom of the Top." *Time* 7 Dec. 1959: 48.

Nochimson, Martha. "*Ally McBeal:* Brightness Falls from the Air." *Film Quarterly* 53.3 (2000): 25–32.

O'Connor, John E., ed. *American History/American Television: Interpreting the Video Past*. New York: Ungar, 1983.

O'Connor, Pat. *Friendships between Women: A Critical Review*. New York: Harvester, 1992.

Ode, Kim. "After All These Years, It's Hats Off to Mary." *Star Tribune* [Minneapolis] 5 Feb. 2000: E1+.

Omi, Michael, and Howard Winant. "Racial Formations." *Race, Class and Gender in the United States: An Integrated Study*. Ed. Paula S. Rothenburg. New York: St. Martin's, 1998. 13–22.

Oxford English Dictionary at http://www.oed.com.

Oppenheimer, Jess. "Lucy's Two Babies." *Look* 21 Apr. 1953: cover, 20–24.

Oppenheimer, Jess, with Gregg Oppenheimer. *Laughs, Luck . . . and Lucy: How I Came to Create the Most Popular Sitcom of All Time*. Syracuse, NY: Syracuse UP, 1996.

Owen, Rob. *Gen X Television:* The Brady Bunch *to* Melrose Place. Syracuse, NY: Syracuse UP, 1997.

Ozzie and Harriet: Adventures of America's Favorite Family. Dir. Peter Jones. A&E. 1998.

Perigard, Mark. "Race and Reality; Four New Shows Are Adjusting the Color Balance of Prime Time." *Boston Herald* 29 Mar. 1998: 6.

Peters, Art. "What the Negro Wants from Television." *TV Guide: Southeast and Gulf Coast Editions* 16 Jan. 1968: 140–42.

Peterson, Kyle. "*Ally McBeal:* George Greenberg." *Advertising Age* 28 June 1999: 16+.

Poniewozik, James. "Color Crosses Over." *Time* 25 Feb. 2002: 64.

———. "Ozzy Knows Best: The Osbournes Has a Bleeping Thing or Two to Teach the Networks About Comedy—and Decorating with Crucifixes." *Time* 15 Apr. 2002: 64+.

Press, Andrea Lee. *Women Watching Television: Gender, Class, and Generation in the American Television Experience*. Philadelphia: U of Pennsylvania P, 1991.

"Program and Production Report." *Television Index*. New York: Television Index, Inc. May 27–June 2 1968.

Putterman, Barry. *On Television and Comedy: Essays on Style, Theme, Performer and Writer*. Jefferson, NC: McFarland, 1995.

Rabinovitz, Lauren. "Ms.-Representation: The Politics of Feminist Sitcoms." *Television, History and American Culture: Feminist Critical Essays*. Ed. Mary Beth Haralovich and Lauren Rabinovitz. Durham: Duke UP, 1999.

"Ratings." *Cable World* 21 July 2003: 29.

Ray, Robert. *A Certain Tendency of the Hollywood Cinema, 1930–1980*. Princeton: Princeton UP, 1985.

Reed, Rex. "*Women's Wear Daily* Television Reviews." Reprinted in *Big Screen Little Screen* by Rex Reed. New York: Macmillan, 1971.

Rich, Adrienne. *Blood, Bread, and Poetry, Selected Prose 1979–1985*. New York: Norton, 1986.

Richmond, Ray. "TV Sitcoms: The Great Divide—Few Shows Bridge Black, White Audiences." *Variety* Apr. 1998: 1.

Riggs, Marlon, dir. *Color Adjustment*. San Francisco: California Newsreel, 1991.

Ringer, Jeffrey R., ed. *Queer Words, Queer Images: Communication and the Construction of Homosexuality*. New York: New York UP, 1994. 107–21.

Romano, Allison. "*Osbournes* Get Another Turn at Bat." *Broadcasting & Cable* 14 July 2003: 14.

Ross, Chuck. "Funny About HBO . . . It Works." *Advertising Age* 6 Dec. 1999: 20+.

Rowe, K. "*Roseanne:* Unruly Woman as Domestic Goddess." *Screen* 31.4 (1990): 408–19.

———. *The Unruly Woman: Gender and the Genres of Laughter*. Austin: U of Texas P, 1995.

Rutenberg, Jim. "Father Knows Best, Including Ozzy." *New York Times* 21 Jan. 2002: C7.

Sanders, Coyne Steven, and Tom Gilbert. *Desilu: The Story of Lucille Ball and Desi Arnaz*. New York: Morrow, 1993.

"Sassafrassa, the Queen." *Time* 26 May 1952: cover, 62–68.

Scharrer, Erica. "From Wise to Foolish: The Portrayal of the Sitcom Father, 1950s–1990s." *Journal of Broadcasting and Electronic Media* 45.1 (2001): 23–40.

Schatz, Thomas. "Desilu, *I Love Lucy* and the Rise of Network Television." *Making Television: Authorship and the Production Process*. Ed. Robert J. Thompson and Gary Burns. New York: Praeger, 1990.

———. *Hollywood Genres: Formulas, Filmmaking, and the Studio System*. New York: McGraw, 1981.

Schneider, Michael. "TV Racial Divide Narrows." *Daily Variety* 11 Feb. 2000: 1.

———. "Where Are All the Minorities?" *Electronic Media* 19 Apr. 1999: 23.

Schulman, Bruce J. *The Seventies: The Great Shift in American Culture, Society, and Politics*. New York: Free, 2001.

Schwichtenburg, C. "Sensual Surfaces and Stylistic Excess: The Pleasure and Politics of *Miami Vice*." *Journal of Communication Inquiry* 10.3 (1987): 45–65.

Scodari, Christine. "'No Politics Here': Age and Gender in Soap Opera 'Cyberfandom.'" *Women's Studies in Communication* 21 (1998): 168–87.

———. "Possession, Attraction, and the Thrill of the Chase: Gendered Myth-Making in Film and Television Comedy of the Sexes. *Critical Studies in Mass Communication* 12 (1995): 23–29.

Scodari, Christine, and Jenna L. Felder. "Creating a Pocket Universe: 'Shippers,' Fan Fiction, and *The X-Files* Online." *Communication Studies* 51 (2000): 238–57.

Scott, James C. *Domination and the Arts of Resistance: Hidden Transcripts*. New Haven, CT: Yale UP, 1990.

Scully, Alan. "A Few Moments with Metal's Big [Expletive] Daddy." *Providence Journal Bulletin* 14 July 2002: I1.

See, Carolyn. "'I'm a Black Woman with a White Image': Diahann Carroll Explains Some of the Reasons Behind Her Success." *TV Guide: Southeast and Gulf Coast Editions* 18 (1970): 27–30.

Seldes, Gilbert. "The Errors of Television." *Atlantic Monthly* May 1937: 531–41.

Shales, Tom, and James Andrew Miller. *Live from New York: An Uncensored History of Saturday Night Live*. New York: Little, 2002.

Shalit, Ruth. "*Cagney and Lacey:* Betrayal of Postfeminism in Television Portrayals of Women." *New Republic* 6 Apr. 1998: 24+.

Shalit, Wendy. "Sex, Sadness, and the Sex and the City." *City Journal* Autumn 1999. 28 July 2000 <http://www.city-journal.org/html/9_4_a4.html>.

Shayon, Robert Lewis. "*Julia:* Breakthrough or Letdown?" *Saturday Review* 51 Apr. 1968: 49.

———. "*Julia* Symposium: An Opportunity Lost." *Saturday Review* 51 May 1968: 36.

Shugart, Helene, Catherine Waggoner, and D. Lynn Hallstein. "Mediating Third-Wave Feminism: Appropriation as Postmodern Media Practice." *Critical Studies in Mass Communication* 18 (2001): 194–210.

Silvian, Leonore. "Laughing Lucille." *Look* 3 June 1952: 7–8.

Simon, George T. *The Big Bands*. New York: Macmillan, 1971. 378–79.

Simonds, C. H. "Wanted: Black Jackie: Electronic Pipeline." *National Review* 20 (1968): 917.

Skolnick, Arlene. *Embattled Paradise: The American Family in an Age of Uncertainty*. New York: Basic, 1991.

Smith, Anna Deavere. *Fires in the Mirror*. New York: Anchor, 1993.

"Speaking Out." *People-Weekly* 15 Sept. 1997: 208.

Spigel, Lynn. *Make Room for TV: Television and the Family Ideal in Postwar America*. Chicago: U of Chicago P, 1992.

Spock, Benjamin. *The Common Sense Book of Baby and Child Care*. New York: Duell, 1946.

Staiger, Janet. *Blockbuster TV: Must-See Sitcoms in the Network Era*. New York: New York UP, 2000.

Stallybrass, Peter, and Allon White. *The Politics and Poetics of Transgression*. Ithaca, NY: Cornell UP, 1986.

Stanley, Allesandra. "No Rest for Family Values on Black Sabbath." *New York Times* 2 Apr. 2002, late ed.: E1.

Staples, Robert, and Terry Jones. "Culture, Ideology, and Black Television Images." *Black Scholar* 16 (1985): 10–20.

Stark, Steven D. *Glued to the Set: The 60 Television Shows and Events That Made Us Who We Are Today*. New York: Free, 1997.

Stark, Steven. "Cheers! It's Been Fun." *Boston Globe* 17 May 1993: 11.

Starr, Michael. "'South Park' Net Cries 'Foul'" *New York Post* 20 Mar. 1998: 120.

Stein, Ben. *The View from Sunset Boulevard*. New York: Basic, 1979.

Sterngold, James. "A Racial Divide Widens on Network TV." *New York Times* 29 Dec. 1998: A1.

Strauss, Neil. "The Osbournes Plan for Summer." *New York Times* 20 Feb. 2003: E3.

Strinati, Dominic. *An Introduction to Theories of Popular Culture*. New York: Routledge, 1995.

Stroman, Carolyn A., Bishetta D. Merrit, and Paula W. Matabane. "Twenty Years After Kerner: The Portrayal of African Americans on Prime-Time Television." *Howard Journal of Communications* 2 (Winter 1989–90): 44–56.

"Study Shows How Blacks Differ from Whites in TV Choices." *Jet* 23 May 1994: 58–62.

Sullivan, Andrew. *Virtually Normal: An Argument About Homosexuality*. New York: Knopf, 1995.

Taylor, Ella. *Prime-Time Families: Television Culture in Postwar America*. Berkeley: U of California P, 1989.

Television History Collections of the Center for the Study of Popular Television, Syracuse U Library.

Thomas, Karen. "Friars Take the Heat for Their Tradition of Tasteless Humor." *USA Today* 12 Oct. 1993: 3D.

Thompson, Robert J. *Television's Second Golden Age: From* Hill Street Blues *to* ER. Syracuse, NY: Syracuse UP, 1996.

Thompson, Robert, and Gary Burns, eds. *Making Television: Authorship and the Production Process*. New York: Praeger, 1990.

Toll, Robert. *Blacking Up: The Minstrel Show in 19th Century America*. New York: Oxford UP, 1974.

Tucker, Ken. "The Osbournes." *Entertainment Weekly* 15 Mar. 2002: 124–25.

Tueth, Michael V. "Fun City: TV's Urban Situation Comedies of the 1990s." *Journal of Popular Film and Television* 28.3 (2000): 98–107.

Turcotte, Louise. Foreword. *The Straight Mind and Other Essays*. By Monique Wittig. Boston: Beacon, 1992. vii–xii.

Turner, Victor. "Process, System, and Symbol: A New Anthropological Synthesis." *Daedalus* 106:3 (1977): 61–79.

Turner, Victor Witter. *The Drums of Affliction*. Oxford: Clarendon, 1968.

Turow, Joseph. *Breaking Up America: Advertisers and the New Media World*. Chicago: U of Chicago P, 1997.

TV Guide (N.Y. Metro ed. 23 Oct. 1953), p. 19, as cited in the *Online Oxford English Dictionary* under "situation comedy" <http://dictionary.oed.com/cgi/entry/00225872/00225872se6?single=1&query_type=word&queryword=situation+comedy&edition=2e&first=1&max_to_show=10&hilite=00225872se6>

Valletta, Robert G. "Changes in the Structure and Duration of U.S. Unemployment, 1967–1998." *Economic Review—Federal Reserve Bank of San Francisco* 3 (1998): 29–40.

Valverde, Mariana. Sex and the City, *Power, and Pleasure*. Toronto, Ontario: Women's, 1985.

Van Deburg, William L. *The Black Power Movement and American Culture, 1965–1975: New Day in Babylon*. Chicago: U of Chicago P, 1992.

Van Gelder, Lawrence. "Arts Briefing." *New York Times* 2 June 2003, late ed.: E2.

Vidmar, Neil, and Milton Rokeach. "Archie Bunker's Bigotry: A Study in Selective Perception and Exposure." All in the Family: *A Critical Appraisal*. Ed. Richard Adler. New York: Praeger, 1979. 123–38.

Waldron, Vince. *Classic Sitcoms: A Celebration of the Best in Prime-Time Comedy*. New York: Collier, 1987.

Walker, Dave. "Surreality TV: MTV Cameras Move In with Ozzy Osbourne's Family, and No, We're Not Sure Why." *New York Times* 5 Mar. 2002: Living 1.

Walters, Suzanna. *Material Girls: Making Sense of Feminist Cultural Theory*. Berkeley: U of California P, 1995.

Wandersee, Winifred D. *On the Move: American Women in the 1970s*. Boston: Twayne, 1988.

Warner, Michael. *The Trouble with Normal: Sex, Politics, and the Ethics of Queer Life*. Cambridge, MA: Harvard UP, 1999.

Watkins, Mel. *On the Real Side: Laughing, Lying, and Signifying*. New York: Simon, 1994.

Weinberg, G. "What Is Television's World of the Single Parent Doing to Your Family?" *TV Guide: Southeast and Gulf Coast Editions* 11 July 1970.

Weiss, Jessica. *To Have and to Hold: Marriage, the Baby Boom and Social Change*. Chicago: U of Chicago P, 2000.

Weissman, Ginny, and Coyne Steven Sanders. The Dick Van Dyke Show: *Anatomy of a Classic*. New York: St. Martin's, 1983.

Welsford, Enid. *The Fool: His Social and Literary History*. Gloucester, MA: Smith, 1966.

Whitney, D. "All Sugar, No Spice," *TV Guide*, 28 Dec. 1968: 2.

"Who's Watching What." *Austin American-Statesman*. 24 Apr. 2000: E10.

Whyte, William H. Jr. *The Organization Man*. New York: Doubleday Anchor Books, 1956.

Wilde, David. "South Park's Evil Geniuses and the Triumph of No-Brow Culture" *Rolling Stone* 19 Feb. 1998: 34.

Wilk, Max. *The Golden Age of Television Comedy*. New York: Delacorte Press, 1976: 176–77.

Wilke, Michael. "'Ellen' Legacy: Gay Television Roles Are More Acceptable: But Number Drops for Fall Season." *Advertising Age* 22 June 1998: 31.

Williams, Jeannie. "Whoopi's Shock Roast/Danson in Blackface Leaves Many Fuming." *USA Today* 11 Oct. 1993: 2D.

Williams-Harold, Bevolyn. "Not All Channels Are in Color." *Black Enterprise* Dec. 2000: 38.

Wittig, Monique. *The Straight Mind and Other Essays*. Boston: Beacon, 1992.

Wolcott, James. "Twinkle, Twinkle, Darren Star." *Vanity Fair* Jan. 2001: 64–72.

Wolters, Larry. "They All Love Lucy!" *Chicago Sunday Tribune* 23 Mar. 1952: 6+.

Zaret, David. "Religion, Science, and Printing in the Public Spheres in Seventeenth-Century England." *Habermas and the Public Sphere*. Ed. Craig Calhoun. Cambridge, MA: MIT P, 1992. 212–35.

Zook, Kristal Brent. *Color by Fox: The FOX Network and the Revolution in Black Television*. New York: Oxford UP, 1999.

Zynda, Thomas H. "The *Mary Tyler Moore Show* and the Transformation of Situation Comedy." *Media, Myths, and Narratives: Television and the Press*. Ed. James W. Carey. Beverly Hills, CA: Sage, 1988. 126–45.

Contributors

KAREN ANIJAR is Associate Professor of Curriculum and Cultural Studies at Arizona State University. She is the author of *Teaching Towards the 24th Century: The Social Curriculum of Star Trek in the Schools*, the co-editor of *Science Fiction Curriculum, Cyborg Teachers, and Youth Culture(s)*, and co-editor of *Culture and the Condom*.

ROBERT S. BROWN is Associate Professor and Director of the Sport Communication program in the Department of Communication Arts at Ashland University. His interests include the use of popular culture references in State of the Union addresses and the influence of popular sport in American society.

HSUEH-HUA VIVIAN CHEN is Assistant Professor at Nanyang Technological University, Singapore. Her research interests focus on cultural identity, cross-cultural communication, Whiteness, and intercultural conflict.

MARY M. DALTON is Assistant Professor of Communication at Wake Forest University and author of *The Hollywood Curriculum: Teachers in the Movies*. She has recently published articles in the *Journal of Film and Video*, *Women and Language* and the *Journal of Media Practice*; she is also a documentary filmmaker and a media critic for WFDD-FM.

PAUL R. KOHL is Associate Professor of Communication and Fine Arts at Loras College in Dubuque, Iowa. Kohl teaches courses in media studies, including film and popular music, and has been published in the *Journal of Popular Culture* and *Popular Music and Society*.

JUDY KUTULAS is Professor of History and American Studies and Director of Women's Studies at St. Olaf College, as well as a founding member of

St. Olaf's Media Studies program. She is currently writing a book about 1970s popular culture.

LORI LANDAY is Associate Professor at Berklee College of Music in Boston, teaching Visual Culture in the General Education Department and Film Scoring Department. She is the author of *Madcaps, Screwballs, and Con Women: The Female Trickster in American Culture* as well as essays on *I Love Lucy*, the flapper, and digital culture; she consulted on and appeared in the PBS American Masters documentary, *Finding Lucy*.

LAURA R. LINDER is Associate Professor of Media Arts at Marist College. She is the author of the book *Public Access Television: America's Electronic Soapbox*. Her interest in situation comedies began at a very early age while she watched *The Adventures of Ozzie and Harriet*; sitcoms were the topic of her masters thesis.

AMANDA DYANNE LOTZ is Assistant Professor of Communication Studies at the University of Michigan. Her research examines gender and feminism on U.S. television and institutional adjustments related to the transition to a post-network era.

DAVID MARC is a writer, editor, and occasional teacher at Syracuse University and Le Moyne College. He is a member of the editorial board of *Television Quarterly*. His most recent book is *Television in the Antenna Age* (2005), co-written with Robert J. Thompson.

CHARLTON D. McILWAIN is Assistant Professor of Culture and Communication at New York University. He is the author of *Death in Black and White: Death, Ritual and Family Ecology* and *When Death Goes Pop: Death, Media and the Remaking of Community*; he is pursuing research interests in the areas of race, media, and politics and also heads the Project on Race in Political Communication.

ROBIN R. MEANS COLEMAN is Associate Professor in the Department of Communication at the University of Pittsburgh. She is the author of *African American Viewers and the Black Situation Comedy: Situating Racial Humor* and *Say It Loud! African American Audiences, Media and Identity*. She has also published scholarly articles on race and representation.

JOHN O'LEARY is Assistant Professor in the Communication Department and Director of Internships for the College of Arts and Sciences at Villanova University. His research focuses on the relationship between media institutions and narrative forms.

VALERIE V. PETERSON is Assistant Professor in the School of Communications at Grand Valley State University in Michigan. Her research interests include rhetorical theory and criticism, discourses of love and sexuality, visual rhetoric, and relationships between popular culture and identity. Her work has been published in the *Southern Communication Journal*, *Communication Studies*, and the *Journal of Communication Inquiry*.

DAVID PIERSON is Assistant Professor of Media Studies at the University of Southern Maine. His research interests include the aesthetic and discursive dimensions of broadcast and cable TV programming. His work has been previously published in the *Journal of Popular Culture* and *Film & History*.

DENIS M. PROVENCHER is Assistant Professor in the Department of Modern Languages and Linguistics at the University of Maryland Baltimore County. He completed a UW-System Fellowship at the Center for 21st Century Studies at the University of Wisconsin-Milwaukee in 2001–02. His work has appeared in *French Cultural Studies*, *Contemporary French Civilization*, and in the anthology *Speaking in Queer Tongues*.

SHARON MARIE ROSS is Assistant Professor at Columbia College in the Television Department where she teaches TV history, criticism, and programming strategies. Her work focuses on gender and sexuality, particularly representations of female friendships on television.

CHRISTINE SCODARI is Associate Professor of Communication and Women's Studies Associate at Florida Atlantic University. In addition to her 2004 book, *Serial Monogamy*, in which she explores age and gender in soap operas and their audiences, she has recently published journal and anthology articles on age and/or gender in science fiction and romantic comedy film and television as well as teen girl cyberculture.

DEMETRIA ROUGEAUX SHABAZZ is a Ph.D. candidate in Mass Communication at the University of Alabama in Tuscaloosa and is completing her dissertation on the 1968 television series *Julia*. She received a 2003–2004 Visiting Dissertation Fellowship from Northeastern University, which was awarded for her work on the series.

H. PETER STEEVES is Associate Professor of Philosophy at DePaul University where he specializes in ethics, social/political philosophy, and phenomenology. He is author of *Founding Community: A Phenomenological-Ethical Inquiry* and *The Things Themselves: Essays in Applied Phenomenology* and editor of *Animal Others: On Ethics, Ontology, and Animal Life*.

MICHAEL V. TUETH is Associate Professor in the Communication and Media Studies Department at Fordham University. He recently published a survey of television comedy and its relationship to the domestic ethos of American society entitled *Laughter in the Living Room: Television Comedy and the American Home Audience.*

THOMAS E. WALKER is a Senior Program Coordinator and Trainer with the Intergroup Relations Center at Arizona State University where he coordinates diversity training, dialogue, and research programs. His research focus is on Whiteness, social justice, ally, and other identity issues.

RICK WORLAND is Associate Professor in the Division of Cinema-Television in the Meadows School of the Arts at Southern Methodist University. His research has concentrated on popular film and television in the Cold War period; he is currently completing a survey of the horror genre for Blackwell Publishing.

PHYLLIS SCROCCO ZRZAVY is Professor of Mass Communication at the Marlin Fitzwater Center for Communication at Franklin Pierce College in Rindge, New Hampshire. She founded the center's Media Studies program and teaches courses in media theory, criticism, media culture, and gender studies. Her research focuses women in media representation and media literacy.

Index

ABC. *See* networks
ABC Entertainment, 195
Abercrombie and Fitch, 195
abortion, 26, 130, 168
Absolut vodka, 195
abstinent. *See* sexuality
absurd, absurdist, 29, 42, 43, 45, 59, 106, 248
Academy Award, 34
Academy of Television Arts and Sciences, 227
Acker, Joan, 215
Action, 27
Action for Children's Television, 27
activists, 166
actors, actresses, 19, 30, 34, 52, 62, 64, 70, 73, 75, 79, 88, 91, 93, 94, 95, 104, 109, 128, 130, 134, 135, 139, 142, 143, 144, 145, 146, 147, 148, 149, 157, 159, 160, 161, 165, 178, 184, 186, 188, 227, 232, 236, 237, 255. *See also under* race and ethnicity
Addams Family, The, 71
Adler, David. *See* Frank Tarloff, 24
adolescent, adolescence, 27, 31, 52, 192, 236
adopt, adoption, adopted, adoptive, 3, 46, 78, 121, 196
adultery, adulterous, 35, 183
Adventures of Amos 'n' Andy: A Social History of an American Phenomenon, 24

Adventures of Ozzie and Harriet, The, 20, 25, 52, 56, 61–71, **63**, 95
"An Evening with Hamlet," 68
Hillside, 62
"Music Appreciation," 68
Nelson, David, **63**
Nelson, Harriet, 3, **63**, 90
Nelson, Ozzie, 3, 4, 20, 62, **63**, 69, 90
Nelson, Ricky (Rick), 20, 56, 59, 61, **63**, 70
the Nelsons, 61, 62, **63**, 64, 67, 68, 69, 70, 71
"Wedding Picture," 68
ads, advertisements, 53, 115, 177, 195, 196, 199, 222, 223
advertisers, advertising, 10, 34, 49, 52, 53, 104, 117, 135, 143, 145, 148, 149, 150, 153, 154, 166, 168, 184, 194, 195, 196, 200, 218, 219, 223, 227, 249. *See also* sponsor(s), sponsorship
aesthetics, 45, 88, 146, 152, 154, 155, 160, 161, 199
African, 154
African American. *See* race and ethnicity
African American Viewers and the Black Situation Comedy: Situating Racial Humor, 136n
agency, 6, 111, 112, 114, 116, 118, 119, 120, 121, 126, 196, 216
aging, 16, 64, 248, 250
AIDS, 201

Airplane!, 271

Albrecht, Chris, 112

alcohol, alcoholic, alcoholism, 31, 183, 258

Alda, Alan, 223

Alexander, Jason, **41**. See also *Seinfeld*

alienation, alienated, 11, 52, 140, 219, 221, 229, 231, 232, 237

All-American, 52

Allen, Debbie, 126. See also *A Different World*

Allen, Gracie, 90. See also *The George Burns and Gracie Allen Show*

Alley, Kirstie, **256**. See also *Cheers*

All in the Family, 4, 26, 30, 34, 53, 54, 84, 219
    Bunker, Archie, 26, 30, 53
    Bunker, Edith, 53
    Bunker family, 4, 54
    Stivic, Gloria Bunker, 26, 53, 54
    Stivic, Mike, 26, 53, 54

Ally McBeal, 2, 11, 241–252, **243**
    Cage and Fish & Associates, 247
    Cage, John, 244, 247, 249. *See also* Peter MacNicol
    Cone, Whipper, 249, 250. *See also* Dyan Cannon
    "face bra," 249
    Fish, Richard, 244, 249, 250. *See also* Greg Germann
    "girls' sleepover," 245
    happy hour ritual, 244
    McBeal, Ally, 242–251, **243**. *See also* Calista Flockhart
    Porter, Nelle, 247, 249. *See also* Portia de Rossi
    Radick, Renee, 248, 249. *See also* Lisa Nicole Carson
    Thomas, Billy, 244. *See also* Gil Bellows
    Thomas, Georgia, 244. *See also* Courtney Thorne-Smith
    "unisex restroom," 244
    Vassal, Elaine, 249. *See also* Jane Krakowski
    "vi-bra," 249
    "wattles," 249, 250

Woo, Ling, 247, 249. *See also* Lucy Lui

amen, 270, 271

Amen, 126, 143

American, Americans, American society, 1, 7, 15, 16, 17, 19, 21, 28, 36, 43, 45, 51, 53, 58, 59, 78, 79, 81, 88, 90, 105, 125, 162, 173, 180, 182, 205, 225, 262

American Airlines, 195

American Dream, 9, 64, 83

American Dream, 34

American Dreams, 251

American family, 62, 70, 126, 269

American Family, 149

American Heritage Dictionary, 23

American mythology/narratives, 20, 40, 83

American National Biography, 24

American pop culture, 27, 128

American television, 1, 3, 23, 24, 35, 36, 45, 49, 76, 188

American University, 189

American values, ideals, beliefs, 75, 76, 82, 220

Amos 'n' Andy, 6, 15, 16, 17, 19, 20, 24, 51, 125, 127, 128, **129**, 136, 159
    Brown, Andy, 127, **129**. *See also* Spencer Williams Jr.
    Calhoun, Algonquin J., 19. *See also* Johnny Lee
    Jones, Amos, 127, **129**. *See also* Alvin Childress
    Mama, 19. *See also* Amanda Randolph
    Sam 'n' Henry, 17, 127, 128
    Stevens, George "The Kingfish," 19, **129**. *See also* Tim Moore
    Stevens, Sapphire, 19, 126. *See also* Ernestine Wade

Amsterdam, Morey, **230**. See also *The Dick Van Dyke Show*

Andersen, Robin, 116

Anderson, Christopher, 97

Anderson, Loni, 223. See also *WKRP in Cincinnati*

Andy Griffith Show, The, 4, 20, 24, 73–84, **74**, 255, 263
   Bailey, Ron, 76
   "Bailey's Bad Boy," 76
   "Barney Hosts a Summit Meeting," 80
   "Big House, The," 79
   Campbell, Otis, 75, 78, 79. *See also* Hal Smith
   "Christmas Story, The," 82
   Fife, Barney, **74**, 75, 77, 78, 79, 80, 82. *See also* Don Knotts
   "Man in a Hurry," 77, 80
   Mayberry, 4, 73, 75, 76, 77, 78, 79, 80, 81, 82, 83, 84, 255, 263
   "Mayberry Goes Bankrupt," 83
   "Mayberry Goes Hollywood," 78, 79
   Juanita, 75
   Lawson, Floyd, 75, 78. *See also* Howard McNear
   Pyle, Gomer, **74**, 75. *See also* Jim Nabors
   Sarah, 75
   "Sheriff Without a Gun," 79
   Sprague, Howard, 75. *See also* Jack Dodson
   Taylor, Andy, 20, 73, **74**, 75, 76, 77, 78, 79, 80, 81, 82, 83, 84. *See also* Andy Griffith
   Taylor, Aunt Bee, 75, 77, 79, 80. *See also* Frances Bavier
   Taylor, Opie, **74**, 75, 76, 77, 78, 79, 82. *See also* Ronny Howard
   Tucker, 77
   "TV or Not TV," 79
   "Visit to Barney Fife, A," 80
   Walker, Ellie, 82. *See also* Elinor Donahue
   Weaver, Ben, 82
Anijar, Karen, 9, 191–202, 293
animal rights groups, 249
animated, animation, 2, 12, 26, 34, 146, 192, 244, 249, 264, 269. *See also* cartoon
Anna and the King, 108
anomie, 79

anthology dramas, 76
antiauthoritarian, 56, 57
antisocial, 34
apolitical, 128, 198
appropriate, appropriation, 29, 96, 162, 195, 250
architecture, 264
Arden, Eve, 6, 100, 102, **103**, 105, 218. See also *Our Miss Brooks*
Aristotle, 102
Arnaz, Desi, 5, **89**, 93, 95, 105. See also *I Love Lucy*
Arsenio, 143
Ashkenazic Jewish, 17. *See also* race and ethnicity
Asian, Asian American, 6, 7, 139, 150, 197, 259. *See also* race and ethnicity
Asner, Edward, **233**. See also *The Mary Tyler Moore Show*
assassination(s), 127, 130, 209
assimilate, assimilation, 19, 130, 160, 161
atheism, 26
Atlantic Monthly, 24
attitudes, 26, 28, 43, 53, 148, 153, 173, 206, 235, 258, 259, 268
audience(s), 1, 2, 3, 4, 7, 8, 9, 19, 22, 23, 27, 30, 34, 45, 49, 52, 53, 54, 56, 57, 58, 59, 62, 64, 68, 75, 88, 90, 91, 94, 95, 96, 101, 104, 106, 112, 118, 128, 134, 135, 136, 152, 153, 163, 165, 173, 174, 186, 187, 206, 217, 219, 220, 222, 223, 227, 232, 234, 236, 237, 241, 251, 252, 255, 258
   crossover, 126, 127, 147, 159
   demographics, 7, 26, 52, 54, 55, 56, 57, 58, 59, 84, 142, 143, 144, 147, 149, 191, 228, 241, 242, 252
   live, studio audience, 2, 64, 88, 93, 95, 236
   niche programming, 6, 149
   racial polarization, 148
   segmentation, 11, 242
   segregation, 7, 139–150
audiovisual, 88, 251
Austrian-German, 268

authentic, authenticity, 62, 78, 79, 165, 170, 183, 184, 185, 186, 263, 266, 268, 269
authoritarian, 51
autobiography, 91, 237. *See also* biography

baby boomer(s), boomers, 4, 10, 52, 53, 54, 55, 56, 57, 58, 219, 220
Baby I'm Back, 126, 136
  Ellis, Olivia, 136
  Ellis, Raymond, 136
bachelor(s), 55, 75
backlash, 115, 246
Baer, Max Jr., **38**. See also *The Beverly Hillbillies*
Baker, Keith Michael, 12, 254, 255, 260
Bakhtin, Mikhial, 234, 235
Ball, Alan, 34
Ball, Lucille, 5, 6, 87, **89**, 90, 91, 92, 93, 94, 95, 96, 97, 105, 206, 213. See also *I Love Lucy* and *My Favorite Husband*
Bamboozled, 148
bandleader, 5, 62, 64, 70, 90
Barbie, 160
Basinger, Janine, 218
battle of the sexes, 51, 93
Bavier, Frances, 75. See also *The Andy Griffith Show*
Beacon Hill, 259
Beatles, The, 52
Beaumont, Hugh, **50**. See also *Leave It To Beaver*
Beavis and Butthead, 34
Behind the Music, 34
Being, 262
Belafonte, Harry, 159
Bellafante, Ginia, 245
Bellows, Gil, 244. See also *Ally McBeal*
Belton, John, 205
Benny, Jack, 21
Berg, Gertrude, 17, **18**, 19, 108. See also *The Goldbergs* and *Molly*
Bergson, Henri, 12, 262
Berle, Milton, 16, 25, 232, 237
Bernie Mac Show, The, 133, 144
Berry, Ken, 83. See also *Mayberry, RFD*
Better Days, 108

Between Brothers, 108
Beulah, 19, 24, 127, 128, 130, 156
  Hurt, Marlin, 128
  Waters, Ethel, 124, 128
Beverly Hillbillies, The, 3, 36, 37–40, **38**, 45, 53, 71, 76, 219
  Bodine, Jethro, **38**. *See also* Max Baer Jr.
  Bodine, Cousin Pearl, 37
  Clampett, Elly May, 37, **38**, 39, 40. *See also* Donna Douglas
  Clampett, Jed, 37, **38**, 39, 40, 46. *See also* Buddy Ebsen
  "Cool School is Out, Part 2," 46
  Drysdale, Margaret, 37
  Drysdale, Milburn, 37, 40, 46
  "Granny vs. the Weather Bureau," 39
  Hathaway, Miss Jane, 37, 40
  Moses, Daisy (Granny), 37, **38**, 39. *See also* Irene Ryan
Beverly Hills, 37, 39
Bianco, Robert, 132
bias(es), biased, 8, 152, 160, 165
bifurcated. *See* dichotomy
big band singer, 207
Big Brother, 185
"big four." *See* networks
Big Mac, 263, 264
bigotry, 26, 30, 132. *See also* racism
big screen, 101, 155, 184
Big Story, The, 109
Big Three. *See* networks
Billboard Top Ten, 20
Bill Cosby Show, The, 102, 105, 108, 109, 130
  Kincaid, Chet, 105. *See also* Bill Cosby
Billingsley, Barbara, **50**. *See also* June Cleaver
Bing Crosby Show, The, 20
  Collins, Bing, 20. *See also* Bing Crosby
  Collins, Ellie, 20. *See also* Beverly Garland
  Collins, Janice, 20
  Collins, Joyce, 20
biography, 24. *See also* autobiography

binary. *See* dichotomy
Birds, The, 269
Birmingham, Alabama, 80
bisexual, bisexuality. *See* sexuality
Black. *See* race and ethnicity
Blacks and White Television, 24
Black Entertainment Television
    Network, 30
Black Panther, 209
Black Sabbath, 59, 61, 64
*Blacking Up: The Minstrel Show in 19th
    Century America*, 23
Blackmon, Edafe, **141**. See also *For Your
    Love*
Bledsoe, Tempestt, **131**. See also *The
    Cosby Show*
Blockbuster, 118, 119
Bob Newhart Show, The, 54, 101, 108,
    220, 221
    Hartley, Bob, 221
    Hartley, Emily, 101
    Kester, Carol, 220
Bodroghkozy, Aniko, 161
body, bodies, 30, 94, 95, 155, 156, 157,
    160, 161, 172, 184, 219, 236, 248,
    249, 250
    breast, 68, 236, 248, 249
    no-nudity clause, 248
    nudity, 248
    penis, 247
Bogle, Donald, 160
bonding, 115, 117, 119, 122, 174
Bonet, Lisa, **131**. See also *The Cosby
    Show*
boomers. *See* baby boomers
Booth, Wayne, 45
Boskin, Joseph, 136
Boston, 24, 244, 251, 255, 258, 259
Boston Common, 108
Boston Globe, 255
Boston Red Sox, 257
boundaries, 2, 29, 88, 90, 97, 101, 102,
    119, 122, 151, 160, 162, 166, 174,
    175, 176, 206, 229
bourgeois. *See* social class
Bowlby, Rachel, 117
Bowser, Yvette Lee, 147, 148

boycotts, 26, 127, 135, 168
Boyd, Todd, 145
boyfriend, 42, 43, 44, 114, 118, 174, 180,
    183, 184, 186, 187, 218, 224, 248
Boy Meets World, 108
bra, bras, brassiere, 222, 249
    bra burning, 222
    braless, 222
brand names, 264
Brady Bunch, The, 271
Breaking Up America, 251
Bridget Loves Bernie, 108
broadcast, broadcasting, 7, 17, 20, 21,
    22, 23, 24, 27, 54, 64, 88, 100, 128,
    142, 149, 151, 155, 170, 185, 186,
    205, 214, 220, 231, 236, 237. *See also*
    network(s)
Broadcasting & Cable, 150
Broadway, off-Broadway, 84, 235, 237
Bronx, 17, 19. *See also* New York City
Brooklyn, 188. *See also* New York City
Brooks, James L., 232, 237
Brooks, Tim, 71, 75, 76. See also *The
    Complete Directory to Prime Time
    Network and Cable TV Shows*
Brother's Keeper, 108
Brown, Philip, 207. See also *The Doris
    Day Show*
Brown, Robert S., 11, 12, 253–260, 293
Bruce, Donald, 43
Bruni, Frank, 180
Buffy the Vampire Slayer, 147
Built to Last, 143
Bullock, Harvey, 81
Bullough, Vern L., 175
Burns, Allan, 232
Bush, George W., 67
Bushnell, Candace, 112, 242
business, 1, 33, 78, 83, 231, 258, 259,
    264. *See also* show business
Butler, Judith, 184
Butterfinger candy, 266, 267
Byrne, Terry 159

cable, 2, 6, 7, 21, 26, 27, 34, 59, 66, 67,
    122, 140, 147, 149, 180, 192, 241,
    242, 249. *See also* networks

Cagney and Lacey, 251
Cagney, James, 80
Caldarola, V., 216
Caldwell, John, 156, 157
California, 24, 27, 37, 198, 207
Calloway, Vanessa Bell, 136
cameo(s). *See under* narrative(s)
Cameron, Kirk, 57
camp, 29, 99
Candies shoes, 222
cancer, 69, 121
Canfield, Douglas, 36
Cannavale, Bobby, 188. See also *Will &
    Grace*
Cannon, Dyan, 249. See also *Ally
    McBeal*
capitalism, capitalist, 37, 83, 112, 115,
    116, 120, 195, 196, 201, 202, 220,
    225, 228, 231, 232, 234, 237, 262,
    266
    democratic capitalism, 154, 162, 201
Capra, Frank, 4, 20, 79, 80, 81, 82, 83
career(s), 10, 36, 39, 43, 54, 55, 64, 66,
    67, 71, 88, 91, 93, 94, 96, 116, 137,
    160, 207, 208, 209, 210, 213, 214,
    215, 218, 220, 221, 224, 231, 236, 255
caricature, 30, 78, 127, 136, 202
Car 54, Where Are You?, 127
carnival, carnivalesque, 11, 33, 229, 232,
    234, 235, 238
Carroll, Bob Jr., 88
Carroll, Diahann, 8, 151–161, **158**. See
    also *Julia*
Carson, Lisa Nicole, 248. See also *Ally
    McBeal*
Cartland, Barbara, 268, 269
cartoon, 26, 52, 76, 191, 192, 194, 202,
    263, 264. *See also* animated, anima-
    tion
category, categorical, 9, 96, 142, 144,
    145, 146, 147, 175, 195, 196, 216,
    258, 263
Catch-22, 176
cathode ray tube, 24
Catrall, Kim, **113**. See also *Sex and the City*
CBS. *See* networks
CBS Sunday Movie, The, 144

celebrity, 4, 16, 64, 68, 70, 105, 174, 264,
    266
censors, censorship, 28, 66, 94, 121
centrist, 198, 225
Center for the Study of Popular
    Television, Syracuse University, 23, 24
*Certain Tendency of the Hollywood
    Cinema, 1930–1980, A*, 81
Chafe, William, 91
character. *See under* narrative
Charlie and Co., Charlie and Company,
    108, 127, 132
Charlie's Angels, 222
Charmed, 147
Charren, Peggy, 27
chauvinist(s), 220
Check and Double Check, 24
Cheers, 11, 12, 224, 253–260, **256**
    Boston city council, 258
    Boyd, Woody, **256**, 257, 258. *See also*
        Woody Harrelson
    "Boys in the Bar," 258
    Chambers, Diane, 224, 225, **256**,
        257, 258. *See also* Shelley Long
    "Cliff's Rocky Moment," 259
    Colcord, Robin, **256**, 257. *See also*
        Roger Rees
    Crane, Dr. Frasier, 224, 225, **256**,
        257, 258. *See also* Kelsey
        Grammar
    Gary, Gary's Tavern, 257
    Gavin, Cliff, **256**. *See also* John
        Ratzenberger
    Howe, Rebecca, **256**, 257, 259. *See
        also* Kirstie Alley
    Kenderson, Tom, 258
    LeBec, Carla Tortelli, **256**, 257. *See
        also* Rhea Perlman
    Lewis, 259
    Malone, Sam, 224, 225, **256**, 257,
        258, 259. *See also* Ted Danson
    "Norm, is that you?," 259
    Peterson, Norm, 255, **256**, 257, 259.
        See also George Wendt
    "Rebecca's Lover . . . Not," 259
    Sternin, Dr. Lilith, 224, **256**, 257. *See
        also* Bebe Neuwirth

Tortelli LeBec, Carla, **256**, 257. *See also* Rhea Perlman

Chen, Hsueh-hua Vivian, 9, 191–202, 293

Chicago, 16, 17, 19, 24, 140, 209

Chicago Sunday Tribune, 93

"chick flick," 117

childless, 55, 84, 93, 101

children. *See under* family

Childress, Alvin, 128, **129**. See also *Amos 'n' Andy*

Chinatown, 210

Chris Rock Show, The, 262

Christian, 32

Chrysler, 168

church, 32, 44, 127

Church Lady, 266

cigarette, 93, 222

cinema, 5, 81, 88, 155, 157. *See also* film and movies, motion pictures

Citizen Kane, 83, 269

City of Angels, 136, 142

civil rights, civil rights movement, 17, 19, 80, 81, 127, 128

civil union, 181, 183. *See also* wedding

Civil War, 133

Class of 1984, The, 99

class, class status. *See* social class

Cleveland, 24

cliché, 132, 136, 166, 268, 270, 271

clique, 246

Clueless, 108

Code, Lorraine, 118

code(s). *See* social codes

Cold War, 51

collaboration, collaborative, 10, 94, 96, 227, 228

collective
    action, 81, 135
    social interest, 258

college students, 52, 54

Colorado, 26

comedy, 2, 7, 17, 23, 25, 26, 27, 31, 34, 75, 78, 87, 88, 91, 139, 205, 237. *See also* transgressive comedy and *under* work, workplace
    comedy-variety, 2, 16, 20, 23, 24, 142

physical comedy, 91, 95, 126

theory of comedy. *See under* theory

Comedy Central, 192, 195, 198. *See also* networks

Comedy of Manners, 3, 35–46

coming out. *See* sexuality

commentary, 9, 32, 33, 148, 168, 173, 174, 191, 225, 229, 269

commercial(s), 15, 34, 68, 104, 152, 153, 168, 219, 223, 241, 249, 266

commercial television, 7, 21, 34, 107, 126, 144, 149, 153, 162, 178, 180, 186, 187, 188, 189, 225, 242, 251, 252

commercial sponsors. *See* sponsors

commercialism, commercialization, 121, 264, 266

commodity, commodities, commodification, 9, 91, 92, 115, 116, 191, 192, 195, 199, 200, 222, 223, 224, 225, 232, 248, 250, 263, 269

communication, 21, 200, 253
    mass communication, 15, 27, 135, 263

Communism, 51, 96

community, 5, 6, 11, 43, 75, 78, 81, 82, 83, 84, 117, 128, 135, 154, 171, 198, 220, 254, 255, 257, 259, 263, 264, 267

"comparative worth," 215

Complete Directory to Prime Time Network and Cable TV Shows, The, 71, 75, 108, 109

complexion, 157, 160

congregation, 32, 183

Congreve, William, 3, 36, 42

con men, 37, 79

Connecticut, 51

Connick, Harry Jr., 188. See also *Will & Grace*

Connor, "Bull," 80

Conrack, 99

conservative, 40, 81, 153, 184, 206, 220, 245

consumer, consumerism, consumerist, 51, 64, 111, 112, 114, 115, 116, 117, 119, 120, 121, 122, 134, 135,

consumer, consumerism, consumerist (*continued*)
  148, 149, 152, 153, 194, 195, 214, 219, 222, 223, 225, 242
  bourgeois consumer culture, 154
  conspicuous consumption, 249
  consumer culture, 9, 12, 75, 117
  consumer-friendly, 10, 220, 224
  consumer identities, 51, 224
  consumer niches, 195
  consumption, 6, 9, 112, 116, 195, 196, 202, 249, 264
  liberated consumerism, 223
  subject-consumers, 194
consumption. *See under* consumer
context, 2, 3, 4, 6, 7, 8, 9, 12, 26, 29, 30, 31, 35, 90, 93, 101, 106, 142, 147, 150, 157, 170, 206, 241, 246, 254, 262, 268
contextualize, 2, 11, 12, 134, 246
controversy(ies), 9, 30, 140, 143, 153, 168, 173, 195, 214
conventions, conventions of the genre. *See* sitcom conventions
conversation(s), 111–122, 178, 185, 218, 248, 255, 259, 260, 268
Coontz, Stephanie, 49
Cooper, Brenda, 246, 248, 250, 252
Copage, Marc, **158**. See also *Julia*
Corbett, John, 245. See also *Sex and the City*
corporate, corporations, 11, 21, 51, 77, 134, 145, 152, 195, 215, 228, 229, 234, 236, 263, 264
  corporate culture, 51. *See also* culture
  corporate sponsors. *See* sponsors
Correll, Charles, 17, 19, 24, 127, 128
Cosby, Bill, 104, 127, 130, **131**, 132, 137. See also *Cosby, The Bill Cosby Show, The Cosby Show, I Spy*
Cosby, 143, 147
Cosby Show, The, 6, 56, 102, 105, 108, 109, 126, 128, 130, **131**, 132, 136, 143, 144, 148, 178, 264
  Huxtable, Clair, 56, **131**. *See also* Phylicia Rashad

Huxtable Kendall, Denise, **131**. *See also* Lisa Bonet
Huxtable, Dr. Cliff, 4, 56, 57, 59, **131**. *See also* Bill Cosby
Huxtable, Rudy, **131**. *See also* Keshia Knight Pulliam
Huxtable, Sondra Tibideaux, **131**. *See also* Sabrina Le Beauf
Huxtable, Theodore, **131**. *See also* Malcolm Jamal-Warner
Huxtable, Vanessa, **131**. *See also* Tempestt Bledsoe
Huxtable, Denise Kendall, **131**. *See also* Lisa Bonet
cosmopolitan, cosmopolitanism, 199, 263
Cotten, Joseph, 269
counterculture. *See* culture
couple, couples, "couplehood," 9, 25, 62, 84, 90, 92, 93, 94, 118, 119, 140, 146, 180–188, 199
creative, 10, 28, 78, 95, 126, 148, 178, 227, 229, 231, 232
  creative process, 134, 135, 151
Crenna, Richard, **103**. See also *Our Miss Brooks*
Cribs, 64
crime, 54, 79
Cripps, Thomas, 19
critical media studies. *See* media
critics, 3, 9, 45, 67, 114, 130, 146, 150, 155, 160, 162, 166, 205, 208, 212, 213, 246, 250, 252, 258, 259, 263
Crosby, Bing, 16, 20. See also under *Bing Crosby Show, The*
crossover. *See* programming
Cuban, 51, 90, 93
cult, 115, 191, 222
cultural studies. *See* culture
culture, cultural, 1, 2, 3, 4, 8, 9, 10, 11, 19, 27, 29, 31, 37, 43, 51, 53, 55, 61, 75, 77, 91, 94, 96, 102, 107, 115, 116, 119, 125, 126, 127, 130, 132, 133, 134, 142, 143, 145, 146, 149, 154, 160, 161, 162, 175, 184, 192, 196, 197, 198, 205, 206, 207, 214, 215,

216, 221, 223, 229, 234, 246, 251, 253, 254, 255, 257, 266, 271
African American, Black culture, 145, 150, 154, 159, 160
American culture, 17, 21, 23, 45, 76, 88, 91, 96, 107, 116, 128, 160, 205
bourgeois culture, 154, 235
capitalist culture, 37, 120
consumer culture. *See* consumer
contemporary culture, 5, 209, 215
counterculture, 52, 54, 55, 195, 220
cultural artifacts, 1, 45, 195
cultural change, 9, 205
cultural context, 3, 90
cultural critics, 146, 250, 253
cultural dialogue, 206, 214, 216, 218
cultural elite, 112–114, 258
cultural ideal, 59, 91
cultural identity, 194
cultural norms, 159
cultural practices, 31, 132
cultural reference, 220
cultural relevance, culturally relevant, 132, 213, 214
cultural representations, 111, 259
cultural resistance, 33
cultural significance, 7, 99, 205
cultural studies, 1
cultural taboos, 3, 34
cultural texts, 106, 229
dominant culture, 160, 264
folk culture, 31, 77
global culture, 264
high culture, 234, 258, 260
learned culture, 254
local culture, 264, 266
low culture, 258, 260
popular culture, 6, 12, 16, 24, 25, 27, 91, 101, 107, 128, 136, 160, 205, 218, 220, 222, 228, 258
postwar culture, 3, 19, 52, 68, 78, 96, 217
socio-cultural, 114, 125, 133, 145, 206, 214
customs, 36, 39, 43, 264
Curb Your Enthusiasm, 262

Curry, Mark, 105. See also *Hangin' with Mr. Cooper*
cynicism, 82, 245, 266

D'Acci, Julie, 251
Dalai Lama, 31
Dallas, 269
    "Who Shot J.R.?," 269
Dalton, Mary M., 6, 99–110, 293
Dancing in September, 148
Dandridge, Dorothy, 160
Dangerous Minds, 109
Daniels, Stan, 234
Dann, Mike, 234, 236
Danny Thomas Show, The (syndicated as *Make Room for Daddy*), 19, 20, 21, 24
    Williams, Danny, 20, 51. *See also* Danny Thomas
Danson, Ted, 30, 255, **256**. See also *Cheers*
dating. *See* relationships
D'Augelli, Anthony R., 166
David, Larry, 235, 236, 237, 262
Davis, Cristin, **113**, 244. See also *Sex and the City*
Dawson's Creek, 147, 180
Day, Doris, 10, 206, 207, 208, 209, 211, 214. See also *The Doris Day Show*
Deacon, Richard, **230**. See also *The Dick Van Dyke Show*
Dear John, 108
Dear Phoebe, 108
De Cecco, John, 172
decode, 182
deconstruct, deconstruction, 119, 199, 206, 214
Defining Women, 251
DeGeneres, Ellen, 8, 165, 166, **167**, 168, 173, 174, 187. See also *Ellen*
Delta House, 108
democratic, democracy, 4, 27, 51, 56, 57, 79, 82, 135, 201, 254, 260, 262
    democratic capitalism, 154, 162
Democratic National Convention, 209
demographics. *See* audience
Demographic Vistas, 24, 77

Denoff, Sam, 231

D'Erasmo, Stacey, 246

Designing Women, 244, 246

Desilu, 5, 93, 95, 97, 105

desire, 3, 6, 29, 37, 42, 43, 44, 45, 57,
    90, 91, 97, 104, 106, 111, 112,
    114, 115, 116, 117, 118, 119, 120,
    121, 122, 172, 177, 181, 199, 205,
    209, 219, 220, 221, 246, 257, 258,
    269
  same-sex desire, 180, 247
  subversive desire, 248

Destry Rides Again, 84

dialect, "dialect comedies," 2, 16–19. *See
    also* stereotypes

dialogue. *See under* narrative(s)

diaspora, 134

dichotomy, dichotomies, dichotomize,
        dichotomous, 81, 142, 144, 172,
        196, 241
  bifurcated, 57, 140
  binary,
        either/or, 196
        gay/straight binary, 172, 174, 175
  highbrow versus lowbrow, 258
  high culture, low culture, 258, 260
  high/low relationships, high/low jux-
        taposition, 235
  love-hate relationships, 225
  public and private, 92
  representation and social experience,
        92
  truth and artifice, 92
  work-family, 208

Dickens, Charles, 82

Dick Van Dyke Show, The, 11, 24, 210,
    215, 218, 229–232, **230**, 234, 237,
    262
  Alan Brady Show, The, 231
  Brady, Alan, 231, 232
  "Coast-to-Coast Big Mouth," 231,
        232
  Cooley, Melvin, **230**, 231. *See also*
        Richard Deacon
  Pay as You Go, 231
  Petrie, Laura, **230**, 231. *See also* Mary
        Tyler Moore
  Petrie, Rob, **230**, 231, 232, 237. *See
        also* Dick Van Dyke
  Rogers, Sally, 215, 218, **230**. *See also*
        Rose Marie
  Sorrell, Maurice "Buddy," **230**. *See
        also* Morey Amsterdam

diegetic, 95

Different World, A, 109, 126, 132, 143
  Allen, Debbie, 126

Diff'rent Strokes, 132
  Drummond family, 132

dilemma, 115, 118, 119, 127, 168

dime novels, 27

Dinkins, Mayor David, 30

director(s), 142, 151, 154, 212, 227

discourse(s), 5, 16, 88, 91, 120, 150, 156,
        159, 160, 166, 168, 196, 198, 212,
        214, 216, 244, 259, 268
  "assimilationist" discourse, 160
  cultural discourse, 88, 133. *See also
        under* culture
  pluralist discourse, 159
  quotational discourse, 267, 268, 269,
        271

discrimination, 128, 130, 166, 198

discrimination lawsuit, 236

disenfranchisement, 130

Disneyland, 79

disposable income(s), 195

Doctor, Doctor, 108

Doctors Without Borders, 188

Dodson, Jack, 75. See also *The Andy
        Griffith Show*

domesticity, domestic, 20, 34, 40, 51,
        52, 54, 55, 70, 78, 84, 87, 88, 90,
        91, 92, 94, 95, 96, 97, 100, 105,
        107, 117, 146, 156, 157, 180,
        207, 209, 217, 218, 219, 224,
        250, 251
  domestic realm. *See under* sphere

dominant ideology. *See under* ideology

Domination and the Arts of Resistance,
    229

Donahue, Elinor, 82. See also *The Andy
        Griffith Show*

Donahue, Phil, 223

Donna Reed Show, The, 19, 264, 267

Doris Day Show, The, 9, 152, 154, 160, 205–216, **211**
  "Byline . . . Alias Doris," 214
  "Billy's First Date," 213
  "Chocolate Bar War, The," 210
  "Colonel Fairburn, Jr.," 213
  "Cover Girl," 215
  "Date, The," 208
  "Doris and the Doctor," 214
  "Doris at Sea," 214
  "Doris Gets a Job," 210
  "Doris Hires a Millionaire," 212, 215
  "Doris Leaves *Today's World*," 213, 215
  "Doris, the Model," 210
  "Doris the Spy," 213
  "Doris vs. Pollution," 213
  Fairburn, Colonel, 213
  "Feminist, The," 213
  "Fine Romance, A," 214
  "Flyboy, The," 208
  "Frog Called Harold, A," 212
  Gibbons, Myrna, 210, **211**, 212. *See also* Rose Marie
  "Great Talent Raid, The," 215
  Harvey, Ron, 212
  "Have I Got a Fellow For You," 214
  "Job, The," 207, 209
  Jonathan, 214, 215
  Juanita, 208
  "Just a Miss Understanding," 215
  "Kidnapped," 212
  Ladies World Magazine, 207
  Lord Nelson (family's Old English Sheepdog), 207
  Martin, Billy, 207, 210, 213
  Martin, Doris, 10, 207–216, **211**. *See also* Doris Day
  Martin, Toby, 207, 210, 212
  "Meant for Each Other," 215
  "New Boss, The," 214, 215
  Nicholson, Michael, 210, 212, 213. *See also* McLean Stevenson
  NOW Magazine, 215
  "Office Troubleshooter, The," 210
  Peter, 214
  "Press Secretary, The," 215
  "Relatives, The," 208
  Simpson, Leroy B., 214
  "Singles Only," 212
  "Today's World Catches Measles," 210
  Today's World Magazine, 210, 212, 215
  "Togetherness," 210
  "Two-Family Christmas, A," 210
  Tyler, William, 212
  Webb, Buck, 207, 208, 210
  "When in Rome, Don't," 214
  "Woman Hater, The," 212, 213
  "Young Love," 213
Dorothy, 108
double standard, 222, 248
Douglas, Donna, **38**. See also *The Beverly Hillbillies*
Dow, Bonnie, 166, 246
Dow, Tony, **50**. See also *Leave It To Beaver*
drama, 35, 36, 39, 40, 42, 76, 126, 136, 139, 142, 143, 147, 156, 157, 160, 216, 241, 244, 251, 252
  comic-drama, 16, 23
dramatic, 20, 35, 36, 42, 45, 94, 102, 212, 244
"dramedy," 242
Drew Carey Show, The, 133
Drexell's Class, 108
drugs, 66, 69, 183
  Ecstasy, 192
Dryden, 29
DuBarry Was a Lady, 97
Duke, Patty, 20, 52. See also *The Patty Duke Show*
Duncan Hines, 208
DVD, 122
dystopia, 83

Ebsen, Buddy, **38**. See also *The Beverly Hillbillies*
Ebony magazine, 159
Eco, Umberto, 12, 267, 268
ecology, 214
economics, 12, 132, 149, 150, 254
  socioeconomic, 154, 229

Ed Sullivan Show, The, 23
egalitarian, 36, 44, 91, 201
egg donation, 250
Ehrenreich, Barbara, 115
1800s, 117
eighteenth century, 12, 254
elite, elitist, 42, 44, 79, 81, 82, 114, 122,
   253, 257, 258
Ellen, 8, 165–176, **167**, 177, 187, 205
   Clark, Paige, **167**. *See also* Joely
      Fisher
   Farrell, Joe, **167**, 173. *See also* David
      Anthony Higgins
   Morgan, Ellen, 8, 165–174, **167**. *See
      also* Ellen DeGeneres
   Penney, Audrey, **167**, 171. *See also*
      Clea Lewis
   Novak, Spence, **167**. *See also* Jeremy
      Piven
   Pete, 171, 173
   "puppy episode," 8, 165
   Richard, 169, 172
   Susan, 169, 170, 171
Ellen Show, The, 187, 189
Ellison, Bob, 234
Ely, Melvin Patrick, 24
emancipation, 209
emasculating, 236, 219, 222
Emmy
   Emmy Award, 67, 178
   Emmy-winner, 75, 231, 234
Empire State Building, 198
empirical, 1, 252
empowerment, disempowerment, 29,
   121, 127, 130, 166, 219, 237, 246
encoding, 8, 152
Engel, Georgia, **233**. See also *The Mary
   Tyler Moore Show*
Enfants-sans-souci, 33
engagement, 42, 120, 214, 216
English, 30, 32, 36, 42, 52, 104, 172
   English-language, 17, 23
   English Restoration comedies, 3, 36,
      43, 44
   gay English. *See under* sexuality
Enter Laughing, 237
Entertainment Weekly magazine, 195

entitlement, 246
episodic series, 76, 108, 216
equality, equal rights, 53, 127, 175, 196,
   201, 220, 221, 224
ER, 144, 180, 244, 251
Ernie Kovacs Show, The, 25
   Kovacs, Ernie, 25
essential, essentialism(s), essentializing,
   8, 9, 165, 166, 173, 174, 175, 176,
   196, 197, 198, 224. *See also* sexuality
ethnicity. *See* race and ethnicity
Etheridge, Melissa, 168
ethics, 262
Eurocentric, 155, 159, 161
Europe, European, 12, 17, 31, 88, 117,
   253, 254, 255
Evans, David S., 191
Evening Shade, 108
Evers, Merlie, 159
Everybody Loves Raymond, 58
exploit, exploitation, exploitative, 17,
   128, 161, 169, 220

Facts of Life, 108
Faculty, The, 108
Fairbanks, Jerry, 97
false, 21, 36, 42, 48, 78, 264, 268
   false assumptions, 263
   false constructions, 263
Falwell, Jerry, 31
family, families, 1, 3, 4, 5, 6, 10, 12, 19,
   26, 27, 30, 37, 40, 88, 90, 93, 94,
   115, 116, 126, 153, 217, 251, 252,
   263, 269
   aunt(s), 52, 75, 77, 79, 80, 81, 82
   baby, 5, 57, 94, 95, 115, 116, 120,
      121, 192, 196, 244, 247, 250
   Black, 126, 130, 132, 136, 137, 143,
      144, 146, 149, 151, 152, 157,
      161
   blended, 3, 49
   children, 3, 4, 6, 10, 20, 27, 30, 33,
      35, 49, 51, 52, 53, 55, 56, 57, 58,
      59, 64, 68, 69, 100, 104, 115, 116,
      136, 152, 183, 196, 207, 208, 210,
      217, 219, 250, 266
   constructed, 55, 56

dad, father, 3, 4, 20, 21, 22, 39, 49, 51, 52, 54, 55, 56, 58, 64, 66, 68, 70, 75, 76, 82, 83, 94, 154, 198, 207, 213, 214, 218, 224
daughter(s), 26, 37, 39, 53, 55, 64, 70, 82, 93, 101, 208, 221, 224, 250
dysfunctional, 52, 57, 68
extended, 5, 37, 49, 75, 84, 136
farm, 10, 37, 76, 83, 206, 207, 208, 209, 210, 215
grandchildren, 115
grandfather, 96, 207
grandmother, 97, 115
great-grandmother, 97
husband, 5, 10, 20, 25, 39, 51, 53, 54, 56, 62, 90, 94, 97, 116, 120, 136, 154, 181, 183, 186, 206, 207, 213, 215, 217, 218, 219, 231, 234, 245, 247, 248
kin, 245
mom, mother, mama, 3, 5, 27, 31, 49, 51, 52, 54, 55, 58, 64, 66, 68, 70, 75, 97, 100, 101, 115, 116, 120, 136, 153, 156, 159, 173, 198, 199, 203, 208, 212, 213, 218, 219, 220, 222, 223, 245, 257
    stay-at-home mom, 3, 51, 64, 218
mother-in-law, 19
nuclear, 3, 5, 49, 55, 84, 136, 152
parent(s), 4, 10, 27, 29, 43, 51, 52, 53, 55, 56, 57, 58, 59, 62, 69, 71, 95, 108, 152, 153, 171, 173, 192, 194, 217, 219, 221, 245, 268
relatives, 75, 208, 245
single-parent, single mother, 152, 153
sitcom, 8, 26, 49–84, 95, 104, 106, 107, 130, 132, 137, 143, 144, 146, 151, 152, 154, 157, 161, 171, 180, 181, 207, 210, 213, 217, 218, 219, 224, 245, 250, 269
son(s), son-in-law, 5, 20, 26, 37, 51, 52, 53, 57, 62, 69, 70, 75, 82, 101, 107, 153, 207, 213, 214, 270
suburban, 5, 19, 20, 37, 51, 62, 68, 76, 84, 90, 154, 207, 218
traditional, 3, 40, 49, 67, 73, 219, 224

uncle(s), 17, 26, 52, 55
values, 4, 9, 56, 66, 67, 77, 82, 83, 180, 183, 188
wife, housewife, 4, 5, 20, 23, 25, 37, 40, 53, 55, 59, 62, 64, 70, 87, 90, 91, 94, 96, 101, 104, 107, 120, 136, 181, 199, 220, 223, 224, 231, 232, 244, 268, 269
work, 208, 220, 221, 244, 246
Family, 109
Family Law, 251
Family Matters, 126, 136, 143, 144
    Urkel, Steve, 136
Family Ties, 56, 57
    Keaton, Elyse 56
fantasy, fantasies, fantasize, 6, 27, 34, 40, 68, 79, 80, 90, 93, 96, 201, 244, 245, 246, 247, 248, 250
farce, farcical, 76, 78, 135
Farnsworth, Philo T., 24
fashion, fashionable. *See* style
Fast Times, 108
Father Knows Best, 15, 19, 20, 25, 56, 58, 59
FCC. *See* Federal Communications Commission
Feagin, Joe, 126
Feast of Fools, 32, 33
Federal Communications Commission, FCC, 24, 26
Felder, Jenna, 250
Felicity, 147
female, feminine, feminist. *See also* "post-feminist"
    female, 5, 6, 24, 33, 43, 55, 91, 96, 97, 100, 101, 105, 106, 107, 112, 115, 116, 117, 118, 120, 121, 152, 153, 154, 155, 156, 157, 159, 160, 170, 172, 178, 180, 181, 184, 188, 214, 218, 219, 220, 221, 223, 224, 225, 242, 244, 246, 247, 248, 249, 250, 251, 252, 260
    female audience, 112, 153, 223, 241, 251, 252
    female character(s), 24, 112, 153, 154, 157, 160, 178, 242, 248, 249, 251, 257

female, feminine, feminist *(continued)*
  female friendship, 6, 112, 115, 116,
    117, 120, 121, 122, 245
  female icons, 159, 160
  female sexual agency, 6, 111, 112,
    114, 116, 118, 119, 120, 121
  female sexual desire, 6, 111, 112, 114,
    115, 119
  female sexuality, 6, 114, 112, 116,
    117, 120, 121, 156, 157, 161, 208,
    212, 215, 222, 223, 225, 227
  feminine, femininity, 5, 11, 90, 91,
    96, 106, 117, 156, 159, 162, 215,
    217, 224, 241, 242, 246, 250, 251,
    252
  feminism, 6, 10, 26, 91, 112, 121,
    215, 217, 219, 220, 221, 223,
    224, 225, 245, 246, 247
    second wave feminism, 216
  feminist theory. *See* theory
  feminine sphere. *See* sphere
  "popular feminist" representation,
    215
Feminine Mystique, The, 91, 209, 217
Ferris Bueller, 108
fetish, fetishism, fetishize, fetishization,
  33, 157, 248, 249, 250
fifteenth century, 32
film, 4, 6, 16, 17, 19, 20, 22, 27, 57, 62,
  64, 69, 78, 79, 80, 81, 83, 87, 88, 93,
  94, 95, 96, 99, 100, 101, 102, 107,
  108, 109, 117, 148, 149, 151, 155,
  159, 177, 206, 207, 208, 218, 236,
  237, 263. *See also* movies, motion pictures
First Amendment, 31
Fisher, Joely, **167**. See also *Ellen*
Fiske, John, 33, 34, 101, 228, 229, 237
Flintstones, The, 52
Flockhart, Calista, 242, **243**. See also
  Ally McBeal
Flying Nun, The, 76
Flynt, Larry, 31
food, 81, 194, 264
"Fools Rush In," 61. *See also* Ricky
  Nelson
format. *See* sitcom conventions

For Your Love, 140, **141**, 142, 143,
  145–147
  Ellis, Malena, 140, **141**. *See also*
    Holly Robinson Peete
  Ellis, Reggie, 140, **141**. *See also* Edafe
    Blackmon
  Ellis, Mel, 140, **141**. *See also* James
    Lesure
  Seawright, Bobbi, 140, **141**. *See also*
    Tamala Jones
  Winston, Dean, 140, **141**. *See also*
    D. W. Moffett
  Winston, Sheri, 140, **141**. *See also*
    Dedee Pfeiffer
Ford, Glenn, 80
format, 10, 17, 19, 20, 25, 68, 83, 104,
  115, 128, 206, 213, 214, 242
formula, formulaic, 3, 29, 61, 90, 92, 95,
  128, 151, 153, 161, 218
Foucault, Michel, 195
413 Hope Street, 142
FOX. *See* networks
FOX Files, 143
Fox, Michael J., 57
France, 32
Frank's Place, 127, 132, 143
Frasier, 140, 145, 146
Fresh Prince of Bel Air, 109, 125, 126, 143
Freud, Sigmund, 28, 29, 122
Freund, Karl, 88, 97
Friars Club, 30
Friedan, Betty, 91, 209, 217
Friends, 58, 140, 148, 242, 244, 255,
  263, 267
  Bing, Chandler, 58
  coffeehouse (Central Perk), 244
  Green, Rachel, 225
  Tribiani, Joey, 58
Frito's, 198
Fromm, Erich, 231, 232
funny, 12, 19, 125, 133, 145, 187, 261,
  262, 267, 268, 270
Funny Face, 108
Fuss, Diana, 175

gag, 16, 45, 133, 136. *See also* jokes
gag jokes. *See* jokes

Garcia, Andy, 109
Garland, Beverly, 20
Garnets, Linda D., 166
gatekeepers, 161
gay. *See* sexuality
Gay and Lesbian Alliance Against
    Defamation (GLAAD), 189, 195
gay pride, 197, 198
gender, 1, 5, 6, 9, 10, 11, 44, 70, 87–122,
        128, 151, 154, 155, 177, 184, 198,
        201, 217, 218, 219, 220, 221, 222,
        224, 241, 252. *See also* female and
        male
    gender difference, 215, 259
    gender expectations, 206
    gender ideals, 217
    gender inequality, 215
    gender-neutral, 220
    gender representation, 85, 87–122,
        245
    gender roles, 3, 6, 40, 51, 90, 91, 93,
        100, 104, 109, 112, 116, 118, 120,
        184, 217, 218, 219, 258
    gender-segregated workplace, 218
    gender stereotypes, 223
    gender stratification, 216
    "gendered hierarchies," 215
General Foods, 152
generation(s), 11, 17, 19, 46, 52, 53, 54,
        56, 57, 58, 106, 189, 192, 216,
        219, 221, 222
    generation(al) gap, 4, 52, 55, 219
    generational identity, 56, 222
        generation *sui generic* (the only
            one of its kind, unique), 221
        Generation X (Gen X), 4, 57, 58,
            59
        Generation Y, 59
        multigenerational, 3, 75
generic, 4, 20, 21, 108, 144, 263, 266
genre, 2, 3, 4, 5, 7, 8, 10, 11, 15, 16, 17,
        19, 20, 21, 23, 24, 35, 36, 37, 42, 43,
        44, 45, 66, 67, 68, 87, 88, 104, 108,
        133, 152, 153, 156, 159, 161, 205,
        217, 241, 247
Germann, Greg, 244. See also *Ally
    McBeal*

George, 108
George Burns and Gracie Allen Show, The,
        20, 22, 23, 90, 95
Georgetown, Virginia, 225
Gertrude Berg Show, 108
ghetto, ghettoization, ghettoize, 37, 117,
        126, 146, 252
Gideon's Crossing, 136
Gidget, 52
Gilligan's Island, 76
Gilmore Girls, 147
Gimme a Break, 196
girlfriend. *See* relationships
Girlfriends, 143, 147, 252
Gitlin, Todd, 34, 102, 104, 228, 229,
        234, 235, 250
globalism, 263
Goethe, 257
Goldberg, Whoopi, 30
Goldbergs, The, 16, 17, **18**, 19, 20, 51
    Goldberg, Molly, **18**. *See also*
        Gertrude Berg, *Molly*
    Uncle David, 17
Golden Gate Bridge, The, 10, 210
Golden Girls, The, 205
Goldman, Robert, 224
Goldsmith, Oliver, 36
Good Housekeeping magazine, 159, 160
Good Life, The, 108
Good News, 143
Good Times, 54, 125, 130, 132, 136, 144,
        151
    Evans family, 130
    Evans, J. J., 132
Goode Behavior, 132, 133, 143
Gordon, Gale, **103**. See also *Our Miss
    Brooks*
Gosden, Freeman, 19, 24, 127
gossip, 117, 118, 119, 120, 229
Goth, 59
Gould, Jack, 92
government, 207, 262
Grammar, Kelsey, **256**. See also *Cheers,
    Frasier*
Gray, Herman, 160
Great Depression, 21
Great Escape, The, 269

Great Gatsby, The, 83
Great Lakes rim, 24
Green Acres, 45, 53, 54, 76, 78, 219
Greenbaum, Everett, 23
Greenpeace, 236
Greenwich Village Halloween Parade, 195, 198
Griffith, Andy, 20, **74**, 84. See also *The Andy Griffith Show*
Groening, Matt, 58. See also *The Simpsons*
grotesque, 11, 229, 235, 236, 238
groundbreaking, 8, 26, 168, 176
Growing Pains, 57
gun-rights, 26, 77, 79, 84

Habermas, Jurgen, 11, 12, 253, 254, 255, 257, 258, 259
Half and Half, 143
Halls of Ivy, 108
Hall, Stuart, 136, 200
Hallstein, D. Lynn, 246, 252
Hamamoto, Darrell, 75
Hamptons, The, New York, 115
Hangin' In, 108
Hangin' with Mr. Cooper, 102, 105, 108, 109, 143
    Cooper, Mark, 105. *See also* Mark Curry
    Lee, Geneva "Cousin Principal," 102
Happy Days, 56, 57
Harlem, 17
Harper Valley PTA, 108
Harrelson, Woody, **256**. See also *Cheers*
Harris, Richard Jackson, 127
Hartley, John, 228
Hayes, Sean, **179**. See also *Will & Grace*
HBO. *See* networks
Head of the Class, 99, 105, 108, 109
    Samuels, Dr. Harold, 102
    Moore, Charlie, 105. *See also* Howard Hesseman
Head of the Family, 232
Heche, Anne, 173, 174
Hecht, Michael L., 200
Hedge, Radha S., 200
hegemony, hegemonic, 5, 33, 139, 152, 246, 247, 248, 250, 252

Heller, Joseph, 29
Henning, Paul, 22, 23, 45, 76, 77
Herbal Essence shampoo, 222
Here Is Television, Your Window on the World, 88
hero, 80, 81, 82, 83, 101, 102, 191
heroine, 96, 215, 245, 249, 250
Hess, Elizabeth, 115
Hesseman, Howard, 105. See also *Head of the Class*
He's the Mayor, 127
heterogeneous, 28, 261
heteronormative. *See* sexuality
heterosexual. *See* sexuality
Higgins, David Anthony, **167**. See also *Ellen*
Hilmes, Michelle, 258, 259
Hirst, David, 35, 42, 44
Hispanic. *See under* race and ethnicity
historian, 10, 91, 160
Hitchcock, Alfred, 207, 269
Hobbes, Thomas, 12, 262
Hochstein, Rollie, 160
Hogan's Heroes, 127
Holleran, Andrew, 177, 186
Hollywood, 5, 62, 76, 77, 78, 79, 81, 88, 91, 92, 93, 100, 102, 156, 160, 207, 227, 228
Hollywood Curriculum: Teachers in the Movies, The, 100
"Hollywood model," 102, 108
Hollywood TV: The Studio System in the Fifties, 97
home, 5, 27, 28, 56, 59, 64, 68, 73, 75, 78, 80, 83, 88, 90, 91, 92, 97, 104, 106, 128, 132, 153, 154, 178, 194, 198, 207, 210, 217, 218, 219, 223, 255, 263, 270
Homeboys in Outer Space, 132, 143
Home Improvement, 146
Homeroom, 108, 109
"homey," 29
Homicide, Life on the Street, 136
homophobia. *See* sexuality
homogenized, 177, 199
homosexual. *See* sexuality
Honey, I'm Home!, 62

Honeymooners, The, 25
  Gleason, Jackie, 25
Hope, Bob, 16
Horne, Lena, 160
House of Buggin', 142
House Un-American Activities
  Committee, 96
housewife. *See* family
Howard, Ronny, **74**, 75. See also *The*
  Andy Griffith Show
Hughleys, The, 133, 143, 146
Hughes-Freland, Felicia, 216
human condition, 262
humor, 11, 17, 19, 27, 28, 30, 31, 34, 39,
    45, 76, 102, 106, 108, 118, 125,
    133, 136, 142, 145, 169, 237, 259,
    261, 262, 264, 267
  Black, racial humor, 133, 145
  purposive humor, 28
  sophomoric humor, 191, 236
  transgressive humor, 3, 29, 31, 33
Hurt, Marlin, 128. See also *Beulah*
husband. *See* family
Hustler magazine, 31
hyperreality, 216
hypocrisy, 36

icon, iconic, iconography, 5, 12, 159,
  160, 245
ideal, idealized, 3, 4, 6, 11, 12, 32, 49,
    51, 56, 57, 58, 59, 64, 67, 73, 78,
    80, 81, 82, 84, 90, 91, 94, 116,
    152, 161, 217, 224, 251, 253, 254,
    255, 258, 259, 260, 263
  ideal womanhood, 157, 159, 160,
    209, 215, 250
identification, 88, 93, 95, 100, 152, 159,
  216, 254
identity, identities, 6, 7, 8, 9, 21, 34, 43,
    58, 78, 152, 154, 155, 166, 194,
    195, 196, 199, 200, 202, 214, 216,
    217, 224, 228, 237, 257, 263
  Black identity, 7, 8, 125, 146, 151,
    154, 160, 161
  female identity formation, 214
  gay identity, 169–175, 184, 186, 192,
    195, 198

generational identity, 56, 222
identity-as-product, 199, 200
identity politics, 9, 175, 176
identity shopping, 194, 195
marginal nonheterosexual identity,
  195
"queer" identity, 175, 195
sexual identity, 58, 166, 170, 172,
  173, 174, 175, 184
ideology, 1, 11, 26, 79, 87, 88, 90, 91,
    115, 116, 117, 121, 122, 125, 130,
    152, 156, 173, 174, 175
  dominant ideology, 11, 34, 175, 237,
    239
  dominant sexual ideology, 174
I Love Lucy, 15, 16, 17, 20, 51, 87–97,
    89, 105, 212
  "Freezer, The," 92
  "Job Switching," 92
  Lopez, Larry (Ricky Ricardo's pilot
    character), 90
  "Lucy Does a TV Commercial," 92
  "Lucy Goes to the Hospital," 92,
    95
  Ricardo, Lucy, 5, 6, 20, 87–97, **89**,
    105, 212. *See also* Lucille Ball
  Ricardo, Ricky, 17, 20, 51, 87, 88, 89,
    91, 92, 94, 95, 97. *See also* Desi
    Arnaz
  "Rockabye Baby," 94
  Vitameatavegamin, 92
  "We're Having a Baby," 94
Incredible Hulk, The, 109
independent, 6, 11, 81, 82, 217, 219,
  222, 225, 246, 254
individualism, individual, individualist,
    31, 43, 45, 46, 49, 52, 75, 77, 81, 83,
    106, 126, 135, 172, 175, 184, 200,
    216, 231, 232, 236, 262, 263
industry
  broadcast industry, 151
  entertainment industry, 1, 10, 16,
    147, 160, 208
  industry executives, 151, 153
  industry, industrial practices, 7, 140,
    149
  media industry, 125, 135, 215

industry *(continued)*
    television industry, 7, 52, 76, 121,
        126, 135, 148, 152, 153, 161, 162,
        227, 229, 231, 237
inequality, 128, 132, 215
injustice, 173, 175. *See also* justice
In Living Color, 142
Inniss, Leslie, B., 126
innocence, 83, 215, 261, 268, 271
innovative, 75, 87, 159, 178, 247
Inside Prime Time, 229
institutional practices, 142, 145
insult, 26, 29, 225, 257
integrate, integration, integrationism, 2,
    7, 16, 130, 142, 143, 150, 151, 161,
    162, 251
international, 77, 80
Internet, 21, 135
intertextuality. *See* text
In the House, 143
Iowa, 168
I Remember Mama, 19, 51
irony, ironic, 30, 31, 34, 39, 44, 45, 94,
    107, 156, 196, 232, 234, 235, 236,
    268. *See also* unironically
I Spy, 130. *See also* Bill Cosby
Italian(s), 19, 214, 215
It's a Wonderful Life, 20, 83

Jack Benny Program, The, 20
Jackee, 126
Jackie Thomas Show, The, 109
Jacobs, Gloria, 115
jail, 76, 79, 80, 82, 255, 257
Jamie Foxx Show, The, 143, 146
Jamal-Warner, Malcolm, **131**. See also
    The Cosby Show
Jar Jar Binks, 266
J. C. Penney, 168
Jeffersonian, 39, 207
Jeffersons, The, 130
    Jefferson, George, 130
Jenkins, Dan, 153
Jenkins, Henry, 135
Jersey. *See* New Jersey
Jesus Christ, 27
Jewish. *See* race and ethnicity

"jiggle television," 222
Jim Crow South, 17, 19
Jimmy Stewart Show, The, 108
John Forsythe Show, The, 108
Johnson, Sharon, 148
jokes, 21, 28, 30, 42, 66, 104, 106, 133,
    172, 229, 257, 262, 269
    gag, 16, 45, 133, 136
    hostile, 28, 29
    visual, 34
    sex-centered, 126
Jones, Gerard, 25, 62, 64, 105
Jones, James Earl, 136
Jones, Lisa, 133
Jones, Tamala, **141**. See also *For Your
    Love*
Jordan, Michael, 266
Judah, Hettie, 117
Judging Amy, 251
Julia, 6, 8, 130, 151–162, **158**
    Baker, Corey, 153, 154, 156, **158**. *See
        also* Marc Copage
    Baker, Julia, 8, 152, 153, 154, 156,
        157, **158**, 159, 161. *See also*
        Diahann Carroll
    Chegley, Dr. Morton, **158**. *See also*
        Lloyd Nelson
    "Eve of Adam, The," 156
    "Mama's Man," 155
    Julia doll, 159
    Spencer, Adam, 156, 157
    "Tanks for the Memories," 159
    Waggerdorns, 154
Just Shoot Me, 225
    DiMauro, Elliot, 225
Just the Ten of Us, 108
justice, 76, 82, 181, 183, 201. *See also*
    injustice
Juvenal, 29

Kansas, 210
Kanter, Hal, 152, 153, 154, 157, 159
Kant, Immanuel, 12, 261, 262
Kaplan, Gabe, 104. See also *Welcome
    Back, Kotter*
KCRG TV9, 168
Keith, Brian, 206

Kelley, David E., 242
Kelly, Kelly, 108
Kelly, Richard, 75, 80
Kennedy, Jackie, 159, 160, 218. *See also* Jackie Kennedy Onassis
Kennedy, John F. Jr., 115
Kennedy, Robert, 209
Kessler, Eric, 242
King, Martin Luther Jr., 209
King of the Hill, 108
kiss, kissing, 68, 69, 178, 180, 182, 183, 184, 187
   gay kiss, 9, 180, 181, 185, 186, 187
   lip lock, 184, 187
   opposite sex kiss(es), 180, 181, 184
   prime-time kiss, 180, 184
   quasi-romantic kisses, 181
   same-sex kiss, 180, 184, 187, 188, 247
   semantic smooch, 181
   straight kiss, 9, 181, 183, 187
Kitzinger, Celia, 174
Kohl, Paul R., 10, 227–238, 293
Knight, Ted, **233**. See also *The Mary Tyler Moore Show*
Knotts, Don, **74**, 75, 80. See also *The Andy Griffith Show*
Krakowski, Jane, 249. See also *Ally McBeal*
Kubrick, Stanley, 29
Kunkel, Dale, 27
Kutulas, Judy, 3, 4, 10, 49–59, 217–225, 293–294

label, labeling, labels, 4, 92, 96, 166, 169, 170, 171, 174, 185, 224, 242, 244, 249, 267
   self-labeling, 8, 165, 170, 172
labor, 11, 152, 228, 232, 236, 237, 251
L.A. Examiner, 93
L.A. Law, 180
Landay, Lori, 5, 87–97, 106, 294
language, 8, 16, 20, 26, 27, 29, 33, 69, 149, 151, 152, 170, 199, 264, 267, 269, 271
Larry Sanders Show, The, 247
Late Night with Jay Leno, 185

Latino/as. *See* race and ethnicity
lavender. *See under* sexuality, gay
laugh track, 17
Laverne & Shirley, 205
Learning the Ropes, 108
Lear, Norman, 25, 26, 30, 34, 54, 130, 132, 195
Leave It To Beaver, 49, **50**, 52, 56, 57, 108
   Cleaver, Theodore Beaver, **50**. *See also* Jerry Mathers
   Cleaver, June, **50**, 53, 55, 56, 221, 223. *See also* Barbara Billingsley
   Cleaver, Wally, **50**. *See also* Tony Dow
   Cleaver, Ward, 4, **50**, 53, 54, 55, 56, 59. *See also* Hugh Beaumont
   Haskell, Eddie, 52
Lebanese, 51
Le Beauf, Sabrina, **131**. See also *The Cosby Show*
Lee, Johnny, 19. See also *Amos 'n' Andy*
legitimation, 253
leisure, 75, 244
Leno, Jay, 191, 192
Leonard, Sheldon, 24, 232
lesbian. *See* sexuality
Lesure, James, **141**. See also *For Your Love*
Letterman, David, 262
Lewis, Clea, **167**. See also *Ellen*
Levy, Ralph, 23
liberal, liberalism, 26, 54, 150, 162, 174, 201, 219, 263
liberation, liberated, liberating, liberatory, 9, 175, 195, 198, 201, 206, 223, 231, 246, 267
   liberated consumerism, 223
   liberated woman, 10, 212, 217, 220–225, 247, 250
   sexual liberation, 222
   television liberation, 221
   women's liberation, women's liberation movement, 52
libido, 166
Life magazine, 16, 20
Life of Riley, The, 15
Life with Luigi, 19

Lincoln, Abraham, 133
Linder, Laura R., 3, 4, 61–71, 294
linguistic(s), linguistically, 12, 175, 177, 184, 185, 269
Lion Tamer, The, 24
Lipsitz, George, 96
literature, 1, 237, 258
Liu, Lucy, 247. See also *Ally McBeal*
Living Single, 142, 143, 147
Lloyd, David, 234
local, 17, 21, 27, 75, 77, 79, 133, 212, 255, 263, 264
    local culture, 264, 266
    local products, 263, 264, 266
London, 29
London Times, The, 117
Long, Shelley, **256**. See also *Cheers*
Look magazine, 90, 93
Loot, 44
Los Angeles, LA, 1, 24, 198
    L.A. circuit-queen, 177
Los Angeles–Herald Express, 96
Lost Horizon, 80
Lotz, Amanda Dyanne, 7, 139–150, 294
Louis-Dreyfus, Julia, **41**. See also *Seinfeld*
Louis XIV, 29
love, 40, 52, 58, 66, 67, 68, 69, 92, 93, 94, 101, 105, 108, 115, 116, 120, 122, 169, 172, 173, 174, 182, 183, 187, 206, 214, 216, 225, 250, 266, 267, 268, 269, 271
Lovell, T., 33
Lucian, 31
Lucy Show, The, 153
Lupino, Ida, 16

MacDonald, J. Fred, 24, 128
machismo, 225
MacLeod, Gavin, 79, **233**. See also *The Mary Tyler Moore Show*
MacMurray, Fred, 16
MacNicol, Peter, 244. See also *Ally McBeal*
mainstream, non-mainstream, mainstreamed, 8, 9, 27, 28, 57, 94, 111, 116, 117, 128, 137, 153, 154, 155, 160, 161, 162, 165, 166, 174, 176, 178, 191, 195, 217, 220, 223, 225
Make Room for Daddy. See *The Danny Thomas Show*
Making the Grade, 108
Malcolm and Eddie, 132, 133, 143
male, 9, 68, 91, 100, 101, 102, 104, 105, 108, 115, 119, 128, 136, 143, 155, 156, 159, 169, 170, 172, 174, 178, 180, 181, 184, 188, 196, 212, 222, 224, 225, 236, 241, 242, 245, 246, 247, 248, 249, 251, 252, 254, 259, 260
    male gaze, 40, 155, 156, 222, 246, 247, 250
masculine, 5, 11, 96, 155, 218, 242, 245, 247, 251, 252
    masculine sphere. *See* sphere
Manhattan, 93, 115, 178, 218. *See also* New York City
Manhattanites, 112
Man Ray, 191
Man Who Knew Too Much, The, 207
Many Loves of Dobie Gillis, The, 108
Marc, David, 2, 6, 15–24, 45, 69, 77, 108, 130, 207, 232, 234, 294
Mad About You, 146
marginal, marginalization, marginalized, margins, 6, 28, 57, 82, 133, 195, 199, 247, 249, 251, 257
Marie, Rose, 210, **211**, **230**. See also *The Doris Day Show* and *The Mary Tyler Moore Show*
market, 56, 58, 62, 106, 112, 114, 121, 133, 168, 194, 195, 218, 225, 264
    market forces, 201
    marketing, marketers, marketed, 9, 27, 34, 67, 115, 147, 194, 195, 196, 199, 242
    marketplace, 195, 196, 199, 257, 262
    market share. *See* share
Marney. See *I Remember Mama*
marriage. *See* relationships
Married . . . with Children, 26, 57
Mars, 224
Marsh, Earle, 71, 75, 76. See also *The Complete Directory to Prime Time Network and Cable TV Shows*

Martin, 132, 142, 144
Marx, Karl, 11, 17, 228, 229, 231, 232, 237
Marxist(s), 199, 228
Mary Hartman, Mary Hartman, 26, 56
Mary Tyler Moore Show, The, 11, 55, 84, 106, 133, 151, 206, 212, 215, 219, 220, 229, 232, **233**, 234, 236, 237, 244
   Baxter, Georgette Franklin, **233**. *See also* Georgia Engel
   Baxter, Ted, **233**, 234. *See also* Ted Knight
   Franklin Baxter, Georgette, **233**. *See also* Georgia Engel
   Grant, Lou, **233**, 234. *See also* Edward Asner
   Lindstrom, Lars, 56
   Lindstrom, Phyllis, 55
   Morgenstern, Rhoda, 222
   Richards, Mary, 55, 106, 210, 215, 220, 221, 223, 224, 225, **233**, 234
   Slaughter, Murray, **233**, 234. *See also* Gavin MacLeod
   Nivens, Sue Ann, **233**. *See also* Betty White
   WJM-television, 220, 234
"*Mary Tyler Moore Show* and the Transformation of Situation Comedy, The," 234
M*A*S*H, 54, 55, 84, 222, 223, 255
   Houlihan, Margaret "Hot Lips," 222
mass communication(s). *See* communication
mass media. *See* media
mass-produced, 264
Material Girls, 156
materialistic, 46
maternal, 101, 105, 115, 156
matriarchs, 49
Mathers, Jerry, **50**. See also *Leave It To Beaver*
Mathews, Gordon, 194
Mattel, 152, 159
Matthau, Walter, 96
Maude, 26, 54, 168, 206, 219, 220
   Findley, Maude, 219

Mayberry RFD, 53, 83
   Sam Jones, 83. *See also* Ken Berry
May, Elaine Tyler, 90
McCarthy, Anna, 68
McConnell, Frank, 40
McCormack, Eric, 178, **179**. See also *Will & Grace*
McDonald's, 263, 264
McDowell, Jeanne, 166
McIlwain, Charlton D., 7, 125–137, 294
McKeever and the Colonel, 108
McLuhan, Marshall, 27
McNear, Howard, 75. See also *The Andy Griffith Show*
Means Coleman, Robin R., 7, 125–137, 142, 294
media, 8, 11, 15, 39, 40, 75, 80, 94, 96, 101, 112, 120, 125, 126, 127, 134, 135, 153, 155, 157, 165, 166, 178, 192, 206, 215, 216, 223, 228, 229, 237, 238, 259, 260
   mass media, 2, 5, 27, 78, 101, 102, 166, 216
   media critics, 205
   media culture, 102, 192
   media image, 161
   media ownership, 149
   media portrayals, 99, 100, 166, 186
   media practices, 166
   media scholars 151
   media studies, 1, 2, 112
   popular media, 159
   print media, 168
medieval,
   late-medieval Europe, 253
   medieval festivals, 234
Melba, 127, 132
Melcher, Marty, 206
men, 10, 32, 53, 55, 70, 79, 90, 91, 100, 114, 116, 117, 118, 119, 120, 121, 127, 128, 130, 133, 155, 175, 176, 178, 180, 181, 184, 185, 186, 187, 196, 212, 213, 217, 218, 220, 221, 222, 223, 224, 225, 232, 235, 245, 246, 247, 248, 249, 251, 255, 257
menopause, menopausal, 248
merchandise, merchandising, 192, 194

Mere-Folie, 32
Messing, Debra, **179**. See also *Will &*
Grace
metaphor(s), 56, 92, 96, 100, 173, 200,
201, 220, 262, 267
metaphysics, 262
Metropolis, 97
MGM, 19, 97, 206
Miami, 76
Miami Vice, 33
Mickey Mouse Club, The, 52
Midwestern, 90
Milwaukee, Wisconsin, 24
miniseries, 180
Minneapolis, 220, 225
minority, 175, 242, 259
minstrel, 17, 23, 127, 132, 136
miscarriage, 93
modern, modern-day, modernist, moder-
nity, 3, 11, 29, 35–48, 49, 51, 55, 56,
76–82, 112, 136, 154, 196, 197, 222,
225, 250, 253, 255, 259, 262, 263,
263, 266, 267, 268, 270, 271
Moesha, 109, 143
Moffett, D. W., **141**. See also *For Your*
Love
Moliere, 29, 36
Molly, 19
Berg, Gertrude, 17, **18**, 19, 108. See
also *The Goldbergs*
Monday Night Football, 144
money, 22, 35, 37, 39, 40, 43, 46, 52, 62,
66, 67, 82, 87, 92, 115, 120, 172, 207,
219, 223, 228, 236, 249
Mo'Nique, 133. See also *The Parkers*
Monty Python and the Holy Grail, 271
Monty Python's Flying Circus, 264
monogamous, 188, 245
Moonlighting, 242
Moore, Demi, 168
Moore, Mary Tyler, 54, **230**, **233**. See
also *The Dick Van Dyke Show* and *The*
Mary Tyler Moore Show
Moore, Tim, 19, **129**. See also *Amos 'n'*
Andy
moral(s), morality, 29, 31, 36, 39, 42, 44,
58, 82, 101, 152, 194, 197, 218

mores, 6, 36, 75. *See also* social codes
Morgenthau, Henry III, 22
Morton, Joe, 136
Mothers-in-Law, The, 52
Mother Teresa, 31
motherhood, 115, 116, 208
movies, motion picture(s), 6, 24, 52, 79,
80, 83, 100, 101, 102, 104, 107, 108,
118, 119, 160, 208, 258, 263, 269. *See*
also film and cinema
Mr. Deeds Goes to Town, 4, 81, 82
Mr. Ed, 76
Mr. Peepers, 109
Mr. Smith Goes to Washington, 4, 81, 82
Mr. Sunshine, 109
MTM Productions, 54, 234
MTV, 34, 59, 64, 66, 67, 69
MTV Real World, 185
Mullally, Megan, **179**. See also *Will &*
Grace
multicultural, 3, 150, 259
Mulvey, Laura, 155, 156, 246
Mumford, Laura, 247, 252
Murphy Brown, 205, 244, 246
Brown, Murphy 224
Museum of Television and Radio, 108,
149
music, musical, 4, 20, 21, 34, 61, 62, 64,
66, 68, 69, 70, 84, 90, 95, 97, 156,
210, 264
music videos, 34, 70
musical specials, 160
My Favorite Husband, 87, 88, 90. *See also*
Lucille Ball
My Favorite Martian, 76
My Mother the Car, 76
My Three Sons, 54, 57
My Wife and Kids, 143, 144

NAACP, 17, 133, 148
Nabors, Jim, **74**, 75. See also *The Andy*
Griffith Show
naïve, naïvely, 40, 261, 264, 268, 269
Nanny and the Professor, 109
narrative(s), 3, 4, 6, 7, 9, 16, 20, 24, 37,
43, 45, 76, 77, 82, 83, 99, 100, 101,
102, 107, 108, 109, 114, 121, 122,

134, 139, 144, 146, 152, 153, 154, 155, 156, 157, 159, 166, 177–189, 210, 213, 216, 236, 241, 242, 244, 245, 246, 247, 250, 251, 252, 270

character(s) characterization, 3, 5, 6, 7, 8, 9, 10, 17, 27, 30, 34, 35, 36, 37, 39, 40, 42–45, 58, 70, 73, 75, 76, 78, 80, 81, 88, 99, 100, 101, 102, 104, 106, 107, 108, 109, 112, 125, 128, 130, 132, 134, 135, 136, 137, 139, 140, 142, 143, 146, 147, 149, 152, 153, 154, 157, 159, 160, 165, 166, 173, 177, 178, 180, 183, 184, 186, 187, 188, 194, 195, 196, 202, 207, 214, 216, 220, 221, 222, 223, 224, 225, 234, 235, 236, 242, 244, 245, 246, 248, 251, 255, 257, 259, 263, 264, 266

alter ego, 235

cameos, 127, 168, 269

developmentally quiescent characters, 214

ensemble casts, 19, 140, 148, 219, 255

eponymous, eponymous character, 81, 178, 188

foils, 90, 258

gay, lesbian, homosexual characters, 8, 139, 166, 171, 178, 180, 187, 188, 194, 195, 196, 198, 200, 202, 254

lead characters, 68, 83, 84, 101, 102, 116, 165, 174, 220, 250, 259

narrator, narration, 134, 244, 245, 270

protagonist(s), 68, 83, 84, 101, 102, 220, 250

spectator-characters, 186–187

counter-hegemonic narrative structures and genres, 247, 250

cumulative narrative, "cumulative narrative" traits, 244, 245, 251

denouement, also anagnorisis, 212, 214

deus ex machina, 187

dialogue, 42, 205–216, 255, 259
banter, 16, 259

dominant narratives, 188

dramatic coherence, 212

escapist, escapism, 57, 76, 208, 267, 269

fantasy interludes, 246, 247, 248

foreshadowing, foreshadowed, 94, 168, 212, 214

formulaic declensions, 214

heteronormative narrative strategies, 9, 177–188

linearity, 261, 264, 270

locations, 1, 102, 104, 162, 210, 255, 263

malgré lui (in spite of itself television series), 206

narrative *à thèse*, 216

narrative device, 153

narrative flow, 270

narrative language, 155, 161

narrative mechanisms, 155

narrative reversal (of the male gaze), 246, 250

narrative spaces, 188

narrative violation, 247

plasticity of narrative, 270

plot, 17, 23, 49, 51, 54, 69, 76, 77, 78, 95, 106, 121, 130, 135, 146, 152, 168, 177, 187, 209, 210, 212, 216, 235, 236, 245, 252, 263

multiple episode arcs, multiple episode tales, 184, 244, 245, 247

multiple story arcs, 244

narrative arc, 236

narrative twist, 183

play within a play, 186

plot line(s), 69, 152, 236

plot twist, 168

production within a production, 186

relational story arcs, 245

story line(s), 69, 101, 102, 104, 115, 121, 177, 178, 181, 187, 212, 227, 249, 271

narrative(s) *(continued)*
  subplot(s), 114, 212, 236
  vignette(s), 156, 247
same-sex narratives, 189
season and series finale(s), 121, 122, 189, 212, 271
season and series premiere(s), 4, 16, 17, 53, 92, 96, 126, 132, 133, 140, 147, 150, 206, 224, 242, 271
stylized repetition of acts, 184
theme, thematic treatments, 4, 8, 20, 36, 42, 43, 45, 69, 71, 75, 77, 78, 117, 119, 121, 122, 136, 154, 156, 177, 201, 209, 212, 213, 214, 223, 264, 269
traditional, "masculine" conventions, 91, 96, 247, 252
national, 16, 21, 80, 92, 185
National Broadcasting Company. *See* networks
National Organization for Women (NOW), 209
NBC. *See* networks
Nearly Departed, 109
negotiate, negotiation, 7, 11, 67, 76, 80, 118, 120, 121, 122, 145, 146, 151–163, 188, 199, 200, 205, 206, 212, 214, 215, 216, 244
Negroes. *See* race and ethnicity
neighbors. *See* relationships
Nelson, Lloyd, **158**. See also *Julia*
neo-Jeffersonian, 207
Nervous Laughter: Television Situation Comedy and Liberal Democratic Ideology, 75
network(s), 2, 6, 7, 8, 10, 12, 15, 16, 17, 19, 21, 25, 26, 27, 34, 52, 53, 57, 59, 62, 66, 75, 80, 81, 83, 84, 102, 125, 126, 127, 128, 132, 133, 134, 135, 136, 137, 140, 142, 143, 144, 145, 146, 147, 148, 149, 150, 153, 178, 180, 184, 185, 218, 219, 224, 225, 227, 228, 229, 232, 234, 235, 241, 242, 249, 251. *See also* broadcast and cable
  ABC, 21, 24, 109, 136, 140, 142, 143, 144, 146, 149, 150, 152, 168,
177, 195, 242, 244
  "big four," 241
  Big Three, 137, 143, 147
  CBS, 16, 17, 21, 24, 53, 54, 73, 76, 83, 87, 90, 93, 96, 109, 136, 137, 140, 142, 143, 144, 149, 150, 187, 189, 206, 231, 232, 234, 242, 244, 246, 251
  Comedy Central, 26, 192, 195, 198
  FOX, 27, 57, 132, 137, 140, 142, 143, 144, 146, 149, 150, 241, 242
  HBO, 6, 34, 111, 112, 121, 241, 242, 247, 249, 262
  NBC, 9, 16, 21, 109, 126, 128, 135, 136, 137, 140, 142, 143, 144, 146, 147, 149, 150, 152, 153, 177, 178, 185, 187, 188, 235, 242, 244, 247, 251, 271
  PBS, 149, 180
  Showtime, 149, 241
  start-up networks, 6
  UPN, 132, 133, 140, 143, 146, 147, 148, 148, 241, 252
  The WB, 132, 133, 143, 251, 252
network programming executives. *See* program executives, programmers
network standards and practices. *See* standards and practices
Neuman, David A., 168
Neuwirth, Bebe, **256**. See also *Cheers*
New Attitude, 126, 127
New Jersey, Jersey, 27, 269
New Republic magazine, 246
New York City, 22, 51, 52, 90, 108, 112, 114, 118, 186, 188, 195, 198, 207, 234, 236, 237, 244, 251, 263. *See also* Bronx, Brooklyn, Manhattan
New York World's Fair, 22
N.Y. Yankees, 46
New York Daily Mirror, 96
New York Observer, 242
New York Times, 246
New York Times Magazine, 92
New York Undercover, 143
Newcomb, Horace, 205, 244
Newhart, 224
  Vanderkellen, Stephanie, 224

news programs, 80, 127, 168, 219, 220, 224

NewsRadio, 238

Newsweek magazine, 90, 95, 166

Nick Freno: Licensed Teacher, 109

Nielsen ratings, Nielsen Media Research, 17, 54, 73, 80, 150, 168, 213

1910s, 21

1920s, 21, 128

1930s, 4, 16, 23, 62

1940s, 16, 17, 22, 62

1950s, 3, 4, 6, 7, 8, 15, 22, 25, 51, 52, 53, 54, 55, 56, 58, 59, 66, 68, 69, 70, 71, 73, 76, 84, 90, 91, 97, 104, 105, 128, 132, 153, 156, 157, 161, 217, 218, 222, 264

1960s, 1, 3, 4, 6, 7, 10, 16, 36, 45, 52, 53, 56, 58, 61, 69, 70, 73, 76, 79, 80, 81, 84, 91, 96, 153, 161, 162, 198, 214, 216, 217, 219, 220, 222, 264

1970s, 4, 7, 8, 10, 26, 34, 54, 55, 56, 84, 91, 96, 115, 132, 214, 216, 217–226, 264

1980s, 4, 5, 7, 10, 26, 56, 57, 84, 114, 115, 127, 140, 178, 224, 229, 251, 264

1990s, 3, 7, 8, 24, 26, 36, 42, 45, 58, 119, 127, 137, 140, 142–150, 199, 234, 236, 264, 266

nineteenth-century, 17, 23, 27, 82, 127

Nixon, Cynthia, **113**, 244. See also *Sex and the City*

Nochimson, Martha, 244, 246, 247, 248, 252

non-Black. *See* race

non-White. *See* race

normalize, normative, 10, 55, 156, 157, 166, 174, 178, 183, 184, 195, 199, 225

North Carolina, 73

Northern Exposure, 242

Norwegians, 19

Noth, Chris, 245. See also *Sex and the City*

Now magazine, 215

nuptials, 245

N.Y.P.D. Blue, 144, 244

objectification, objectify, 106, 155, 156, 157, 201, 223, 224, 225, 231, 248

O'Connor, Pat, 116

O.K. Crackerby, 109

O'Leary, John, 4, 73–84, 294

Onassis, Jackie Kennedy, 160. *See also* Kennedy, Jackie

One Day at a Time, 54, 55

one-dimensional, 159, 196

One on One, 143

online bulletin boards, 252

online fan sites, 122

On Television and Comedy, 152

Oppenheimer, Jess, 88, 94

oppositional, 3, 33, 34, 96

oppress, oppressed, oppression, oppressors, 174, 175, 199, 200, 228, 229, 237

"Organization Man," 4, 73–84

orgasm, 111, 114

Original Programming and Independent Production, 112

orthodoxy, 246

Orton, Joe, 42, 44

Osborne, John, 42

Osbournes, The, 3, 34, 49, 59, 61, 64–71, **65**

  "A Very Ozzy Christmas," 69

  "Bark at the Moon," 69

  Osbourne, Aimee, 64

  Osbourne, Jack, 64, **65**, 66, 68, 70

  Osbourne, Kelly, 64, **65**, 66, 67, 68, 70

  Osbourne, Ozzy, 3, 4, 59, 61, 64, **65**, 66, 67, 68, 69, 70, 71

  Osbourne, Sharon, 3, 64, **65**, 66, 67, 68

  "Won't You Be My Neighbor," 69

Other, "other," "otherness," 159, 175, 267

Our Miss Brooks, 6, 99–109, **103**, 215, 218

  Boynton, Philip, 6, **103**, 104, 105, 106, 107. *See also* Robert Rockwell

  Brooks, Connie, 5, 6, 100, 102, **103**, 104, 105, 106, 107, 218. *See also* Eve Arden

Our Miss Brooks (continued)
  Conklin, Osgood, 102, **103**. *See also*
    Gale Gordon
  Davis, Mrs. Margaret, 105
  Denton, Walter, **103**, 104, 105. *See*
    also Richard Crenna
  "frog boy," 6, 106
  Madison High School, 102
  "Model Teacher," 108
  Snodgrass, Stretch, 104
Out All Night, 143
outlaw, 81, 82
Out of This World, 109
outsider(s), 40, 77, 80, 81, 102, 108, 119
ownership, 10, 149, 227, 228, 234
Oxford English Dictionary, 15, 23
Oz, 34
Ozarks, 39
Ozzfest, 71

"Papa, Don't Preach," 67
paparazzi, 246
paradigm, 3, 108
paradigm shift, 241
Paramount "road" pictures, 16
parental authority, 55, 57
Parent 'Hood, The, 137, 143
Parker Lewis Can't Lose, 109
Parker, Sarah Jessica, **113**, 242. *See also*
    Sex and the City
Parker, Trey, 26. *See also South Park*
Parkers, The, 133, 143, 145
Paris, 29, 121, 122
parody, parodic, 11, 31, 37, 183, 184, 229
Parsonian separation, 210
patriarch, 32, 39, 40, 51, 53, 70, 112,
    136, 174, 225, 247, 249
Partridge Family, The, 57
patriotic, 194
Patty Duke Show, The, 20, 52
  Lane, Patty, 20. *See also* Patty Duke
  Lane, Cathy, 20. *See also* Patty Duke
PBS. *See* networks
Peanuts, 191, 192
Pearl, 109
Peete, Holly Robinson, **141**. *See also For*
    Your Love

penny-presses, 27
People magazine, 173
Pepsi, 266
period (menstruation), 116
Perlman, Rhea, **256**. *See also Cheers*
Peterson, Valerie V., 8, 9, 165–176, 295
Persky, Bill, 231
perspective, 1, 6, 40, 91, 101, 116, 117,
    118, 119, 122, 140, 145, 200, 205,
    219, 221, 222, 224, 241, 250
Petticoat Junction, 45, 54, 76, 77, 78
  Hooterville, 77
Pfeiffer, Dedee, **141**. *See also For Your*
    Love
Pfeiffer, Michelle, 109
Philips, Irna, 24
Phillip Morris, 93, 94
philosopher(s), 17, 39, 267
Photoplay magazine, 91
Phyllis, 54
Picket Fences, 54
Pierson, David, 2, 3, 35–46, 295
Pillow Talk, 208
Pinter, Harold, 42
Pittsburgh, Pennsylvania, 170
Piven, Jeremy, **167**. *See also Ellen*
PJs, The, 146
Platonic, 267
Pleasantville, 57
Please Don't Eat the Daisies, 109
pleasure, 28, 29, 33, 42, 43, 92, 114, 115,
    156, 187, 218, 222, 224, 225, 262,
    268
plot. *See under* narrative(s)
Poetics, 102
politics, political, 5, 6, 8, 9, 24, 26, 33,
    40, 51, 53, 56, 73, 80, 112, 116,
    125, 128, 130, 132, 135, 142, 151,
    162, 166, 168, 173, 174, 175, 186,
    187, 194, 196, 197, 198, 199, 201,
    209, 212, 213, 219, 244, 248, 251,
    253, 254, 258, 262, 263. *See also*
    apolitical
  identity politics, 9, 175, 176, 191,
    198
  political action, 198
  political change, 176

political correctness,43
sexual politics, 244
Poniewozik, James, 68
Pope, Alexander, 29, 32
populism, populist, 4, 79, 234
pornography, pornographic, 198, 201
Poitier, Sidney, 161
positivist, 196
"postfeminist," 246
Post-its, 267
postmodern, postmodernism, postmodernity, 12, 68, 198, 199, 201,
246, 252, 261, 262, 263, 264, 266,
267, 268, 269, 270, 271
postwar, 3, 5, 19, 52, 64, 68, 78, 88, 90,
91, 94, 96, 97, 217
Poussaint, Alvin, 132
poverty, 130, 152
power, 54, 55, 70, 107, 135, 166, 198,
199, 201, 216, 255
Black power. *See under* race
cultural power, 149
female power, 112
gay power, 175
"girl power," 117
power relations, 5, 96, 114, 119, 120
social power, 33
practice(s), 20, 56, 88, 91, 96, 106, 147,
202, 229
pregnancy, pregnant, 92, 93, 94, 95, 115,
120, 250
prejudice(s), 29, 133, 192
prenuptial agreement, 120, 248
President of the United States, 67, 194
Press, Andrea, 221
Preston Episodes, The, 109, 142
preteen, 52, 57, 236
prime-time, 4, 8, 16, 17, 21, 108, 126,
154, 157, 177, 178, 180, 181, 184,
186, 188, 196, 214, 215, 259
Primetime Live, 168
Prince des Sots, 32
Prince of Darkness, 59, 67
printing, 12, 254
private, 5, 37, 69, 94, 95, 106, 107, 251
private domain. *See* sphere
private sphere. *See* sphere

Private Secretary, 218
privilege(d), 42, 53, 119, 121, 136, 149,
166, 174, 196, 225, 228, 242
producer(s), 8, 19, 22, 23, 24, 27, 57, 62,
67, 69, 76, 68, 81, 88, 93, 94, 96, 112,
134, 142, 147, 148, 149, 152, 156,
159, 160, 168, 178, 188, 209, 213,
220, 228, 231, 232, 235, 242, 246,
250
product(s), 11, 16, 21, 33, 34, 70, 71, 92,
135, 149, 152, 195, 199, 200, 216,
223, 229, 237, 249, 250, 263, 264,
266, 267
product placement, 64, 114
product tie-ins, 67, 266
Production Design for Television, 157
production, 1, 5, 7, 16, 93, 116, 184,
186, 188, 213, 264
mode of production, 155, 227, 228,
229, 231, 234, 237
production executives 10, 227
production practices, 7–8, 151–162
black-and-white film, 104
camera, 10, 56, 64, 66, 70, 95,
116, 118, 148, 151, 181,
183, 208, 250
backgrounded, 245
camera angles, 8, 154, 155,
156, 157
cinema verite, 155
close-ups, closeups, 88, 94,
156, 207, 208, 210
filters, 208
intimate shooting, 155
lighter-weight cameras, 155
live camera, 185
multiple-camera, 155
single-camera, 2, 155
stop-action, 68
televisual cinematography,
155
three-camera, 2, 88, 97
color, 104, 157, 161
color symbolism, 156, 159
costuming, 136, 154, 156, 160,
201, 210
haute couture clothing, 156, 159

production *(continued)*
    editing, 88, 155, 210
      continuity editing, 88
      edited sequences, 155
      montage, opening montage,
        156, 207, 210
      rhythmic edits, 156
      segmented editing, 155
      stylized edited sequences, 156,
        207, 210
      30-degree cutting rule, 156
    lighting, 8, 88, 154, 157, 161
      heavily backlit visuals, 207
      high-key lighting, 157
      lighting composition, 154
      lighting design, 157
      lighting arrangement, 157
    live audience, 2, 64, 88, 93
    makeup, 4, 106, 210
    mise-en-scène, 95, 156, 208, 214
    point of view, 155, 156, 186
    production meetings, 227
    production techniques, 161
    program tapings, 227
    rushes, 210
    set(s), 2, 23, 68, 78, 88, 102, 104,
      153, 154, 155, 186, 237
      set décor, 8, 153, 154, 161
      set design, 8, 153, 154, 155,
        210
    sound, 21, 22
      direct-address(es), 20, 116, 118
      laugh track, 183, 187, 209
      music, 20, 61, 62, 68, 69, 156,
        210, 264
      narration, 134, 244, 245
      opening song, 207
      theme song, 52, 66, 68, 75,
        156
      voiceless, 245
      voice-over, 68, 118
    studio audience, 88, 95, 236
    voice-over, 68, 118
production process, 56, 57, 134
television aesthetics, 88
visual(s), 23, 104, 122, 155, 157, 180,
    184, 207, 208, 218, 223, 250,

    269. *See also* televisual and
    audiovisual
    visual integrity, 212
    visual jokes, 34
    visual level, 188
    visual narrative devices, 156
    visual style, 104, 155, 250
program executives, programmers, 10,
    52, 142, 149, 227, 235 242
programming, 1, 2, 3, 7, 10, 16, 23, 26,
    33, 34, 45, 56, 67, 76, 104, 125,
    126, 132, 133, 134, 136, 142, 143,
    144, 147, 149, 152, 218, 219, 229,
    232, 234, 241, 252
    "Adult Western" era, 76
    crossover, 1126, 127, 147, 159
    counter-programming, 142
    "Idiot Sitcom" era, 76
    "narrowcasting," 241
    network era, 144, 150
    niche programming, 6, 149
    practices, 229
    programming blocks, 146
    scheduling, 142, 146, 147, 149
    specialization, 241
progressive, 8, 9, 195, 196
proselytizing, 246
protagonist(s). *See under* narrative(s)
proto-feminist, 40, 96
Provencher, Denis M., 9, 177–189,
    295
Prozac, 118, 119
public, 5, 8, 11, 12, 21, 28, 29, 30, 31,
    32, 44, 64, 75, 79, 92, 93, 94, 95,
    100, 107, 108, 153, 159, 161, 166,
    170, 173, 182, 244, 250, 251, 254,
    255, 257, 259
    public address, 260
    public house, 11, 253–260
    public morality, 194, 197
    public person, 257
    public policy, 130, 251
    public sphere. *See* sphere
publicity, public relations, PR, 5, 16, 92,
    93, 152, 153, 185, 237
    publicity agents, 152, 153
Pugh, Madelyn, 88, 91

Pulliam, Keshia Knight, **131**. See also
  The Cosby Show
Pursuit of Happiness, 109
Putterman, Barry, 152
Pyle, Denver, 207. See also *The Doris
  Day Show*

queen, 117, 187
queer. *See* sexuality
  queerness, 198
  queer theory. *See* theory
"Que será será," 207, 210
Queer as Folk, 180

race and ethnicity, 1, 6, 7, 8, 17, 19, 51,
    53, 76, 90, 93, 121, 125–162, 198,
    232, 241, 262, 263
  African American, 6, 7, 17, 19, 24,
    26, 27, 30, 125–162, 178, 199,
    252, 259
  Ashkenazic Jewish, 17
  Asian, Asian American, 6, 7, 139,
    150, 197, 259
  Black, 6, 7, 24, 29, 30, 81, 125–162,
    196, 218, 249, 259
  anti-Black, 160
  Black actors, 134, 139, 142–149,
    157, 161
  Black arts movement, 154
  Black empowerment, 29, 127, 130
  Black erasure, 128, 161, 199
  blackface, 17, 23, 24, 30, 127, 128
  Black identity, 7, 125, 151, 160
  Black images, 17–19, 134, 151
  Black language, 142, 152
  Black nationalism, Black cultural
    nationalism, 160, 161
  Blackness, 7, 125–162
  Black power, 128
  Black sitcom, Black cast sitcom,
    6, 7, 125–151
    Assimilationist Era, 7, 19, 130,
      160, 161
    Black Family and Diversity
      Era, 7, 132
    Minstrelsy Era, 7, 127, 128,
      130, 132, 133

  Neo-Minstrelsy Era, 132, 133
  Nonrecognition Era, 7, 127
    blackvoice, 127, 128, 136
  ethnicity, 1, 6, 90, 93, 121, 144, 232,
    241
  Hispanic, 6, 17, 259
  Jewish, Jews, 17, 188, 232, 236, 237
  Latino/as, 7, 139, 150, 199
  Negro, Negroes, 17, 159
  non-Black, 132, 134, 136, 144, 150
  non-White, 139, 142, 149, 150, 249
  phenotypic norms, 160
  "race humor," 7, 17
  racial
    racial advancement, 156
    racial bias and discrimination, 8,
      128, 130, 152, 160
    racial determinancy, 7, 146
    racial difference, 157, 159
    racial hierarchy, 162
    racial inclusion, 146, 155
    racial inequalities, 128, 132
    racial invisibility, 6, 7, 127, 130,
      160
    racial "otherness," 159
    racial polarization, 148
    racial segmenting (programming
      and audience), 7, 19, 135
    racial segregation, 7, 132,
      139–150, 152
    racial tensions, 161
    racially pluralistic, 154, 159
  racism, 6, 8, 17, 19, 24, 26, 29, 30,
      130, 135, 136, 148, 149, 150,
      152, 160, 162. *See also* stereo-
      types
    bigotry, 26, 30, 132
  reverse racism, 26
  White, 6, 7, 9, 17, 19, 24, 81, 115,
      126, 127, 128, 130, 132, 133,
      139–162, 196, 199, 207, 242,
      249
    White as rice, 162
    whitening, 157, 160
    "Whiteout," 6
radio, radio sitcoms, 2, 3, 5, 15–24, 27,
    51, 61, 62, 64, 67, 70, 87, 88, 90, 99,

radio, radio sitcoms *(continued)*
    100, 104, 105, 107, 108, 127, 128,
    142, 168, 215, 220
Radio Corporation of America (RCA),
    21, 22, 24
Radio's Second Chance, 22
Raleigh, North Carolina, 78, 80
Randolph, Amanda, 19. See also *Amos 'n'*
    Andy
Rashad, Phylicia, **131**. See also *The*
    Cosby Show
Rasslin' Match, The, 24
rating, 15, 16, 17, 19, 23, 26, 27, 43, 54,
    67, 73, 80, 83, 88, 92, 104, 105,
    126, 128, 133, 137, 140, 168, 208,
    213, 228. *See also* share
    sweeps, 213, 247
rational, 88, 254, 257
Ratzenberger, John, **256**. See also
    Cheers
Ray, Robert, 81
Ray Milland Show, The, 109
reactionary, 196
Reagan-era, 224
realism, 88, 90, 114, 153, 224, 235, 242
    magical realism, 242
reality, 10, 54, 92, 94, 95, 96, 97, 118,
    152, 153, 159, 188, 205, 209, 218,
    219, 225, 235, 237, 249, 263, 267
    hyperreality, 216
    reality sitcom, 61, 66, 67, 71
    reality com, 66
    reality programming, 34, 68, 143
Real McCoys, The, 76
reception, 7, 139–150
Redd Foxx Show, 127
red scare, 96
Reed, Donna, 16, 264
Rees, Roger, **256**. See also *Cheers*
reflexively, 168
    self-reflexively, 11, 229
Rehnquist, Chief Justice William, 31
Reid, Tim, 137, 149, 150
relationship(s), 16, 30, 35, 43, 44, 45, 53,
    105, 106, 114, 116, 117, 118, 120,
    121, 146, 169, 174, 178, 183, 184,
    186, 187, 188, 200, 217, 222, 225,

    228, 242, 244, 245, 251, 258. *See*
    also family
boyfriend, 42, 43, 44, 114, 118, 174,
    180, 183, 184, 186, 187
codependent relationship, 178
dating, dates, 42, 43, 54, 106, 122,
    140, 168, 172, 178, 180, 208, 213,
    214, 221, 223, 247, 248
fiancé, fiancée, 220, 235, 245
friend(s), friendship, 3, 6, 35, 42, 43,
    44, 52, 55, 80, 92, 93, 112,
    114–122, 140, 168, 169, 171, 180,
    181, 200, 208, 215, 222, 224, 235,
    244, 245, 246, 249, 259, 263
girlfriend(s), 26, 43, 44, 82, 107, 247,
    249
neighbor(s), 23, 37, 52, 64, 71, 75,
    154, 199, 263
marriage, married, 5, 6, 20, 35, 36,
    49, 51, 53, 55, 62, 88, 90, 91, 92,
    93, 94, 95, 96, 100, 101,105, 106,
    107, 114, 115, 116, 119, 120, 136,
    140, 146, 160, 178, 181, 183, 188,
    189, 209, 215, 218, 221, 222, 223,
    246, 247, 248, 249
nuptials, 245
owner/worker, 11
relational story arcs, 245
weddings, 68, 114, 120, 121, 178,
    181, 182, 183, 215, 235
relativism, 201
relevancy. *See* social relevancy
religion, 12, 53, 254
    religious hypocrites, 29
    religious festivals, 32
    religious groups, 168
Renaissance, 31
representation(s), 5, 6, 7, 8, 20, 21, 32,
    40, 57, 58, 90, 92, 94, 96, 101,
    111, 112, 116, 117, 120, 121, 127,
    133, 136, 137, 139, 142, 146, 148,
    149, 151, 152, 155, 157, 161, 178,
    180, 186, 188, 199, 200, 205, 206,
    207, 208, 215, 216, 217, 218, 220,
    221, 245, 248, 251, 255, 259, 263
gay representation, 186, 188
reproducing gayness, 198

reruns, 16, 49, 57, 59, 96, 242
Resurrection Blvd., 149
resistance, resistant, resistive, 11, 33, 34, 40, 112, 135, 148, 149, 170, 175, 228, 229, 237, 246, 248, 249, 251, 252
collective resistance, 160
resistance appeal, 199
Restoration comedies, 3, 36, 43, 44
reverse racism. *See under* race and ethnicity
reviews, 117, 147, 150
Reynolds, Burt, 30
Rhoda, 54, 55
Rich, Adrienne, 173
Richards, Michael, **41**. See also *Seinfeld*
Rickles, Don, 262
Ricky Nelson Sings "For You," 61
right wing, 196
Rise of the Goldbergs, The, 16. See also *The Goldbergs*
Robert Guillaume Show, The, 126, 127
Roc, 142
rock 'n' roll, 4, 61, 62, 64, 68, 70, 71, 238
Rockwell, Robert, **103**. See also *Our Miss Brooks*
Rogers, Will, 76
Roker, Al, 185
romance, romantic, 5, 10, 35, 40, 42, 44, 109, 112, 116, 117, 118, 121, 122, 152, 156, 160, 177, 181, 207, 208, 212, 214, 215, 221, 224, 242, 244, 245, 246, 247, 249, 250
romantic comedy, 87
romance novelists, 268
Rome, 29
Roosevelt, Eleanor, 22
Roseanne, 26, 180, 205
Ross, Sharon Marie, 6, 111–122, 295
Rossi, Portia de, 247. See also *Ally McBeal*
Rowan and Martin's Laugh-In, 208
Rukeyser, M.S. Jr., 153
rural, 39, 53, 79. *See also* farm families
rural sitcoms, rural situation comedies, 4, 45, 75–77, 83
rural-wisdom, 75, 81
rustic, 37, 75

Russian, 24, 121, 122, 234
Ryan, Irene, **38**. See also *The Beverly Hillbillies*

salon, 12, 254, 255
Sam 'n' Henry, 17, 127, 128. See also *Amos 'n' Andy*
Sanford and Son, 26, 54, 130
Sanford, Fred, 130
San Francisco, 19, 24, 210, 213, 215
San Salvadorian, 178
Sapphire/sapphire, 126, 132, 135, 136. See also *Amos 'n' Andy*
sarcasm, sarcastic, 44, 56, 218, 270
Sarnoff, David, 21, 22
Sassa, Scott, 135
satellite, 7, 241
satire, satirical, 28, 29, 30, 31, 32, 33, 37, 42, 44, 45, 78, 192, 235
Saturday Night Live, 56, 185
Saturnalia, 31, 33
Saved by the Bell, 262
Saved By The Bell: The College Years, 109
Savel, Dava, 168
scholar, scholarship, 1, 2, 45, 67, 69, 99, 112, 120, 128, 140, 151, 166, 183, 205, 245, 246
Schwichtenburg, C., 33
science, 12, 39, 234, 254
Scodari, Christine, 11, 241–252, 295
Scott, James C., 154
Scottish, 32
scriptwriters. *See* writers
Scrooge, 82, 83
second-class citizens, 188
Secret Diary of Desmond Pfeiffer, The, 133, 143
segmentation, 11, 156, 157, 242, 251
segregation, segregated, 130, 218
Seinfeld, 11, 24, 36, 40–45, **41**, 133, 140, 229, 231, 234, 235–236, 237, 247, 255, 264, 267
Audrey, 44
Benes, Elaine, 36, **41**, 42, 43, 44, 46, 236. *See also* Julia Louis-Dreyfus
"Conversation, The," 44

Seinfeld (continued)
  Costanza, George, 36, **41**, 43, 44, 46,
    235, 236, 271. *See also* Jason
    Alexander
  Dalrymple, Russell, 235, 236
  Jujyfruit, 42, 46
  "Junior Mint, The," 43
  Junior Mints, 266
  Kramer, Cosmo, 36, **41**, 44, 235, 236.
    See also Michael Richards
  La Cosina, 235
  "Nose Job, The," 44
  "Opposite, The," 46
  "Pen, The," 43
  "Pitch, The," 235
  "Red Dot, The," 43
  Seinfeld, Jerry, 36, **41**, 42, 43, 44,
    235, 236, 237, 271
Seldes, Gilbert, 24
self
  self-aware, 262
  self-deprecation, 262
  self-determination, 81, 160, 166
  self-fulfilling prophecy, 147, 148
  self-identity, 224
  self-images, 218
  self-reference, self-referential, 34,
    192, 267, 269
  self-reflexive, self-reflexively, 11, 68,
    70, 229, 235, 236
  self-sufficient, 263
semiotic, 33, 198, 201
"servant of the state," 257
servants, 19, 53, 133, 157, 160
seventeenth century, 12, 32, 36, 254,
    255
7th Heaven, 147, 251
sexuality, 6, 8, 28, 112, 114, 116, 117,
    120, 121, 156, 157, 161, 166, 168,
    169, 170, 172, 173, 174, 175, 176,
    177, 195, 196, 198, 201, 208, 212,
    215, 222, 223, 225, 247
  abstinent, 208
  asexual, asexuality, 215, 222
  bisexual, bisexuality, 6, 121, 170,
    173
  cult of virginity, 222

coming out, out of the closet, outing,
    outed, 8, 165–176, 188, 196,
    210
  announcing, 8, 166, 169, 170,
    171, 172
  confiding, 8, 165, 169, 171, 172
  self-labeling, 8, 165, 170, 172
  shared meaning, 8, 165, 169
closeted, 9, 188
gay, gayness, 8, 9, 114, 196, 199, 252,
    259
  antigay behavior, 180
  Gay and Lesbian Alliance
    Against Defamation
    (GLAAD), 178, 195
  gay characters, 8, 139, 166, 171,
    178, 180, 187, 188, 194, 195,
    196, 198, 200, 202, 254
  gay comedy, 29
  gay English, 177
  gay identity, 8, 9, 166, 169–176,
    184, 186, 192, 195, 198
  gay issues, 178
  gay kiss, 9, 181
  gay marriage, 115
  gay power, 175
  gay pride marches, 195, 197, 198
  gay representations, 165–176,
    186, 188, 199
  gay sitcom, 9, 165–176, 176–189
  lavender, 177, 201
heteronormative, 9, 177, 178, 181,
    183, 184, 187, 188
heterosexual, heterosexuality, 9, 114,
    115, 116, 121, 122, 166, 169, 170,
    172, 173, 174, 175, 177, 188, 195,
    196
homosexual, homosexuality, 8, 9, 26,
    130, 165–175, 180, 184, 187,
    194, 195, 196, 198, 201, 258,
    259, 262
homoeroticism, 195
same-sex affection, 9, 180, 187, 188
same-sex desire, 180, 247
same-sex narratives, 189
homophobia, homophobic, 184, 199,
    258

lesbian, lesbianism, 6, 8, 116, 121,
139, 165, 166, 168–175, 187,
188, 195, 198, 199, 245, 248
lesbian chic, 195
lesbian continuum, 173
lesbian sexual identity, 166,
170–175, 195
essential, essentialism, essentialist, 8, 165, 166, 173,
174, 175, 176, 196–200,
224
latent, 166, 172, 173, 174,
213
liberal constructions of lesbianism, 174
natural, 166, 172, 173, 174,
183, 184, 201
preexistent, 166, 172, 173, 174
radical feminist lesbianism,
174
mature sexuality, 208, 215
nonheterosexual, 195
promiscuous, 222, 245
queer, 1, 29, 175, 183, 185, 188, 195,
198, 199, 200–202
"flaming," 184
sex, 6, 8, 9, 10, 11, 27, 28, 30, 31, 35,
42, 44, 45, 58, 66, 69, 79, 100,
105, 106, 107, 111–122, 133,
156–157, 161, 163–189,
195–201, 205, 208, 212, 215,
222–225, 241–252, 259, 263
battle of the sexes, 51, 93
romantic encounters, 42, 112,
117, 121, 212, 214, 242, 244,
245
sex appeal, sexual appeal, sexual
attractiveness, 44, 156, 157,
172, 247, 250
sexcom, 11, 241, 242–252
sexism, sexual discrimination,
166, 175, 221, 246. See also
feminism
sexuality, 6, 8, 28, 112, 114, 116,
117, 120, 121, 130, 156,
157, 161, 166, 168, 169,
170, 172–180, 195–198,

201, 208, 212, 215, 222,
223, 225, 247
dominant sexual ideology, 174
polymorphous sexuality, 173
sexual activity, 28, 180
sexual aggressiveness, 157, 212
sexual attitudes, 53, 173, 206, 259
sexual engagements, 42, 214
sexual harassment, 118, 119, 225
sexual humor, 126, 169
sexual identity, 8, 58, 166, 169,
170, 172, 173, 174, 175, 184,
186, 192, 195, 198
sexual liberation, 10, 52, 198,
217–225, 247, 250
sexual orientation, 1, 8, 163–176
sexual politics, power relations, 5,
40, 112, 166, 174–176,
198–199, 201, 244, 263
sexual preference, 174, 249, 259
sexual revolution, 52, 114
straight, 8, 9, 171–188, 192, 196,
199
Tantric, 118
workplace-related liaisons, 215,
225
Sex and the City, 6, 11, 34, 111–122,
113, 205, 241–252
"Baby Shower, The," 115, 121
Blatch, Stanford, 114, 115
Bradshaw, Carrie, **113**, 114, 115, 116,
117, 118, 119, 120, 121, 122, 242,
244, 245, 248, 251. See also Sarah
Jessica Parker
"The Drought," 118, 119
"girls lunch," 244
gummy bears, 119
Hobbs, Miranda, 111, **113**, 114, 115,
116, 117, 118, 119, 120, 121, 122,
244, 245, 248, 250. See also
Cynthia Nixon
Jones, Samantha, **113**, 116, 117, 118,
119, 120, 121, 122, 244, 245, 248,
249. See also Kim Catrall
McDougal, Charlotte York, **113**, 114,
115, 116, 122, 244, 245, 246, 247,
248, 249. See also Cristin Davis

Sex and the City (continued)
  Mr. Big, 114, 118, 119, 120, 122,
    245. *See also* Chris Noth
  Paris, 121, 122
  Rabbit, the, 111, 114, 115
  Shaw, Aidan, 245. *See also* John
    Corbett
  "Turtle and the Hare, The," 114, 115
  York McDougal, Charlotte. *See*
    Charlotte York McDougal
  "Woman's Right to Shoes, A," 121
Shabazz, Demetria Rougeaux, 7, 8,
  151–162, 295
Shalit, Ruth, 246, 250
Shalit, Wendy, 245
Shangri-La, 80
share, 23, 140, 144, 168, 196, 201. *See*
  also rating
Shaw, George Bernard, 125
Sheridan, Richard B., 3, 36
Shively, Michael G., 172
Six Feet Under, 34, 180
shock, 3, 4, 26, 28, 34, 171
shopping, 6, 77, 111–122, 178, 194,
  198, 219. *See also* consumer, con-
  sumerism
show business, 5, 16, 20, 62, 64, 66, 70,
  90, 133, 148, 228, 229, 232, 236
Showtime. *See* networks
Shugart, Helene, 246, 252
Shut Up!, 67
Sibs, 109
Siepmann, Charles A., 22
signify, signified, signifier(s), significa-
  tion, 2, 8, 29, 70, 154, 156, 157, 159,
  160, 161, 170, 184, 187, 199, 201,
  224, 232, 244
Simpsons, The, 12, 34, 57, 58, 71, 109,
  196, 261–271, **265**
  Ayn Rand Daycare Center, 269
  "Blood Feud," 270
  Burns, Charles Montgomery (Mr.
    Burns), 262, 269, 270
  "Burns Verkaufen der Kraftwerk,"
    263
  Comic Book Guy, 269
  Duff Beer, 263

Fat Tony, 269
Flanders, Ned, 267
Groening, Matt (creator), 58
Itchy and Scratchy, 263–264
Krusty the Klown, 264, 266, 267
Krusty Burger, 264
Krusty-O's, 266
"Lisa the Iconoclast," 263
Mr. T, 271
nuclear power plant, 263
"Poppa's Got a Brand New Badge,"
  269
"'Round Springfield," 267
Simpson, Bart, 199, **265**, 266, 269,
  270
Simpson, Homer, 58, 59, 262, **265**,
  269, 270
Simpson, Lisa, 263, **265**, 269, 270
Simpson, Maggie, **265**, 269
Simpson, Marge, **265**, 269, 270
Smithers, Waylon, 196, 262
Mr. Sparkle, 263
Springfield, 12, 58, 262, 263, 264,
  266, 269
Springfield, Jebediah, 263
"Streetcar Named Marge, A," 269
"Summer of 4 Ft. 2," 267
"Who Shot Mr. Burns," 269
Wiggum, Chief Clancy, 262
Wolfcastle, Rainer, 263
simulacra, 216
Sinbad Show, The, 142
single(s), 42, 53, 54, 55, 101, 106, 115,
  153, 219, 224, 245
  single women, 54, 106, 114, 115,
    209, 215, 221, 242, 248
Sister, Sister, 137, 143
sitcom, situation comedy
  Black sitcom. *See* race and ethnicity,
    Black
  "buddy" series, 242, 244, 246, 251,
    252
  domestic sitcoms, 5, 20, 40, 52, 54,
    61–71, 78, 84, 87–97, 146, 156,
    157, 180, 207, 217, 218, 219
  family sitcom. *See under* family
  gay sitcom. *See under* sexuality, gay

pilot, 62, 77, 90, 93, 133, 152, 153, 156, 206, 207, 209, 214, 132, 135–136

radio sitcoms, 5, 15–24, 51, 61, 62, 64, 67, 70, 87, 88, 90, 99, 100, 104, 105, 107, 108, 127, 128, 142

sexcom, 11, 241, 242, 244, 246, 247, 250, 251, 252

sitcom conventions
"cumulative narrative" traits. *See* narrative
episodes, 2, 68, 214, 244, 245, 247, 271
half-hour, 8, 16, 17, 68, 87, 191, 242
installments, 242
sixty-minute format, 242
story arcs. *See* narrative

sitcom structure, 2, 17, 55, 56, 68, 69, 87, 213, 214, 241, 247, 250, 252

workplace comedy. *See under* work, workplace

Six Feet Under, 34, 180

sixteenth century, 32

60 Minutes, 144

Skelton, Red, 25, 62

Skolnick, Arlene, 51, 57, 58

slapstick, 25

small screen, 5, 101, 104, 155, 180, 181, 186, 188

small-town, 4, 51, 73–84, 192, 263

Smallville, 147

Smart Guy, 109, 143

Smith, Anna Deavere, 202

Smith, Hal, 75. See also *The Andy Griffith Show*

soap opera, 17, 24, 33, 117, 247, 250, 268

social
social change, 8, 10, 217
social class, 1, 9, 39, 42, 45, 203
social class, status
blue-collar, 228
bourgeois, 154, 159, 196, 198, 235, 251, 254, 255, 257
lower classes, 32
manual workers, 228
middle-class, 36, 42, 43, 90, 92, 93, 115, 126, 152, 153, 154, 156, 159, 184, 207, 221
pink collar, 249
ruling class, 36, 228
upper-class, 32, 36, 42, 255
upper-middle-class, 42, 126
white-collar, 51
working-class, 25, 42, 228, 249, 251, 257, 260

social code(s), 36, 43, 45, 201, 214, 229. *See also* mores

social context, 35, 254

social contradictions, 218

social construct, socially constructed, a construct, 5, 6, 8, 9, 11, 12, 45, 55, 56, 88, 101, 108, 111, 112, 154, 159, 174, 196, 197, 199, 205, 217, 220, 251, 263

social control, 33, 34, 136

social criticism, 32, 255, 260

social discourse, 214

social group, 42, 45, 257

social influences, 255

social interaction, 200

social justice, 201

social milieu, 254

social order, 9, 175, 196

social participation, 216

social pattern, 200

social realism, social realist, social reality, 91, 153, 209

social reform movements, 148, 209
Black empowerment. *See under* race and ethnicity
empowerment movements, 219
gay power, gay pride marches. *See under* sexuality

social ritual, 216

social relevancy, socially relevant, relevancy programs, television, 4, 8, 10, 55, 219
Social Relevancy and Ridiculed Black Subjectivity Era, 7, 130, 132

social *(continued)*
   social roles, 96, 216
   social rules, 35, 36, 42, 44, 51, 52
   social "superiors," 257
   socially responsible, 153
   sociocultural, 114, 125, 133, 145,
      206, 214
   socioeconomic, 154, 229
Something So Right, 109
Sopranos, The, 34, 269
Soul Food, 149
South, southern 17, 80, 81, 127, 133,
   263
South Central, 142
South Park, 2, 3, 9, 26–34, 191–202, **193**
   Big Gay Al, **193**, 195, 196, 198, 200
   "Big Gay Al's Big Gay Boatride,"
      197, 201
   Broflovski, Kyle, 26, 34, 198, 199
   Cartman, Eric, 26, 27, 37, 191, 192,
      194, 197, 198, 199
   cheesy poofs, 194
   Cowboys, Middlepark Cowboys, 191,
      192, 197
   Garrison, Mr. Herbert, 192, 197, 201
   Marsh, Stan, 26, 34, 192, 197, 198,
      199
   Mr. Hat, 197
   McCormick, Kenny, 26, 34
   McElroy, Jerome "Chef," 27, 192,
      196, 201
   Parker, Trey (co-creator), 26
   Sparky, 200
   Stone, Matt (co-creator), 26
   "Tom's Rhinoplasty," 198
   Testaburger, Wendy, 26
South Park, the Movie: Bigger, Longer, and
   Uncut, 27
Soviet, 80
Spanish-language, 23
Sparks, 132, 143
Spears, Britney, 266
spectator, spectatorship, 88, 135, 155,
   156, 184, 186, 187
   spectator-characters, 186, 187
   spectatorial disappointment, 184
speech(es), 82, 96, 253, 260

Spelling, Aaron, 242
Spencer, 109
sphere(s), 11, 90, 150, 235, 245–252,
   253–260
   bourgeois public sphere, 254, 255
   domestic sphere, realm, space, 51, 54,
      78, 87–97, 117, 251
   feminine sphere, 11, 91, 250
   home sphere, 210, 215
   masculine sphere, 11, 91, 96, 242
   occupational sphere, 210
   private sphere, domain, 11, 12, 92,
      94, 95, 100, 104, 107, 210, 242,
      244–254
   professional sphere, 107, 244, 252
   public sphere, 11, 12, 94, 107, 212,
      242, 244, 247, 253–260
   separate spheres doctrine, 242,
      245–252
   work sphere, 210, 213
Spigel, Lynn, 95
spinster, 5, 105, 107, 215, 221, 223
sponsor(s), sponsorship, 26, 93, 149,
   152, 153, 168, 180, 195, 208, 227
sports, 258
Square Pegs, 109
stage, 4, 17, 20, 21, 95, 128, 132, 151,
   159, 216
Stallybrass, Peter, 234, 235
standards and practices, 2, 26
Stark, Steven, D., 236, 255, 257
Starke, Todd, 207. See also *The Doris
   Day Show*
Starr, Darren, 112, 242, 252
status quo, 58, 69, 130, 149, 160, 218
Steeves, H. Peter, 12, 261–271, 295
Stein, Ben, 228
Stein, Gertrude, 172
Steinberg, Sid, 195
stereotypes, 6, 8, 17, 19, 24, 29, 30, 40,
   53, 56, 75, 109, 135, 136, 148,
   166, 219, 257. *See also* racism
   "babe hound," 224
   braggart, 25, 257
   buffoon, buffoonery, 128, 132, 136
   coon, 128, 132
   dialect, 2, 16–19, 127, 136

dumb blond, 196, 223
elitist, 79, 122, 257
gender stereotypes, 223
hick, 79, 257
husband-hungry spinster, 215
hypersexual Black male, 196
"intellectual ice queen Lilith," 257
mammy (mammy/sambo, modern mammy), 132, 196
"obtuse, gold-digging Rebecca," 37, 257
"pedantic, perky Diane," 257
sambo, "sambo," sambo-ism, 126, 128, 132, 135, 136
Sapphire, 126, 132, 135, 136. See also *Amos 'n' Andy*
sexless widow, 215
sloth, 257
slow-witted jock, "Sam, the dumb jock," 196, 257
Uncle Tom, 136
unmarriageable career woman, 55, 215
"volatile, oft-unwed mother Carla," 257
trickery, 106, 107, 132
"White saviors," 132
wise rube, 39
Steve Harvey Show, The, 109, 143, 146, 147
Stevenson, McLean, 210. See also *The Doris Day Show*
Stewart, Jimmy, 16. See also *The Jimmy Stewart Show*
Stone, Matt, 26. See also *South Park*
Stonewall riots, 197, 198, 201
Strangers with Candy, 109
Streisand, Barbra, 197
Strinati, Dominic, 228
Struck By Lightning, 109
Structural Transformation of the Public Sphere, The, 253, 254
Stu Erwin Show, The, 109
style, 3, 35, 36, 56, 66, 146, 155, 196, 212, 249
Blahnik, Manolo, 249
Choo, Jimmy, 249

designer gowns, designer labels, 159, 224, 225, 249
fad, 37, 40, 173, 195
fashion, 37, 40, 120, 159, 173, 196, 198, 199, 225, 246, 249
fashion status symbols, 249
Fendi, 249
fur, 93, 249
haute couture, 156, 159
Jackie Kennedy suits, 218
Spade, Kate, 249
subgenre, 4, 7, 11, 117, 241, 242, 244, 252
subjective, subjectivity, 132, 155, 161, 197, 246, 252
subordinate, subordination, 33, 107, 237
suburban, suburbanites, 5, 19, 20, 37, 51, 62, 68, 76, 84, 90, 154, 198, 218
"suburban ecstasy period," 207
subversive, subversiveness, subversion, 57, 96, 106, 192, 236, 246, 248
Sugar and Spice, 126, 127
Sullivan, Andrew, 175
Sunday Night Movie, 109
Supreme Court, 31
Survivor, 185
sweeps. *See* rating
syndicated, syndication, 22, 67, 73, 102, 122, 180, 241

taboo(s), 3, 25, 26, 27, 29, 34, 36, 69
Tales of the City, 180
talk shows, 22, 67, 168, 194, 223
Tarloff, Frank, 24
tattoo(s), 59, 66, 69
Taxi, 221, 223
DePalma, Louie, 221
Nardo, Elaine, 221, 223
Reiger, Alex, 223
Taylor, Ella, 54, 106, 152, 153, 155, 161, 215, 219
teacher, 6, 99–109, 197, 198, 218
"good" teacher, 100, 102, 104, 106, 108
Teacher, The, 99
Teachers Only, 109

technical, technology, 2, 15, 22, 37, 39, 152, 155, 263

Teech, 109

teen, teenager, 27, 52, 57, 62, 117, 147, 194, 199

Telepictures, 67

television comedy, 2, 25, 28, 264
    traditionalist, 264
    modern, modernist, 225, 264, 266, 267, 270, 271
    postmodern, 68, 246, 261–271

television families. *See* family sitcoms

televisual, 36, 122, 145, 154, 155, 160, 206, 207, 214. *See also* visual

Televisuality, 156

Terminator, The, 271

Texaco Star Theater, 16

text(s), textual, 3, 4, 8, 9, 10, 11, 21, 33, 75, 96, 101, 106, 107, 108, 117, 120, 121, 145, 150, 181, 186, 192, 194, 206, 214, 229, 234, 237, 241, 250, 266
    first-level text, 186
    intertextual, intertextuality, 101, 229
        horizontal intertextuality, 229
        vertical intertextuality, 229, 232
    secondary texts, 101, 237
    second-level text, 186
    tertiary texts, 101, 237
    textual analysis, 4, 8, 229, 242, 246

That Girl, 52, 206
    Marie, Ann, 52

theater, 62, 127, 136, 258

theory, 11, 12, 156, 202
    feminist theory, 1, 198
    genre theory, 20
    queer theory, 1, 198, 199
    theory of comedy, 2, 28, 29, 30, 261, 264, 267, 269, 270

therapists, 67, 166, 168, 169, 170, 171, 172, 173

3rd Rock from the Sun, 109

thirtysomething, 180

Thomas, Danny, 20, 24. See also *The Danny Thomas Show*

Thompson, Robert J., 130

Thorne-Smith, Courtney, 244. See also *Ally McBeal*

Thornton, Billy Bob, 168

Three's Company, 55, 262, 267

Three Stooges, 262

Time magazine, 68, 159, 168, 245

Tinker, Grant, 54

Toast of the Town, 23

Today Show, The, 185, 186, 187

Toll, Robert, 23

Toms, Coons, Mulattoes, Mammies, and Bucks, 160

To Rome with Love, 109

Touched by an Angel, 144

Townsend, Robert, 137

Townsend Television, 142

tradition, traditional, 2, 3, 25, 29, 30, 31, 32, 36, 37, 40, 44, 45, 49, 52, 54, 56, 66, 67, 73, 78, 81, 82, 90, 91, 92, 93, 104, 126, 145, 148, 155, 157, 159, 161, 180, 205, 209, 212, 218, 219, 220, 222, 224, 228, 234, 247, 251, 261, 264, 266, 267

transformative, 194

transgressive, 3, 29, 30, 31, 39, 194
    transgressive comedy, 2, 3, 25–34
    transgressive humor, 3, 29, 31, 33
    transgressive space, 194
    transgressive status, 194

Travilla, William, 159

trickery, 106, 107, 132

trickster, 94, 96, 97, 106

True Colors, 109

truewit, 39, 44

truth, 30, 31, 35, 39, 44, 92, 125, 126, 170, 237, 263, 267

Tueth, Michael V., 2, 3, 25–34, 69, 296

Turner, Victor Witter, 216

Turow, Joseph, 251

TV Guide, 15, 16, 168, 208, 213

Twain, Mark, 76

'tweens, 57

twelfth-century, 32

twentieth century, 17, 21, 77, 91

twenty-first century, 241, 264

Twilight Zone, 59
2000s, 71
Two of a Kind, 109
227, 126, 127, 132, 143

Under One Roof, 136
    Langston family, 136
Understanding Popular Culture, 237
uneducated, 234, 257
unemployed, unemployment, 46, 54, 68, 178, 235, 257
unironically, 262
United States, US, USA, 22, 23, 67, 80, 100, 114, 115, 116, 140, 142, 144, 148, 153, 154, 160, 161, 178, 180, 194, 199, 219, 241, 262
universal, 96, 195, 254, 262, 267
UPN. *See* networks
urban, 10, 24, 29, 37, 43, 75, 76, 77, 78, 79, 81, 82, 83, 130, 152, 153, 242
    urban-sophistication, 75, 79
US News and World Report magazine, 168
utopia, 83, 234

Valverde, Mariana, 111
values, 4, 9, 11, 27, 36, 46, 56, 57, 66, 67, 75, 76, 77, 78, 81, 82, 83, 130, 152, 154, 155, 161, 180, 183, 184, 188, 206, 209, 220, 224, 225. *See also* family values
Van Damme, Jean-Claude, 263
Van Dyke, Dick, **230**, 231, 232, 234. See also *The Dick Van Dyke Show*
Vanity Fair magazine, 246
Variety magazine, 153
variety, 2, 16, 20–21, 23–24, 76, 142, 231
Vaseline, 208
vaudeville, 17, 20, 23, 25, 87, 90, 93, 104, 127, 237
Venus, 224
Vermont, 181
Vietnam, 26, 53–54, 152, 214
View from Sunset Boulevard, The, 228
Vilanch, Bruce, 30
violence, 79, 209
Virginia Slims, 162, 222

"Visual Pleasure and Narrative Cinema," 155
Vogue magazine, 120
voice, 26, 228–229, 253, 257, 268
Vonnegut, Kurt, 29
voyeur, voyeuristically, 156, 185

Wade, Ernestine, 19. See also *Amos 'n' Andy*
Waggoner, Catherine, 246, 252
Walker, Thomas E., 19, 191–202, 296
Walters, Suzanna, 156
War of the Worlds, 27
Warner Pathé, 206
Washington, DC, 4, 24, 56, 81, 82, 189
Washington, Fredi, 160
WASP, 76, 232
Watching Race, 160
Waters, Ethel, 24, 128. See also *Beulah*
Waverly Wonders, The, 109
Wayans Brothers, The, 132, 133, 143
WB, The. *See* networks
wealth, wealthy, 42, 77, 112, 134, 154, 224, 228, 257
Web site, 185, 195, 249
Webster, 132
    Papadapolis family, 132
wedding, 114, 120, 121, 178, 181, 182, 183, 215, 235
    nuptials, 245
    same-sex civil ceremony, 181
Weinberger, Ed, 232, 234
Weird Science, 109
Welcome Back, Kotter, 99, 102, 104, 108, 109
    Kotter, Gabe, 104. *See also* Gabe Kaplan
    Kotter, Julie, 104
    Woodman, Mr. Michael, 102
    "sweathogs," 104
Welcome Freshmen, 109
Wells Fargo Bank, 195
Welsford, Enid, 31, 32, 33
Wendt, George, **256**. See also *Cheers*
West Wing, The, 244
western(s), 23, 76, 77, 84
Western culture, society, 31, 42, 201

Western Europe, 117
What a Country, 109
What About Joan, 109
What's Back, 143
What's Happening!, 126, 127, 136
    Thomas, Bill, 136
    Thomas, Dee, 136
    Mama, 136
    Thomas, Raj, 136
What's Happening Now!, 127
Wheaties, 266
"Where Everybody Knows Your Name:
    Cheers and the Mediation of
    Culture," 258
*Where Were You When the Lights Went
    Out?*, 206
White. *See* race
White, Allon, 234, 235
White, Betty, **233**. See also *The Mary
    Tyler Moore Show*
White House, 54, 67, 133
widows, widowers, 55, 157
Wilde, Oscar, 36, 42
Will & Grace, 8–9, 58, 177–189, **179**,
    195, 196
    Adler, Grace, 178, **179**. *See also*
        Debra Messing
    Along Came You, 184, 185
    "Coffee and Commitment," 181
    Danny, 180
    Douchette, Ben, 180, 186
    Freeman, Mrs., 186, 187
    Joan, 181
    Joe, 181–183
    Josh, 180, 183, 186, 187
    "justjack" Web site, 185
    Larry, 181–183
    Markus, Dr. Leo, 188. *See also* Harry
        Connick Jr.
    McFarland, Jack, 178, **179**, 181. *See
        also* Sean Hayes
    McFarland, Rosario Salazar, 9, 178,
        183, 184, 189
    Nathan, 180
    Salazar McFarland, Rosario, 9, 178,
        183, 184, 189
    Walker, Stanley (Stan), 183

Truman, Will, 178, **179**. *See also* Eric
    McCormack
Vince, 188. *See also* Bobby Cannavale
Walker, Karen, 178, **179**. *See also*
    Megan Mullally
Williams, Elise A., 30
Williams, Montel, 30
Williams, Spencer Jr., 128, **129**. See also
    Amos 'n' Andy
Winfrey, Oprah, 166, 168, 173
With Six You Get Eggroll, 206
Wittig, Monique, 175
WKRP in Cincinnati, 55, 220–223, 238
    Marlowe, Jennifer, 220, 223
    Quarters, Bailey, 220–221, 224
    Travis, Andy, 223
WMAQ, 17, 128
Wolcott, James, 246
woman, women, womanhood, 5, 6, 10,
        11, 17, 24, 36, 37, 40, 51, 53, 54,
        55, 70, 77, 87, 90, 91, 94, 95, 96,
        100, 101, 105–109, 111–122, 133,
        136, 139, 153–160, 169, 172–174,
        178, 180, 188, 205–225, 236,
        242–251, 254, 268
    super woman, 223
    woman-centered control, 210
    women's issues, 206, 209
    women's liberation. *See under* liberation
    women's movement, 55, 96, 216, 219,
        220
womanizer, 223
Women's Equity Action League, 209
work, workplace, 1, 9, 10, 54, 56, 64, 73,
        75, 78–79, 84, 94–95, 104, 116,
        120, 136, 153, 171–172, 206–225,
        230–232, 244, 252
    male work domain, 212
    work families, 3–4, 90, 94–95
    work-related issues, 244, 247
    workplace sitcoms
        gender-segregated workplace, 10,
            218
        "workbuddy" shows, 244–246,
            252
        workplace comedy, 9–10, 79, 84,
            153, 210, 215, 217–225

workplace etiquette, 220
workplace-related liaisons, 215
Worland, Rick, 4, 73–84, 296
World's Wildest Police Videos, 143
World War I, 21
World War II, 19, 21–22, 51, 53, 64, 90, 209
writing, 1–2, 73, 88, 134, 145, 214, 228, 230–232, 234. *See* also narrative
writers, 10–11, 23–24, 29, 56, 88, 91–92, 112, 121, 183, 185–186, 188, 209, 212, 227–228, 236–237, 259
WTBS, 122
WWE Smackdown, 34

X Files, The, 191

Yankelovich, Daniel, 58
Year of the Barricades, The, 209
yoga, 118, 119
Yorkin, Bud, 130
Young, Robert, 16, 20. See also *Father Knows Best*
Your Show of Shows, 232
You Take the Kids, 126
yuppie, 224

Zaret, David, 12, 254, 255, 257, 258, 260
Zrzavy, Phyllis Scrocco, 9, 205–216, 296
Zworykin, Vladimir, 24
Zynda, Thomas H., 234